THE EMERGENCE OF A DISCIPLINE:
Rochester Symposium on Developmental Psychopathology

Volume 1

THE EMERGENCE
OF A DISCIPLINE:
Rochester Symposium on
Developmental Psychopathology

Volume 1

Edited by
DANTE CICCHETTI
University of Rochester

1989

LAWRENCE ERLBAUM ASSOCIATES, PUBLISHERS
Hillsdale, New Jersey   Hove and London

Lawrence Erlbaum Associates, Inc., Publishers
365 Broadway
Hillsdale, New Jersey 07642

Library of Congress Cataloging-in-Publication Data

The Emergence of a Discipline: Rochester Symposium on Developmental Psychopathology
   (1st : 1987 : University of Rochester)
   Rochester Symposium on Developmental Psychopathology / edited by
Dante Cicchetti.
      p.   cm.
   Includes bibliographical references.
   ISBN 0-8058-0553-2
   1. Child psychopathology—Congresses.   2. Psychology,
Pathological—Congresses.   3. Developmental psychology—Congresses.
I. Cicchetti, Dante.   II. University of Rochester.   III. Title.
RJ499.R625   1987
618.92'89—dc20   89-17233
                                                           CIP

Printed in the United States of America

10   9   8   7   6   5   4   3   2   1

Contents

  Psychobiological Vulnerability and
  Psychosocial Stressors   212
Conclusion   214
References   214

10. **Age of Onset, Temporal Stability, and Eighteen-
    Month Course of First-Episode Psychosis**   **221**
    William G. Iacono and Morton Beiser

    Overview of the MAP Project   222
    Age of Onset and Sex Distribution   227
    Nine and Eighteen Month Outcomes of First
      Episode Psychosis   242
    Final Remarks   254
    References   256

11. **Resilience in Development: Implications of the
    Study of Successful Adaptation for Developmental
    Psychopathology**   **261**
    Ann S. Masten

    The Roots of Resilience as a Focus of
      Research   262
    Project Competence: Studies of Competence
      Under Adversity   268
    Conclusion   289
    References   290

    Author Index   295
    Subject Index   307

Foreword

Edward Zigler
Yale University

The birth of a discipline, like that of a baby, is an exciting event. It is a time of unlimited promise, a time in which all roads are open, all things possible. On some level, however, it is also a time of uncertainty, as one wonders what the child is to become and how it can best be nurtured and cared for.

The field of developmental psychopathology has truly been born over the past few years. Under the enthusiastic leadership of Dante Cicchetti, the past 5 years has seen the emergence of the discipline: the special edition of *Child Development* in 1984, the inauguration of the journal *Development and Psychopathology* in 1989, and the first annual Rochester Conference on Developmental Psychopathology in 1987.

This volume comprises the proceedings of that first annual conference. The conference, held from October 19 to 21, 1987 at the University of Rochester, was a landmark event. Featuring such workers as Cicchetti, Sroufe, Sameroff, Weisz, Masten, and others, developmental psychopathology was "put on the map" by this conference. Indeed, the very act of holding such a conference implies the field's inauguration and increased status—similar in many ways to child development's increased status due to the annual Minnesota symposium series.

But what is this child called "developmental psychopathology"? At its most basic level, developmental psychopathology is a joining of developmental psychology and child and adult psychopathology. Developmental psychology provides the theoretical orientation, the organismic developmental views of Werner (1948, 1957), Piaget (1954) and others, but also the more recent inclusion of transactional (Sameroff & Chandler, 1975) and ecological (Bronfenbrenner, 1979) perspectives on the environment. In short, developmental psychology provides the perspective of the "whole person" (Zigler, 1971) throughout development. The interrelationships of both intrinsic and extrinsic factors are considered over time as the organism develops.

Developmental psychopathology provides an organizational framework that applies equally to normal and atypical development. Knowledge of normal development enhances understanding of deviant development just as knowledge about maladaptive behavior illuminates principles underlying adaptive functioning. Indeed, it is a central tenet of developmental psychopathology that individuals move between pathological and nonpathological forms of functioning and that, even in the midst of pathology, patients display adaptive mechanisms (Zigler & Glick, 1986). This organizational perspective moreover cuts across particular pathological syndromes to reveal commonalities underlying diverse disorders. There is thus a complex and ever-changing relationship between pathology and normality, adaptive and maladaptive behavior, intrinsic and extrinsic factors.

These relationships and tensions can clearly be seen in the chapters that follow. Sroufe's emphasis on psychopathology as deviation from normal patterns of development implies that one has identified and judged the significance of those normative patterns. His discussions of the continuity of adaptation further highlight the idea of continuities and discontinuities over time, a central problem for the discipline. In a similar way, the interplay between intrinsic and extrinsic factors is emphasized both in this book and in the field at large. Sameroff's concept of the environment over time; Weisz's discussion of the effects of different environments from one culture to another; and the discussions about the effects of stress by Gunnar and her colleagues all highlight exogenous factors, how different environments and environmental influences affect individuals as they develop. Others discuss the effects of endogenous factors. Asarnow and his colleagues's discussion of psychobiological vulnerability in schizophrenia, Masten's on resiliency, and Tucker's on the relationship of brain development and psychopathology all emphasize endogenous factors, although the importance of the environment is also apparent.

It is evident, then, that the field of developmental psychopathology can be characterized in several ways. First, it is a field that values its "world view" (Pepper, 1942) or "frame of reference" (Zigler, 1963). Facts about child or adult psychopathology are understood within a broader context that includes organismic-developmental theory, expansions of that theory (especially as concerns the environment), and knowledge about normative sequences and processes. Second, developmental psychopathology is concerned with lifespan development in many types of psychopathology. The developmental lens can be used to understand child and adult functioning across a variety of disorders: autism (Sigman, this volume), schizophrenia (Asarnow, Asarnow, & Stradburg, this volume; Zubin & Spring, 1977), brain damage (Tucker, this volume), maternal depression and high-risk infants (Field, this volume; Tronick & Field, 1982), and mental retardation (Cicchetti & Beeghly, in press; Hodapp, Burack, & Zigler, in press; Zigler & Hodapp, 1986). Third, the approach is both multi-method and multidisciplinary. As this book shows, researchers in developmental psychopathology employ both longitudinal and cross-sectional studies, in one or several cultures, using a variety of behavioral, biological, and neurological measures of the pathological individual as well as measures of that person's environment over time. The field draws upon findings from many disciplines, including general developmental psychology, adult and child psychiatry, abnormal psychology, and clinical child psychology.

Such a listing, preliminary as it may be, also implies what developmental psychopathology is not. Developmental psychopathology is not simply the characterization of childhood or adult psychopathology—either at one moment or over time—nor is it exclusively a taxonomic enterprise. At the same time, one must know the "facts" about the onset and course of particular disorders, and studies of homogeneous (or nearly homogeneous) populations are useful. As such, developmental psychopathology, while it uses information from a variety of disciplines, is a field in its own right, an emerging discipline that incorporates but goes beyond traditional perspectives.

These are, then, the basics, the outline of a field that has begun to emerge. How successful developmental psychopathology will become cannot be predicted, but the early indications—as exemplified by this volume—are encouraging. And, like anyone meeting a new baby and its parents, we can only express our congratulations and best wishes.

REFERENCES

Bronfenbrenner, U. (1979). *The ecology of human development.* Cambridge, MA: Harvard University Press.

Cicchetti, D., & Beeghly, M. (Eds.). (in press). *Children with Down Syndrome: A developmental perspective.* New York: Cambridge University Press.

Hodapp, R. M., Burack, J. A., & Zigler, E. (Eds.). (in press). *Issues in the developmental approach to mental retardation.* New York: Cambridge University Press.

Pepper, S. (1942). *World hypotheses.* Berkeley, CA: University of California Press.

Piaget, J. (1954). *The construction of reality in the child.* New York: Ballantine.

Sameroff, A. & Chandler, M. (1975). Reproductive risk and the continuum of caretaker casualty. In F. Horowitz, M. Hetherington, S. Scarr-Salapatek, and G. Sigel (Eds.), *Review of Child Development Research.* (Vol. 4). Chicago: University of Chicago Press.

Tronick, E., & Field, T. (Eds.). (1982). *Maternal depression and infant disturbance: New directions for child development.* No. 34. San Francisco: Jossey-Bass Press.

Werner, H. (1948). *Comparative psychology of mental development.* New York: Follett.

Werner, H. (1957). The concept of development from a comparative and organismic point of view. In D. Harris (Ed.), *The concept of development.* Minneapolis: University of Minnesota Press.

Zigler, E. (1963). Metatheoretical issues in developmental psychology. In M. Marx (Ed.), *Theories in contemporary psychology.* New York: Macmillan.

Zigler, E. (1971). The retarded child as a whole person. In H. E. Adams & W. K. Boardman (Eds.), *Advances in experimental clinical psychology*. New York: Pergamon.

Zigler, E., & Glick, M. (1986). *A developmental approach to adult psychopathology*. New York: Wiley.

Zigler, E., & Hodapp, R. M. (1986). *Understanding mental retardation*. New York: Cambridge University Press.

Zubin, J., & Spring, B. (1977). Vulnerability: A new view of schizophrenia. *Journal of Abnormal Psychology, 56*, 103–126.

This volume is dedicated to Norman Garmezy, Michael Rutter, and Edward Zigler. Without their pioneering efforts, developmental psychopathology would not be such a compelling area of inquiry.

1 Developmental Psychopathology: Past, Present, and Future

Dante Cicchetti
University of Rochester

In October of 1987 the Rochester Symposium on Developmental Psychopathology was initiated. This volume is noteworthy in that it marks not only the inauguration of this annual symposium with its accompanying presentations, but also serves as a chronicle of the current state of theorizing and research in the discipline of developmental psychopathology. The impetus for organizing this meeting and the intention to ensure its occurrence on a yearly basis arose from recognition of the productivity and associated excitement generated by researchers in the field. A similar landmark event last took place in 1984, when a special issue of the journal *Child Development* was devoted exclusively to developmental psychopathology. At that time, I discussed the "coming of age" of the discipline (Cicchetti, 1984). With scholars such as Thomas Achenbach, Norman Garmezy, Marian Radke-Yarrow, Lee Robins, Michael Rutter, Alan Sroufe, and Edward Zigler providing guidance and direction, developmental psychopathology has indeed joined the ranks of other mature scientific disciplines. As such, it is critical that investigators have a forum in which to gather and discuss new developments and to question the overall direction of the field.

A danger inherent in the developmental course of a relatively new, exciting discipline is that its core identity may be lost in the onslaught of enthusiasm which it generates. That is, it is possible that the popular use of the term will not accurately reflect the original tenets of the discipline. It is therefore important to examine the key components which differentiate developmental psychopathology from other areas of scientific endeavor. To this end, an historical perspective is presented, followed by identification of definitional elements encompassed by developmental psychopathology.

In reviewing the writings of noted systematizers in psychology and psychiatry,

1

the interrelation between the study of normal functioning and the study of psychopathology emerges (Cicchetti, in press-a). A consensus exists that a knowledge of normal development can inform the understanding of psychopathology, and that reciprocally, the exploration of atypical populations can shed light on normal functioning (Cicchetti, 1984; Rutter, 1986). This principle emerges clearly in the writings of Sigmund Freud (see, for example, 1927/1955a, 1937/1955b, 1940/1955c, 1940/1955d), but also is evident in the work of Anna Freud (1946, 1965, 1974, 1976), Kurt Goldstein (1939, 1940, 1943, 1948), David Rapaport (1951, 1960), and Heinz Werner (1948, 1957). Because these theorists viewed pathology as a deviation from normality, the study of pathology was seen as enhancing one's knowledge of normal processes (Cicchetti, in press-b).

While these systematizers played an important role in the genesis of developmental psychopathology, the historical roots of this discipline extend far beyond psychology and psychiatry. In fact, the interdisciplinary nature of those involved in the field mirrors the origins of the discipline. For example, influence from work conducted in neurophysiology by Jackson (1884/1958) and Sherrington (1906), in embryology by Waddington (1957, 1966) and Weiss (1961, 1969), in physiological psychology by Teitelbaum (1971, 1977; Teitelbaum & Stellar, 1954), and in neurobiology by Jacobson (1978) and Rakic and Goldman-Rakic (1982) all can be seen in the writings of developmental psychopathologists. It was through these historical endeavors that the groundwork for the importance of differentiation, organization, and hierarchical integration, principles at the cornerstone of developmental psychopathology, was laid. For example, Herbert Spencer's (1862/1900) "Developmental Hypothesis" or "Doctrine of Evolution" has had a predominant influence upon the social and scientific ideologies of the 19th and 20th centuries. Spencer conceived of the developmental process as one of an integration of successively higher stages that occurred in an invariant sequence. He likewise considered these stages to be hierarchical while coexisting in time. Because through the process of hierarchic integration an organisms' early structures are not lost in development, the organism can maintain feelings of integrity and continuity in the face of change so rapid that it might otherwise create problems for the sense of internal continuity.

Although these brief illustrations highlight the long and diverse history that has contributed to the emergence of developmental psychopathology, it was not until the 1970s that developmental psychopathology was delineated as a separate field of inquiry. As such, it is a young discipline which has strived to incorporate and build upon a wealth of knowledge. For a more indepth historical perspective, the reader is referred to Rutter and Garmezy (1983) and Cicchetti (in press-a).

Moving beyond the historical origins of this discipline, it is necessary to clarify its content and boundaries. That is, what exactly is developmental psychopathology and how does it *differ* from other disciplines such as developmental and clinical psychology and psychiatry? To begin, developmental psychopathology is unique in its emphasis on the importance of recognizing the interplay between normal and abnormal development (Cicchetti, 1984; Rutter, 1984; Sroufe & Rutter, 1984). As such, a knowledge of normal development is considered to be critical to understanding abnormality and, similarly, examining deviant development is seen as a necessary enhancement of knowledge of normal functioning (Cicchetti, in press-b; Cicchetti & Toth, in press; Rutter, 1986; Sroufe & Rutter, 1984). In order to achieve this integration, developmental psychopathologists address the mechanisms and processes by which various developmental outcomes occur. This requires attention to developmental continuities and discontinuities across the lifespan rather than an emphasis on rates of psychopathology (Cicchetti & Schneider-Rosen, 1986; Rutter, 1988; Rutter & Garmezy, 1983; Zigler & Glick, 1986). In addition, the effect of experience on modifying or maintaining behavior is also central to the developmental psychopathology approach (Cicchetti & Schneider-Rosen, 1986; Gottlieb, 1976; Rutter, 1986). Thus, developmental psychopathology can be defined as "the study of the origins and course of individual patterns of behavioral maladaptation, whatever the age of onset, whatever the causes, whatever the transformations in behavioral manifestation, and however complex the course of the developmental pattern may be" (Sroufe & Rutter, 1984, p. 18). The interest of developmental psychopathologists in high risk nondisordered populations is, therefore, equal to their interest in disordered populations.

With this framework in mind, differences between the discipline of developmental psychopathology and seemingly related areas of endeavor begin to emerge. Rather than focusing exclusively on normal or abnormal functioning, developmental psychopathologists maintain a dual focus. In addition, a belief in the importance of employing a life-span perspective is central to this approach. Finally and perhaps most significantly, developmental psychopathologists are committed to bridging the dualisms that have separated scientific research from clinical application. Clearly, a central premise of this discipline calls for mutually beneficial growth through a working interface between research and clinical practice.

Due to the newness of the discipline of developmental psychopathology, a theme was not chosen for the current volume. Rather, I chose to solicit contributions from those individuals whose work reflects the goals of developmental psychopathology. Although a thematic focus therefore was not possible, all of the chapters are unified by their attention to the principles embodied by developmental psychopathology. In fact, despite the diversity of the contributions, several themes recur. Throughout the volume, authors attend to the importance of the interface between normal and atypical development. Regardless of the nature of the population under investigation, an incorporation of principles of normal development is evidenced. Perhaps most compelling in this regard is the attention directed toward the implications of the work reported for clinical populations. Issues related to continuity and discontinuity, as well as to the processes by which behavior is modified or maintained also are in evidence throughout the volume. Finally, a recognition of the need to conceptualize functioning within the context in which it occurs is manifested. To this end, many of the authors stress the importance of employing multidomain, multicontextual methods of assessment. As a whole, this volume reflects a departure from a simple main effects causal model of functioning and addresses the multiplicity of dynamic transactions which impact upon normal, as well as disordered behavior. In reading the chapters contained in this volume, the reader is advised to keep these unifying themes in mind, for it is through the maintenance of this perspective that the potential of developmental psychopathology can be realized.

The volume opens, most appropriately, in view of his guiding influence on the development of the discipline, with a contribution by Alan Sroufe. His chapter focuses on the assessment of psychopathology as deviation from normal patterns of development. According to Sroufe, it is this view that contains the major promise of developmental psychopathology. By recognizing prognostically significant developmental deviations before an individual manifests a psychiatric disorder, early identification and preventive efforts can be enhanced. In addition to its relevance for early identification, the developmental deviation approach also has the advantage of providing guidance regarding areas of functioning to examine and what constitutes atypical functioning (see also Rolf, 1985). Moreover, this approach contains clearly delimited outcome criteria.

Following his discussion of the developmental deviation approach, Sroufe addresses the continuity of adaptation, an issue central to the discipline of developmental psychopathology. The importance of examining the continuity of *pathways* and not expecting behavioral isomorphism is stressed. Sroufe cites longitudinal studies and presents data to support this view. The chapter culminates with a discussion pertaining to the fluidity of developmental pathways and emphasizes the importance of this approach to understanding the processes which operate in the development of psychopathology.

In the next chapter, Arnold Sameroff, a pioneer in the area of developmental psychopathology, discusses the requirements for a theory of developmental psychopathology. After critiquing nondevelopmental approaches, Sameroff presents a model of developmental regulation which is rooted in an elaboration of the role of environmental constraints on individual behavior. Specifically, Sameroff argues that the principles espoused by a medical model related to symptomatic and etiological continuity across the lifespan cannot be applied usefully to the study of psychopathology.

Based on data from the Rochester Longitudinal Study (Sameroff, Seifer, & Zax, 1982), Sameroff describes the importance of cumulative environmental risk, emphasizing that the characteristics of a child must be related to the environment's ability to guide the development of the child toward social norms. In fact, Sameroff posits that a disordered social environment might convert biologically normal children into "caretaking casualties". Sameroff describes the role of experience in determining behavior and stresses the dynamic relation between the individual and the internal and external context. Interestingly, the Rochester Longitudinal Study revealed continuities in development. It is the study of linkages over time and the relation to continuities and discontinuities which Sameroff views as the most defining aspect of developmental psychopathology.

Sameroff's premise of the importance of experience in modifying biological predisposition is illustrated brilliantly and elaborated upon in Donald Tucker's chapter. Tucker considers the implications of evidence on brain development for an organismic approach to developmental psychopathology. Accordingly, he suggests that the major issues of early social and emotional development provide a context for understanding brain maturation. This chapter is compelling in its ability to impart a multidomain perspective to the understanding of psychopathology.

After describing structural aspects of the nervous system and the relation between structure and function in the developing brain, Tucker provides illustrations through data on depression and schizophrenia. Tucker's approach emphasizes the importance of early experience for the actualization of genetic potential. Importantly for purposes of continuity/discontinuity, Tucker states that the effects of early experience on neural maturation may not be reversible.

In a different but related vein, John Weisz addresses the importance of cross-cultural research for enhancing our understanding of psychopathology. Cross-cultural research is critical to incorporate into a comprehensive theory of developmental psychopathology as it enables us to assess contextual influences on the etiology, course, and identification of psychopathology. Weisz begins with a warning that in the absence of the incorporation of data from diverse areas of the world, developmental psychopathology risks the stigmatization of being known as a "monocultural science." According to Weisz, we must delimit the extent to which psychological dysfunctions reflect development influences of childhood versus social-environmental factors. After discussing how cross-cultural research should be approached and presenting his findings, Weisz discusses the relevance of the data for a theory of developmental psychopathology. According to Weisz, similarities of problems despite cultural variation raise the possibility of the central role of developmental influences in the manifestation of psychopathology. However, despite these commonalities, identifying differences and exploring their genesis may improve our understanding of how social forces influence developmental psychopathology. Implications of culturally specific beliefs on problem identification and the provision of treatment also are discussed.

The next chapter is unique in its focus on a nondisordered population, but consistent with the tenets of developmental psychopathology in its attention to the relevance of the data for normal, as well as abnormal development. Megan Gunnar, Sarah Mangelsdorf, Roberta Kestenbaum, Sarah Lang, Mary Larson, and Debra Andreas maintain that knowledge of how an individual functions under stress is central to an understanding of both normal and atypical functioning. Consistent with the importance of multidomain assessments to developmen-

tal psychopathology, Gunnar and her colleagues state that an adequate understanding of stress responses requires an analysis of behavior and physiology. She
and her colleagues review three areas relating behavioral, hormonal and relationship systems to our understanding of the developing child's ability to manage
stress and challenge: behavioral competence, relationship security, and the ontogeny of coping strategies. Several of their conclusions are of note. First,
having reviewed the literature they conclude that behavioral competence is often
associated with greater physiological stress-reactivity. They suggest that this is
because competence involves more approach-oriented coping strategies that have
as a cost bringing the individual into greater contact with distressing elements of
situations. Furthermore, they suggest that when lack of competence is associated
with greater stress reactivity, that this may be because less competent individuals
tend to use avoidance coping strategies and when these strategies are not available or functional, intense physiological stress results. A second point made in
this chapter concerns the linkages between attachment and physiological stress.
These researchers point out that there are remarkably few studies with human
infants of either the effects of the attachment figure's presence or of attachment
security on infant physiological stress responding. The data from animal studies,
however, clearly indicate that the mother's presence buffers the infant from
physiological stress, albeit with not well-understood exceptions. The few studies
with human infants also suggest that the security of attachment plays little role in
the infant's physiological stress reaction to separation; however, we do not know
whether attachment quality mediates the buffering effect of the mother's presence. Gunnar and her colleagues point to a number of areas needing additional
study, including the linkages between attachment security, coping strategy development, and physiological stress reactivity. They also note that work on these
issues using infants and children from disordered relationships will be an essential adjunct to our understanding of these issues in normal development.

Shifting the focus from research with a population of normal infants to high
risk infants, Tiffany Field examines data related to the effects of maternal depression on interaction and attachment behavior. In summarizing the data, Field
reports that infants of depressed mothers exhibited depressed affect, increased
heart rate, and increased salivary cortisol levels. Importantly, in comparing the
interactions of infants with depressed mothers with other adults, Field found that
the infant's depressed style of interaction generalized not only to interactions
with nondepressed strangers, but seemed to elicit depression-like behavior in
nondepressed adults. The significance of this for a transactional model of the
development of psychopathology is clear (see Cicchetti & Aber, 1986). Field
discusses the findings of elevated infant heart rate and cortisol as indicative of
sympathetic arousal, and their lower vagal tone as suggestive of lower parasympathetic activity, which may be reflective of a state of stress. These findings with
high risk infants can be compared with Gunnar's work on normal infants. Field
concludes by questioning the stability of the early disturbances manifested by
infants of depressed mothers.

Because developmental psychopathology is concerned with a range of functioning from nondisordered, through high risk conditions, to actual psychopathology, it is fitting that the next several chapters address conditions of abnormality in children and adults. Marian Sigman begins her chapter with an emphatic statement regarding the relevance of normal developmental theory to the study of childhood autism. Sigman advocates the utilization of a developmental perspective so that research on disordered functioning can be guided by an understanding of competencies which are expected to be mastered by nondisordered children of various ages. This approach also is considered to be critical for understanding and integrating research results from various studies.

After discussing methodological considerations, Sigman presents her data on the developmental functioning of autistic children. The sophistication with which Sigman approaches her multidomain assessment of functioning is noteworthy, and underscores the importance of utilizing paradigms such as this in designing research projects within the domain of developmental psychopathology. If a less comprehensive assessment were employed, a valid portrayal of functioning would be precluded (see also Cicchetti & Wagner, in press; A. Freud, 1965). Sigman's description of the normative sequence of development and her utilization of this for the basis of her investigation into the disordered functioning of autistic children also serves as an elegant illustration of a central principle of developmental psychopathology.

In another sophisticated application of developmental psychopathology principles to the understanding of abnormality, Robert Asarnow, Joan Asarnow, and Robert Stradburg examine the development of schizophrenia. Because developmental psychopathology highlights issues related to developmental continuity and discontinuity, Asarnow and his colleagues stress the importance of detailing the antecedents and course of disordered functioning. Accordingly, they believe that an understanding of schizophrenia may require an elucidation of how a genetically transmitted predisposition is expressed at different ages, and how it interacts with the caregiving environment to determine both whether an individual develops a schizophrenic disorder and the quality and level of psychosocial development (see Meehl, 1962, 1972; Zubin & Spring, 1977).

Asarnow and his colleagues present a vulnerability/stress model for the etiology of schizophrenia and describe the research strategy used to identify psychobiological vulnerability factors in efforts to illustrate the application of the developmental perspective to the study of schizophrenic disorders. Studies designed to detail the nature of psychobiological vulnerability factors, psychosocial stressors, and the links between psychobiological dysfunctions and the emergence of schizophrenic disorders prior to twelve years of age are summarized. The interaction between psychobiological vulnerability and psychosocial stressors in the onset and course of schizophrenia is discussed. Asarnow and his colleagues conclude with a stimulating discussion of the importance of this program of research for developmental psychopathology.

In the one article that focuses on adult psychopathology, William Iacono and

Morton Beiser present their data on the onset, stability, and course of first-episode psychosis. Despite the importance of the lifespan perspective, it is interesting that, to date, far more developmental researchers have focused their efforts on childhood functioning. The relative dearth of developmentally relevant research on disordered populations of adults makes this contribution all the more important. The data presented by Iacono and Beiser is embedded within a comprehensive program of research involving an array of predictors of schizophrenia which range from psychophysiological to environmental factors. The comprehensive nature of this approach is consistent with the transactional focus advocated by developmental psychopathologists. In the current chapter, Iacono and Beiser address individual differences in the age of onset, the developmental course of disorder as manifested by temporal stability of diagnosis, and the short-term prediction of outcome. Of note is the finding that, in schizophrenia, there is little change in the symptom picture over a 9-month period.

The work of Iacono and Beiser is illustrative of an epidemiological approach within a developmental perspective. In many ways, Iacono's identification of first episode psychosis capitalizes upon what Rutter describes as "experiments in nature" (Rutter, 1988) to further our knowledge of developmental psychopathology. Moreover, this contribution stresses the relevance of developmental psychopathology for adult functioning (see also Zigler & Glick, 1986).

The volume concludes with a contribution by Ann Masten which describes the implications of resilience for developmental psychopathology. Because resilience can be conceptualized as the ability to cope effectively with conditions of stress and adversity, there are clear links between Masten's work and the findings of both Gunnar and her colleagues and Field. This is an important chapter, as developmental psychopathologists are interested not only in abnormal functioning, but in the pathways by which both normal and abnormal development may occur. Perhaps not surprisingly, successful adaptation in the face of adversity has been largely ignored by students of psychopathology (Garmezy, 1974, 1981; Pavenstedt, 1965; Rutter, 1985; Werner & Smith, 1982). This is unfortunate, as a potentially rich area of intervention knowledge has been overlooked. Masten examines the origins, methodology, results, and future of the study of resilience as it relates to developmental psychopathology. To this end, she presents data obtained from "Project Competence," a longitudinal investigation initiated over 10 years ago at the University of Minnesota by Norman Garmezy. Because competence is considered to be a multidimensional construct, multiple measurement strategies were employed in its assessment. Consistent with other findings reported in this volume, competence, along with the internal and external resources which accompany it, was found to be reasonably stable and predictive of later adjustment. In addition to the corroboration provided for continuity of adaptation, resilience research is significant with regard to its implications for intervention. According to Masten, the prevention of maladaptation can benefit greatly from a knowledge of resilience, as they are different components of the overall picture of adaptation.

As this volume illustrates, developmental psychopathology is a comprehensive and exciting area of scientific endeavor. It holds the promise for increasing communication between researchers and clinicians, thereby benefiting members of each area. By reducing the schism which historically has existed between scientific inquiry and its application, developmental psychopathology's ability to enhance preventive efforts and to encourage the development of effective intervention strategies is vast. Additionally, a discipline that is well grounded in theory and research, as well as cognizant of the needs and demands of the provision of services, promotes the incorporation of this knowledge base into social policy-making decisions. Moreover, as monies available for prevention and intervention in mental health have become scarcer, funding sources are demanding that the efficacy of programs be demonstrated. Inquiries designed within the developmental psychopathology perspective also are relevant to the attainment of this goal. Of course, due to its recent emergence, it is critical that careful thought be directed toward education and training in the area of developmental psychopathology (Cicchetti and Toth, in press). It is only through educational and collaborative efforts such as those embodied in the current volume that the potential of this exciting area will be realized fully.

In concluding, I would like to thank the contributors for making the first symposium a memorable event. In addition, I acknowledge the assistance of the entire staff of the Mt. Hope Family Center and of my graduate students. Their efforts helped make the symposium run smoothly and efficiently. In particular, I would like to single out Douglas Barnett, Debra Bartenstein, Carol Evans, Victoria Gill, Kevin Hennessy, Randi Hess, Gerald Rabideau, and Delbert Smith, for their superb help and hard work. Moreover, I appreciate the phenomenal efforts of my colleague and friend, Sheree Toth. At every step of the way, Sheree offered critical and significant ideas and suggestions and provided important input. Without her energies and competence the quality of the symposium would have been compromised greatly. Furthermore, I thank Sheree for her invaluable insights and help on this manuscript and Victoria Gill for typing it. I also acknowledge the John D. and Catherine T. MacArthur Foundation Network on Early Childhood, the A. L. Mailman Family Foundation, Inc., the Smith Richardson Foundation, Inc., and the Spunk Fund, Inc. for their support of my work on this manuscript.

Finally, I acknowledge Dennis O'Brien, President of the University of Rochester, Brian Thompson, Provost of the University of Rochester, and James Ison, Professor and Chairperson of the Psychology Department, for their support and guidance in bringing this symposium to fruition. Two noteworthy happenings occurred during this 3-day conference (October 19–October 21). First, there was a dedication ceremony for the opening of the new facility for Mt. Hope Family Center. Second, the inauguration of the symposium occurred on Joseph C. Wilson Day, a major yearly celebratory event at the University of Rochester. Wilson Day celebrates the contributions of the late Joseph C. Wilson, a graduate of the University who was Chairman of the Board of the Xerox Corporation,

Chairman of the Board of Trustees at the University of Rochester, and one of the University's major benefactors. I want to commend the Wilson family on their continued efforts to improve the quality of life for members of the Rochester community.

REFERENCES

Cicchetti, D. (1984). The emergence of developmental psychopathology. *Child Development, 55,* 1–7.

Cicchetti, D. (in press-a). An historical perspective on the discipline of developmental psychopathology. In J. Rolf, A. Masten, D. Cicchetti, K. Neuchterlein, & S. Weintraub (Eds.), *Risk and protective factors in the development of psychopathology.* New York: Cambridge University Press.

Cicchetti, D. (in press-b). The organization and coherence of socioemotional, cognitive, and representational development: Illustrations through a developmental psychopathology perspective on Down syndrome and child maltreatment. In R. Thompson (Ed.), *Nebraska Symposium on Motivation. Vol. 36. Socioemotional development.* Lincoln: University of Nebraska Press.

Cicchetti, D., & Aber, J. L. (1986). Early precursors to later depression: An organizational perspective. In L. Lipsitt & C. Rovee-Collier (Eds.), *Advances in infancy, Vol. 4* (pp. 81–137). Norwood, NJ: Ablex.

Cicchetti, D., & Schneider-Rosen, K. (1986). An organizational approach to childhood depression. In M. Rutter, C. Izard, & P. Read (Eds.), *Depression in young people: Clinical and developmental perspectives* (pp. 71–134). New York: Guilford.

Cicchetti, D., & Toth, S. (in press). The making of a developmental psychopathologist. In J. Cantor, C. Spiker, & L. Lipsitt (Eds.), *Child behavior and development: Training for diversity.* Norwood, NJ: Ablex.

Cicchetti, D., & Wagner, S. (in press). Alternative assessment strategies for the evaluation of infants and toddlers: An organizational perspective. In S. Meisels & J. Shonkoff (Eds.), *Handbook of early intervention.* New York: Cambridge University Press.

Freud, A. (1946). *The ego and mechanisms of defense.* New York: International Universities Press.

Freud, A. (1965). *Normality and pathology in childhood.* New York: International Universities Press.

Freud, A. (1974). A psychoanalytic view of developmental psychopathology. *Journal of the Philadelphia Association for Psychoanalysis, 1,* 7–17.

Freud, A. (1976). Psychopathology seen against the background of normal development. *British Journal of Psychiatry, 129,* 401–406.

Freud, S. (1955a). Fetishism. In J. Strachey (Ed.), *The standard edition of the complete psychological works of Sigmund Freud* (Vol. 21). London: Hogarth. (Originally published, 1927).

Freud, S. (1955b). Analysis terminable and interminable. In J. Strachey (Ed.), *The standard edition of the complete works of Sigmund Freud* (Vol. 23). London: Hogarth. (Originally published, 1937).

Freud, S. (1955c). An outline of psycho-analysis. In J. Strachey (Ed.), *The standard edition of the complete works of Sigmund Freud* (Vol. 23). London: Hogarth. (Originally published, 1940).

Freud, S. (1955d). Splitting of the ego in the process of defense. In J. Strachey (Ed.), *The standard edition of the complete works of Sigmund Freud* (Vol. 23). London: Hogarth. (Originally published, 1940).

Garmezy, N. (1974). Children at risk: The search for the antecedents of schizophrenia. *Schizophrenia Bulletin, 8,* 14–90. (With the collaboration of S. Streitman).

Garmezy, N. (1981). Children under stress: Perspectives on antecedents and correlates of vulnerability and resistance to psychopathology. In A. I. Rubin, J. Arnoff, A. M. Barclay, & R. A. Zucker (Eds.), *Further explorations in personality*. New York: Wiley Interscience.

Goldstein, K. (1939). *The organism*. New York: American Book Company.

Goldstein, K. (1940). *Human nature in the light of psychopathology*. Cambridge, MA: Harvard University Press.

Goldstein, K. (1943). The significance of psychological research in schizophrenia. *The Journal of Nervous and Mental Disease, 97*, 261–279.

Goldstein, K. (1948). *Language and language disturbances*. Orlando, FL: Grune & Stratton.

Gottlieb, G. (1976). The roles of experience in the development of behavior and the nervous system. In G. Gottlieb (Ed.), *Neural and behavioral specificity*. New York: Academic Press.

Jackson, J. H. (1958). Evolution and dissolution of the nervous system. In J. Taylor (Ed.), *The selected writings of John Hughlings Jackson* (Vol. 2). New York: Basic Books. (From the Crooniam Lectures, Originally published in 1884).

Jacobson, M. (1978). *Developmental neurobiology*. New York: Plenum.

Meehl, P. E. (1962). Schizotaxia, schizotypy, schizophrenia. *American Psychologist, 17*, 827–838.

Meehl, P. E. (1972). Specific genetic etiology, psychodynamics, and therapeutic nihilism. *International Journal of Mental Health, 1*, 10–27.

Pavenstedt, E. (1965). A comparison of the child-rearing environment of upper-lower and very low-lower class families. *American Journal of Orthopsychiatry, 35*, 89–98.

Rakic, P., & Goldman-Rakic, P. S. (1982). Development and modifiability of the cerebral cortex. *Neurosciences Research Program Bulletin, 20*, 433–438.

Rapaport, D. (1951). *Organization and pathology of thought*. New York: Columbia University Press.

Rapaport, D. (1960). Psychoanalysis as a developmental psychology. In B. Kaplan & S. Wapner (Eds.), *Perspectives in psychological theory*. New York: International Universities Press.

Rolf, J. (1985). Evolving adaptive theories and methods for prevention research with children. *Journal of Consulting and Clinical Psychology, 53*, 631–646.

Rutter, M. (1984). Psychopathology and development: I. Childhood antecedents of adult psychiatric disorder. *Australian and New Zealand Journal of Psychiatry, 18*, 225–234.

Rutter, M. (1985). Resilience in the face of adversity: Protective factors and resistance to psychiatric disorder. *British Journal of Psychiatry, 147*, 598–611.

Rutter, M. (1986). Child Psychiatry: The interface between clinical and developmental research. *Psychological Medicine, 16*, 151–160.

Rutter, M. (1988). Epidemiological approaches to developmental psychopathology. *Archives of General Psychiatry, 45*, 486–495.

Rutter, M., & Garmezy, N. (1983). Developmental psychopathology. In E. M. Hetherington (Ed.), *Carmichael's manual of child psychology, (Vol. 4): Social and personality development* (pp. 775–912). New York: Wiley.

Sameroff, A. J., Seifer, R., & Zax, M. (1982). Early development of children at risk for emotional disorder. *Monographs of the Society for Research in Child Development, 47*. Chicago: University of Chicago Press.

Sherrington, X. (1906). *The integrative action of the nervous system*. New York: Scribners.

Spencer, H. (1900). *First Principles* (6th edition). New York: Appleton. (Originally published, 1862).

Sroufe, L. A., & Rutter, M. (1984). The domain of developmental psychopathology. *Child Development, 54*, 173–189.

Teitelbaum, P. (1971). The encephalization of hunger. In E. Stellar & J. Sprague (Eds.), *Progress in physiological psychology* (Vol. 4). New York: Academic Press.

Teitelbaum, P. (1977). Levels of integration of the operant. In W. K. Honig & J. Staddon (Eds.), *Handbook of operant behavior*. Engelwood-Cliffs, NJ: Prentice-Hall.

Teitelbaum, P., & Stellar, E. (1954). Recovery from the failure to eat produced by hypothalamic lesions. *Science, 120,* 894–895.

Waddington, C. H. (1957). *The strategy of the genes.* London: Allen and Unwin.

Waddington, C. H. (1966). *Principles of development and differentiation.* New York: Macmillan.

Weiss, P. A. (1961). Deformities as cues to understanding development of form. *Perspectives in Biology and Medicine, 4* 133–151.

Weiss, P. A. (1969). *Principles of development.* New York: Hafner.

Werner, E., & Smith, R. (1982). *Vulnerable but invincible: A study of resilient children.* New York: McGraw-Hill.

Werner, H. (1948). *Comparative psychology of mental development.* New York: International Universities Press.

Werner, H. (1957). The concept of development from a comparative and organismic point of view. In D. B. Harris (Ed.), *The concept of development.* Minneapolis: University of Minnesota Press.

Zigler, E., & Glick, M. (1986). *A developmental approach to adult psychopathology.* New York: Wiley.

Zubin, J., & Spring, B. (1977). Vulnerability: A new view of schizophrenia. *Journal of Abnormal Psychology, 56,* 103–126.

2

Pathways to Adaptation and Maladaptation: Psychopathology as Developmental Deviation

L. Alan Sroufe
University of Minnesota

Developmental psychopathology is concerned with the origins and course of maladaptive patterns of behavior, some forms of which represent traditional psychiatric disorders. It involves more than the study of disturbed children, including also the discovery and study of developmental pathways which are the *forerunners* of disorders both in children and adults. It also includes study of the course of disorders once manifest (their phases and sequelae).

Moreover, this field involves comparison between normal and maladaptive courses of development. Herein lies the major uniqueness of the developmental approach to psychopathology. Disorder is viewed as *developmental deviation*. The focus then becomes one of defining, tracing, and understanding normal pathways of development, specifying significant deviations from these normal pathways, outlining the sequential behavioral transformations that occur as individuals follow these atypical developmental courses, and uncovering the factors that deflect and return individuals to any given pathway. Developmental psychopathologists are interested in those individuals who consistently follow a pathway leading to disorder. But they are just as interested in those individuals who, having deviated from normal developmental pathways, ultimately resume normal development and achieve adequate adaptation and those who resist stresses that usually lead to developmental deviation (Cicchetti, 1984; Sroufe & Rutter, 1984). Such a dual focus on competence in the face of early adversity, on the one hand, and continuity in maladaptation in other cases is the essence of risk research (Garmezy & Streitman, 1974; Masten, this volume). Such comparative studies will provide important clues for prevention and intervention.

When developmental psychopathology is defined in this way, understanding the nature of developmental pathways becomes critical. This understanding will

13

come from considering a number of interrelated questions. One set of questions concerns what might be called equivalencies and variations. Which pathways are essentially equivalent in that they lead to a similar outcome (i.e., a particular disorder or pattern of adaptation)? In current terminology this is referred to as the idea of a "final common pathway." There may be numerous routes to a given disorder, such as depression, with various factors playing a greater or lesser etiological role in different cases. But in the end the adaptational picture presented by the individuals is similar.

A complementary question is, what are the likely variations in outcome associated with a given developmental pathway? Differentiation always occurs in development (Santostefano, 1978), and this applies equally to abnormal development. Conduct disorder in middle childhood, for example, has been associated not only with adult antisocial behavior and alcoholism, but with schizophrenia and depression as well (Robins, 1978; Zeitlin, 1982). It is reasonable to assume that any pathway will lead to a set of outcomes rather than to a single linear endpoint. Generally, this set of outcomes should be coherent and specifiable in advance. Thus, some boys who have histories of seductive relationships with their mothers are hyperactive and undercontrolled (Jacobvitz & Sroufe, 1987). Others are passive, coy, and appealing to opposite gender adults and children (Sroufe & Fleeson, 1986). Only some show frankly inappropriate sexual behavior as young children and only some are exploited by others, as is discussed in a later section. Patterns which combine these features also exist. Any one of these patterns selected as a sole outcome variable would yield only modest results. When a family of conceptually related outcomes are taken together the power of predictive variables becomes much greater. As illustrated below, the problem of continuity in adaptation over time hinges on defining related patterns of adaptation at various ages. Defining such patterns and their transformations over time becomes one of the most pressing tasks for developmental psychology.

A second set of questions concerns factors influencing the origins and course of particular developmental pathways. What factors, both endogenous and environmental, determine the "choice" of a given pathway? Similarly, what are the factors that support continuance on a given path, deflection to some other pathway, and/or the particular outcome "chosen" from among the array of outcomes for a given path? Causal and mediating variables may be both biological or environmental, with each influencing the other. Genes and environment must, of course, always be considered together. For example, various "internalizing" pathways in adolescence (anorexia, depression, passivity) are strongly influenced both by biologically given gender and culturally given socialization practices (Sroufe & Rutter, 1984). Thus, the pubescent female's emerging sense of vulnerability and self-protectiveness is biologically induced, but feelings of low self-worth and helplessness are culturally mediated (Block, 1979).

But it will also be important to keep in mind the "third" ingredient in development. Genes and current environment are never enough to explain development. The third major influence is *preceding development* itself. One striking example of the mediating role of preceding development comes from embryology (Arms & Camp, 1987). If at an early stage of development of a chick embryo, a section of tissue that would have become part of a thigh is placed at the tip of a bud that is going to become a wing, the tissue becomes a normal part of the wing tip. This shows the impact of both genes (it is compatible chick tissue) and environment or context (it is induced to be a part of the tip by surrounding cells). But the precise point in development is also critical. If done too late, this transplantation will not take. Most striking of all is what happens when this transplant is done at an intermediate point. It does not become a normal part of a wing tip nor anomalous thigh tissue. Rather it becomes a claw-like structure. Its genetic instructions and developmental history lead it to already be "committed" to being leg tissue. But it is not yet fully committed, and local cells induce it to be tip-like, so it becomes the *tip* of a leg; that is, a claw! So it is with human psychological development; at each point development turns both upon current circumstances and development to that point (Bowlby, 1973). Thus, for example, early loss (Brown, Harris, & Bifulco, 1986) and "learned helplessness" (Seligman, 1970) also relate to depression, in addition to genetic and cultural factors.

The final set of questions which lead to clarification of a developmental viewpoint concerns the early manifestations or precursors of later patterns of maladaptation. The nature of development is complex, with early patterns undergoing a series of transformations to outcomes which, while logically tied to the original forms, are in no simple way identical. How, then, are precursors of later pathology to be detected? Are there patterns of adaptation which indicate that infants or young children are on the pathway to attention deficit/hyperactivity disorder, conduct disorder, adolescent depression, or adult schizophrenia? How flexible or mobile are these early pathways? When do pathways for various disorders become rather strongly channeled or "canalized" (Waddington, 1957)? This is an alternative way of asking the question: By what criteria, short of the emergence of a formal disorder, can we determine that a certain pathway represents a true and significant developmental deviation? Unlike early childhood autism, few developmental deviations are obviously apparent. Yet, early detection of developmental deviations, probabilistically associated with later disorder, is critical for primary prevention and early intervention. In fact, the key promise of a developmental approach is the recognition of prognostically significant developmental deviations well before the person fits the criteria for the ultimate psychiatric disorder.

The Waddington/Bowlby Developmental Model

Bowlby (1969/1982; 1973) drew his model of developmental pathways from Waddington (1957). The basic metaphor is that of a tree lying on its side. In using any metaphor, there is the risk of oversimplification. Still, this one has a number of insightful features which appear to be useful for developing theory and conducting research.

First, this branching tree model alerts developmental psychopathologists to the possibility of change. Relevant concepts are differentiation in adaptation, deviation within the normal range, and *equifinality*. Thus, individuals may all begin on the same major pathway and, because of subsequent "choices," ultimately show quite different patterns of adaptation. The "mainstream" is represented by a family of pathways and not just one. Moreover, individuals who begin on a path deviating from the mainstream may nonetheless return to adaptation within the normal range, through subsequent corrective changes. "Pathology," then, would be viewed as the result of a series of deviations, always taking the individual further from normal patterns of adaptation. Finally, two individuals may at an early point be taking quite different directions, yet through a series of changes ultimately show quite similar adaptation. Thus, there are multiple pathways to the same outcome.

Second, the model makes the rather bold suggestion that, despite the possibility of change, subsequent adaptation is constrained by previous development. Normal pathways are considered "healthy" partly because they leave open the greatest array of future choices. On the other hand, the more consistently a deviating pathway is followed over time, the more unlikely it becomes that a normal pathway can be reclaimed. This proposition cannot be accepted completely because improved functioning sometimes occurs at every stage of development and because some disorders seem to emerge rather suddenly in adulthood. Still, as a generalization, it has considerable validity. When deviant behavior has been chronic and present from early life, change becomes quite difficult to accomplish in the years beyond middle childhood, and those individuals most easily changed in adulthood are those who have shown the least deviant patterns of adaptation.

This model, then, obviously suggests considerable continuity or coherence in development. Such continuity derives from environmental factors, individual factors, and the interplay of the two (Sroufe, 1979). First, environments tend to have stability in certain ways, such as the quality of parenting provided (Pianta, Egeland, & Sroufe, in press). Thus, environmental features that tend to influence development in a certain direction often continue to exert such an influence. Second, the experiences garnered by individuals in the context of a given developmental pathway influence the way they engage and interpret subsequent experiences (therefore influencing adaptational "choices"). This is Bowlby's provocative idea of *internal working models* (Bowlby, 1973). Based on experience, individuals form models of self, other, and relationships, and this set of basic expectations and beliefs colors the new relationships individuals form and how they interpret their experience within them (Bretherton, 1985; Main, Kaplan, & Cassidy, 1985). Finally, and closely related, these model-based ways of perceiving and interacting with the environment influence environmental reactions. A child that has been rejected by caregivers isolates himself from peers and so is neglected by them, or, in anger lashes out and is actively rejected by peers and punished by teachers. Both peer relationships and teacher relationships may be predicted from earlier attachment relationships (Sroufe, 1988; Sroufe & Fleeson, 1987). In a later section we review what is now considerable evidence for the coherence of individual adaptation over time.

Developmental Deviation as a Criterion of Pathology

Traditionally, two approaches to defining psychopathology have been dominant. In the first, clinical consensus is used to describe syndromes and their associated clusters of symptoms. This is the basis for the influential Diagnostic and Statistical Manuals of the American Psychiatric Association (e.g., APA, 1987). The second, commonly referred to as the empirical approach, utilizes statistical techniques to summarize large amounts of descriptive data on discrete problems and symptoms of children (Achenbach, 1982; Achenbach & Edelbrock, 1986). Quite robust, broad dimensions of behavior emerge from such studies, such as the externalizing/internalizing dimension—those children whose problem is manifest in outwardly expressed behavior (e.g., aggressiveness) and those whose problem is expressed in more private symptoms (somatic complaints, social withdrawal). Such broad characterizations of children do have predictive power. It is externalizing problems in children that are most predictive of later problems, including severe pathology. More specific factors and clusters have also been identified, but the prognostic value of these is less well established, and the same children may score high on factors which seemingly are quite dissimilar. It is the case, however, that scores on such factors show moderate stability during the elementary school years (Renkin et al, in press).

Neither of these two traditional approaches has been very developmental. In its early forms the DSM system had few categories pertinent to children and these were primarily downward extentions of adult categories. Recent versions do have child categories (attention deficit/hyperactivity disorder, reading disorder, etc), but other than mention of age of onset little concern has been shown for varying manifestations of the disorder with development, developmental precursors, or developmental relationships among disorders. Normal development is brought in to some extent by addressing the child's highest level of adjustment (on Axis 5), but disorders are not really considered in terms of salient developmental issues or tasks; that is, disordered behavior is not considered in light of normal development.

The empirical approach, too, while not necessarily so, has made little connection with a developmental viewpoint. The primary agenda of the empirical researchers was to demonstrate that meaningful groupings of children could be made empirically. Rather than keying to age appropriate issues (e.g., fantasy play, identification, reciprocal peer relations), the effort has been to select a series of problem behaviors and symptoms which might apply across much of childhood. Moreover, the symptom checklist approach does not readily yield access to *patterns* of adaptation; that is, the child's particular way of managing impulses and feelings and particular style of coping with environmental challenges in various circumstances. (Frequency, not behavioral context, is the focus of the rating.) From this approach, one certainly can get an overall index of how well a child is doing and broad characterizations of his or her problems, but the information obtained is probably not sufficiently precise to forecast with accuracy future specific problems or to guide intervention. For example, externalizing problems have been linked to virtually every major adult disorder (Sroufe & Rutter, 1984). Because it is without theoretical guidance, this approach also may not be the most efficient for tracing the course of individual children, that is, for defining developmental pathways.

The third approach to defining psychopathology, namely in terms of developmental deviation, has received little emphasis, perhaps because adequate description of patterns of adaptation across phases of development is only recently being achieved. This viewpoint does have a history within psychoanalytic theory, most notably in the work of Anna Freud (1965). Freud's concept of ''developmental lines'' could be used as a starting point for a developmental approach to assessing pathology. In her scheme she identifies some key developmental issues. Some lines concern the child's acquisition of mastery over his own actions (body hygiene, prevention of injury). Other lines, such as the movement from emotional dependency to independence and from egocentrism to social partnerships, are concerned with mastery of the environment. The entire profile of lines is examined, and pathology is assessed in terms of large discrepancies among the lines and notable lags with respect to normal progress along each line.

There are the roots of an adequate developmental approach here. Freud proposed that in the case of ego development there were no fixation points. Individuals could move back along a developmental line to the extent necessary to deal with some current, potentially overwhelming challenge, then move forward again (so-called ''regression in the service of the ego''). And she noted that one could not infer disorder from a given behavior, because it could reflect a temporary or circumstantial perturbation rather than being a true symptom. These two ideas—mobility of function and the meaning of behavior—are key assumptions in developmental approaches to psychopathology (Santostefano, 1978; Sroufe & Rutter, 1984). Still, Anna Freud's conceptualization remained mired in psychic structure and energy terminology (the balance between id and ego, drive fixation, etc.). Moreover, there is an emphasis on progress along a line (level of maturity, attainment of stages) in defining pathology. Such a quantitative focus on level of maturity is often seen in more modern developmental approaches as well. I would argue instead that an emphasis on qualitative aspects of adaptation rather than quantitative, level approaches will be more fruitful in defining developmental pathways. For example, the child who is highly attuned to detecting and exploiting the vulnerabilities of others may be just as advanced in cognitive perspective taking as the empathic child.

Despite these criticisms, Anna Freud's work serves as a starting point for a conceptualization of developmental deviation by underscoring the following features: (1) a focus on phase (age) appropriate developmental issues, (2) assessment of current behavior in terms of those issues, and (3) insistence upon an analysis of the profile of adaptation shown by the child, cutting across aspects of development. Were one to then broaden the developmental issues away from drive management, and emphasize qualitative aspects of functioning with respect to these issues rather than level of functioning or age of achievement, the beginnings of a new approach to defining pathology may be seen. Individuals manifesting developmental deviation are those whose manner of dealing with the set of issues for a given period of development puts them at a disadvantage for dealing with the issues of a subsequent period. Some of these individuals are disordered. Some are on a developmental pathway leading to disorder. The judgment of whether they are now or likely will later be disordered depends on the particular nature of the deviation, as does the particular set of disorders likely to be manifest.

One illustrative set of developmental issues is shown in Table 2.1. Patterns of adaptation—both normal patterns and deviations—have been sketched for only a

TABLE 2.1
Issues in Early Development[a]

Period	Age in Months	Issues	Role for Caregiver
1	0 - 3	Physiological Regulation (Turning Toward)	Smooth Routines
2	3 - 6	Management of Tension	Sensitive, Cooperative Interaction
3	6 - 12	Establishing an Effective Attachment Relationship	Responsive Availability
4	12 - 18	Exploration and Mastery	Secure base
5	18 - 30	Individuation (Autonomy)	Firm support
6	30 - 54	Management of Impulses, sex-role identification, Peer Relations	Clear roles, values, Flexible self-control
7	72 - 144	Physical and academic competence, social competence, friendship formation	Recognition, modeling of competent behavior, appropriate role relations

[a]Adapted from Sroufe (1979).

few. For example, Ainsworth's (Ainsworth, Blehar, Waters, & Wall, 1978) patterns of secure attachment and two basic patterns of anxious attachment (each with two subtypes) represent normal adaptations and deviations, respectively, with regard to the issue, "forming an effective attachment relationship." The "rejected"/"neglected" subtypes of social withdrawal, and their varieties, represent beginning attempts to define deviations in relation to the salient developmental issue of peer group entry (Asher & Wheeler, 1985; Rubin, LeMare, & Lollis, in press). Clearly, much work needs to be done, but illustrations of the developmental deviation concept exist. Some of these are based on qualitative assessments. Anxiously attached infants are not more or less attached or less advanced in their attachment compared to securely attached infants. Rather, the organization of their attachment behavior puts them at a disadvantage with respect to environmental exploration and the development of coordinated, reciprocal social exchanges (see Table 2.2). Later self-efficacy and peer relations

TABLE 2.2
Patterns of Attachment Behavior[a]

Infants Secure in Their Attachment

A. Caregiver is a secure base for exploration
 1. readily separate to explore toys
 2. affective sharing of play
 3. affiliative to stranger in mother's presence
 4. readily comforted when distressed (promoting a return to play)

B. Active in seeking contact or interaction upon reunion
 1. If distressed
  (a) immediately seek and maintain contact
  (b) contact is effective in terminating distress
 2. If not distressed
  (a) active greeting behavior (happy to see caregiver)
  (b) strong initiation of interaction

Anxious/Resistant Attachment

A. Poverty of exploration
 1. difficulty separating to explore, may need contact even prior to separation
 2. wary of novel situations and people

B. Difficulty settling upon reunion
 1. may mix contact seeking with contact resistance (hitting, kicking, squirming)
 2. may simply continue to cry and fuss
 3. may show striking passivity

Anxious/Avoidant Attachment

A. Independent exploration
 1. readily separate to explore during preseparation
 2. little affective sharing
 3. affiliative to stranger, even when caregiver absent (little preference)

B. Active avoidance upon reunion
 1. turning away, looking away, moving away, ignoring
 2. may mix avoidance with proximity
 3. avoidance more extreme on second reunion
 4. no avoidance of stranger

---

[a]Adapted from Ainsworth et al. (1978).

are thereby compromised. Likewise rejected preschoolers are not best thought of as more or less competent than neglected children. Rather, they evidence qualitatively different patterns or "developmental pathways" (Rubin et al., in press).

An emphasis on normal and deviating patterns of adaptation with respect to salient developmental issues has a number of advantages for developmental psychopathology. First, such an approach is primed for early detection. Developmental deviations may be defined not only before there is clear-cut psychopathology but before *any* problem may be obvious in the child. This is accomplished by examining adaptation of the caregiver-child dyad with respect to the developmental issues of early infancy and toddlerhood. Second, the approach provides guidance concerning what areas of functioning to examine and what may be considered atypical functioning. And because fundamentally different issues are defined at each phase, developmental transformations pose no inherent problem for this approached. There is no assumption of linear continuity (e.g., an overly dependent preschooler emerging from a dependent infant; an aggressive child emerging from a tantrumy infant). Rather, complex developmental relationships are assumed; for example, an effectively dependent infant becoming a self-reliant preschooler (Bowlby, 1973), a prediction which has been confirmed by research (Sroufe, Fox, & Pancake, 1983). Finally, suitable outcome criteria are built right into the approach. If one has correctly identified a significant developmental deviation (a particular pattern of maladaptation with respect to a given salient issue), such a pattern should be related probabilistically to maladaptation with respect to subsequent salient issues. By definition, maladaptation (developmental deviation) in this scheme reflects compromised development and therefore less than usual likelihood of negotiating subsequent issues well (Waters & Sroufe, 1983). I next examine research support for this critical tenet of the developmental approach.

THE COHERENCE OF ADAPTATION

How clear, defined in terms of salient developmental issues, is the link between adaptation at one period and adaptation at a later period? Recent research provides quite strong evidence for cross-time continuity in adequately designed studies. When robust assessments are carried out at both early and later time points, powerful relationships have been supported over periods of 30 or more years and from early childhood to adulthood. For example, in a 30-year follow-up of subjects in their classic studies of childhood conduct disorders, McCord (1988) found notable continuity. Likewise, the Eron/Huesman group (Huesman, Eron, Lefkowitz, & Walder, 1984) found continuity in aggressive behavior over a 25-year period. Farington and West showed that they could predict conduct disordered behavior quite strongly up to age 32 from indices at age 8 (e.g., West, 1982). Lee Robins (1978) also found impressive evidence of continuity for such externalizing behavior, but found much less continuity for internalizing problems. The Berkeley longitudinal study by Jeanne and Jack Block has now revealed continuity in an impulse control variable from age 4 to age 18 (Block, 1987). And recent studies in England have documented powerful effects of early institutionalization, including the inability to achieve intimate peer relationships in adolescence and parenting difficulties in early adulthood (Rutter, in press). This latter work may be used to illustrate the point that the more appropriate focus is on the coherence and logic of developmental pathways rather than on strict continuity per se. Not all of the early institution-reared girls showed parenting difficulties. In fact, those who achieved adequate partnerships did quite well as parents. Of course, the adequacy of the marital partnership was forecast by the planfulness of the partner selection, which was related to other aspects of adolescent adaptation. The coherence of developmental pathways goes beyond the direct connection between functioning at early and later developmental phases.

The series of longitudinal studies we have carried out at Minnesota (with Byron Egeland, Brian Vaughn, and Everett Waters) have been directly addressed to the problem of determining salient developmental issues, devising qualitative assessments specifically tailored to these issues, and determining the degree of stability/coherence of individual functioning across time. Some of this work has been presented previously in a number of publications and is reviewed only briefly here. A major focus is on the presentation of new data examining the continuity of individual adaptation from infancy to preadolescence of 32 children studied intensively.

In an early study we assessed the continuity of adaptation from infancy to toddlerhood (Matas, Arend, & Sroufe, 1978). It was found that assessments of attachment in infancy predicted key aspects of toddler functioning including persistence, flexibility, enthusiasm in approaching problems, positive affectivity, and cooperation with the caregiver—all aspects of emerging autonomy. There were two striking things about this demonstration. First, these strong links were found despite notable transformations in development. As predicted by numerous theorists (Bowlby, Erikson, Mahler, Yarrow, Kohut), it was those infants who had emotionally close relationships with their caregivers, who sought them out when needed, actively achieved physical contact when distressed, and used this contact to support encounters with novelty (i.e., those who were effectively dependent) who by age two had made the movement toward more autonomous functioning. Second, the attachment assessments in infancy (see Table 2.2) were actually assessments of the effectiveness of the infant-caregiver *relationship,* not of the infant per se (Sroufe, 1985). In support of this, infant attachment classifications just as strongly predicted independently assessed maternal behavior at age two (emotional support for the toddler, quality of assistance) as they predicted child behavior. The claim is that one may forecast an incipient developmental pathway of a child even before such manifestations would be apparent in observations of the child in isolation, by an adroit assessment of the dyadic regulation which precedes emergence of the self (Sroufe, in press).

Subsequent studies have extended the process of linking sequential adaptation with respect to the series of developmental issues. Several showed that assessments of attachment in infancy predicted competence with peers during the preschool period (Waters, Wippman & Sroufe, 1979; LaFrenier & Sroufe, 1985) or with aspects of curiosity and self-management (Arend, Gove, & Sroufe, 1979; Sroufe, 1983; Waters et al., 1979). The Arend study also explicitly revealed the link between assessments of toddler autonomy and later curiosity and self-management in kindergarten.

One intensive, detailed study concerned examination of the range of salient aspects of preschool functioning with respect to prior adaptation (Sroufe, 1983). Peer competence, for example, was accessed through composited teacher ratings and rankings, peer sociometrics, and numerous forms of direct observation. Children with histories of secure attachment were clearly more effective in the peer group and also formed deeper relationships with individual partners (Pancake, 1985; Sroufe, 1983). Likewise, emotional dependency was measured by observations of frequency of child-initiated contacts with teachers, specific seeking of nurturance, amount of physical contact in group meetings, frequency of teacher guidance and discipline, and overall ratings and rankings across the set of teachers. All measures revealed that children who had been in anxious attachment relationships in infancy were more dependent on their preschool teachers. This included those who had shown the anxious/avoidant pattern of attachment (ignoring, failing to go to their mothers or even retreating from them when under stress). Such infants might have been viewed by some to be precociously independent (Clarke-Stewart & Fein, 1983). But from the viewpoint of developmental deviation and developmental pathways, the later dependency of those in this avoidant group is fully predictable (Sroufe et al., 1983). (This pattern also had seen in the Matas study of toddler functioning.) Based on composited Q-sort descriptions by the teachers, those children with histories of secure relationships also were higher on self-esteem and on the Block's ego-resiliency construct (Block, 1987), with almost no overlap between the secure and avoidant groups. They also were judged by the teachers to be less aggressive, less depressed, and less noncompliant. Direct observation showed them to be less often victims and less often to victimize their peers (Troy & Sroufe, 1987). Independent observations of their fantasy play showed their play to be more elaborate, more flexible, and overall of higher quality. Most notably, when conflict themes arose in the play, such conflicts were significantly more likely to be brought to a successful resolution (Rosenberg, 1984). (Oh no! He broke his leg. . . Here comes the ambalenz. . . Take him to the hospital. . . They fixed it.) Their manner of coping with problems that arose in everyday transactions was also observed to be more flexible and more enhancing of their social relationships (Erez, 1987).

More germain to the present paper than these differences between the preschool functioning of those with histories of secure or anxious attachment are the particular patterns of adaptation shown by the various groups. Those children who were functioning well in preschool, even considering only those who had had secure histories, were not all the same. For example, physical dominance had a very different influence on popularity within the boys group compared to the girl's group. Also, some of these children were reserved and quiet; others were quite boisterous and energetic. Healthy adaptation consists of numerous pathways. What these children had in common was the ability to manage themselves (adjust their behavior in keeping with the requirements and opportunities of given circumstances), to effectively utilize resources in the environment (including teachers) and to be emotionally engaged with peers. Characteristically they were emphatic, affectively positive (especially in engaging and responding to others), and eager for new experiences (Kestenbaum, Farber, & Sroufe, in press).

Those who had histories of anxious attachment relationships also showed variety in their patterns of preschool adaptation. Probabilistically, they conformed quite well to behavioral profiles defined *a priori* (see Table 2.3). It was reasoned that those with histories of anxious/resistant attachment, presumed to result from inconsistent, chaotic care (with households often characterized by disorganization and neglect in our poverty sample), would likely fit one of two patterns, either being hyperactive, impulsive, easily frustrated and inept with peers or passive, dependent, weak, and teacher-oriented. These children, it was thought, would be oriented toward social contact, but would not have the necessary expectations or skills for successful peer relations. They would not be emotionally disengaged from their environments but they might be wary, constrained or generally needy of support to deal with the environment. Those with avoidant histories, on the other hand, were expected to be antisocial and hostile/aggressive, emotionally isolated, or disconnected and poorly oriented. These patterns were derived from the connection between avoidant attachment and emotional unavailability or active rejection by the caregiver (Ainsworth et al., 1978; Egeland & Sroufe, 1981). Of course not all of the children with anxious

TABLE 2.3
Hypothetical Behavioral Profiles

A Groups

A_a Hostile, mean, aggressive, antisocial (lying, stealing, devious).

A_b Emotionally insulated, asocial, isolated.

A_c Disconnected, spaced out, psychotic-like. May be oblivious or bizarre, or just not know what is going on.

C Groups

C_a Overstimulated (hyper), easily frustrated, tense or anxious, impulsive, flailing out, rather than hostile.

C_b Dependent, passive, weak, helpless, teacher oriented.

histories fit the predicted patterns. Individual children with avoidant histories fit one of the two "resistant" patterns and vice versa, and an occasional child (4 of 22 with anxious histories in the two preschool classes) showed a healthy pattern of adaptation. Still, the placements of blind judges, using descriptions of 3 teachers, placed children within the expected patterns well beyond chance (Sroufe, 1983).

We present these latter findings in some detail for two reasons. First, they demonstrate the usefulness of the idea of branching pathways of development. Were only one pattern of adaptation assumed, notably fewer cases would have been correctly predicted. In fact, prior to moving to this level of profile analysis very few differences between the children with different types of anxious attachment history were found. Both groups were dependent on teachers, both lacked competence with peers, neither was judged to be ego-resilient or have high self-esteem or enthusiasm in engaging tasks. Only when we moved beyond global measures and toward configurations of behavior with attention to meaning were meaningful differences between these two deviating developmental pathways found. The second reason for describing these families of preschool patterns of adaptation is that they will be useful as we next turn our attention to the problem of predicting adaptation at the end of middle childhood. The model we are developing suggests that certain kinds of change are more likely than others. In particular, it should be more likely that a child will reveal another member of the family of patterns for a given major pathway than a pattern from some other grouping. Further differentiation of patterns also seems likely with development. Therefore, these descriptions from the preschool period can serve as a backdrop for a consideration of patterns of maladaptation in middle childhood.

THE MINNESOTA SUMMER DAYCAMP PROJECT

The most compelling data on the continuity and coherence of adaptation over time that we have gathered were obtained in a recent series of observational studies made in the context of a summer recreation program. Of three programs planned, two have been completed. Sixteen children are involved each summer, so the total N will be 48, 24 boys and 24 girls. The children are all being drawn from our longitudinal study, so that detailed information exists on the history of family circumstances, child adaptation and parent-child interaction, including attachment history, behavior in a dyadic problem-solving situation, incremental stress and other measures described on subsequent pages. The majority of the children will have attended the earlier nursery school project, so quite detailed data concerning their adaptation at that age will be available for longitudinal comparison as well. All subjects in the longitudinal studies were originally selected on the basis of poverty (public assistance for prenatal care and delivery). Half the mothers were teenagers, two-thirds were unmarried. Living conditions often were unstable. Most continue to live at or near poverty by age 10. However, some (about 25%) now live in stable middle class or lower middle class families.

The children were selected so that histories of anxious and secure attachment are equally represented, with the two subtypes of anxious attachment also equally represented. Most of the children had the same attachment classifications at 12 and 18 months. But for some, roughly in the same proportion as the total sample, attachment classification changed between the two infant assessments. In these cases, profiles of adaptation in the tool problem situation at age two, previously validated against infant attachment assessments, were used to reach a final classification. In the end all children were classified as secure (B), anxious/resistant (C), or anxious/avoidant (A) before being included in the camp.

Each daycamp lasts 4 weeks, with children present daily for 4 hours. The programming is highly recreational with swimming, games, crafts, and outings. There are structured activities, including group meetings and the inevitable song circle. Lunch and 2 snack times are also highlights. There is a great deal of opportunity for peer social interaction, and this is a key focus of the study. The level of supervision is high. At least 4 counselors were always present, and often the ratio of counselors to children was about 1 : 4. The counselors were highly qualified child experts (advanced graduate students in applied programs or professionals) who generally had a great deal of experience with children. The program was very high quality, and in some ways this worked against the hypothesis of continuity in adaptation. We saw, for example, less bullying and less aggression, less isolation, and more positive affect than we see when we observe the same children on their elementary school playgrounds. Children thrived at these camps, some looking better than they ever have previously. Nonetheless, significant differences between groups remained obvious.

The supportiveness of the camp context may have blunted the differences among children. On the other hand, the richness and power of the observational opportunities more than outweighed this potential problem. We had done school observations in the past, but in that circumstance we were never able to observe the child more than three times. Moreover, the children were in 139 different classrooms (100 schools), with widely varying atmospheres, including different teachers and different children, none of whom we knew. In contrast, the current study to a large extent controls context. Each child in the camp has the same counselors, and, with the exception of himself or herself, the same peers. Therefore, a great deal of extraneous variance is removed. Also, it is possible to gather certain unique data, such as the way developmental histories go together. For example, one cannot only identify the history of a bully, but the history of the victim, the histories of both friends and so forth. One also can composite the ratings and other evaluations of the multiple counselors, thus removing to a large extent idiosyncratic features. Finally, and most important, it was possible to do daily observations (and filming) using teams of trained observers. Not surprisingly, the summer camps are yielding far more powerful results than our school observations even though the N for the latter study was twice as large.

In keeping with the developmental perspective underlying this work (Sroufe, 1979; Waters & Sroufe, 1983), the assessments in the daycamp project are specifically keyed to the issues of the late middle childhood period, just as our assessments of attachment, emerging autonomy, and entry into the peer group were keyed to infancy and early childhood. The children are now 10–11 years-old. One key domain concerns social competence. By this age children are expected to be able to function well within the peer group with all its demands for negotiation and conflict resolution. The child who is rejected by, or removes him- or herself from the same-gender peer group arena is showing clear maladaptation, which forecasts later problems, even into adulthood (Cowen et al., 1973; Robins, 1978; Roff, Sells, and Golden, 1972; Kohlberg, Ricks, & Snarey, 1984). Beyond this successful participation in the peer group, the child of this age is expected to show the capacity for genuine friendship, complete with a sense of loyalty and emotional sharing, with one or two other children of the same gender. Another domain concerns a sense of agency, mastery, and confidence (what Erikson calls "industry"). A child of 10 should not only obviously expect to do well in new or challenging tasks, but should throw him- or herself into activities with an enthusiasm and confidence. Well functioning 10-year-olds have a notable level of comfort both with their bodies and their abilities. They enjoy a challenge. They try hard. And commonly they are successful. This capacity is also related to a more abstract sense of well being and self-esteem. By age 10 a child should have a clear sense of himself or herself and be in "command" of his or her own behavior. These children, then, have an advanced capacity for self-management, which is not dependent on continual adult direction (what Jeanne and Jack Block, 1980, have called "ego-resiliency"). Finally, in keeping with this, such children have left emotional dependency far behind. They do not constantly need nurturance and attention from adults in order to function. Relationships with adults may obviously be warm and caring, and they are able to use adults appropriately as resources, but the business at hand clearly is peer relationships. Well functioning 10-year-olds were expected to spend relatively little time engaging the adults at the camp.

As was the case with our earlier preschool project (Sroufe, 1983), data in this project were collected at several levels. For each child 4 counselors completed a California Q-sort, describing the child by sorting 100 statements into 9 categories denoting congruence or noncongruence with the child in question (i.e., from extremely characteristic to extremely uncharacteristic of the child). These sorts, then, may be referred to criterial sorts for high ego-resiliency, high self-esteem, and so forth. In addition, where a Q-sort exists from an earlier period (e.g., nursery school), the child may be compared with him- or herself. Counselors also made ratings of each child on agency, dependency, social competence, positive and negative affect, compliance, and self-confidence, and they made a series of rank orderings, including one for emotional health/self-esteem.

Three teams of observers (all blind to attachment history or any other data) provided behavioral data at different levels of detail and across several domains. One was concerned with dependency data, noting every contact between a child and the counselor of focus during a given observation, including who initiated the contact and the nature of the contact. They rotated around the counselors using a counselor-sampling procedure. In addition, this team made seating charts during every circle meeting over the course of the camp. From this data, the frequency with which a child sat next to a counselor could be determined. A second team focused on social association patterns. Association data was based on a child-sampling procedure. Each child was watched just long enough to determine if the child was engaged with someone and if so who that partner was. These observations were used to generate isolation scores, frequency of having counselors as partners, and frequency of being engaged with other children. It also provided an objective measure of friendships to accompany judgments by counselors obtained weekly. The final observation team concentrated on affect expression and aggression.

The most global indices of middle childhood competence in this daycamp setting showed a clear advantage for those children having had a history of secure attachment, for each summer separately and, overwhelmingly, for the first two camps combined. For example, a summary formula was generated across 4 counselors and across all ratings (agency + self-confidence + social competence + positive affect + compliance with counselor requests − dependency − negative affective tone). In the first summer camp 7 of the 8 top-ranked children had been securely attached. In the second camp, the top 5 children all had been securely attached. Each of these results is significant at the .01 level of significance, and the difference between anxious and secure groups across the two camps was highly significant. Likewise, the Q-sort based ego-resiliency scores significantly discriminated secure from anxious groups, as did molar rankings on emotional health, social competence, and dependency. Specific rating scales for self-confidence, dependency, and social skills also yielded significant results.

The behavioral observation data confirmed and expanded these findings from the ratings. For example, not only was it the case that behavioral measures and ratings of dependency were highly correlated (in the .60s), but the behavioral indices of dependency (e.g., number of child–counselor contacts, frequency of sitting by counselor, etc.) all distinguished secure from anxious groups in each camp. Those with anxious histories sought and got more nurturance from their counselors, and they received more intervention from the counselors. In accord with this, association pattern observations made by another team of observers showed that those with anxious histories were more often "paired" with a counselor. They also were more often isolated. Reciprocally, those with secure histories were more often paired with other children.

Both counselor judgments and association observations revealed that those with secure histories were more likely to have friendships, and to obtain the leading ranks in terms of frequency of being together. While not yet formally analyzed, interviews with the children also suggest that those with secure histories more often indicate reciprocal friendships and discuss their friendships in emotionally deeper terms (e.g., "We tell each other things we wouldn't tell anyone else."). These same interviews also revealed that those with secure histories tend to have higher sociometric status; i.e., they are more frequently named by their peers as liked.

One other finding concerning friendships is especially noteworthy, although with one camp remaining it is only marginally significant. There is a clear trend for friendships to form within basic attachment groups; that is, those with secure histories tend to form friendships with others with secure histories, while those with anxious histories find partners with similar backgrounds. To some extent this may be a function of anxious partners being all that is left after the secure children pair up. However, at least some of the anxious/anxious partnerships formed rather early in the camp. We are actively pursuing this lead and also information we have concerning qualitative aspects of relationships, including cross-gender relationships. The rules concerning gender boundaries were rather strictly observed. Therefore when these boundaries were traversed, it is interesting to note which children are involved.

Findings for affect expression and aggression have not yet been analyzed for the second daycamp. Two significant findings from the first camp are worthy of mention, however. Those children with anxious histories more often were observed to show no positive affect during a 3-minute observation period than those with secure histories, and they also were significantly more likely to exhibit a passive response to aggression. (Based on teacher behavior checklist data, we also have found anxious attachment to be related to aggression and antisocial behavior at school; Renken et al., in press).

Analyses of behavioral profiles are only now underway and really must await completion of the third camp to be dealt with fully. Some preliminary results are clear enough to merit reporting, however. When as a first approach we classified each child with an anxious history into one of the five profiles derived from our earlier preschool research, considerable fit was apparent. All but 2 of the 16 anxiously attached children could be placed in one of the 5 categories in Table 2.3, although the one case placed in the "disconnected/bizzarre" group was not nearly as psychotic-like as the earlier preschool members of this class had been. As can be seen in Table 2.4, all 7 of the children placed in the Passive and Hyperactive/Impulsive (tense) groups in fact had histories of anxious/resistance attachment, along with one child with a secure attachment history. Children

TABLE 2.4
Children of Different Attachment Histories
Grouped According to Counselor Judged Patterns of Maladaptation

Passive*	Hyperactive*	Aggressive**	Isolated**	Bizarre**
C	C	C	A	A
C	B	B	A	
C	C		A	
C	C		A	

*Patterns predicted for Anxious/Resistant (C) infants.
**Patterns predicted for Anxious/Avoidant (A) infants.

placed in the Isolated (from peers) group consistently had histories of anxious attachment. One child placed in the Hostile/Aggressive group had a resistant attachment history and one had a secure history, both contrary to prediction. This group was also expected to be much larger. In fact, two of the children in the Isolated group have been observed in other contexts to be quite hostile and aggressive. One is, in fact, the leading bully at his school. This seems to be an instance where our positive camp context reduced certain forms of negative behavior.

Patterns Related to Seductive Care

More striking with respect to the notion of branching developmental pathways are the observations concerning current adaptation of children at the daycamp who during the toddler and early preschool periods had experienced patterns of seductive care and/or notable blurring of generational boundaries. As suggested in the introduction, such a pattern of early care, where the parent is meeting sensual or emotional needs through a child, is overstimulating and ill-prepares the child for normal patterns of adaptation to the peer group (Jacobvitz & Sroufe, 1987; Sroufe et al., 1985). Yet, following our developmental perspective, a family of outcomes rather than one single outcome is to be expected from such a developmental history. Patterns that we had defined at the end of the preschool period included the following:

1. *Sexually inappropriate behavior.*   At age 10/11 this could include inappropriate touching or fondling of another, exposing oneself, preoccupation with sexuality, precocious cross-gender behavior.

2. *Hyperactive/Impulsive/Tense.*   At age 10/11 impulse control issues would be especially notable, though intense anxiety is also possible

3. *Coy/Cute/Appealing.*   These children are especially appealing to adults of the opposite gender. They may be quite shy or clownish, or they may be strikingly attractive

4. *Victimized.*   These children are scapegoated by others, and may even be

TABLE 2.5
Children Showing Patterns of Maladaptation
Expected to Derive from Seductive Care

Sexually Inappropriate	Exploited	Hyperactive	Coy/ Cute
KS*	TS	KS	HJ
EJ	DM	EJ	(YT)
	DA	KD	

*Letters refer to code names for individual subjects.

the targets of "sexual" exploitation (the child that the inappropriate toucher touches).

Of the 36 children who have participated in the 2 daycamps, 9 had histories of seductive/overstimulating care. Table 2.5 shows the behavioral patterns exhibited by 8 of these children. It can be seen that two children showed both the highly impulsive and the sexually inappropriate patterns. The case in parentheses under coy/cute was designated as marginal because, while he was indeed viewed by all of the female counselors as very attractive, he showed only hints of coyness, shyness, clownishness or passivity that we think will often be associated with this pattern. One case with a seductive history fit none of the patterns (though he clearly had fit pattern 1 as a preschooler). This child seems to have changed his pattern of adaptation. Still, excluding these 2 cases, 7 of 9 were clearly hits, and only one child of the other 27 fit any of these patterns (pattern 3). This clearly is a dramatic result, and it underscores the value of defining multiple outcomes. Were only one of the possible outcomes considered (e.g., inappropriate sexual contact), significant results would not have been obtained and valid developmental pathways would have been obscured.

DISORDERS AS DEVELOPMENTAL DEVIATION: THE CASE OF AD/HD

Within our research program we are only beginning to trace out pathways to disorder, describing them as developmental deviations. We have shown some links between attachment history (and our toddler and preschool measures of adaptation) and assessments of depressive symptomatology and aggression during the first 3 grades of elementary school (Bacon, 1988; Garber et al., 1985; Renkin et al., in press). Seriously disturbed children who already have had extensive psychiatric care also have been found to have negative early histories. But, generally, the numbers are not yet great enough to allow systematic analysis. Formal detection of troubled children lags behind the emergence of problems, and, of course, many problems of interest do not become apparent until adolescence or early adulthood.

One exception is the case of Attention Deficit/Hyperacticity Disorder (AD/HD). We already have a handful of subjects that have been given this diagnosis formally, and we have a sizeable number that we have determined to fit quite closely the agreed upon clinical picture of this disorder (e.g., Barkley & Cunningham, 1978). AD/HD is, of course, one of the most common childhood diagnoses, especially among boys, with estimates ranging up to one in ten. While this estimate probably is high, there is no doubt that a large number of children may be reliably assigned this label. Therefore, AD/HD represented a suitable starting point for an attempt to apply a developmental perspective to a recognized, early emerging disorder.

Traditionally AD/HD has not been considered within a developmental perspective, with the exception that the symptom picture is viewed as changing in adolescence (APA, 1987). Such children often are viewed as qualitatively different from other children, due to an organic aberration. The condition is thought to be inherent in the child, with little influence from family factors. This accounts for the former labels given these children (e.g., minimal brain dysfunction), and to the current widespread practice of pharmacological intervention (Wender & Klein, 1986). Yet, the assumption of organicity remains unfounded, and environmental determinants have been virtually unexplored (Jacobvitz & Sroufe, 1987). It remains likely that many cases of this heterogeneous condition are due to history of care and current environmental factors. Moreover, even in those cases when organic factors play a large role or those cases (many more) where there is a combination of biological and environmental factors, a consideration of normal developmental pathways and developmental deviation would still be pertinent for understanding children with these problems.

The relevant developmental issue for our conceptualization of AD/HD concerns the acquisition of self-management or self-control. This issue is listed under those for the preschool period in Table 2.1. However, as is the case with any developmental issue, its roots precede the period of its ascendancy, and its elaboration continues throughout development. Therefore, in tracing this line, and the normal pathways and deviations with respect to it, we will begin in the infant period. Basically, this issue concerns the developing capacity to manage one's impulses and behavior in the face of changing arousal and the modulation of arousal itself. The key developmental question concerns how dyadic modulation of arousal and control of behavior effects the development of, or becomes, self-control.

One prototypic normal developmental pathway with respect to this issue might be described as follows (adapted from Sroufe, in press): In the early months of life, modulation of arousal and maintainence of organized behavior is largely under the control of the caregiver. To be sure, very young infants have certain built-in capacities to regulate arousal (e.g., crying or falling asleep when overstimulated), and by 4–6 months they have an array of capacities for pacing or modulating stimulation. They may, for example, turn away from something unpleasant or turn away simply to pace an interaction. However, if they are to succeed, these capacities must rely heavily on responsiveness in the social environment. The caregiver may accurately read the turn away as a signal to reduce stimulation or may, in fact, pursue the infant with intensified inputs. In general, caregivers must frame, pace, and be responsive to the infant's signals for arousal to stay within the limits that insure ongoing and well-organized infant behavior (Hayes, 1984; Sroufe & Ward, 1984). When the infant plays alone, she or he of course has great control over stimulation, but critical experiences with peaks and valleys of arousal and arousal modulation occur in the course of dyadic interaction.

When such interactive episodes are well choreographed by the caregiver, they provide a cumulative learning experience for the infant of unparalleled importance. In this setting the infant learns to "hold himself as he is being held" to "pay attention" and, in general to experience the maintainence of behavioral organization even in the face of high arousal (Brazelton, Koslowski, & Main, 1974; Sroufe, 1977; Stern, 1974). Thus, the infant is brought to peaks of arousal and excitement, but just before disorganization occurs, often in response to a "signal" from the infant, the caregiver deescalates and composure is regained. Again arousal is built up, ever higher over time, with the infant's capacities (and ultimately confidence) expanding. In time, too, the young child becomes a more active participant in the process, purposefully signaling the caregiver, purposefully varying his or her own response, and doing a larger share of the arousal modulation. In fact, one way of summarizing the developmental issues of the toddler period is in terms of the giving over of behavioral control—within limits—to the child. Within boundaries monitored and maintained by the caregiver, the toddler expresses feelings and impulses, at times coming to the edge of loss of control and at times crossing it. Caregivers provide feedback, guidance, limits, and discipline when necessary to assure that the toddler commonly stays within the boundaries of appropriate expression. All of this paves the way for the preschool period and beyond, when the child is expected to manage arousal and behavioral expression much more on his or her own, at times even when outside of the purview of caregivers.

When this developmental course is proceding normally, young children learn that high arousal or high stimulation need not lead to behavioral disorganization and total loss of control. They also learn that when they do in fact become overstimulated, and they do lose control, that organization can be regained. They develop, first, the belief that arousal can be modulated and that behavioral organization can be maintained or reclaimed, and, ultimately, the capacities and techniques for self-management of arousal. These children have control over deployment of attention, strategies for coping with stimulating circumstances, and the capacity to monitor and regulate the expression of impulses. Because they have been part of a well-regulated system, a system designed to progressively pass control on to the child, they now have the capacity for flexible self-regulation (Sroufe, in press).

The origins of AD/HD may be conceived (in many cases) as a deviation from the developmental pathway just described (e.g., Jacobvitz & Sroufe, 1987). The developmental progression of many of these children, we have reasoned, has followed a very different course. In the early phase of dyadic interaction, they did not experience responsive, smoothly orchestrated care. Stimulation was not paced and geared to the states and "signals" of the infant. Rather, stimulation was orthogonal to infant readiness, being based on the independent desires, moods, and needs of the caregiver. Care was, in Ainsworth's terms, "interfering." When the infant reached a peak of arousal, this may often have been precisely when he or she was stimulated further, either because signals were misread or because they were not attended at all. Stimulation often was pushed on an infant in an intrusive manner. Conceptually, of course, the infant may play a role in this scenario, perhaps due to inborn differences in arousability. Such a role remains to be demonstrated empirically. In any case, overstimulated infants would acquire little sense of the organization and flow of rises and falls of arousal and of the coordination of behavior within them. In addition, such infants likely would have numerous experiences of overarousal and total behavioral disorganization. From the infancy period then, such infants would take forward neither the expectations for nor the experiences with routine arousal modulation.

The movement toward autonomy in the toddler period presents new opportunities for acquiring self-modulating capacities but also new ways of being overtaxed. Having well developed intentionality and purposefulness—the capacity to keep a goal in mind—the toddler has a greatly expanded capacity for frustration. Acting more on his own impulses the toddler can overarouse himself and is much more vulnerable to being drawn into highly arousing interchanges with the caregiver. Despite the movement toward autonomy (or perhaps because of it) the child remains quite dependent on parental controls, for he can take arousal to heights from which he cannot return. The term "terrible twos" is not without meaning. There are thus new vulnerabilities for overstimulation during the toddler period. Sometimes this takes the form of simply not recognizing the legitimacy of the child's needs; more often we observe deliberate provoking, teasing, parent-initiated power struggles and/or refusal of the parent to set boundaries. Also, gender issues commonly emerge during the toddler period; the male child, for example, is no longer an infant but now is a boy. We see parental control techniques emerge which are tinged with sensuality, and we see seductive maternal behavior taking various forms (flirting, teasing, inappropriate sensual contact), largely reserved for sons in the case of mothers (Sroufe & Ward, 1980). Such behavior is notably overstimulating of the child, often resulting in further noncompliance and/or frustration. Often this renewed frustration is met with threats or punishments, further stimulating the already highly overaroused child.

Such patterns may be elaborated at age 3½ when, normally, children have acquired the rudiments of self-management. Children provoked and overstimulated during the toddler period may be shaky in their ability to manage their impulses now. They may still be engaged in negotiating control issues with their caregivers and may be quite vulnerable to frustration and loss of control. If, as their emerging capacities for self-regulation and arousal modulation are taxed by challenging circumstances, they are subject to teasing, provocation or distracting, self-serving engagement by the caregiver, they may again experience bouts of loss of control. As with the toddler period, a clear, calm parental presence supports the child's acquisition of self-control; an abdication of the parental role, deliberate provocation, or untimely stimulation, hampers the child's development of these critical capacities.

Caregiving Origins of AD/HD

In the context of the Egeland/Sroufe longitudinal study, assessments were available which were keyed to developmental deviations with respect to these issues. At 6 months we had home-interaction based ratings on Ainsworth's Cooperation/Interference Scale (a measure of intrusiveness). At 24 months we had observational data on maternal seductive behavior in a toy clean-up situation. (It was observation of these patterns of behavior and their apparent effects on the child that first alerted us to this particular pathway; Sroufe & Ward, 1980.) And at 42 months we had measures of "non-responsive intimacy" (physical contact pushed on the child) and "generational boundary dissolution" in a maternal teaching situation. The latter, which included abdication of the parental role, peer-like giggling and teasing with the child and the like (at times when the child needed calming), was specifically developed as a prediction of AD/HD type problems (Sroufe et al., 1985). The basic outcome variable in these studies was derived from teacher ratings using the Achenbach Behavior Problem Checklist (Achenbach & Edelbrock, 1986). A "hyperactivity" factor already existed from the original validation studies. In addition, both we and the Achenbach group created scales by selecting items from the checklist which corresponded to established criteria for AD/HD. These scales were then validated by comparing large clinical groups with control groups. Measures at all 3 ages yielded powerful confirmation of our predictions. Two of the 3 predictor variables were significant independently, including the 6-month assessment, both at kindergarten (Jacobvitz & Sroufe, 1987) and, in a follow-up, up to 3rd grade (Jacobvitz, 1987).

Thus, this elementary school-age problem was forecast by a developmental deviation as early as age 6 months. Assessments of child behavior (either observations or maternal report) at that time, including ratings of hyperactivity, did not predict later attention or hyperactivity problems, although, by age 3½ measures of child distractibility in the mother-child teaching task also predicted later hyperactivity. Cases predicted by maternal and child variables at this later age overlapped very little. In terms of early infant measures, only 1 of 42 measures predicted later AD/HD (a composite measure from two assessments with the Brazelton neonatal assessment procedure). While as one isolated variable, this finding requires replication, it is worth noting that cases predicted by this newborn neurological status measure overlapped little with cases predicted from early care measures, nor was this variable predictive of maternal overstimulation.

In summary, beginning by mapping out a usual developmental pathway with respect to a key issue in early development, then providing a sequential definition of a common deviation from this pathway, we were able ultimately to move to the level of assessment. In our view, this would not likely be the only pathway leading to AD/HD, though it seems to be a common one. Others have reported that minor physical anomalies predict AD/HD (Waldrop, Pederson, & Bell, 1968) although these were not a significant predictor in our study.

CONCLUSION

Researchers are only just beginning to consider the implications of viewing psychopathology in terms of developmental deviation; yet, within such a view lies the major promise of the developmental psychopathology discipline. It is clear that with appropriately complex approaches considerable coherence in individual adaptation over time can be demonstrated. This was pivotal, for unless this maintains we would have little hope of tracing pathways to particular disorders. And in this paper we have provided a beginning example of how one set of common childhood problems (labeled Attention Deficit/Hyperactivity Disorder in current psychiatric nomenclature) may be conceived in terms of developmental deviation. Implications of this research would seem clear. Children who will follow this pathway may be identified quite early in development, apparently well before the problem is manifest in the child per se. Related to this, prevention or early intervention in such cases would seem prudently directed at the caregiver–child relationship, rather than at the child alone.

Many questions remain, however, both in the case of our AD-HD example and more generally. We still know little about what protects certain individuals from continuing on the pathway to disorder once started, and we know little about varieties of pathways to the same disorder and how they are related. About half of the cases we identified as AD-HD were accounted for by our caregiving variables, with a few more (with little overlap) accounted for by our infant neurological status assessments. Many remained unaccounted for. At the same time, not all children experiencing intrusive, seductive, or overstimulating care showed hyperactivity and attention problems. As we pointed out in the case of seductive care, some children showed either a coy, passive pattern, a tendency to be victimized, and/or some sexually inappropriate behavior. At present we have little understanding of what determines whether one or another of these is followed.

In general, we know little about how fluid developmental pathways are, how and to what extent the fluidity changes with development, the uniqueness or commonality of factors which influence deviation from various pathways and at various points in development. These are some of the pressing issues that face our young field in the near future.

REFERENCES

Achenbach, T. (1982). *Developmental psychopathology* (2nd ed.). New York: Wiley.

Achenbach, T., & Edelbrock, C. (1986). *Manual for the Teacher's Report Form and Teacher Version of the Child Behavior Profile*. Burlington: Department of Psychiatry, University of Vermont.

Ainsworth, M., Blehar, M., Waters, E., & Wall, S. (1978). *Patterns of attachment*. Hillsdale, NJ: Lawrence Erlbaum Associates.

American Psychiatric Association. (1987). *Diagnostic and statistical manual of mental disorders* (3rd ed., rev.), Washington, D.C.: Author.

Arend, R., Gove, F., & Sroufe, L. A. (1979). Continuity of individual adaptation from infancy to kindergarten: A predictive study of ego-resiliency and curiosity in preschoolers. *Child Development, 50*, 950–959.

Arms, K., & Camp, P. (1987). *Biology* (3rd ed.). Philadelphia: Saunders.

Asher, S., & Wheeler, V. A. (1985). Children's loneliness: A comparison of rejected and neglected peer status. *Journal of Consulting and Clinical Psychology, 53*, 500–505.

Bacon, M. (1988). *The origins of depression in childhood*. Unpublished doctoral dissertation, University of Minnesota.

Barkley, R., & Cunningham, C. (1978). Do stimulant drugs improve the academic performance of hyperkinetic children? A review of outcome research. *Clinical Pediatrics, 17*, 85–93.

Block, J. (1987, April). *Longitudinal antecedents of ego-control and ego-resiliency in late adolescence*. Paper presented at the biennial meeting of the Society for Research in Child Development, Baltimore.

Block, J. H. (1979). *Personality development in males and females: The influence of different socialization*. Master Lecture Series of the American Psychological Organization, New York.

Block, J. H., & Block, J. (1980). The role of ego-control and ego-resiliency in the organization of behavior. In W. A. Collins (Ed.), *Minnesota symposia on child psychology, 13*. Hillsdale, NJ: Lawrence Erlbaum Associates.

Bowlby, J. (1973). *Separation*. New York: Basic Books.

Bowlby, J. (1982). *Attachment and loss* (2nd ed.). New York: Basic Books.

Brazelton, T. B., Koslowski, B., & Main, M. (1974). The origins of reciprocity: The early mother-infant interaction. In M. Lewis & L. Rosenblum (Eds.), *The effect of the infant on its caregiver*. New York: Wiley.

Bretherton, I. (1985). Attachment theory: Retrospect and prospect. In I. Bretherton & E. Waters (Eds.), *Growing points in attachment theory and research*. *Monographs of the Society for Research in Child Development, 50* (Serial No. 209).

Brown, G., Harris, T., & Bifulco, A. (1986). Long-term effects of early loss of parent. In M. Rutter, C. Izard, & P. Read (Eds.), *Depression in young people*. New York: Guilford Press.

Cicchetti, D. (1984). The emergence of developmental psychopathology. *Child Development, 55*, 1–7.

Clarke-Stewart, K. A., & Fein, G. (1983). Early childhood programs. In M. Haith & J. Campos (Eds.), P. H. Mussen (Series Ed.), *Handbook of child psychology: Infancy and developmental psychology*. New York: Wiley.

Cowen, E., Pederson, A., Babijian, H., Izzo, L., & Trost, M. (1973). Long-term follow-up of early detected vulnerable children. *Journal of Consulting and Clinical Psychology, 41*, 438–446.

Egeland, B., & Sroufe, L. A. (1981). Developmental sequelae of maltreatment in infancy. In D. Cicchetti & R. Rizley (Eds.), *New directions in child development: Developmental approaches to child maltreatment*. San Francisco: Jossey-Bass.

Erez, T. (1987). *Individual patterns of coping*. Unpublished doctoral dissertation, University of Minnesota.

Freud, A. (1965). The concept of developmental lines. *Psychoanalytic Study of the Child, 18*, 245–265.

Garber, J., Cohen, E., Bacon, P., Egeland, B., & Sroufe, L. A. (1985). *Depression in pre-schoolers: Reliability and validity of a behavioral observation measure*. Paper presented at the Society for Research in Child Development, Toronto.

Garmezy, N., & Streitman, S. (1974). Children at risk: The search for antecedents of schizophrenia. Part I: Conceptual models and research methods. *Schizophrenia Bulletin, 8*, 14–90.

Hayes, A. (1984). Interaction, engagement, and the origins of communication: Some constructive concerns. In L. Feagans, C. Garvey, & R. Golinkoff (Eds.), *The origins and growth of communication*. Norwood, NJ: Ablex.

Huesmann, L., Eron, L., Lefkowitz, M., & Walder, L. (1984). The stability of aggression over time and generations. *Developmental Psychology, 20*, 1120–1124.

Jacobvitz, D. (1987). *The early caregiver-child relationship and attention deficit hyperactivity disorder in school children*. Unpublished doctoral dissertation, University of Minnesota.

Jacobvitz, D., & Sroufe, L. A. (1987). The early caregiver-child relationship and attention deficit disorder with hyperactivity in kindergarten: A prospective study. *Child Development, 58*, 1496–1504.

Kestenbaum, R., Farber, E., & Sroufe, L. A. (in press). Individual differences in empathy among preschoolers: Concurrent and predictive validity. In N. Eisenberg (Ed.), *New directions in child development: Empathy*. San Francisco: Jossey Bass.

Kohlberg, L., Ricks, D., & Snarey, J. (1984). Childhood development as a predictor of adaptation in adulthood. *Genetic Psychology Monographs, 110*, 91–172.

LaFrenier, P., & Sroufe, L. A. (1985). Profiles of peer competence in the preschool: Interrelations between measures, influence of social ecology, and relation to attachment history. *Developmental Psychology, 21*, 56–69.

Main, M., Kaplan, N., & Cassidy, J. (1985). Security in infancy, childhood, and adulthood: A move to the level of representation. In I. Bretherton & E. Waters (Eds.), *Growing points in attachment theory and research. Monographs of the Society for Research in Child Development, 50*, 66–104 (Whole No. 209).

Matas, L., Arend, R., & Sroufe, L. A. (1978). Continuity of adaptation in the second year: The relationship between quality of attachment and later competence. *Child Development, 49*, 547–556.

McCord, J. (1988). Parental behavior in the cycle of aggression. *Psychiatry, 51*, 14–23.

Pancake, V. (1985, April). *Continuity between mother-infant attachment and ongoing dyadic peer relationships in preschool*. Paper presented at the biennial meeting of the Society for Research in Child Development, Toronto.

Pianta, R., Egeland, B., & Sroufe, L. A. (in press). Continuity, and discontinuity in maternal sensitivity at 6, 24, and 42 months in a high risk sample. *Child Development.*

Renkin, B., Egeland, B., Marvinney, D., Mangelsdorf, S., & Sroufe, L. A. (in press). Early antecedents of aggression and passive-withdrawal in early elementary school. *Journal of Personality and Social Psychology.*

Robins, L. (1978). Sturdy childhood predictors of adult antisocial behavior: Replications from longitudinal studies. *Psychological Medicine, 8,* 611–622.

Roff, M., Sells, S., & Golden, M. (1972). *Social adjustment and personality development in children.* Minneapolis: University of Minnesota Press.

Rosenberg, D. M. (1984). *The quality and content of preschool fantasy play: Correlates in concurrent social-personality function and early mother-child attachment relationships* Unpublished doctoral dissertation, University of Minnesota.

Rubin, K., LeMare, L., & Lollis, S. (in press). Social withdrawal in childhood: Developmental pathways to peer rejection. In S. Asher & J. Coie (Eds.), *Children's status in the peer group.* Cambridge, England: Cambridge University Press.

Rutter, M. (in press). Functions and consequences of relationships: Some psychopathological considerations. In R. Hinde & J. Stevenson-Hinde (Eds.), *Towards understanding families.* Oxford, England: Oxford University Press.

Santostefano, S. (1978). *A biodevelopmental approach to clinical child psychology.* New York: Wiley.

Seligman, M. E. P. (1970). On the generality of the laws of learning. *Psychological Review, 77,* 406–418.

Sroufe, L. A. (1977). *Knowing and enjoying your baby.* Engelwood Cliffs, NJ: Prentice-Hall.

Sroufe, L. A. (1979). The coherence of individual development. *American Psychologist, 34,* 834–841.

Sroufe, L. A. (1983). Infant-caregiver attachment and patterns of adaptation and competence. In M. Perlmutter (Ed.), *Minnesota symposia in child psychology* (Vol. 16). Hillsdale, NJ: Lawrence Erlbaum Associates.

Sroufe, L. A. (1985). Attachment classification from the perspective of infant-caregiver relationships and infant temperament. *Child Development, 56,* 1–14.

Sroufe, L. A. (1987). The role of infant-caregiver attachment in development. In J. Belsky & T. Nezworski (Eds.), *Clinical implications of attachment.* Hillsdale, NJ: Lawrence Erlbaum Associates.

Sroufe, L. A. (in press). An organizational perspective on the self. In D. Cicchetti & M. Beeghly (Eds.), *Transitions from infancy to childhood: The self.* Chicago: University of Chicago Press.

Sroufe, L. A., & Fleeson, J. (1986). Attachment and the construction of relationships. In W. Hartup & Z. Rubin (Eds.), *Relationships and development.* Hillsdale, NJ: Lawrence Erlbaum Associates.

Sroufe, L. A., & Fleeson, J. (1988). The coherence of family relationships. In R. Hinde & J. Stevenson-Hinde (Eds.), *Relationships within families: Mutual influences* (pp. 27–47). Oxford: Oxford University Press.

Sroufe, L. A., Fox, N., & Pancake, V. (1983). Attachment and dependency in developmental perspective. *Child Development, 54,* 1615–1627.

Sroufe, L. A., Jacobvitz, D., Mangelsdorf, S., DeAngelo, E., & Ward, M. J. (1985). Generational boundary dissolution between mothers and their preschool children: A relationship systems approach. *Child Development, 56,* 317–325.

Sroufe, L. A., & Rutter, M. (1984). The domain of developmental psychopathology. *Child Development, 55,* 17–29.

Sroufe, L. A., & Ward, M. J. (1980). Seductive behavior of mothers of toddlers: Occurrence, correlates, and family origins. *Child Development, 51,* 1222–1229.

Sroufe, L. A., & Ward, M. J. (1984). The importance of early care. In D. Quarm, K. Borman, & S. Gideonse (Eds.), *Women in the workplace: The effects on families.* Norwood, NJ: Ablex.

Stern, D. N. (1974). The goal and structure of mother and infant play. *Journal of the American Academy of Child Psychiatry, 13,* 402–421.

Troy, M., & Sroufe, L. A. (1987). Victimization among preschoolers: Role of attachment relationship history. *Journal of the American Academy of Child and Adolescent Psychiatry, 26,* 166–172.

Waddington, C. H. (1957). *The strategy of the genes.* London, England: Allen & Unwin.

Waldrop, M., Pederson, F., & Bell, R. (1968). Minor Physical anomalies and hyperactive behavior in young children. *Child Development, 39,* 391–400.

Waters, E., & Sroufe, L. A. (1983). A developmental perspective on competence. *Developmental Review, 3,* 79–97.

Waters, E., Wippman, J., & Sroufe, L. A. (1979). Attachment, positive affect, and competence in the peer group: Two studies in construct validation. *Child Development, 50,* 821–829.

Wender, P., & Klein, D. (1986). *Mind, mood, and medicine: A guide to the new psychobiology.* New York: Farrar, Straus & Giroux.

West, D. (1982). *Delinquency: Its roots, careers, and prospects.* London: Heinemann Educational.

Zeitlin, H. (1982). *The natural history of psychiatric disorder in children.* Unpublished doctoral thesis. University of London, England.

3 Models of Developmental Regulation: The Environtype

Arnold J. Sameroff
Brown University and E. P. Bradley Hospital

The emerging field of developmental psychopathology has begun to impact on a number of the traditional problem areas by illuminating new possibilities for understanding the etiology, future course, and treatment of many childhood problems. Such new possibilities are contained in the dynamic models of development that are implicit in the new discipline. After a short discussion of the requirements for a theory of developmental psychopathology, data are presented highlighting the difficulties of a nondevelopmental approach to understanding psychopathology. A model of developmental regulation is suggested that is rooted in an elaboration of environmental constraints on individual behavior. Further data illustrate the importance of analyzing the constraints on development, if an understanding of individual growth is to be achieved. One of the more articulate redefinitions of psychopathology in developmental terms has been provided by Sroufe & Rutter (1984) who saw the discipline as "the study of the origins and course of individual patterns of behavioral adaptation" (p. 18). Cicchetti (1986) enlarged this concept by rooting it in the organismic-developmental approach elaborated by Werner (1948):

> Consequently, it is necessary to engage in a comprehensive evaluation of those factors that may influence the nature of patterns, and the different pathways by which the same developmental outcomes may be achieved. It is important to map out the processes whereby the normal course of development in the social, emotional, and or cognitive domains, in dynamic transaction with the "inner" constitutional and "outer" environmental characteristics, may lead to outcomes that either inhibit or exacerbate early deviations or maintain or disrupt early adaptation. (Cicchetti, 1986, p. vii)

Rutter and Garmezy (1983) elaborate the difference between developmental psychopathology and other disciplines. They argue that developmental psychologists assume an essential continuity in functioning such that severe symptoms (e.g., depression), are placed on the same dimensions as normal behaviors (e.g., sadness or unhappiness). In contrast, traditional psychiatry is based on an implicit assumption of discontinuity such that disordered behavior is interpreted as different in kind from normal behavior. Developmental psychopathologists make no prior assumptions about either continuity of discontinuity. They are concerned centrally with both the connections and lack of connections between normality and disorder.

Theories of Psychopathology

There is a need for a new orientation to the etiology of psychopathology because of the failure of more customary models to explain how disorders arise and are maintained. The traditional medical model of disorder is based on the presumption that there are identifiable somatic entities that underlie definable disease syndromes. Within traditional psychiatry the current dominant view of disease is still strongly biomedical, with little role allowed for social and psychological factors in the etiology of mental illness (Engel, 1977), although they may have an important role in the maintenance and perhaps treatment of mental disorder. In this view individuals are not seen as integrated systems of biological, psychological, and social functioning, but rather as divided into biological and behavioral selves. If the biology changes, either through infection or cure, the behavior changes. Three principles emerge from this model that are frequently applied to the study of psychopathology:

1. The same entity will cause the same disorder in all affected individuals, whether they be children or adults.
2. The same symptoms at different ages should be caused by the same entity.
3. Specific disorders of children should lead to similar adult disorders.

Diabetes is an example of a disease that approximates this model: (1) Any individual that has the same degree of insulin deficiency will exhibit similar symptoms independent of age. (2) If one has symptoms of increased urination, thirst, and problems of growing or maintaining weight, then the underlying cause is generally diabetes. (3) Almost always if one develops diabetes during childhood, one will continue to have the disorder through adulthood. However, there are many medical disorders that do not fit this model. Chicken pox will have different effects and symptoms depending on the age of the individual; the symptoms of fever can be caused by a wide variety of factors; and having the flu in childhood does not lead to having the flu in adulthood.

The failure of this disease model is evident in the fact that none of these three principles can be generalized, especially with respect to the study of psychopathology. Regarding the first principle, the same underlying problem can be related to quite different behaviors in children and adults, for example, the genetic deficit thought to underlie schizophrenia. Research on children at high risk for the disorder is focused on the identification of early markers of a process leading to schizophrenia. These markers are not schizophrenia but given a certain unique set of developmental experiences they could lead to schizophrenia (Watt, Anthony, Wynne, & Rolf, 1984).

Second, the same symptoms may be caused by quite different processes at different ages. The sadness that is a primary characteristic of adult affective disorders is a common reactive condition in childhood. The proportion of unhappy, miserable children increases from 10% at age 10 to 40% by age 15, when adolescence is taking its toll (Rutter, Tizard, & Whitmore, 1981). For most of these cases there is little evidence that depression in childhood has the same biological causes as depression in adult life.

Finally, for many emotional and behavioral problems in childhood, there is little evidence of continuity into adulthood. Most childhood emotional problems do not persist and there is little empirical evidence that connects adult neuroses with childhood conditions. Even when continuities of symptoms are found, the connection to underlying entities is complex. Of those children with depression who did go on to have a psychiatric problem in adulthood, depression was generally a component of the later disorder; however, in only a minority of cases was depression the primary adult diagnosis (Rutter & Garmezy, 1883).

Theories of Development

The developmental approach expands upon traditional models of mental disease by incorporating biological and behavioral functioning into a general systems model of developmental regulation. Within this approach underlying entities do not exist independent of developmental organization. The expression of biological vulnerabilities can occur only in relation to the balance between coping skills and stresses in each individual's life history (Zubin & Spring, 1977). Continuities in competence or incompetence from childhood into adulthood cannot be simply related to continuities in underlying pathology or health. The relations between earlier and later behavior have to be understood in terms of the continuity of ordered or disordered experience across time interacting with an individual's unique biobehavioral characteristics. To the extent that experience becomes more organized, problems in adaptation will diminish. To the extent that experience becomes more chaotic, problems in adaptation will increase. What the developmental approach contributes is the identification of factors that influence the child's ability to organize experience and, consequently, the child's level of adaptive functioning.

Although there is some consensus on the contents of the field of developmental psychopathology, there is less agreement on a theoretical framework. Sroufe and Rutter (1984) believe that there is no single developmental theory that can encompass the field, but suggest that there are a number of accepted guiding principles that underlie all major "developmental" positions. These include concepts of holism, directedness, differentiation of means and ends, and mobility of behavioral functions (Santostefano, 1978). These principles overlap significantly with a developmental model based on general systems theory that includes principles of wholeness and order, adaptive self-stabilization, adaptive self-organization, hierarchical interactions, and dialectical movement (Sameroff, 1983). Obviously there is a great gap between such principles and the data collected in typical empirical studies of psychiatric disorder. The Rochester Longitudinal Study (Sameroff, Seifer, & Zax, 1982) is an example of a study that was conceived as a linear analysis of the effects of parental psychopathology on child behavior and not as a study of the interaction of complex dynamic processes. During the course of the study, however, adaptive changes were forced upon the investigators because of the lack of congruence between hypotheses and data. This dialectical process produced changes in the analytic strategy as well as the investigator's understanding of development. These changes will become clear as the data from the longitudinal study are described below. Bridging the gap between the unlimited complexity of dynamic developmental conceptualizations and the limited complexity of possible empirical investigations becomes the scientific agenda for a discipline of developmental psychopathology. The continuing task is to relate a general theory of development to the data of both normality and deviance.

Rochester Longitudinal Study

In 1968, we (Sameroff & Zax, 1973; Sameroff, Seifer, Zax, & Barocas, 1987) initiated a study applying the high-risk approach to the study of schizophrenia in adolescence developed by Mednick and Schulsinger (1968) in Denmark to infancy and early childhood. Fish and her colleagues (Fish, 1984; Fish, Shapiro, Halpern, & Wile, 1956) already had provided a clinical picture of the development from birth of a group of children born to schizophrenic women. The absence of control groups, however, made it impossible to determine if the behaviors she observed were the result of the mother's schizophrenia or some other characteristic of her poor sample. Because a diagnosis of schizophrenia is usually associated with chronic and severe mental disturbance, high anxiety, social incompetency, and a variety of demographic variables, and since all these factors may have an effect on the newborn condition and later development of a child, they must be adequately controlled in any study devoted to understanding the singular effect of a schizophrenic heritage. Mednick and Schulsinger did include a nonschizophrenic control group in their study, but they assessed the offspring of their subjects only after they had reached adolescence.

In contrast, we felt that the ideal point in time to search for constitutional differences would be at birth, when the infant had not yet been subject to the social consequences of life with a schizophrenic mother. Accordingly, we began our study with pregnant schizophrenic women and planned to follow their offspring through the first 4 years of life. In addition, we felt that it was necessary to use additional control groups. As Mednick and McNeil (1968) pointed out in their original justification of the high-risk strategy for studying schizophrenia, many of the characteristics that have been attributed to schizophrenia have really been the *consequences* of the diagnosis rather than of the disorder itself. The consequences include the effects of labeling and institutionalization. Similarly, we felt that a schizophrenic mother might influence her offspring in many ways that might be a consequence of the chronicity or severity of her mental illness per se, rather than something specifically related to her diagnosis. In short, our strategy was to include control populations that would allow us to assess the effects of separate aspects of psychiatric diagnosis, chronicity of disturbance, severity of disturbance, and social competency, as well as the general characteristics of social class, race, educational level, and family constellation.

For our study 337 pregnant women were recruited over a 4-year period. Before delivery the women underwent a clinical interview. From the interview and case records each woman was given a diagnosis, a chronicity rating, a severity of illness rating, and a social competence score.

The chronicity of psychological disturbance was defined by the frequency of psychiatric contact plus the need for, and length of, institutionalization. The least chronic category involved subjects who had had no previous psychiatric contact and were diagnosed as having no mental illness on the basis of the interview. The most chronic category included cases which had in excess of four psychiatric contacts or more than 1 year of institutionalization. The severity of mental illness score was based on an evaluation of emotional state, current functioning at home, at work, and the general level of social adjustment.

For our analysis of the specific effects of a schizophrenic mother on the development of her child, a subset of four groups were formed from the larger total sample based on the psychiatric diagnosis: (1) a schizophrenic group, with 29 mothers, (2) a neurotic-depressive group, with 57 mothers, (3) a personality-disordered group, with 41 mothers, and (4) a no-mental-illness group, with 80 mothers. The no-mental illness control group was matched to the other groups on the basis of age, race, socioeconomic status, number of children, education, and sex of child. The total sample was used for analyses of the effects of social status and the chronicity and severity of mental illness.

As we expected when the four groups were compared on mental-health criteria other than diagnosis, it was found that the schizophrenic women as a group were more chronically ill, more severe in their current symptomatology, and more socially noncompetent. As a control for chronicity all the women in our sample were divided into four groups based on their psychiatric histories. Similarly four groups were formed based on the severity of psychopathology rating. Any differences we would find between the schizophrenic and other diagnostic groups could then be evaluated in terms of either chronicity or severity of mental illness independent of diagnosis, in order to determine which factor was making the greatest contribution to the outcome measures.

OUTCOME MEASURES

The assessments in the longitudinal study through early childhood were made during pregnancy, at birth, and then at 4-, 12-, 30-, and 48-months-of-age both in the home and in the laboratory. At each age assessment variables were divided into four sets, each focused on domains of behavior related to potential mental-illness outcomes. These were (1) perceptual-motor functioning, (2) cognitive functioning, (3) affective functioning, and (4) social functioning.

Perceptual-motor functioning was tested at birth with the Brazelton (1973) Neonatal Behavioral Assessment Scales. The newborns were also monitored for autonomic responsivity in a sensory stimulation task. At 4-, 12-, and 30-months-of-age they were tested with the Bayley Infant Development Scales, which included scores for psychomotor performance. Physical health was assessed from birth records and also from a medical history form filled out by the mothers when the children were 30 and 48 months-of-age.

Cognitive performance at birth was measured by tests of alertness and habituation on the Brazelton scales. At 4, 12, and 30 months the mental-developmental index of the Bayley scales was used and at 48 months the Verbal Scales of the Wechsler Preschool and Primary Scale of Intelligence (WPPSI). The Peabody Picture Vocabulary Test (PPVT) was also given at both 30-and 48-months-of-age.

Emotional responsivity of each child was assessed at birth from irritability and associated scores on the Brazelton scale. At 4 months, mood, threshold to stimulation, and intensity of response were scored from a temperament questionnaire. Observations of emotionality were recorded during mother-infant interactions in the home at 4 and 12 months-of-age. During the psychometric testing in the laboratory, the examiner scored measures of emotional responsivity during the 4-, 12-, 30-, and 48-month laboratory sessions. At 30 and 48 months-of-age additional information was obtained from the Rochester Adaptive Behavior Inventory (RABI), a detailed maternal interview (Seifer, Sameroff, & Jones, 1981).

The social behavior of a newborn is hard to define but we judged alertness and consolability measured by the Brazelton Scales to be its primary constituents. At

4 and 12 months, the mother-infant social interactions were observed and recorded in the home setting. At 4, 12, 30, and 48 months, ratings of the child's social responsiveness were made by the examiner during the psychometric evaluation. At the later testings, the child's reactions to separation from his or her mother were scored. A social history and the results of the RABI provided us with additional sources of information on the child's social behavior.

SOURCES OF RISK

At the outset we considered three major hypotheses: (1) that deviant behavior would be attributed to variables associated with a specific maternal diagnosis, e.g., schizophrenia; (2) that deviant behavior would be attributable to variables associated with mental illness in general, but no diagnostic group in particular; and (3) that deviant behavior would be associated with social status, i.e., race and SES, exclusive of maternal psychopathology.

Psychiatric Diagnosis Effects

In general, the first hypothesis found little support. Most of the significant differences found for the schizophrenic group occurred during the prenatal period, and these differences were in the mothers, not in the children. The schizophrenic mothers were the most anxious and least socially competent. They also had the worst prenatal obstetric status, but this was primarily due to a single item, the use of antipsychotic medication.

After the birth of their children, the schizophrenic group was nearly indistinguishable from the control group during evaluation of both mother and child behavior. The infants showed almost no differences on behavioral or psychological measures during the newborn period. The only finding was the children of schizophrenics had the lowest birthweights. At 4 months the schizophrenic group again showed few differences. The infants' Bayley developmental scores were slightly lower and two indices of mother behavior during home observations indicated less involvement with their child by schizophrenics. No differences in infant behavior were noted in the home, nor were there any differences in temperament ratings. By 12 months the only differences found were on the Bayley. Home and laboratory observations revealed no differences in mother or infant behavior. At 30 months Bayley scores of children in the schizophrenic group were not different from controls. Only one adaptive behavior scale (Depression) and one Bayley laboratory observation scale (Reactivity) showed the schizophrenics' children to be behaving more poorly than controls. Finally, at 48 months one temperament scale and one adaptive behavior scale were related to parental schizophrenia.

In contrast to the paucity of differences between the schizophrenic groups and the no-mental-illness control group, the neurotic depression group showed many significant effects. At all ages, the mothers and children in the depression group showed a variety of differences from controls. The depressed mothers were more anxious and lower in social competence. Their newborns had by far the worst obstetric status, and exhibited poor functioning on measures during the newborn laboratory examination. At 4 months the mothers showed less involvement with their infants at home, and the infants in turn had poorer responsivity to people in the laboratory and lower activity and distractibility temperament ratings from a maternal questionnaire. No differences were found between the neurotic depressive and other groups at 12 months, but at 30 months these infants were reported by the mothers to have a variety of less adaptive behaviors in the home. At 48 months the neurotic depression group looked worse than controls on one temperament scale and four adaptive behavior scales. It should be noted that after the newborn period almost all of the differences found between the depression and control groups were in mothers' behavior or mothers' reports of their children's behavior, but were not in direct measures of the children.

To summarize these diagnostic comparisons, if one were to choose a diagnostic group where children were at most risk, it would be neurotic depression rather than schizophrenia. Further, the impact of a schizophrenic parent appears to decrease somewhat with age as the child moves from biological or simple motor functioning to more complex behavior, while the impact of maternal depression remains constant throughout the first few years. The personality disorder group showed few effects throughout.

In some respects this finding is surprising. The schizophrenic mothers were, on average, more severely ill than the depressed mothers. Thus, one might expect the more severely ill schizophrenic mothers to have children who fared more poorly, and (if the high-risk model is correct) that the small portion of preschizophrenic children of the schizophrenic mothers should have skewed their group means downward relative to the other diagnosis group. Recent evidence, however, has suggested that it may not be simply the fact of a mother's schizophrenia that predicts illness in the child, but that one must also consider the affective relation between mother and child. For example, child incompetence in a school-age sample was related to symptoms of depression and withdrawal in mothers, regardless of whether they received a diagnosis of schizophrenia or depression (Kokes, Harder, Fisher, & Strauss, 1982). In our sample it may be that the affective nature of the maternal relationship, characterized by withdrawal and depression, contributed to the poorer outcomes in the depressive group. The effect may be particularly striking in our sample because relationships between younger children may be more sensitive to affective cognitive interactions with their mothers than are older children. The emotional unavailability of depressed mothers may be relatively more damaging to young children than the primary cognitive disorganization of schizophrenic mothers (Cicchetti & Schneider-Rosen, 1986).

This is not to say that the children of schizophrenic mothers performed exceptionally well. On the contrary, if one were to select a group of children who were at risk for many developmental problems, they would be an appropriate choice. When compared with children of middle class white mothers who had no illness, the children of schizophrenic parents showed many deficits. The important etiological point highlighted by our data is that children of their mentally ill mothers showed equal or larger differences from normal controls.

Severity and Chronicity of Mental Illness Effects

The second general hypothesis, that mental illness in general would produce substantial effects, was supported more strongly than the hypothesis regarding specific diagnosis effects. In almost every instance where there was an effect due to one or another diagnostic group there was a corresponding effect for severity and/or chronicity of illness. Further, there were a large number of variables that had severity and/or chronicity effects, but did not have corresponding specific diagnosis differences.

These general effects of maternal psychopathology, i.e., severity and chronicity, were ubiquitous throughout the study. Children of more severely or chronically ill mothers had poorer obstetric and newborn status. At 4 months they had more difficult temperaments, lower Bayley scores, and less adaptive behavior in the laboratory. These mothers were less involved and more negative in affect during home observations. At 12 months their infants were less spontaneous and mobile when observed in the home and less responsive in the laboratory. The ill mothers remained less involved and less positive during home observations. At 30 and 48 months their children were again less responsive in the laboratory, had lower developmental test scores, and were reported by their mothers as having a variety of nonadaptive behavior patterns at home.

Social Status Effects

The third hypothesis regarding social status effects was also strongly supported. Like the general psychopathology findings, the social status effects are apparent, throughout the first 4 years of life. The low-SES Blacks in our sample exhibited the poorest development, the high-SES Whites showed the best, and the low-SES Whites were generally in between these two groups. Specifically, the low-SES Black children had poorer obstetrical status, more difficult temperaments and lower Bayley test scores at 4 months, less responsivity during the home and laboratory observations at 12 months, and less adaptive behavior in the home and laboratory at 30 and 48 months-of-age. Like their children, the low-SES Black mothers were less positive in affect and less involved during our observations.

Comparing Risk Factors

When the number of significant contrasts was compared for the diagnostic, mental illness, and social status dimensions, the highest density was found in the social class and race contrasts. One of the more interesting results was the lack of specificity of these differences. The differences found between offspring of women with psychiatric diagnoses and those without were almost the same as those between lower and higher social status women. To assess the relative contribution of specific maternal characteristics, further statistical analyses were done.

Hierarchical multiple regression directly compared the predictive strength of social status, severity of illness, and diagnosis on child outcomes in four general categories: obstetrical and newborn status, developmental quotients, home observations, and adaptive behavior (Sameroff & Seifer, 1983). In all of these realms social status explained the greatest proportion of variance when entered first in the regression equations. In three of these four realms (developmental quotients, home observation, and adaptive behavior) social status was most often significant when entered first, when entered second after severity of illness or diagnosis, or when entered third after both severity and diagnosis. In the fourth area (perinatal status) social status was equal in predictive power to either of the other two dimensions regardless of the step when entered in their regression equation.

From these analyses a relatively clear picture can be seen. Among the mental illness measures, severity and chronicity of maternal disturbances were better predictors of risk than were specific diagnoses. With respect to diagnosis, it was not the schizophrenic mothers who produced the worst outcomes in their children, but the neurotically depressed mothers who proved most pathogenic.

The excitement of the decade of the 1970s was devoted to high-risk research targeting the offspring of schizophrenic women. As with most fads the achievements rarely match the expectations and the high risk study of schizophrenia was no exception. The last two major conference reports of the Risk Research consortium (Watt, Anthony, Wynne, & Rolf, 1984; Goldstein & Tuma, 1987) contain sobering appraisals of the difficulties inherent in such research. The inability of the RLS to find the roots of schizophrenia was not an exception in this research area. The decade of the 1980s has seen a shift in high-risk targets to the offspring of parents with affective disorders. The RLS data showing early difficulties in the behavior of the offspring of neurotic depressives has been followed by a new wave of research on the offspring of depressed women (for reviews see Trad, 1987; and Tronick & Field, 1986). The increased theoretical sophistication of the field (Cicchetti & Aber, 1986) hopefully will permit a closer approximation between aspiration and achievement in this area by making developmental concerns a central part of each of these studies.

But in addition to developmental concerns, of overriding importance is attention to the context of development. In the RLS social status was a more powerful risk factor than any of the mental illness measures. To produce more sophisticated studies of the role of social status more differentiated views of environmental influences must be taken. Diagnosis and symptoms are characteristics of the individual. Social status is a function of the environment. In order to translate this sociological measure into something that would have direct impact on the child, we needed to analyze the social status factor into behaviorally relevant units. We have attempted a variety of techniques for translating environment into its component parts. The most important of these units was the environment's ability to properly regulate the development of the child. Unfortunately, we did not have a direct measure of this variable, but we were able to make some headway in our analyses of other factors.

Cumulative Environmental Risk

In defining the developmental risk associated with any specific child, the characteristics of the child must be related to the ability of the environment to regulate the development of that child toward social norms. In extreme cases of massive biological abnormality such regulations may be ineffectual. At the other extreme, disordered social environments might convert biologically normal infants into caretaking casualties.

The Kauai study of Werner and her colleagues (Werner, Bierman, & French, 1971; Werner & Smith, 1977; Werner & Smith, 1982) provides a good description of the interplay among those risk factors in the child and those in the environment. A sample of children were followed from birth through adolescence. Assessments were made of the birth condition of the children and their developmental progress at 2-, 10-, and 18-years-of-age. From the predominantly lower SES sample, more than half had learning or emotional problems by 18-years-of-age. The first two books reporting this study (Werner et al., 1971; Werner & Smith, 1977) helped to dispel the notion that birth complications had a determining effect on behavioral outcomes. Children with severe early trauma frequently showed no later deficits unless the problems were combined with persistently poor environmental circumstances such as chronic poverty, family instability, or maternal mental health problems.

In the third report of the Kauai study Werner and Smith (1982) divided all the children who had been at a high clinical risk at 2-years-of-age into three groups: those who developed problems by 10-years-of-age, those who did not develop problems until 18-years-of-age, and those who did not develop problems at all. This latter ''resilient'' group was the target of analyses to determine what factors in development protected them from the disorders that characterized the children who did have problems. Most of the protective factors that were identified were not surprising: good temperament, favorable parental attitudes, low levels of family conflict, counseling and remedial assistance, small family size, and a smaller load of stressful life experiences. What was surprising was the variety of interactions among the factors and the degree of complexity of analysis needed to match the complexity of variables that affected the course of a child's development. For example, Werner and Smith attempted to separate those factors that led to healthier outcomes both in the presence or absence of risk conditions from those factors that only had an interactional effect, i.e., a positive impact in the presence of risk factors but no impact when risk factors were absent. These latter protective factors were not found to discriminate between positive and negative outcomes for middle-class children whose lives were relatively free of stress, but they were very important in the lives of children who were growing up in poverty and subject to a large number of negative life events.

The Kauai study is in tune with many others (Sameroff & Chandler, 1975) in targeting SES and family mental health as important moderators of child development. Both mental health and social status are summary variables that incorporate a wide range of factors that may interfere with optimal child rearing. The Kauai study was able to isolate a number of variables that are associated with social class but were not the same as social class. In our previous analyses comparing children from various groups of mothers we demonstrated that both parental mental illness and social status factors were directly related to child performance (Sameroff et al., 1982). Although these results are meaningful, they do not fully address the issue of what psychological mechanisms are responsible for the individual and group variation observed in the children's development. We became interested in identifying factors in the RLS that were associated with developmental risk (Sameroff & Seifer, 1983). These included the cognitive capacities, attitudes, beliefs, and values of the mother, as well as the stresses that impact on the family.

An additional issue that concerned us was that child behavior typically has been studied using causal models in which singular variables are hypothesized to uniquely determine outcomes. However, a series of studies in a variety of domains have found that it is the *number* of risk factors rather than their *nature* that is the best determinant of outcome. Studies of biological disorders, e.g., heart disease (Dawber, 1980), and behavioral disorders, e.g., mental illness (Rutter, Tizard, Yule, Graham, & Whitmore, 1976), have found that the more risk factors, the worse the outcome, independent of the particular nature of the variables. We decided to examine the effects of multiple risks on the development of the children in our sample.

A set of 10 risk factors was identified among the variables assessed during the 4 years of the RLS (Sameroff, Seifer, Barocas, Zax, & Greenspan, 1987). Each measure was chosen based on two criteria. The first was that there was a significant basis in the literature validating the variable's potential negative impact on developmental outcomes. The second was that the variable was highly reliable or that there were a sufficient number of assessments of that variable during the RLS to assure reliability. These 10 risk variables are listed in Table 3.1. The

TABLE 3.1
Summary of Risk Variables

Risk Variables	Low Risk	High Risk
Chronicity of illness	0-1 contact	More than 1 contact
Anxiety	75% least	25% most
Parental perspectives	75% highest	25% lowest
Spontaneous interaction	75% most	25% least
Education	High school	No high school
Occupation	Skilled	Semi- or unskilled
Minority status	White	Nonwhite
Family support	Father present	Father absent
Stressful life events	75% fewest	25% most
Family size	1-3 children	4 or more children

From Sameroff, Seifer, Barocas, Zax, and Greenspan (1987).

definition of the high risk group for each variable is described below. In the case of continuous variables where a categorical definition of risk was not possible, families in the top quartile were placed in the hazardous category.

Maternal Mental Health.   The mental health status of the mother was determined from three principal sources: a structured psychiatric interview (Endicott & Spitzer, 1972) conducted when the mother was pregnant with the study child, a second psychiatric interview conducted when the study child was 30-months-of-age, and information obtained from a psychiatric registry. For the purpose of the present analysis high risk was defined as a mother who was diagnosed as emotionally disturbed at least twice during her life. Using this criteria about 40% of the sample was in the high risk group.

Maternal Anxiety.   The mental health risk factor was most sensitive to variations in the clinical range of emotional functioning. In contrast, anxiety measures were used to assess variation in the subclinical range. We averaged the standardized scores of three measures of maternal anxiety: the total score from the IPAT anxiety scale (Cattell & Scheier, 1963), the Eysenck neuroticism scale (Eysenck & Eysenck, 1969), and the Malaise scale (Rutter, 1977). The high risk group contained the most anxious 25% of the sample.

Parental Perspectives.   For this dimension we combined the standardized scores of three measures that reflected rigidity vs flexibility in the attitudes, beliefs and values that parents had in regard to their child's development. The Concepts of Development Questionnaire (Sameroff & Feil, 1983) evaluates parents' understanding of development on a dimension ranging from categorical to perspectivistic. At the *categorical* end, child development is seen as a determined expression of single causes like constitution or environment. At the *perspectivistic* end, child behavior is seen as the outcome of complex, transactional processes. The Kohn (1969) parental values scale measures the behaviors that parents desire for their children. The primary dimension derived from this scale ranges from conformity to self-direction. An orientation toward child *conformity* emphasizes values of obedience, neatness, good manners, and appropriate sex role behavior. An orientation toward child *self-direction* emphasizes values of responsibility, consideration of others, and curiosity. The third assessment was the Parental Attitude Research Instrument (Schaefer & Bell, 1958). The dimension used was the *authoritarian-control* scale (Becker & Krug, 1965) that accounts for most the variance in the items. High scores reflect parenting styles that emphasize parental control and minimize acceptance of child-initiated behavior. The high risk group was the 25% who scored highest on the combined categorical, conforming, and authoritarian dimensions.

Mother Interactive Behaviors.   The parental perspectives instruments just described measured the mothers' cognitive representation of the developmental process. In contrast, home observations of mother-child interaction when the children were 4- and 12-months-of-age measured the way that mothers actually behaved. A composite variable was created by standardizing a measure of mother spontaneous behavior at each age and averaging them with unit weights. Spontaneous behavior included mother smiling, vocalizing, or touching the child. The high risk group included the 25% least spontaneous mothers.

Maternal Education.   The level of mothers' education was determined during the prenatal interviews. Mothers with less than a high school education were considered high risk, about 40% of the sample.

Occupation of Head of Household.   The occupation(s) of family members were also determined during the prenatal interviews. While occupational status in itself is not a risk factor, to the extent that it reflects the financial resources of the family, it can be interpreted as one. The father's occupation was used if he was present in the household, otherwise the mother's occupation was used. The high risk group were unemployed, unskilled, or at best semiskilled, and consisted of about 20% of the sample.

Minority Group Status.   In addition to low SES, membership in a disadvantaged minority adds risk elements related to prejudice and segregation. Blacks and Puerto Rican families were included in the high risk group was formed from the minority status families (about 40%).

Family Social Support.   Social support involves many dimensions of the mother's relation to other members of her family and both formal and informal social institutions. However, for these analyses family social support was defined simply as the presence or absence of a father in the home.

Family Size. The number of children in the family was judged to be a risk factor for intellectual competence (Zajonc, 1976). The presence or absence of other children determines the degree to which there is competition for social and physical resources that are at a premium in at-risk families. Families with 4 or more children were placed in a high-risk group that consisted of about 20% of the sample.

Stressful Life Events. During the 4 years of the RLS mothers were questioned about events that affected the child and the family. A measure of stressful negative life events was developed patterned after the inventories of Holmes and Rahe (1967) that included events such as loss of job, deaths in the family, or physical illness. The high-risk group consisted of the 25% of families who experienced the greatest number of stressful life events.

Outcome Measures. The two outcome criterion measures of child performance were the Wechsler Primary and Preschool Scales of Intelligence (WPPSI) Verbal IQ and the Rochester Adaptive Behavior Inventory (RABI), a measure of social-emotional competence (Seifer, Sameroff, & Jones, 1981). The RABI was developed during the course of the RLS and consisted of a 90-minute interview of the mother by a trained interviewer about the adaptive behavior of her child. We used the global rating which is a summary score given by the interviewer on a 5-point scale where one indicated superior adjustment and five indicated clinical disturbance.

Consequences of Environmental Risk

Our subcomponents of social status were doing a better job than the demographic variable alone. All comparisons for the verbal IQ scores were significantly different, and in all cases the low-risk group had higher scores than the high-risk group. The largest absolute difference was for minority status (about 18 points) but most differences were about 7 to 10 IQ points, about ½ to ⅔ of a standard deviation. On the RABI global rating the low-risk group performed significantly better than the high-risk group for all but one of the comparisons. This exception was for mother-child interaction where no difference was found. The differences between groups on these comparisons was generally about ½ of a standard deviation.

Although there were many significant effects for the individual risk factors there are two major shortcomings in such analyses. First, any one particular risk group consists of a relatively large number of individuals, and the discrimination between the two groups is not large enough to accurately predict poor outcome based on risk status alone. Second, it is not clear if the many risk factors are totally overlapping in their effects or if there are additive components when these risk variables are viewed in unison.

To alleviate these shortcomings a multiple-risk score was created that was the total number of risk groups any individual family was a member of. The sample was well distributed between scores of 0 and 8. Only 1 family had a multiple risk score of 9 and they were combined in all analyses with those whose score was 8. The largest resulting group contained 36 families and the smallest group had 10 families. The relation between the multiple risk scores and the 4-year IQ outcome criterion is summarized graphically in Fig. 3.1, and between the score and social-emotional outcome in Fig 3.2. It is clear from these figures that the effect of combining the 10 risk variables was to strongly accentuate the differences noted for the individual scores described above. As the number of risk factors increases, performance decreases for children at 4-years-of-age.

In addition to the clear downward linear trend, the size of the effect for multiple risk factors was much larger than for individual risk factors. For the IQ and RABI scores, the difference between the lowest and highest groups was about 2 and 1½ standard deviations, respectively. Thus the combination of risk factors resulted in a nearly threefold increase in the magnitude of differences found among groups of children relative to the effect of single variables.

These data support the view that verbal IQ scores for 4-year-old children are multidetermined by variables in the social context, but the possibility exists that poverty may still be an overriding variable. To test for this possibility, two additional analyses were completed. The first analysis was to determine if there were consistencies in the distribution of risk factors, i.e., were there always the same factors present? The second analysis was to determine if the multiple risk scores were predictive of VIQ scores within SES groupings.

For the first type of analysis data from the 79 families that had a moderate

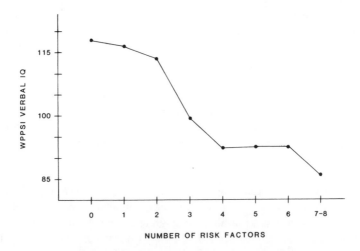

FIG. 3.1.   Effects of multiple risk scores on four-year verbal IQ. From Sameroff, Seifer, Barocas, Zax, and Greenspan (1987).

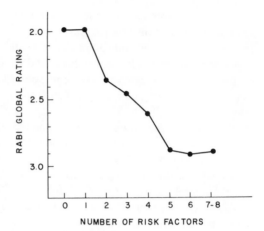

FIG. 3.2. Effects of multiple risk scores on four-year social-emotional competence. From Sameroff, Seifer, Zax, and Barocas (1987).

multiple risk score of 3, 4, or 5 were cluster analyzed. The families fell into five clusters with different sets of high-risk conditions that are listed in Table 3.2. Different combinations of factors appear in each cluster. Cluster 2 has no over-lapping variables with clusters 3, 4, or 5. Minority status is a risk variable in clusters 3, 4, and 5, but does not appear in clusters 1 or 2. Despite these differences the mean IQs were not different for children in the five clusters ranging from 92.8 to 97.7. Thus is seems that it was not any single variable but the combination of multiple variables that reduced the child's intellectual performance. Similar results were found for the RABI score differences.

For the second analysis, the sample was split into high (SES = I, II, III) and low (SES = IV, V) SES groups based on the Hollingshead scale (1957). Because occupation and education levels are used in the SES calculation, these variables

TABLE 3.2
Cluster Analysis of Families with Moderate Multi-Risk Scores

Cluster 1	Mental Health
	Family Support
	Mother Education
Cluster 2	Mother-Infant Interaction
	Mental Health
	Anxiety
Cluster 3	Family Support
	Minority Status
Cluster 4	Mother Education
	Minority Status
	Occupation
Cluster 5	Parental Perspectives
	Minority Status
	Mother Education

From Sameroff, Seifer, Barocas, Zax, and Greenspan (1987).

were removed from the multiple risk score to reduce redundancy. The reduced score had a maximum of 8 risk factors. To assure a sufficient N in each group families were combined into a low (0–1), medium (2–3), or high (4 or more) risk group and the mean VIQ scores calculated for each group.

The effects of the multiple risk score were as clear within SES groups as well as for the population at large. Trend analyses were significant for both high- and low-SES groups. The more risk factors the worse the child outcomes. When the RABI scores of the children were examined, there were similar relationships between risk factors and social-emotional competence within SES groups, as well. Multiple-risk scores were found to be linearly related to these social-emotional outcomes within SES groups just as they were for intellectual competence (Sameroff, Seifer, Zax, & Barocas, 1987).

These analyses of the RLS data were attempts to elaborate environmental risk factors by reducing global measures, e.g., SES, to component social and behavioral variables. We were able to identify a set of risk factors that were predominantly found in lower SES groups, but affected child outcomes in all social classes. Moreover, no single variable was determinant of outcome. Only in families with multiple risk factors was the child's competence placed in jeopardy. In the analyses of intellectual outcomes none of the children in the low multiple-risk group had an IQ below 85, whereas 24% of the children in the high multiple-risk group did.

The multiple pressures of environmental context in terms of amount of stress from the environment, the family's resources for coping with that stress, the number of children that must share those resources, and the parents' flexibility in understanding and dealing with their children all play a role in the fostering or hindrance of child intellectual and social competencies.

Regulatory Systems in Development

What kind of theory would be necessary to integrate our understanding of pathology and development? It must explain how the individual and the context work together to produce patterns of adaptive or maladaptive functioning and relate how such past or present functioning influences the future.

The first principle to emerge in such a general theory of development is that individuals can never be removed from their contexts. Whether the goal is understanding causal connections, predicting outcomes, or intervention, it will not be achieved by removing the individual from the conditions that regulate development. There has been a great deal of attention given to the biological regulators of development. What has now become necessary is the giving of equal attention to the environmental regulators of development.

The development of each individual is regulated by interactions with regulatory systems acting at different levels of organization. The two most prominent of these are the biological and social regulatory systems. From conception to birth interactions with the biological system are most prominent where the changing contemporary state of the organism's embryonic phenotype triggers the genotype to provide a series of new biochemical experiences. These experiences are regulated by the turning on and off of various gene activities directed toward the production of a viable human child. These processes continue less dramatically after birth with some exceptions, for example, the initiation of adolescence and possibly senility.

The period from birth to adulthood is dominated by interactions with the social system. Again the state of the child triggers regulatory processes but now in the social environment. Examples of such coded changes are the reactions of parents to their child's ability to walk or talk, and the changes in setting provided when the child reaches preschool or school age. These regulations change the experience of the child in tune with changes in the child's physical and behavioral development.

The result of these regulatory exchanges is the expansion of each individual's ability for biological self-regulation and the development of behavioral self-regulation. Advances in motor development permit children to maintain thermal regulation and nutrition that initially could only be provided by caregivers. They soon are able to dress themselves and reach into the refrigerator. Through psychological development on one hand, they are able to self-regulate cognition with the growth of perceptual constancy and the conceptual organization required for representation, and on the other, self-regulate affect with the growth of social referencing and defense mechanisms. Despite this burgeoning independence in thought and deed, each individual is never freed from a relationship to an internal and external context. Should we forget this connectedness, it only takes a bout of illness or a social transgression to remind us of our constraints.

The Environtype

Just as there is a biological organization, the genotype, that regulates the physical outcome of each individual, there is a social organization that regulates the way human beings fit into their society. This organization operates through family and cultural socialization patterns and has been postulated to compose an "environtype" (Sameroff, 1985, Sameroff & Fiese, 1989) analogous to the biological genotype (see Fig. 3.3).

The environtype is composed of subsystems that not only transact with the child but also transact with each other. Bronfenbrenner (1977) has provided the most detailed descriptions of environmental organizations that impact on developmental processes within categories of microsystems, mesosystems, exosystems, and macrosystems. The *microsystem* is the immediate setting of a child in an environment with particular features, activities, and roles, e.g., the home or the school. The *mesosystem* comprises the relationships between the major settings at a particular point in an individual's development, e.g., between

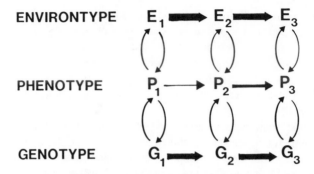

FIG. 3.3.   Regulation model of development with transactions among genotype, phenotype, and environtype. From Sameroff (1985).

home and school. The *exosystem* is an extension of the mesosystem that includes settings that the child may not be a part of but affect the settings in which the child does participate, for example, the world of work and neighborhoods. Finally, the *macrosystem* includes the overarching institutional patterns of the culture including the economic, social, and political systems of which the micro-systems, mesosystems, and exosystems are concrete expressions. Bronfenbren-ner's ecological model has been fruitfully applied in the analysis of a number of clinical issues including the effects of child abuse (Belsky, 1980) and divorce (Kurdek, 1981).

Despite the promising consequences for understanding behavior by using the ecological models (Bronfenbrenner & Crouter, 1983), most behavioral research on the effects of the environment have focused on analyses of dyadic interaction patterns in which the focus is on the participating individuals. Only recently, have these relationships themselves become empirical issues of inquiry. Parke and Tinsley (1987) in an extensive review of family interaction research have pointed to the important new trend of adding not only father-child interaction to the study of mother-child interaction, but the combination of these into studies of triadic interactions and entire family behavioral patterns. The behavioral research is slowly overcoming the technological difficulties embodied in analyses of multiple interacting individuals. Another growing empirical base comes from the direction of beliefs rather than behavior (Sigel, 1985). Investigators have become increasingly articulate at defining the dimensions of parental belief systems with the ultimate goal of describing the effects of these belief systems on parental behavior and ultimately, the behavior of the child. For the present, however, these research domains have provided primarily promissory notes of important future contributions to successful intervention efforts.

For our present purposes we will restrict the discussion to the organization of environmental factors contained within the culture, the family, and the individual parent. These codes are hierarchically related in their evolution and in their current influence on the child. The experience of the developing child is partially determined by the beliefs, values and personality of the parents, partially by the family's interaction patterns and transgenerational history, and partially by the socialization beliefs, controls, and supports of the culture. Developmental regulations at each of these levels are carried within codes that direct cognitive and social-emotional development so that the child ultimately will be able to fill a role defined within society.

Although at any point in time the environtype can be conceptualized independently of the child, changes in the abilities of the developing child are major triggers for regulatory changes and in most likelihood were major contributors to the evolution of a *developmental agenda* that is each culture's timetable for developmental milestones.

Cultural Code

The ingredients of the cultural code are the complex of characteristics that organize a society's childrearing system incorporating elements of socialization and education. These processes are embedded in sets of social controls and social supports based on beliefs that differ in the amount of community consensus ranging from mores and norms to fads and fashions. It would be beyond the scope of this paper to elucidate the full range of cultural regulatory processes that are potentially relevant to intervention efforts. As a consequence only a few points will be highlighted to flesh out the dimensions of the cultural code.

Although the common biological characteristics of the human species have acted to produce similar developmental agendas in most cultures, there are differences in many major features that often ignore the biological status of the individual. In most cultures formal education begins between the ages of 6 and 8 (Rogoff, 1981) when most children have reached the cognitive ability to learn from such structured experiences. On the other hand, informal education can begin at many different ages depending on the culture's attributions to the child. The Digo and Kikuyu are two East African cultures that have different beliefs about infant capacities (deVries, & Sameroff, 1984). The Digo believe that infants can learn within a few months after birth and begin socialization at that time. The Kikuyu wait until the second year of life before they believe serious education is possible. Closer to home some segments of middle-class parents have been convinced that prenatal experiences will enhance the cognitive development of their children. Such examples demonstrate the variability of human developmental contexts.

One of the major contemporary risk conditions toward which many programs are being directed is the elimination of adolescent pregnancy. Although for certain young mothers, the pregnancy is the outcome of individual factors, for a large proportion it is the result of a cultural code the defines maturity, family relationships, and socialization patterns with adolescent motherhood as a normative ingredient. In such instances to focus on the problem as one that resides wholly at the individual level would be a gross misrepresentation.

Family Code

Just as cultural codes regulate the fit between individuals and the social system, family codes organize individuals within the family system. Family codes provide a source of regulation that allow a group of individuals to form a collective unit in relation to society as a whole. As the cultural code regulates development so that an individual may fill a role in society, family codes regulate development to produce members that fulfill a role within the family and ultimately are able to introduce new members into the shared system. Traditionally, new members are incorporated through birth and marriage, although more recently, remarriage has taken on a more frequent role in providing new family members.

The family regulates the child's development through a variety of forms that vary in their degree of explicit representation. Families have rituals that prescribe roles, stories that transmit orientations to each family member as well as to whomever will listen, shared myths that influence individual interactions, and behavioral paradigms that change individual behavior when in the presence of other family members. Reiss (in press) has contrasted the degree to which these forms regulate family behavior through explicit prescriptions, i.e., the knowledge of family rules that each member has, with the degree to which each family members behavior is regulated by common practice, i.e., the behavior of the family members when together. The most represented regulations are exemplified by family rituals and the least by family paradigms. At intermediate levels are stories and myths. Research efforts are only beginning to explore the exact nature of how these forms are transmitted behaviorally among family members and how they are represented in cognition.

Individual Code

There is good evidence that individual behavior is influenced by the family context. When operating as part of a family, the behavior of each member is altered (Parke & Tinsley, 1987), frequently without awareness of the behavioral change (Reiss, 1981). However, there is also no doubt that individuals bring their own contribution to family interactions. The contribution of parents is much more complexly determined than that of young children, given the multiple levels that contribute to their behavior. Although the socializing regulations embodied in the cultural and family codes have been discussed, the individualized interpretations that each parenting figure imposes on these codes has not. To a large extent these interpretations are conditioned by parents' past participation in their own family's coded interactions, but they are captured uniquely by each member of the family. These individual influences further condition each parent's responses to their own child. The richness of both health and pathology embodied in these responses are well described in the clinical literature. In terms of early development, Fraiberg (1980) and her colleagues have provided many descriptions of the attributions that parents' bring to their parenting. These "ghosts" of unresolved childhood conflicts have been shown to "do their mischief according to a historical or topical agenda, specializing in such areas as feeding, sleep, toilet-training or discipline, depending upon the vulnerabilities of the parental past" (Fraiberg, Adelson, & Shapiro, 1980).

Parental psychopathology has long been recognized as a contributor to the poor developmental status of children. Although we acknowledge that influence, we must also be careful to note the effects of the contexts in which parental behavior is rooted, the family and cultural codes. It is important to recognize the parent as a major regulating agency of child development, but it is equally important to recognize that parental behavior is itself embedded in regulatory contexts.

UNDERSTANDING CONTEXTS OF DEVELOPMENT

The preceding discussion has been aimed at understanding the complexity of contextual influences on development. Through an ecological analysis, some aspects of the environtype were highlighted as providing the regulatory framework for healthy child development. The environment is an active force in shaping outcomes. However, the shaping force is constrained by the state and potentialities of the individual (Sameroff, 1983).

Developmental psychopathology has introduced an important reorientation within psychiatry. The principles of development that apply to the achievement of healthy growth are now seen as the same ones that apply to the achievement of illness (Sroufe & Rutter, 1984). In this view most illnesses are indeed achievements that result from the active strivings of each individual to reach an adaptive relation to his or her environment. The nutrients or poisons that experience provides will flavor that adaptation. No complex human accomplishment has been demonstrated to arise without being influenced by experience. For young children, these experiences are either provided or arranged by the family and the culture.

Developmental psychopathology applies developmental approaches to understanding maladaptive individual differences in behavior. Where developmental psychology tries to understand the continuities between normal and deviant behavior to reveal general laws of development and psychiatry seeks to define the discontinuities between normal and disordered behavior in order to categorize individuals, developmental psychopathology combines the two approaches by utilizing general principles of development to explain why some individuals develop disorders that are discontinuous with normal functioning. Thus the scientific program for developmental psychopathology is to explain both the continuities and discontinuities in individual patterns of behavioral adaptation.

Within the RLS our attention has been captured much more by the continuities than by the discontinuities. We have recently completed a new assessment of the sample when the children were thirteen years of age. We were especially interested in those children from multiple risk families who had managed to overcome their handicaps and reach normal or above average levels of intellectual or social emotional competence. We were very disappointed to find little evidence of these resilient or invulnerable children. When we recreated our multiple risk score at age thirteen we found the same powerful relationship between environmental adversity and child behavior, those children with the most environmental risk factors had the lowest competence ratings (Sameroff, Seifer, Baldwin & Baldwin, 1989). The typical statistic found in longitudinal research is the correlation between early and later performance. We found such correlations. Intelligence at 4 years correlated .72 with intelligence at 13 years, and the social competence scores at the two ages correlated .43. The usual interpretation of such numbers is that there is a continuity in the child of competence or incompetence. In our study we were able to correlate environmental characteristics as well as child ones. The correlation between multiple risk scores at the two ages was .76, as great or greater than any continuity within the child. Those children who had poor environments at 4 still had them when they were 13 and probably would continue to have them for the foreseeable future. Whatever the child's ability for achieving high levels of competence, it was severely undermined by the continuing paucity of environmental support. Whatever the capabilities provided to the child by the genotype or his or her own accomplishments, it is the environtype that controls the opportunities for development.

The importance of the regulatory function of parents became clear when we examined discontinuities in our data. These discontinuities were not between early performance and later but between expected outcome and actual outcome. We were able to identify a small group of children (20%) from demographically high-risk families who were doing better than average on their cognitive outcome scores (Baldwin, Baldwin, & Cole, 1989). The differences between these children and their poorly achieving peers were in the attitudes and practices of their parents. A pattern of restrictiveness, clarity of rules, warmth but little democracy characterized these families. The parents had constructed a safe environment in the midst of chaos in which their children could develop. The environtype was modified to foster development rather than hinder it.

Continuity and Discontinuity

The discussion of developmental psychopathology that began this chapter provided a definition characterized by three components: (1) an adaptational process, (2) a linkage between constitution and experience, and (3) a linkage across time. The study of the adaptational process emphasizes the constructive aspect of development in which each individual comes to terms with the opportunities and limitations of experience to produce a uniquely integrated outcome. The study of the linkage between constitution and experience contains the recognition that no individual can be understood apart from the context in which he or she lives. The analysis of the environtype provided a description of the many levels of influence at both family and societal levels that potentially regulate the adaptational process. The study of linkages across time is perhaps the most defining of developmental psychopathology in that it contains the basis for continuities and discontinuities.

The perspective taken by developmental psychopathology offers a powerful alternative to nondevelopmental approaches because principles of process are integrated into an understanding of behavioral deviancy. Where traditional views have seen deviancy as inherent in the individual, developmental views place deviancy in the dynamic relation between the individual and the internal and external context.

ACKNOWLEDGMENTS

Research reported here was supported by funds from the National Institute for Mental Health and the W. T. Grant Foundation.

REFERENCES

Baldwin, A. L., Baldwin, C., & Cole, R. E. (1989). Stress-resistant families and stress-resistant children. In J. Rolf, D. Masten, D. Cicchetti, K. Neuchtherlin, & S. Weintraub (Eds.), *Risk and protective factors in the development of psychopathology.* Cambridge, England: Cambridge University Press.

Becker, W. C., & Krug, R. S. (1965). The parent attitude research instrument—A research review. *Child Development, 36,* 339–361.

Belsky, J. (1980). Child maltreatment: An ecological integration. *American Psychologist, 35,* 430–435.

Brazelton, T. B. (1973). Neonatal behavioral assessment scale. *Clinics in Developmental Medicine* (No. 50). Philadelphia: Lippincott.

Bronfenbrenner, U. (1977). Toward an experimental ecology of human development. *American Psychologist, 32,* 513–531.

Bronfenbrenner, U., & Crouter, A. C. (1983). The evolution of environmental models in development research. In W. Kessen (Ed.), *History, theories, and methods.* Vol. I of P. H. Mussen (Ed.), *Handbook of child psychology* (pp. 357–414). New York: Wiley.

Cattell, R. B., & Scheier, I. H. (1983). *Handbook for the IPAT anxiety scale questionnaire* (2nd Edition). Champaign, IL: Institute for Personality and Ability Testing.

Cicchetti, D. (1986). Foreword in E. Zigler & M. Glick (Eds.), *A developmental approach to adult psychopathology.*

Cicchetti, D., & Aber, J. L. (1986). Early precursors of later depression: An organizational perspective. In L. P. Lipsitt & C. Rovee-Collier (Eds.), *Advances in infancy research* (Vol. 4). Norwood, NJ: Ablex.

Cicchetti, D., & Schneider-Rosen, K. (1986). An organizational approach to childhood depression. In M. Rutter, C. E. Izard, & P. B. Read (Eds.), *Depression in young people: Developmental perspectives* (pp. 71–134). New York: Guilford.

Dawber, T. R. (1980). *The Framingham study: The epidemiology of atherosclerotic disease.* Cambridge, MA: Harvard University Press.

deVries, M. W., & Sameroff, A. J. (1984). Culture and temperament: Influences on temperament in three East African societies. *American Journal of Orthopsychiatry, 54*, 83–96.

Endicott, J., & Spitzer, R. L. (1972). Current and past psychopathology scales (CAPPS). *Archives of General Psychiatry, 27*, 678–687.

Engel, G. L. (1977). The need for a new medical model: A challenge for biomedicine. *Science, 196*, 129–136.

Eysenck, H. J., & Eysenck, S. B. G. (1969). *Personality structure and measurement.* San Diego: Robert R. Knapp.

Fish, B. (1984). Characteristics and sequelae of the neurointegrative disorder in infants at risk for schizophrenia: 1952–1982. In N. F. Watt, J. Anthony, L. C. Wynne, & J. E. Rolf (Eds.), *Children at risk for schizophrenia* (pp. 423–439). Cambridge, England: Cambridge University Press.

Fish, B., Shapiro, T., Halpern, F., & Wile, R. (1965). The prediction of schizophrenia in infancy: 3. A ten-year follow-up report of neurological and psychological development. *American Journal of Psychiatry, 121*, 768–775.

Fraiberg, S. (1980). *Clinical studies in infant mental health: The first year of life.* New York: Basic Books.

Fraiberg, S., Adelson, E., & Shapiro, V. (1980). Ghosts in the nursery: A psychoanalytic approach to the problems of impaired mother-infant relationships. In S. Fraiberg (Ed.), *Clinical studies in infant mental health: The first year of life.* New York: Basic Books.

Goldstein, M., & Tuma, S. (1987). High risk research: Editors' introduction. *Schizophrenia Bulletin, 13*, 369–372.

Hollingshead, A. B. (1957). *Two factor index of social position.* New Haven, CT: Yale University.

Holmes, T. H., & Rahe, R. H. (1967). The social readjustment rating scale. *Journal of Psychosomatic Research, 11*, 213–218.

Kohn, M. L. (1969). *Class and conformity: A study in values.* Homewood, IL: Dorsey.

Kokes, R. F., Harder, D. W., Fisher, L., & Strauss, J. S. (1982). Child competence and psychiatric work: V. Sex of patient and dimensions of psychopathology. *Journal of Nervous and Mental Disease, 168*, 348.

Kurdek, L. A. (1981). An integrative perspective on children's divorce adjustment. *American Psychologist, 36*, 856–866.

Mednick, S. A., & McNeil, T. F. (1968). Current methodology in research on the etiology of schizophrenia: Serious difficulties which suggest the use of the high-risk group method. *Psychological Bulletin, 70*, 681–693.

Mednick, S. A., & Schulsinger, F. (1968). Some premorbid characteristics related to breakdown in children with schizophrenic mothers. In D. Rosenthal & S. S. Kety (Eds.), *The transmission of schizophrenia* (pp. 267–292). Oxford: Pergamon Press.

Parke, R. D., & Tinsley, B. J. (1987). Family interaction in infancy. In J. Osofsky (Ed.), *Handbook of infant development* (2nd edition, pp. 579–641). New York: Wiley.

Reiss, D. (1981). *The family's construction of reality.* Cambridge, MA: Harvard University Press.

Reiss, D. (1989). The represented and practicing family: Contrasting visions of family continuity. In A. J. Sameroff & R. N. Emde (Eds.), *Relationship disturbances in early childhood: A developmental approach.* New York: Basic Books.

Rogoff, B. (1981). Schooling and the development of cognitive skills. In H. C. Triandis & A.

Heron (Eds.), *Handbook of cross-cultural psychology: Developmental psychology* (Vol. 4, pp. 233–294). Boston: Allyn & Bacon.

Rutter, M. R. (1977). Protective factors in children's responses to stress and disadvantage. In M. W. Kent & J. E. Rolf (Eds.), *Primary prevention of psychopathology Vol. 3: Social competence in children.* Hanover, NH: University of New England Press.

Rutter, M. R. & Garmezy, N. (1983). Developmental psychopathology. In M. Hetherington (Ed.), *Social development.* Volume 4 of P. H. Mussen (Ed.), *Handbook of child psychology* (pp. 775–911). New York: Wiley.

Rutter, M., Tizard, J., & Whitmore, K. (1981). *Education, health and behaviour.* Huntington, NY: Krieger.

Rutter, M., Tizard, J., Yule, W., Graham, P. J., & Whitmore, K. (1976). Research report: Isle of Wight studies 1964–1974. *Psychological Medicine, 6,* 313–332.

Sameroff, A. J. (1983). Developmental systems: Contexts and evolution. In W. Kessen (Ed.), *History, theories, and methods.* Volume 1 of P. H. Mussen (Ed.), *Handbook of child psychology* (pp. 237–294). New York: Wiley.

Sameroff, A. J. (1985). Environmental factors in the early screening of risk. In W. K. Frankenburg & R. N. Emde (Eds.), *Early identification of the child at risk: An international perspective* (pp. 21–44). New York: Plenum.

Sameroff, A. J., & Chandler, M. J. (1975). Reproductive risk and the continuum of caretaking casualty. In F. D. Horowitz, M. Hetherington, S. Scarr-Salapatek, & G. Siegel (Eds.), *Review of child development research* (Vol. 4, pp. 187–244). Chicago: University of Chicago Press.

Sameroff, A. J., & Feil, L. (1983). Parental concepts of development. In I. Sigel (Ed.), *Parent belief systems: The psychological consequences for children* (pp. 83–104). Hillsdale, NJ: Lawrence Erlbaum Associates.

Sameroff, A. J., & Fiese, B. H. (1989-b). Transactional regulation and early intervention. In S. J. Meisels & J. P. Shonkoff (Eds.), *Early intervention: A handbook of theory, practice and analysis.* New York: Cambridge University Press.

Sameroff, A. J., & Seifer, R. (1983). Familial risk and child competences. *Child Development, 54,* 1254–1268.

Sameroff, A. J., Seifer, R., Baldwin, C., & Baldwin, A. L. (1989, April). *Continuity of risk from early childhood to adolescence.* Paper presented at the biennial meetings of the Society for Research in Child Development, Kansas City.

Sameroff, A. J., Seifer, R., Barocas, R., Zax, M., & Greenspan, S. (1987). IQ scores of 4-year-old children: Social-environmental risk factors. *Pediatrics, 79,* 343–350.

Sameroff, A. J., Seifer, R., & Zax, M. (1982). Early development of children at risk for emotional disorder. *Monographs of the Society for Research in Child Development, 47,* (7, Serial No. 199).

Sameroff, A. J., Seifer, R., Zax, M., & Barocas, R. (1987). Early indicators of developmental risk: Rochester longitudinal study. *Schizophrenia Bulletin, 13,* 383–394.

Sameroff, A. J., & Zax, M. (1973). Neonatal characteristics of offspring of schizophrenic and neurotically-depressed mothers. *Journal of Nervous and Mental Diseases, 157* 191–199.

Santostefano, S. A. (1978). *A biodevelopmental approach to clinical child psychology: Cognitive controls and cognitive control therapy.* New York: Basic Books.

Schaefer, E. S., & Bell, R. Q. (1958). Development of a parental attitude research instrument. *Child Development, 29,* 339–361.

Seifer, R., Sameroff, A. J., & Jones, F. (1981). Adaptive behavior in young children of emotionally disturbed women. *Journal of Applied Developmental Psychology, 1,* 251–276.

Sigel, E. (1985). *Parental belief systems: The psychological consequences for children.* Hillsdale, NJ: Lawrence Erlbaum Associates.

Sroufe, L. A., & Rutter, M. (1984). The domain of developmental psychopathology. *Child Development, 55,* 17–29.

Stern, D. (1977). *The first relationship: Infant and mother.* Cambridge, MA: Harvard University Press.

Trad, P. V. (1987). *Infant and childhood depression: Developmental factors.* New York: Wiley.

Tronick, E. Z., & Field, T. M. (Eds.). (1986). Maternal depression and infant disturbance. *New directions for child development.* San Francisco: Jossey-Bass.

Watt, N. F., Anthony, J., Wynne, L. C., & Rolf, J. E. (1984). *Children at risk for schizophrenia: A longitudinal perspective.* Cambridge, England: Cambridge University Press.

Werner, E. E., Bierman, J. M., & French, F. E. (1971). *The children of Kawai.* Honolulu: University of Hawaii Press.

Werner, E. E., & Smith, R. S. (1977). *Kauai's children come of age.* Honolulu: University of Hawaii Press.

Werner, E. E., & Smith, R. S. (1982). *Vulnerable but invincible: A longitudinal study of resilient children and youth.* New York: McGraw Hill.

Werner, H. (1948). *Comparative psychology of mental development.* New York: International University Press.

Zajonc, R. B. (1976). Family configuration and intelligence. *Science. 192,* 227–236.

Zubin, J., & Spring, B. (1977). Vulnerability: A new view of schizophrenia. *Journal of Abnormal Psychology, 56,* 103–126.

4 Neural and Psychological Maturation in a Social Context

Don M. Tucker
University of Oregon

INTRODUCTION

This chapter outlines a theoretical approach to emotional and social development that considers mechanisms of neural development and that emphasizes the role of emotions in organizing behavior. The complexities of brain development or social development are enough to cause a treatment of either one to be a major challenge. This chapter can be seen as a conceptual exercise. In it, I consider the implications of the evidence on brain development for an organismic approach to developmental psychopathology. I also suggest that the major issues of early social and emotional development frame the context for an understanding of brain maturation.

PRINCIPLES OF NEURAL DEVELOPMENT

For developmental theorists such as Freud and Werner, their knowledge of a course of biological development guided their approach to understanding psychological development (Cicchetti, in press). More sophisticated and mature psychological structures were to be understood through their emergence from more primitive forms. Similarly, for Piaget, the origins of intelligence were to be found in the more elementary biological substrates of sensory and motor complexes. There are several principles of brain development that can inform a model of social and emotional development. Some of these are well known, and obvious enough that it may not seem important to stress them. Other principles are of more recent origin, and are only beginning to be understood in terms of their possible psychological significance.

Perhaps the most remarkable thing we have discovered about biological development is that is recapitulates our phylogenetic heritage. Evolution has operated on a developmental process, and the blueprint of complex organisms contains within it the traces of the historical sequence of more primitive progenitors. This must be a profound discovery, yet it has proven to be difficult to understand its implications. Many writers point out that the parallel is not an exact one, that just because in embryonic form each of us had a tail doesn't mean that we ever took the form of lizards. Although some parents might, no psychologist would propose that children can be understood as passing through a reptilian stage. Yet the implications of embryonic transformations for understanding development are clear. More complex patterns of cellular organization are created only through a program that first assumes more primitive forms. The later structures are transformations of these more primitive forms.

When we examine the anatomy of the brain, we find that the transformation of more primitive structures is only partial; the gross outlines of more primitive neomammalian and reptilian brains are still to be found within the core of the human brain (MacLean, 1970). Furthermore, this process of transformation seems to involve an active inhibition of the behavioral potential of more primitive structures. Thus, as the infant matures, vestigial reflexes are observed to disappear. However, these reflexes may appear again if there is brain damage later in life, suggesting that the maturation process involves not only a reworking of primitive structures toward higher ends, but an active inhibition of at least some of the tendencies of these primitive structures (Brodal, 1969).

Thus we could consider something of a psychological embryology. The process of psychological development could be considered to involve primitive patterns of emotional and social orientation in the early years that then form a foundation for later, more organizationally complex transformations that direct adult social behavior. Reasoning from the biological model, the later more complex patterns of social relation may involve inhibition of aspects of earlier, more primitive forms. Yet with major dysfunction at the adult level, we might see a reemergence of infantile emotional patterns, perhaps not unlike the reemergence of vestigial reflexes in brain damage.

Just as neurophysiologic transformation involves a major reworking of primitive brain structures as they are incorporated in a more complex brain, we must appreciate the extensive transformation of infantile patterns of social emotional functioning as they are incorporated in an adult brain. Thus, the function of brain stem structures in the human brain only bear a vague resemblance to their functions in more primitive early vertebrates, and the transformation process is a major reworking of primitive algorithms to suit the new complexities of higher brain forms. Reasoning by analogy, the childhood patterns of emotionality may have become so thoroughly subsumed within more complex patterns through later childhood and adolescence that it may be a mistake to reason too concretely from early experience to explain even developmentally regressed adult behavior.

In evolution, all transitional forms were required to be adaptive. Thus the continuity between more complex patterns of brain function and the patterns of simpler creatures is required by the fact that no design changes could be allowed that would take even one generation out of commission. Thus, each change had to be a tinkering of an existing, workable form. In psychological development we can consider a much greater aptitude for new strategies for behavior control at new developmental stages. But perhaps the same principle of continuity could be informative. Thus the child encountering a stressful environment will be forced to rely on more primitive coping methods, whereas a child operating under a more permissive and supportive environment would be allowed a greater range of variability in behavior control that could allow wholly new organizational patterns to appear.

Timing of Component Maturation

Another principle suggested by considering neurobiological development is that there may be advantages to having certain components of the brain become functional earlier than others. For example, in the Aplysia, an invertebrate that has been a favorite subject for studies of neural organization and development, it can be shown that habituation mechanisms mature earlier than sensitization mechanisms (Rankin & Carew, 1987). Apparently, the adaptability of the juvenile organism is facilitated by appearance of this habituation mechanism for learning an environmental adaptation, whereas sensitization is only required for more mature functioning. This ability to alter the developmental timing of certain response modes may be important for understanding more complex neural networks as well.

The Structures of Social Behavior

Although for neurobiologists the neurochemistry of learning and adaptation is remarkably similar from simple invertebrates to the big primates, we must recognize that there are major discontinuities in brain organization when it comes to the evolution of social behavior. MacLean's (1970) concept of the triune brain has been particularly informative. The third, highest level is the cortex that is so well developed in humans. Underlying this is a neomammalian brain whose highest level of organization parallels the human limbic system with it paleocortex. Still more primitive is a reptilian level involving striatal, brainstem, and midbrain structures. MacLean was impressed by the emergence of completely new patterns of behavior with the rise of mammals and their paleocortex. One new form of behavior was care for the young. This required a new class of emotional control mechanisms that were not present in the reptilian brain.

In considering the neuropsychological development of the human infant, it is easy to become caught up in aspects of cortical function. Yet if we are to appreciate an evolutionary perspective, it may be important to understand the essential roles of these more recent limbic structures that are unique to social mammals. It is not inconceivable that the ontogenesis of more complex mammalian brains requires adequate social interaction, and if this is lacking, the genetic blueprint defaults to a pattern of organization that in a gross sense could be described as reptilian.

Dorsal and Ventral Patterns

Recent anatomical studies have suggested that an important way of understanding the functions of the neocortex is to appreciate the origins of neocortical structures from more primitive neomammalian cortices of the limbic system. The earliest cortex that appeared associated with limbic structures had primitive lamination, compared to the six layers of the more recent neocortex. Cytoarchitectonic studies by Sanides (1970) suggested that the dorsal or superior surface of the human cerebral hemispheres can be shown to have its phylogenetic and ontogenetic origins in the dorsal or archiocortical structures of the limbic system. These archiocortical limbic areas have a high concentration of pyramidal cells, and this pyramidal quality pervades the cytoarchitectonics of dorsal neocortex. In contrast, the inferior or ventral cortical regions, including occipital-temporal pathways and orbital-frontal regions, have a more granular cellular organization that demonstrates their developmental origins in the more ventral paleocortex of the limbic system (see also Goldberg, 1985). Thus, there is a clear developmental story to explain major divisions of highest level of the brain, the cortex, which is the target of most neuropsychological study. These divisions reflect the limbic origins of the cortical layers. Although the implications of these differentiations for emotion are just beginning to be understood (Bear, 1983; Tucker & Liotti, in press), it is becoming increasingly clear that an appreciation of the primitive, emotional functions of the limbic system will be essential if we are to develop an integrated model of higher cortical functions.

Sprouting and Pruning

Only fairly recently have the methods for characterizing neuronal synapses been sufficiently precise to allow determination of rates of synaptogenesis in the cortex. Remarkably, brains of young mammals appear to undergo a widespread and undifferentiated synaptogenesis, multiplying the interconnections among neurons and cortical networks. The developmental mechanism accompanying this proliferation seems to be a process of adaptive attrition: The undifferentiated sprouting of synapses forms a base upon which experiential usage of neural circuits becomes the mechanism for retention and continued development. Unused connections are not retained.

This is the most specific substantiation of the "use it or lose it" principle of neural development. Not only synapses, but neurons are lost at a high rate in the developing brain. The genetic program creates a brain with rather undifferentiated potential for neural circuitry, and interaction with the environment sets up patterns of function in the circuitry that are then retained in the neuroanatomy. Unused tissue is literally pruned away.

Thus, structure is closely meshed with function in the developing brain. The first implication this principle may suggest is that the brain is a passive recipient of the experience imposed on it from the environment. Yet, an organismic-developmental perspective would view the brain as active, organizing itself in patterns of circuitry and patterns of functioning in the face of the environmental context. Nerve cell proliferation and synaptogenesis would form a set of developmental raw materials upon which the self-organization of circuitry can operate.

Fully appreciating this interdependence of structure and function may be one of the more difficult tasks for the current generation of neuropsychologists. We are all too accustomed to thinking of the biological hardware of brain structure that has been programmed in its software by experience. Rather, the developmental process involves a more fundamental organization of cellular structure dependent upon experience.

For example, occluding one eye of a kitten causes the pathways from the remaining eye to occipital-cortices of both hemispheres to become highly developed (Hubel, Wiesel, & LeVay, 1977). The crossed pathway, because of its abnormal functional use, successfully competes with the uncrossed pathway to the hemisphere ipsilateral to the occluded eye. Differences in experiential contact thereby create differences in wiring. Thus we can expect that the highly interactive combination of genetics and functional development will create substantially different patterns of neuroanatomy for different individuals. As methods of studying anatomy and intact brains, such as magnetic resonance and other forms of imaging are becoming widespread, there is an increasing recognition of parallels between individual differences in functional capacity and individual differences in neuroanatomy (Ojemann, 1983).

Gradients of Cortical Maturation

Judging from the rates of myelination (the formation of the fatty sheath around axons), the cortex does not mature as one piece, but rather along maturational gradients. Primary receptive areas for sensory input appear to mature before the association cortex that is responsible for integrating these modalities (Yakovlev, 1962). In addition, in the early years of human brain development there appears to be a caudal-to-rostral gradient, such that receptive functions of the posterior brain seem to be mature before the motor, and perhaps regulatory, functions of the anterior brain (Yakovlev, 1962). This is consistent with the substantial perceptual competence of the infant in the first months of life, and the relative delay in motor competence. This maturational gradient suggested by traditional methods seems to be confirmed by recent studies of regional brain metabolism with positron emission tomographic methods (Chugani & Phelps, 1986). Thus, we might expect to find the infant has capacity for responsiveness to the environment before it has competence for action, and perhaps before the frontal regulatory influences provide much integration of the developing perceptual capacities.

It has also been suggested that there may be a lateral gradient of maturation, such that the two cerebral hemispheres mature at different rates. Although the evidence is sketchy, and the claims remain controversial, most of the evidence seems to favor an early maturation of the right hemisphere in the first year, while the left hemisphere remains relatively immature. One line of evidence is that seizures are more likely in the left hemisphere in the first year of life (Taylor, 1969), suggesting greater immaturity of the cerebral tissue on the left side. Other evidence is electrophysiological. A more mature photic driving response is observed in the infant's right hemisphere (Crowell, Jones, Kapuniai, & Nakagawa, 1973). Furthermore, the maturation of the spontaneous EEG, which proceeds from slow frequencies toward a greater proportion of alpha, has been observed to occur earlier for the right hemisphere than for the left (Walter, 1950).

Although the direct evidence on maturation rates is still quite tentative (see Whitaker, 1978), it is consistent with what we can infer about functional maturation of the cognitive capacities of the left and right hemispheres in the first and second years. The evidence of right hemisphere specialization for nonverbal emotional communication is now compelling, whether collected from brain lesioned individuals (Borod, Koff, & Buck, 1986), or normal individuals (Tucker & Frederick, in press), or whether in visual or auditory modalities. It is also clear that a major developmental task for the infant is responding to nonverbal communication. It would seem as if the right hemisphere's contributions to nonverbal communication are quite well developed substantially prior to the left hemisphere's burst of language acquisition in the second year.

Another perspective might integrate the caudal-rostral gradient with the right-left gradient. The right hemisphere's specialized skills often involve strong perceptual components; Tucker and Williamson (1984) proposed that the right hemisphere's specialization has involved integration of perceptual components of the posterior brain. In contrast, not only is it clear that left hemisphere damage impairs fine motor control, but the theoretical case can be made that the left hemisphere's language skills are derived from a more fundamental specialization of the left hemisphere for motor control (Kimura, 1961; Tucker & Williamson, 1984). Thus, the gradient from *responsive* toward *active* kinds of attentional control might be consistent with the gradient from nonverbal communication toward verbal communication and increased locomotion and the appearance of left hemisphere controls and motor competence in the second year.

Limbic Microgenesis

Perhaps more than any other of his concepts, Werner's (1957) notion of microgenesis emphasizes the pervasive sense in which he used the term "development." Microgenesis is a developmental sequence that can occur in a short span of a psychological process, such as an idea, a percept, or perhaps a relationship (Tucker, 1973). Recently, this principle has been applied to the functioning of brain systems as a way of considering the relation of limbic structures to cortical ones (Brown, 1985; Goldberg, 1985). Building upon Brown's initial formulation of a neuropsychological model of microgenesis, Goldberg emphasizes that major control pathways into motor regions come from the limbic system. Interestingly, different kinds of controls come from dorsal and ventral limbic routes (Goldberg, 1985). These limbic structures are also the targets of the main pathways of sensory integration, from primary receptive areas, through association areas, to the limbic targets.

Thus, from observing the circuitry we must conclude that whatever affective and motivational processes are being elaborated within the more primitive limbic structures, these are essential not just to long-range patterns of behavior organization, but to each sensation and action. Importantly, the microgenetic process seems to involve an integration of phylogenetically primitive brain structures into more complex, cortical functions in the organization of a single percept or action. Reasoning from anatomy in this way, we have no indication of how ontogenetic sequences may be relevant to more microgenetic ones, but it remains an interesting possibility that more primitive levels of organization of an idea or a percept involve greater influences from ontogenetically primitive levels (see Kragh & Smith, 1971).

EMOTIONS AS NEURAL CONTROL SYSTEMS

The possibility that the two cerebral hemispheres mature at different rates is particularly intriguing given the evidence of differential hemispheric contributions to emotion. This evidence can be approached in at least two ways. One approach might be considered a top-down approach, in which the two hemisphere's differing cognitive functions are helpful in understanding ways that cognitive processes direct and organize more primitive emotional ones. A second approach might be considered a bottom-up perspective, which suggests that there may be primitive forms of emotional arousal and activation that differ for the two hemispheres, and that provide specific kinds of emotional controls on attention and cognition. This second approach is more speculative at the current time, but it suggests a number of interesting ways of thinking about how processes of biological maturation might interact with early social development.

The approaches to the psychology of emotion that emphasize the determining role of cognitions in creating emotional experience often seem to describe a propositional form of cognition. Thus, when emotions are described as attributions made to undifferentiated arousal states (Schachter & Singer, 1962) or inferences made from self-perception, it is difficult to understand how the cognition could be other than in verbal, propositional form. Yet when we consider the neuropsychological evidence, it is the nonverbal right hemisphere that is found to be most important for many of the kinds of communication we would term emotional, including facial expressions of emotion (Borod et al, 1986) and emotional intonations of speech (Heilman, Scholes, & Watson, 1975).

A primary elaboration of emotional experience thus seems to occur within the right hemisphere without the necessity of elaboration by language. If so, we might expect the right hemisphere's skill in holistic organization, and its capacity to integrate information from several sources, to figure in emotional experience (Safer & Leventhal, 1977). These aspects of right hemisphere cognition seem to be relevant to what Werner (1957) termed *syncretic* cognition, in which various aspects of the child's experience are fused in an undifferentiated experiential matrix. Werner described the postural-affective matrix, in which emotion and bodily position serve as key defining contexts for early experience. Consistent with Werner's theorizing, we might expect that right hemisphere cognition is essential to emotional experience early in life, and that it is not simply supplanted by more analytic cognition of the left hemisphere, but remains an integral aspect of emotional life throughout development (Tucker, 1981, 1986). An appreciation of the right hemisphere's syncretic mode of emotional experience has appeared in recent theories of emotion, both those that emphasize a biological foundation for emotional processes (Buck, 1985) and those that emphasize the primacy of cognitive appraisal in the generation of emotion (Lazarus, 1987).

Another approach to lateral specialization for emotion has considered the bottom-up perspective, from which it appears as if the hemispheres differing cognitive skills might be explained as emergent from lateral asymmetries in more basic control modes associated with certain emotional states. This perspective was first suggested by observations on the way that hemispheric cognitive capacities seem to covary with emotional state, both in normals and in psychiatric patients (Tucker & Frederick, in press).

Several lines of evidence suggest there may be impaired functioning of the right hemisphere in depression (Goldstein, Filskov, Weaver, & Ives, 1977; Perris, 1974). It is an attractive hypothesis that the emotional hemisphere is somehow dysfunctional in the affective disorders. Yet several findings suggest that when the depressed mood state is effectively treated, right hemisphere normalizes (Kronfol, Hamsher, Digre, & Waziri, 1978; Brumback, Staton, &

Wilson, 1980). Furthermore, induction of a depressed mood state in normals can also be shown to influence right hemisphere function preferentially (Tucker & Dawson, 1984; Tucker, Stenslie, Roth, & Shearer, 1981). Thus it appears that a certain kind of emotional arousal, perhaps closely related to a depression-elation dimension, preferentially controls the level of function of the right hemisphere.

Not all psychiatric conditions show preferential involvement of the right hemisphere. In schizophrenics, a substantial body of evidence indicates dysfunction of the left hemisphere (Flor-Henry & Gruzelier, 1983). Yet in some cases this may be accompanied by excessive activation of the left hemisphere (Gur, 1978; Walker & McGuire, 1982). The possibility of a parallel between normal emotion and variance of left hemisphere activation has been suggested by studies on anxiety, in which highly anxious individuals show an over activation and a dysfunction of the left hemisphere that parallels in some respects the findings on schizophrenia (Tucker, Antes, Stenslie, & Barnhardt, 1978; Tyler & Tucker, 1982).

Tucker and Williamson (1984) attempted to develop a theoretical model that would account for what seemed to be inherent asymmetries in emotional arousal mechanisms, including a depression-elation mechanism and what might be a relaxation-anxiety mechanism. An important line of evidence guiding their theorizing was the suggestions that neurotransmitter pathways that are thought to be important to both emotion and arousal systems of the brain may be asymmetrical in humans.

In attempting to formulate a model of how these neurochemical mechanisms might lead to controls on both emotional state and attentional processes, Tucker and Williamson drew from the model of attentional control proposed by Pribram and McGuinness (1975). This model made several differentiations, among which were those between a tonic activation system whose primary function is enhancing motor readiness and a phasic arousal system that facilitates orienting to novel stimuli.

Tucker and Williamson proposed that the tonic vs. phasic characteristics of these primitive neural mechanisms could lead to different kinds of attentional control. They argued that these different kinds of attentional control could be relevant to understanding how brain function and cognition are altered by disordered brain chemistry in psychiatric conditions. Reviewing the animal evidence on activating mechanisms of the brain, Tucker and Williamson emphasized that the norepinephrine pathways thought to be important both to altering and to hedonic mechanisms seemed to operate in a phasic fashion. These pathways thus habituate rapidly to repetitive stimuli. This *habituation bias* could serve as an adaptive mechanism by augmenting the brain's response to novel stimuli. Tucker and Williamson formulated several implications of a control mechanism that facilitates response to novelty. One of these applications is the effect of a structure of working memory. By including various sensory elements, and perhaps mnemonic elements, the habituation bias would saturate working memory with a broad range of diverse data. The expansive attentional mode thus produced might be essential for the kind of holistic cognition for which the right hemisphere specialized. Thus Tucker and Williamson speculated that the phasic arousal system, which is important to perceptual orienting processes in general, might be especially important to the right hemisphere's holistic integration of these perceptual processes.

The emotional implications of this model can be seen when it is appreciated that the norepinephrine pathways are strongly implicated in emotional state variation on the depression-elation dimension. Thus depression is thought to be associated with impaired norepinephrine function, and when elation is induced by stimulant drugs, norepinephrine function is implicated (Schildkraut, 1965). Perhaps the most interesting aspect of this theorizing is that the hedonic and emotional characteristics emerged from the same system as do the attentional control characteristics. At least at this primitive level, the differentiation between emotional mechanisms and attentional mechanisms breaks down.

Pribram and McGuinness (1975) emphasized that attentional systems that are closely related to motor functions seem to operate in a more tonic fashion. Tucker and Williamson reviewed the animal evidence on dopaminergic pathways thought to be integral to motor readiness and found several indications that the cybernetics of the motor readiness system are in many ways opposite to those of the phasic arousal system. Specifically, the animals with strong dopaminergic modulation from drug treatments do not simply increase the quantity of motor activity, but rather restrict the range of motor operations until at high doses they show behavioral stereotypy. Thus the tonic quality of motor readiness seems to be associated with what may be a *redundancy bias,* a control mechanism through which routinization of motor actions is facilitated.

By considering this redundancy bias not just in motor control but in attentional control broadly, Tucker and Williamson theorized that this influence on working memory would produce a focused attention. A restricted set of elements would be maintained in working memory. Thus, temporal continuity is enhanced at the price of diversity of informational elements. The attentional control that seems to be more closely associated with motor rather than perceptual elements is thus tight, rather than loose.

The fact that drugs used to treat schizophrenia have their primary neurophysiologic action in blocking dopamine pathways has long suggested that symptoms of schizophrenia could be seen as exaggerated dopaminergic function. Furthermore, increasing evidence suggests that the mesolimbic dopamine pathways may be important to symptoms of anxiety (reviewed by Tucker & Liotti, in press). Although the evidence is still tentative, there are several findings that suggest that the dopamine pathways may be asymmetric, favoring the left side in humans. Tucker and Williamson argued that a case could be made that the left hemisphere's exaggeration in schizophrenia and normal anxiety states could reflect exaggerated dopaminergic function. Perhaps more interestingly, the cognitive characteristics of the left hemisphere, including its focal attention and analytic cognitive organization, could be seen as reflecting the attentional control of the tonic motor readiness system, wherein focusing and analyzing are facilitated by the redundancy bias. Here again, the attentional controls and emotional characteristics seem to stem from common mechanisms at this primitive level of brain organization.

Although they glossed over many aspects of brain function in their theorizing, Tucker and Williamson argued that higher brain systems, perhaps including the left and right hemispheres, are dependent upon more primitive control mechanisms that may be inherently linked to emotional states. Thus the left hemisphere's capacity for sequential reasoning and analytic thinking may require the control mode of tonic motor readiness that has subjective features of anxiety. The right hemisphere's capacity for holistic perception and expansive integration may require modulation by a neural control mode that has the inherent subjective qualities of an elated state. This kind of framework, in which self-regulation of cognitive capacity and self-regulation of emotional state are tightly linked, presents several interesting possibilities for considering mechanisms of early development.

SELF-REGULATION OF BRAIN DEVELOPMENT IN A SOCIAL CONTEXT

If we take the activation and arousal model of primitive attentional controls and apply it to the context of early psychological development it may be possible to consider how specific kinds of attentional control are adapted to the interaction of a child with the environment in the first years of life.

Early Perceptual and Emotional Responsivity

Although perceptual and motor organization is often closely integrated, we might consider that perceptual functions appear to mature earlier. Although both hemispheres of the brain are maturing in the first year, we might also consider the suggestion of early maturation of the right hemisphere. A reliance on the phasic arousal mechanism that seems to underlie the right hemisphere's attentional functioning may be particularly well suited to the tasks faced by the child in the first year. These include developing responsivity to emotional communication with parents as well as developing general competence in perception. The phasic arousal system seems to support a kind of external control of brain function that would be suited to these tasks. By orienting attention to novel events in the environment, the child's psychological functioning is closely responsive to the external context when it is modulated by the phasic arousal system.

If there is a specificity to the attentional control that is predominant in the first year, this would be accompanied by a specificity of the emotional arousal associated with this attentional control. The child would be self-regulating along the depression-elation dimension that is the affective manifestation of the phasic arousal system. Thus strong phasic arousal and strong responsivity to the context would be associated with elation whereas withdrawal and decreased perceptual-hedonic responsivity would be associated with depression. It seems particularly relevant that maternal separation in infant Rhesus monkeys is associated with a specific decrement in norepinephrine function (Suomi, 1987).

Thus the fundamental psychological orientation relevant to dependency and attachment phenomena might be specific in both its attentional features and its emotional qualities. If this early experiential base is to be influential in later functioning, we might expect it to relate not only to the hedonic value of social attachment in a specific sense, but to the interaction between hedonic tone and attentional responsivity to novel events generally. Similarly, pathologies resulting from dysfunctions at this stage, or at later stages that include this attentional orientation, would be associated with disorders in the hedonic value of social interaction.

This model shares much in common with other approaches to social development that emphasize the dependency of the child in the first year. The advantage of a neuropsychological model is that we may begin to characterize the mechanisms through which the social and emotional processes are developing in parallel with attentional processes. An interesting characteristic of attention in the infant has been termed "obligatory attention," in which the infant may examine a stimulus and appears to be unable to withdraw. The infant eventually shows distress, apparently from overstimulation (Posner & Rothbart, 1981). The infant's attention appears completely regulated by external factors at this time, before internal control is fully functional.

The emphasis on the depression-elation dimension and its control of attention in the first year is not meant to underestimate the importance of various other emotional states and processes, including irritability, panic, and other adaptive control mechanisms. Perhaps the best way to emphasize this model of the phasic arousal system and its externally directed control is to suggest that it is a dominant system, one that plays the major role in the baby's interest in objects and in people.

Autonomy and the Motivational Control of Motor Competence

Several developmental trends occur in the second year. The child gains increasing locomotor skills, providing more autonomous movement through the environment. There are also struggles for control with the parent, enough to suggest that separating from the external control mode of the first year is a major developmental task for this period. Finally, there is a remarkable burst of language development, providing the child with the ability not only to generate communication, but to become an independent agent for formulating mental representations.

An observation that may suggest a role of emotional factors in the development of language skills has come from the work of Bloom and Capatides (1987). Their observations of infants' spontaneous emotional displays during their actions with their mothers did not support the notion that language production grows out of emotional communications between mother and child. Rather, infants are often emotionally neutral at the time of their early utterances, and if anything show a tendency to display negative affect, as they seem to struggle with the demands of verbalization.

It may be that the several aspects of development represent a configuration of cognitive, behavioral, and emotional processes that stem from an increasing importance of the tonic motor readiness system in the child's self-control. In considering the cognitive attentional control emergent from the tonic activation system, Tucker and Williamson (1984) found a number of attentional features that seem to be consistent with the left hemisphere's cognitive skills. The redundancy bias of the tonic activation system seems to cause the contents of working memory to become stable, and yet at the same time restricted, since existing elements are favored instead of novel ones. This seems to be the kind of focal attention that is required to support the left hemisphere's analytic perception and cognition. Furthermore, the tonic activation system supports sequential control of actions. Since it introduces a bias against change in motor sequences, the changes that occur must be highly determined. This highly organized or determined control of changes in the motor program may support the sequential organization of actions, in contrast with the more fluid and impulsive behavior that would be facilitated by strong reliance on the phasic arousal system.

In his description of general principles of the development of biological systems, Bertalanffy (1968) emphasized that in earlier stages of development, the components of biological systems appear to interact in dynamic fashion. Only with continued development and greater fixity in the interaction among processes is consistent feedback possible, such that actions are repeated in a regularized enough fashion to allow the outcomes of some actions to feed back and alter the next cycle of behavior of other actions. Thus the developmental sequence is one that proceeds from dynamic flexibility and irregularity to one of increasing routinization and regularization of interactions. It may be that in the cognitive domain of the child the progression from a reliance on phasic arousal, which provides responsivity and flexibility at the cost of impulsivity, toward increasing importance of the tonic activation system, which allows routinization of motor programs and focusing of attention, may reflect the cognitive instantiation of Bertalanffy's biological principles.

Thus in its development of language, the left hemisphere may rely on the cybernetics of the motor readiness system to provide it with the routinization and sequential control required for verbal communication and mental representations in propositional form. If it is correct that the primitive control mode of the motor readiness system has inherent affective as well as attentional qualities, then perhaps it is not surprising that increased anxiety or hostility may be facilitated as the system is becoming fully operational. The implication would be that the same primitive controls required to engage tonic motor readiness in fight–flight situations would be called on for in the more articulate programming of the motor system required for language. This does not mean that extreme emotional states accompany optimal language development; indeed they would probably be counterproductive. However, it does suggest that some optimal amount of anxiety would be required as the young child is structuring articulate productions.

The capacity for autonomy in a positive sense, with locomotor skills and autonomous representations, seems to develop with the emotional substrate that engenders distance in an interpersonal context. These neuropsychological mechanisms would seem to be an important part of the autonomy operations of the second year, particularly when they are placed in the context of the strong degree of external control characterizing the first year. However, it may not be wise to attempt to formulate the autonomy struggle simply as an outgrowth of, or side effect of, these developmental trends. Rather, if the observations on Rhesus monkeys are to be a guide, the separation of the infant from the mother is a highly significant developmental task. It seems to have been actively selected as a developmental mechanism. It was probably fortuitous for the evolution of human developmental biology that individuation could be effected at the time of enhanced motor control, negativism, and language acquisition.

Social Integration and Competence with Peers

The human infant is, of course, not individuated in the sense of being functionally competent after his second year, and so continued integration in parental relations is necessary. Mahler (1968) describes the re-integration of the child with the mother after the autonomy struggles to be a period of "rapprochement." Within psychoanalytic theory this is a period at which time the relations with parents may become sexualized. Again considering the observations of social behavior of Rhesus monkeys, it may be important not to overemphasize the role of the parents at this stage, but rather to consider the attachment to peers that occurs after the initial separation from the mother. Although for monkey and human babies, the mother or caregiver provides a strong base of emotional support throughout childhood, the emotional significance of relations is increasingly directed toward peers.

From a general theoretical vantage, we might suspect that the external mode of attentional control facilitated by the phasic arousal system in the right hemisphere would be important to the older child's emotional attachment both to parents and peers. Success in the peer culture, either in childhood or in adolescence, is no easy task, and some studies of children with apparently normal IQs who fail in peer adjustment have suggested that they may have impaired functioning of the right hemisphere, thus not allowing them the sensitivity to nonverbal cues of accepted behavior (Denckla, 1986). In light of the importance of sexuality for psychoanalytic theory and for formation of adult relations, it is interesting that the right hemisphere seems to be particularly important to sexual behavior (Tucker & Frederick, in press). Consistent with the notion that the depression-elation dimension is integral to the right hemisphere's functioning and to the primitive hedonic value of social interactions, it is relevant that clinically depressed persons are hyposexual, while manics are hypersexual.

SPECULATIONS ON BIOLOGICAL MECHANISMS AND COGNITIVE PROCESSES IN A GENERIC SEQUENCE OF SOCIAL MATURATION

If we consider the process of social development in broad outline, it must be similar for many social animals. The juvenile period is critical for social bonding and some kind of training. This seems to be facilitated by emotions that support the bonding process. Then about the time of sexual maturity, the bonds must be severed and the maturing young animal must leave or be driven off to maintain diversity of the gene pool. In the larger primates, this appears to be accomplished by different mechanisms, such that young Rhesus monkey males are driven off but it is the females that leave the band in Chimpanzees (Suomi, 1987). Finally, the sexually mature animal forms a new kind of bond that supports sexual reproduction and the adult social order.

The developmental programming of this sequence seems to be cycled prematurely in the case of the larger primates. Thus for Rhesus monkeys there is an early stage of bonding and strong dependency, a stage of individuation and separation from the mother, and then a stage of peer interaction and contact, all prior to sexual maturity. This entire sequence occurs within the juvenile period, which is then followed by sexual maturity, individuation from the family or origin, and establishment of adult reproductive bonds. Thus the primordial sequence seems to be cycled early for the Rhesus monkeys, and perhaps for humans as well. It is as if the complex social relations of adulthood require a rehearsal of the emotional orientations and social patterns, and this rehearsal is provided by an early unfolding of the genetic program of social orienting.

Because the evolution of intelligence has occurred in the matrix of the social interactions of our primate ancestors, it may be that the neuropsychology of cognitive development can only be explained through the neuropsychology of emotion and social interaction. In this final section, I speculate that the emotional mechanisms of depression-elation and relaxation-anxiety/hostility operate to control the developmental processes that simultaneously control social orientations and the neural substrate of intelligence.

In a theoretical effort that attempted to integrate aspects of Freudian and Piagetian theory within a modern social cognition framework, Harvey, Hunt, and Schroder (1961) proposed that the development of cognitive complexity must be understood as entailing a sequence of orientations toward the social environment. They argued that the development of concrete and authoritarian attitudes can be linked to a life-long pattern of unilateral dependence on authority. In similar fashion, an adult pattern of negativism and antiauthoritarian attitudes can be traced to a struggle for autonomy in an inconsistent and capricious environment. For Harvey et al., the development of abstract intelligence and the capacity for complex cognitive constructions occurs only as the struggle for dependence and independence is resolved in favor of an interdependent pattern of relating to the social environment.

This emphasis on the social bases of intelligence is lacking in modern cognitive psychology. I suggest, however, that the more we learn about the neuropsychological mechanisms of cognitive development, and how these are closely linked to social and emotional development, the more that a broad and ecological view of intelligence will become important. Ideas and attitudes are not gained primarily through books, or even from school, but through a child's efforts to maintain a relation with the social environment. The emotions that underlie these efforts at social orientation may be integral to the formation of intelligence.

The external mode of the first year, reflecting the environment, may be important in a variety of contexts in which a person comes to orient to a new idea or situation. In fact, this may be the primordial mode, one that establishes the hedonic value of ideas or situations. For the capacity for independent and critical thinking, an opposite emotional orientation may then be required, one that separates self from context and indeed opposes self to the existing order. This is facilitated by emotions of anxiety and hostility that create identity for the self through maintaining constancy of attention and providing internal control of mental representations. In a formal sense this is the attentional control mode that may be required for critical analysis and sequential reasoning. Yet it is not irrelevant that it is also an orientation that is required for autonomy, for separating one's internal representations from the currently established beliefs.

For integrated functioning, these two modes must interplay effectively, and probably not simultaneously but in sequence. This may be a kind of dialectic, in which the child's experience with each of these fundamental modes becomes a formative mechanism for later intellectual development, and later social relations (Tucker, 1973). Stifling of either mode would lead to an imbalance of the dialectic, an inability to form the complex, abstract constructions that arise only from a finely tuned interaction of internal activity and external responsivity.

AFFECTS MODULATING THE STRUCTURE OF
NEURAL NETWORKS

There may be a more direct way that primitive emotional mechanisms shape intelligence—through their influence on the pruning of neural networks in early development. If it is the case that use shapes the viable circuitry of the brain, with unused synapses and nerve cells dying off, then controls on the usage of neural networks would provide controls on the structure of brain tissue. The activation and arousal systems provide qualitatively different controls on the functioning of neural networks, and thus qualitatively different influences on the structure of neural networks that are created by the developmental process.

As the phasic arousal system responds to novelty, it selects for a broad range of information to be active in working memory. Because each element in working memory will have inherent relations to longer term storage or reference memory, the expansive mode or attentional control created by the phasic arousal system would facilitate a broad range of activity in the neural network at any given time. We can thus predict that a neural network strongly modulated by the phasic arousal system would be highly interconnected and less influenced by selective pruning.

On the other hand, the redundancy bias of the tonic activation system would serve to restrict the range of elements that is maintained in working memory, thus, restricting the range of longer term items that are accessed or primed. At any given time only a restricted set of elements of the neural network would be active. Although it is conceivable that this kind of focal control could be sequentially applied to a number of sets or subdivisions of the broader neural network, it seems more likely that this control mode would facilitate the activation of a few restricted subsets of elements in the network, thus enhancing the opportunity for the pruning process to shape the functional networks that are retained. The outcome is a more differentiated pattern of neural organization.

These differing kinds of control modes are proposed by Tucker and Williamson (1984) to be differentially important to the right and left hemispheres, such that a more expansive attentional control facilitates the right hemisphere's holistic cognition, whereas a more restricted attentional control facilitates the focusing of the left hemisphere's analytic capacities. From the above reasoning, we would predict that the anatomical organization of the right hemisphere would be more diffuse, whereas that of the left hemisphere would be more differentiated. Although controversial, there is evidence that supports this contention. Semmes (1968) originally observed that somatosensory functions appear to be more focally organized in the left hemisphere, whereas the somatosensory organization of the right hemisphere appears to be more diffuse, as if organized in a mass action fashion. Consistent findings have come from regional cerebral blood flow methods that allow the delineation of relative amounts of white matter (axons) and gray matter (cell bodies). Gur et al. (1980) found that the relative proportion of white to gray matter was higher in the right hemisphere for most regions, consistent with a high degree of connectivity of its neural networks. Finally, electrophysiologic evidence gathered by my associates and I (Tucker, Roth, & Bair, 1986) also fits this trend. We found that coherence, a measure of covariance of specific frequencies, is higher for electroencephalographic recordings among right hemisphere regions in adults than among homologous regions of the left hemisphere. These findings have been replicated with data from children by Thatcher, Krause, and Rhybyk (1986).

If it is the case that short-term controls on activity of networks produces long term anatomical effects, then there would seem to be important implications for understanding psychopathology from a developmental perspective. This is not to say that hypotheses about genetic defects as manifested in brain structure are not relevant. It may suggest that what is genetically coded is not a fixed system of anatomical interconnections, but rather a predisposition toward certain attentional and emotional modes that then have their effects in shaping or not shaping brain organization. This perspective does underline the importance of early environmental interaction, since it suggests that major defects in the way that genetic potential is actualized in the face of early environmental context simply may not be reversible.

REFERENCES

Bear, D. M. (1983). Hemispheric specialization and the neurology of emotion. *Archives of Neurology, 40,* 195–202.

Bertalanffy, L. von. (1968). *General systems theory: Foundations, development, applications.* New York: Braziller.

Bloom, L., & Capatides, J. B. (1987). Expression of affect and the emergence of language. *Child Development, 58,* 1513–1522.

Borod, J. C., Koff, E., & Buck, R. (1986). The neuropsychology of facial expression: Data from normal and brain-damaged adults. In P. Blanck, R. Buck, & R. Rosenthal (Eds.), *Nonverbal communication in the clinical context.* University Park, PA: Penn State Press.

Brodal, A. (1969). *Neurological anatomy: In relation to clinical medicine.* New York: Oxford University Press.

Brown, J. (1985). Comments on Goldberg's Supplementary motor area structure and function. *Behavioral and Brain Science, 8,* 567–616.

Brumback, R. A., Staton, R. D., & Wilson, A. (1980). Neuropsychological study of children during and after remission of endogenous depressive episodes. *Perceptual and Motor Skills, 50,* 1163–1167.

Buck, R. (1985). Prime theory: An integrated view of motivation and emotion. *Psychological Review, 92,* 349–413.

Chugani, H. T., & Phelps, M. E. (1986). Maturational changes in cerebral function in infants determined by 18 FDG positron emission tonographies. *Science, 231,* 840–843.

Cicchetti, D. (in press). An historical perspective on the discipline of developmental psychopathology. In J. Rolf, A. Masten, D. Cicchetti, K. Neuchterlein, & S. Weintraub (Eds.), *Risk and protection factors in the development of psychopathology.* New York: Cambridge University Press.

Crowell, D. H., Jones, R. H., Kapuniai, L. E., & Nakagawa, J. K. (1973). Unilateral cortical activity in newborn humans: An early index of cerebral dominance? *Science, 180,* 205–208.

Denckla, M. B. (1986, March). *The neuropsychology of social emotional learning disabilities.* Symposium on Brain and Emotion: The Neuropsychology of Affect. New York Neuropsychology Group.

Flor-Henry, P., & Gruzelier, J. (Eds.). (1983). *Laterality and psychopathology. Vol. II.* Amsterdam: Elsevier.

Goldberg. G. (1985). Supplementary motor area structure and function: Review and hypotheses. *Behavioral and Brain Science, 8,* 567–616.

Goldstein, S. G., Filskov, S. B., Weaver, L. A., & Ives, J. (1977). Neuropsychological effects of electroconvulsive therapy. *Journal of Clinical Psychology, 33,* 798–806.

Gur, R. C., Packer, I. K., Hungerbuhler, J. P., Reivich, M., OBrist, W. D., Amarnek, W. S., & Sackeim, H. A. (1980). Differences in the distribution of gray and white matter in human cerebral hemispheres. *Science, 207,* 1226–1228.

Gur, R. E. (1978). Left hemisphere dysfunction and left hemisphere overactivation in schizophrenia. *Journal of Abnormal Psychology, 87,* 226–238.

Harvey, O. J., Hunt, D. E., & Schroder, H. M. (1961). *Conceptual systems and personality organization.* New York: Wiley.

Heilman, K. M., Scholes, R., & Watson, R. T. (1975). Auditory affective agnosia: Disturbed comprehension of affective speech. *Journal of Neurology, Neurosurgery, and Psychiatry, 38,* 69–72.

Hubel, D. H., Wiesel, T. N., & LeVay, S. (1977). Plasticity of ocular dominance columns in monkey striate cortex. *Philosophical Transactions of the Royal Society of London, 278,* 377–409.

Kimura, D. (1961). Cerebral dominance and the perception of verbal stimuli. *Canadian Journal of Psychology, 15,* 166–171.

Kragh, U., & Smith, G. J. W. (Eds.). (1970). *Percept-genetic analysis.* Lund: Gleerup.

Kronfol, Z., Hamsher, K., Digre, K., & Waziri, R. (1978). Depression and hemisphere functions: Changes associated with unilateral ECT. *British Journal of Psychiatry, 132,* 560–567.

Lazarus, R. (1987, August). *Constructs of the mind in adaptation.* Paper presented at symposium on Psychological and Biological Processes in the Development of Emotion, University of Chicago.

MacLean, P. D. (1970). *A triune concept of brain and behavior.* Toronto: University of Toronto Press.

Mahler, M. S. (1968). *On human symbiosis and the vicissitudes of individuation.* New York: International Universities Press.

Ojemann, G. A. (1983). Brain organization for language from the perspective of electrical stimulation mapping. *The Behavioral and Brain Sciences, 6,* 198–230.

Perris, C. (1974). Averaged evoked responses (AER) in patients with affective disorders. *Acta Psychiatrica Scandinavica,* Suppl. 225.

Posner, M. I., & Rothbart, M. K. (1981). The development of attentional mechanisms. In J. H. Flowers (Ed.), *Nebraska symposium on motivation.* Lincoln: University of Nebraska Press, 1–52.

Pribram, K. H., & McGuinness, D. (1975). Arousal, activation, and effort in the control of attention. *Psychological Review, 82*(2), 116–149.

Rankin, C. H., & Carew, T. J. (1987). Development of learning and memory in aplysia. II. Habituation and dishabituation. *Journal of Neuroscience, 7,* 133–143.

Safer, M. A., & Leventhal, H. (1977). Ear differences in evaluating emotional tone of voice and verbal content. *Journal of Experimental Psychology: Human Perception and Performance, 3,* 75–82.

Sanides, F. (1970). Functional architecture of motor and sensory cortices in primates in the light of a new concept of neocortex evolution. In C. R. Noback & W. Montagna (Eds.), *The primate brain: Advances in primatology* (Vol. 1, pp. 137–201). New York: Appleton-Century-Crofts.

Schachter, F., & Singer, J. E. (1962). Cognitive social and physiological determinants of emotional states. *Psychological Review, 69*, 379–399.

Schildkraut, J. (1965). The catecholamine hypothesis of affective disorders: A review of supporting evidence. *American Journal of Psychiatry, 122*, 509–522.

Semmes, J. (1968). Hemispheric specialization: A possible clue to mechanism. *Neuropsychologia, 6*, 11–26.

Suomi, S. (1987, August). *On temperament.* Paper presented at the meetings of the International Society for Research on Emotions, Worcester, MA.

Taylor, D. C. (1969). Differential rates of cerebral maturation between sexes and between hemispheres. *Lancet*, July 19, 140–142.

Thatcher, R. W., Krause, P. J., & Rhybyk, M. (1986). Cortico-cortical associations and EEG coherence: A two-compartmental model. *Electroencephalography and Clinical Neurophysiology, 64*, 123–143.

Tucker, D. M. (1973). Some relationships between individual and group development. *Human Development, 16*, 249–272.

Tucker, D. M. (1981). Lateral brain function, emotion, and conceptualization. *Psychological Bulletin, 89*, 19–46.

Tucker, D. M. (1986). Neural control of emotional communication. In P. Blanck, R. Buck, & R. Rosenthal (Eds.), *Nonverbal communication in the clinical context.* Cambridge, England: Cambridge University Press.

Tucker, D. M., Antes, J. R., Stenslie, C. E., & Barnhardt, T. N. (1978). Anxiety and lateral cerebral function. *Journal of Abnormal Psychology, 87*, 380–383.

Tucker, D. M., & Dawson, S. L. (1984). Asymmetric EEG power and coherence as method actors generate emotions. *Biological Psychology, 19*, 63–75.

Tucker, D. M., & Frederick, S. L. (in press). Emotion and brain lateralization. In H. Wagner & T. Manstead (Eds.), *Handbook of psychophysiology: Emotion and social behavior.* New York: Wiley.

Tucker, D. M., & Liotti, M. (in press). Neuropsychological mechanisms of anxiety and depression. In F. Boller & J. Grafman (Eds.), *Handbook of neuropsychology.* Amsterdam: Elsevier.

Tucker, D. M., Roth, D. L., & Bair, T. B. (1986). Functional connections among cortical regions: Topography of EEG. *Electroencephalography and Clinical Neurophysiology, 63*, 242–250.

Tucker, D. M., Stenslie, C. E., Roth, R. S., & Shearer, S. (1981). Right frontal lobe activation and right hemisphere performance decrement during a depressed mood. *Archives of General Psychiatry, 38*, 169–174.

Tucker, D. M., & Williamson, P. A. (1984). Asymmetric neural control systems in human self-regulation. *Psychological Review, 91*, 185–215.

Tyler, S. K., & Tucker, D. M. (1982). Anxiety and perceptual structure: Individual differences in neuropsychological function. *Journal of Abnormal Psychology, 91*, 210–220.

Walker, E., & McGuire, M. (1982). Intra- and inter-hemispheric information processing in schizophrenia. *Psychological Bulletin, 29*, 701–725.

Walter, W. G. (1950). Normal rhythms—Their development, distribution, and significance. In D. Hill & G. Parr, *Electroencephalography* (pp. 203–227). London: McDonald.

Werner, H. (1957). *The comparative psychology of mental development.* New York: Harper.

Whitaker, H. A. (1978). Is the right leftover? Commentary on Corballis & Morgan, "On the biological basis of human laterality." *Behavioral and Brain Sciences, 1*, 1.

Yakovlev, P. (1962). Morphological criteria of growth and maturation of the nervous system in man. *Research Publications of the Association for Research in Nervous and Mental Diseases, 39*, 3–46.

5 Culture and the Development of Child Psychopathology: Lessons from Thailand

John R. Weisz
University of North Carolina at Chapel Hill

Most research on psychopathology is based in the west, particularly in North America. As a consequence, we risk what Kennedy, Scheirer, and Rogers (1984) call a "monocultural science." Studying mental health problems in but one corner of the world can limit our understanding of the forms, and the determinants, of psychological dysfunction across various social contexts. In addition, monocultural approaches may blur the distinction—so crucial to our understanding of mental health problems—between phenomena that are culture-specific and those that are culture-general (see Draguns, 1982; Jahoda, 1977).

Recognizing the need for a cross-cultural approach, investigators have begun to study psychopathology across ethnic and national boundaries. Even these efforts, though, have been focused mainly on adults. This is surprising, because, for most people, the impact of culture is felt well before adulthood. Cultural differences have a powerful psychological impact in childhood. Data and ideas that I present here constitute one attempt to explore that impact, and in the process to help broaden our base of information about child psychopathology beyond its western foundations.

Cross-cultural research focused on childhood may be especially powerful in its empirical and theoretical impact. Consider, for example, a recurring question that arises in research on etiology: To what extent do various forms of psychological dysfunction reflect general development influences of childhood and adolescence, and to what extent do they represent social-environmental factors? Cross-cultural research can help us address this question. When such research reveals patterns of child dysfunction that are highly similar across very *dissimilar* cultures, culture-general developmental and biological causal processes need to be seriously considered. By contrast, when such research reveals patterns of dysfunction that are quite different from one culture to the next, the search for causes needs to include social-environmental processes that may vary across setting. Of course, such findings may also help us narrow the search for effective means of treatment and prevention, suggesting which social processes may need to be altered, and which groups of youth are at risk.

How should one go about studying child psychopathology cross-culturally? I offer several suggestions, in the form of steps which I believe can enhance the empirical and theoretical value of such research.

STEPS IN THE CROSS-CULTURAL STUDY OF CHILD PSYCHOPATHOLOGY

1. Finding Focal Patterns of Problem Behavior. First, it is helpful to identify dimensions or patterns of child problem behavior that are both clinically significant and relatively prevalent across cultures. Most specific problems (e.g., social isolation, cruelty to animals) or even specific diagnostic categories (e.g., gender identity disorder) pose a problem of low base rates in many cultures.

By contrast, there are two empirically derived broad-band behavior problem dimensions or "syndromes" that appear to be both high in base rate (because they encompass many specific problems) and relatively robust across cultures: *Overcontrolled problems* (e.g., fearfulness, sleep problems, somaticizing), sometimes labeled "internalizing" (Achenbach, 1978), "anxiety-withdrawal" (Quay, 1979) or "anxious-immature" (Conners, 1970); and *Undercontrolled problems* (e.g., disobedience, fighting, arguing), sometimes labeled "externalizing" (Achenbach, 1978), "conduct disorder" (Quay, 1979), or "aggressive-conduct disorder" (Conners, 1970). These syndromes are strong candidates for cross-cultural study. The two have emerged in more than a dozen independent studies of child behavior problems (see Achenbach & Edelbrock, 1978), and in research with Americans (e.g., Achenbach & Edelbrock, 1983), British (e.g., Collins, Maxwell, & Cameron, 1962), Sicilians (Peterson, 1965), Japanese (Hayashi, Toyama, & Quay, 1976), and Greeks, Finns, and Iranians (Quay & Parskeuopoulos, 1972). Therefore, these two syndromes have been chosen as a primary focus of the research described here.

2. Identifying an Appropriate Assessment Approach. Second, one needs a reliable, empirically sound, accurately translatable, means of identifying and classifying child problems. Such complex, committee-derived systems as the recently revised third edition of the *Diagnostic and Statistical Manual* (DSM III-R) may be useful clinically, but they tend to be difficult to translate; moreover, they require special additional procedures to overcome problems of low reliability—procedures that are difficult to replicate across cultures.

An alternative assessment approach that is relatively simple linguistically and relatively noninferential, shows good reliability, and seems particularly amenable to cross-cultural research is illustrated by the work of Achenbach and Edelbrock (1983). Their Child Behavior Checklist (CBCL) lists 118 clinically significant behavior problems, each briefly described in terms of observable behavior (e.g., "physically attacks people," "refuses to talk"); for each problem, parents are asked to make a rating—0 if the problem item is not true of their child, 1 if the problem is somewhat or sometimes true of their child, and 2 if the problem is very true or often true of their child. All of the 118 problem items were originally derived from clinic records of disturbed children or from the input of clinicians, paraprofessionals, and parents. The CBCL is regarded by many investigators as the best validated and most thoroughly researched instrument of its kind for children. It has been used in epidemiologic research exploring the prevalence of each of the 118 problems as a function of children's age, sex, and status as clinic-referred vs. normal, nonreferred.

The CBCL has also been used to develop a classification scheme for child and adolescent behavior problems, a scheme that includes the Over- and Undercontrolled syndromes discussed earlier. Principal components analyses of CBCL ratings have also revealed several narrow-band syndromes (e.g., aggressive, anxious, schizoid) arrayed within each of the broad-band Over- and Undercontrolled syndromes. Much of the research described here follows the general approach to assessment represented by the CBCL.

Ultimately, observational research could be quite useful—research focused on the observed prevalence of various behavior problems in natural settings such as home and school. However, such research requires, first, the identification of target behaviors that are high enough in base rate to warrant observational research. Such identification can take place through the use of the checklist approach described here.

3. Formulating Models of Cultural Influence.   Third, it is useful to construct heuristic models describing ways that culture might have an impact. Such models can serve to guide research, to suggest interpretations, and to stimulate theory development. The models may, in turn, be modified or replaced, as the data warrant. Our research has been guided by two nascent models of cultural influence—both growing out of an important fact about research on child psychopathology.

That fact is this: The study of child psychopathology is actually the study of two phenomena: (1) the behavior of children, and (2) the lens through which adults view child behavior—i.e., the attitudes and beliefs that lead adults to regard some forms of child behavior as disturbed or "pathological." The adult lens is particularly important because it is adults, not children, who make the all-important decisions about child classification, referral, and treatment. If adults are not concerned about a child's behavior or psychological state, that child is not likely to receive clinical attention, no matter how distressed the child may be.

To understand the origins of psychopathology in childhood, then, we need to understand the forces that shape both child behavior and adult attitudes toward that behavior. One such force appears to be culture. Cultures certainly may differ in the patterns of child behavior they foster and discourage. In addition, identical forms of child behavior may be viewed differently by adults of different cultures.

From these general ideas, two models have emerged, one focused on child behavior, the other on adult attitudes. A *problem suppression-facilitation model* holds that cultural forces may directly affect the incidence of certain child problems, suppressing (e.g., via punishment or social pressure) the development of behavior that is disapproved, and facilitating (e.g., via tolerance, or positive reinforcement) the development of behavior that is considered acceptable in the child's society. An *adult distress threshold model* holds that culture may influence adults' attitudes toward child behavior, helping to determine how distressing child problems will be to adults, and what actions adults will take in response to the problems (e.g., whether they will seek professional help for the children involved). We return to these models later.

4. Identifying Cultures for Comparison: Why Compare Thailand and the U.S.? Fourth, it is important to identify cultures that offer theoretically rich contrasts which promise significant information gain. Toward this end, we have focused on Thailand and the U.S. Why are these two cultures of interest, and what value is there in extending the Thai–U.S. comparisons?

First, the comparisons may enrich our understanding of child psychopathology in the U.S. Suppose we want to know the extent to which the patterns of child psychological dysfunction seen in the U.S. relate to characteristics of our own culture, and the extent to which the patterns reflect the problems of developing children *across cultures*? To address this question, we need to compare patterns of child dysfunction in the U.S. to those in a culture that differs quite radically from our own. A particularly striking contrast—in religious base, philosophical perspective, social values, and ideas about childhood—is offered by the culture of Thailand.

Thai culture is remarkably homogeneous in a number of important ways, with 95% of the population subscribing to Therevada Buddhism and a network of related social ideals involving nonaggression and restraint in the expression of emotion (detailed later). Moreover, the fact that Thailand, during its 800-year history, has never been colonized or occupied by a Western country has helped to insure that the social values are not merely a set of easternized westernisms. By contrast, such alternative eastern cultures as Japan and South Korea have had a heavy dose of western influence.

There are also practical reasons for selecting Thailand. As the 16th most populous country in the world, Thailand has a substantial population of youth from which to draw. Access is facilitated by a well-developed transportation system and by the relative absence of international conflict or civil war. In addition, strong child-oriented psychology departments in eight of the nation's universities, and a 35-year tradition of child guidance service and research have created a climate that is highly receptive to research on child issues.

EXPLORING THAI-U.S. CULTURAL DIFFERENCES AND THEIR IMPLICATIONS

Having identified Thailand and the U.S. as the foci for our research, let us now compare the cultures involved and discuss child behavior in those two cultures. Thai and American culture differ in theoretically intriguing ways—ways that may well be associated with differences in the patterns of psychological dysfunction among children. To explain, we return to the two models of cultural influence.

Suppression-Facilitation Model

The prevailing values of a society may lead adults to discourage certain kinds of child behavior while condoning or facilitating other behavior. One result may be cross-cultural differences in the patterns of behavior problems their children show. Consider Thais, 95% Buddhist, and strongly committed to peacefulness and nonaggression in interpersonal relations (Moore, 1974). Thai adults are very intolerant of aggressive, abusive, disrespectful, or other kinds of Undercontrolled behavior in children (Gardiner & Suttipan, 1977; Moore, 1974; Suvannathat, 1979). Instead, children are taught a blend of peacefulness, politeness, and deference. This blend is symbolized by the *wai*—the deep, deferential bow, with palms joined in a prayerful position—which dominates Thai social exchange. A Thai ideal, stressed from early childhood on, is *krengchai*, an attitude of self-effacement and humility that aims to avoid disturbing others (Phillips, 1965; National Identity Office, 1984; Suvannathat, 1979).

If Thai culture discourages Undercontrolled behavior in children, Thai youngsters who are distressed may be likely to develop Overcontrolled problems instead. Some (e.g., dependency, inhibition, and anxiety) may be directly fostered by Thai child-rearing practices (Kingshill, 1960; Moore, 1974; Suvannathat, 1979). For example, in some areas, prolonged dependency in the form of breast feeding may continue into middle childhood. In addition, Thai social values discourage strong overt expression of emotion, and encourage strict self-control and unemotionality (see National Identity Office, 1984). Several researchers (e.g., Boesch, 1977; Sangsingkeo, 1969) have argued that this orientation may foster psychological problems involving excessive inhibition.

In the U.S., by contrast, prolonged dependency often seems to be less a problem than does premature independent behavior. Moreover, in apparent contrast to Thai patterns, American culture appears to encourage open expression of thoughts and feelings. Children and adolescents, like adults, are encouraged to talk about their thoughts and feelings, to "open up," and to "share" their inner experience. A widely held cultural value is that holding feelings inside is bad for mental health, and that negative feelings (e.g., anger, sadness, distress) need to be aired if they are to be resolved. Indeed, these values have fueled a much-increased emphasis on child mental health services in the U.S. over the past 2 decades. In addition to our emphasis on open expression of thoughts and feelings, Americans appear to expect a certain amount of Undercontrolled behavior in children as they pass through certain developmental phases—evidenced by such terms as "the terrible twos," and "typical teenager," catch phrases implying the near-inevitability of at least some degree of difficult-to-control behavior in our youngsters.

If this analysis of differences between Thai and American culture is accurate, one might expect certain cross-national differences in the kinds of problems Thai and American children tend to develop. One possible result of such cultural differences is that Overcontrolled problems might be especially prevalent among Thai youngsters, and Undercontrolled problems more prevalent among American youngsters.

Adult Distress Threshold Model

The threshold model, holds that culture may set adult thresholds for distress experienced in response to child problems, thereby influencing whether such problems are considered serious and, ultimately, what actions will be taken in response. The model has two forms.

General form of the threshold model. A general form holds that cultures may differ in their threshold for child problems generally. In Suvannathat's (1979) analysis of child-rearing research, she concludes that Thai adults are relatively unperturbed by a broad range of child behavior. That attitude may be reinforced by core teachings of Thai Buddhism (see Jumsai, 1980), which encourages people to be "not worried about our worries" (Daksinganadhikorn, 1973). In fact, a Thai ideal is to be serenely unperturbed or *choei choei* in the face of problems, and a favorite expression in response to misfortune is *mai pen rai* (or "never mind, it doesn't matter"). This general attitude of unflappability, if broadly applied, might moderate adults' distress over child behavior problems. Aside from the impact of Thai Buddhist culture, one could argue that general levels of adult concern over child problems will be least pronounced in those cultures least sensitized to child psychological issues. Certainly, there are fewer opportunities for such sensitization (through, e.g., the media) in Thailand than in the U.S.

Pattern-specific form of the threshold model.   A pattern-specific form of the threshold model also can be advanced. That is, cultures may differ *differentially*, with certain types of child problem behavior arousing greater concern in some cultures than in others. Here, too, a Thai–U.S. comparison may prove intriguing, particularly if Over- and Undercontrolled behavior problems are compared. A prominent Thai researcher and former Minister of Public Health (Sangsingkeo, 1969) argued that in Thai society, partly because of Buddhist influence, "quietness, politeness, and inhibition are both expected and accepted [in children]" (p. 292), and that such Overcontrolled behavior is much less likely to be distressing to adults than are aggression and other Undercontrolled behavior. Suvannathat (1979) agreed, noting that despite their overall tolerance, "Thai parents usually disapprove of any type of aggression . . . " (p. 480). [See also Gardiner, 1968; Gardiner & Suttipan, 1977].

CONFLICTING PREDICTIONS FROM THE TWO MODELS

While the suppression-facilitation model and the threshold model (in two forms) may each seem plausible, they actually generate some conflicting predictions about the nature of cross-cultural differences. Consider, for example, the question of clinic referral patterns. The suppression-facilitation model might lead us to expect a predominance of Overcontrolled problems among Thai youngsters and Undercontrolled problems among Americans. On the other hand, the pattern-specific form of the threshold model might lead us to expect that Thai adults would be most *concerned* about *Undercontrolled* behavior, and thus most likely to refer such problems for treatment. So, what pattern should we expect? Should Thai youngsters be more, or *less* likely than Americans to be referred for Overcontrolled behavior problems? The question is an empirical one, of course. It, and other questions bearing on the nature of cross-national differences have been the focus of our research program.

A RESEARCH PROGRAM ON CHILD PROBLEMS AND THEIR CULTURAL CONTEXT

I. Development of the Thai Youth Checklist

The first part of our program involved development of a research instrument, the Thai Youth Checklist. Originally, my Thai colleagues and I had considered simply translating the CBCL into Thai, then using it to assess problems among Thai boys and girls. On further reflection, we decided that such a procedure would not be sufficiently sensitive to Thai culture, and that we needed to identify and include those child problems that are actually considered clinically significant in that country. Toward this end, we sought to identify problems considered significant enough in Thailand to stimulate clinic referral there. We surveyed clinic admissions from three widely separated Thai clinics that served children and adolescents. We focused on the years 1982–1984, to reflect relatively current patterns, and we chose 376 cases blindly, with the constraint that there be equal numbers of boys and girls, children (aged 6–11) and adolescents (aged 12–17). To provide a basis for comparison, we carried out a parallel survey in the U.S., focusing on 1982–1984 admissions to five widely scattered clinics that served children and adolescents. Procedural details follow (see The Clinic Referral Study).

We used the clinic data to develop the Thai Youth Checklist (TYC). We sought to make the TYC (1) sufficiently similar in format and content to the U.S. CBCL to facilitate cross-cultural comparisons, but also (2) sufficiently sensitive to Thai culture to detect psychological problems (and competencies) that might be clinically significant there, but undetectable with the CBCL. We translated the CBCL into Thai, using a process consistent with the views of cross-cultural researchers (e.g., Brislin, 1970; Draguns, 1982; Wagatsuma, 1977). With a professional translation agency, two bilingual Thai clinical psychologists, and one bilingual Thai anthropologist, we took the CBCL through three waves of translation into Thai and back translation into English, until meanings across the two languages seemed as parallel as we could make them. To further enhance parallelism between the TYC and CBCL, we also (1) used the CBCL format (demographic information, then competency items, then problem items with a 0-1-2 rating scale); and (2) made 118 problem items identical to those listed on the CBCL (see what follows for one exception). However, to make the measure sensitive to the phenomena of interest in Thai culture, we (1) adjusted some of the competency items to conform to Thai circumstances [e.g., deleting a question about whether the child is in a "special class," since most Thai schools have no such classes], and (2) added problem items to reflect the referral problems listed in our clinic records survey, and problems noted as significant by Thai clinicians.

For this last step, we produced a frequency table for all problems identified in the Thai clinic referral records. We selected for the TYC all those problems listed for 1% (i.e., 4) or more of the Thai clinic sample. This list included 20 new problems not listed on the CBCL. In addition, we asked Thai clinicians to review a preliminary draft and suggest changes that might enhance the research and clinical value of the instrument. Four additional problems were generated through this process. The final version of the TYC lists 142 specific behavioral and emotional problems, 118 of which correspond to those of the CBCL. [At the recommendation of Thai clinicians, we divided CBCL item No. 105, "Uses alcohol or drugs" into two TYC items, "Uses alcohol" and "Uses drugs;" for

TABLE 5.1
Non-CBCL Problems Reported for More than One Percent of Thai Cases

Problem	Percentage of Cases
1. Absentminded or forgetful	17%
2. Lacks motivation to study or learn	12%
3. Lacking in self-help skills	4%
4. Egotistical, self-centered	3%
5. Uninterested in things around him/her	3%
6. Impolite, rude, disrespectful	3%
7. Naughty (does risky, dangerous things)	3%
8. Irresponsible	3%
9. Feelings easily hurt, feels bad easily	2%
10. Does things slowly, dawdles	2%
11. Likes going out, does not like to stay home	2%

Note. The column at the right indicates the percentage of Thai cases for whom the problem was listed as a reason for referral by parents.

analyses reported here, though, we combined the two, thus forming, in effect, a single item, as on the CBCL.] Table 5.1 conveys some of the flavor of the clinic data used in this process; it shows the non-CBCL problems reported for more than 1% of all the Thai cases sampled.

The TYC appeared to be easily understood by most Thai parents, and its psychometric properties seemed adequate, especially for the problem portion, the part most relevant to our research. Inter-interviewer reliability assessment (i.e., two interviewers interviewing the same parent independently) yielded a correlation of 0.91 for the problem portion; test-retest assessment (same parent, 1-week interval) yielded a correlation of 0.81.

TYC—Teacher Form.   Using similar procedures, we also produced a Teacher Form of the TYC, intended to parallel the CBCL teacher report form. The Teacher Form of the TYC includes (1) a modified list of competency items similar to the CBCL teacher report form, and (2) a problem list, 118 items of which correspond to the CBCL teacher report form list, and 24 of which reflect the added TYC parent form problems which teachers would have occasion to observe. We have gathered the same base of data for the teacher form as for the parent form, but the present report focuses only on parent data.

II. Clinic Referral Problems of Thai and American Youngsters [Weisz, Suwanlert, Chaiyasit, & Walter, 1987].

The clinic data just described formed the basis of The Clinic Referral Study. In this study, our two theoretical models suggested different predictions as to cross-national difference. As noted earlier, the *suppression-facilitation model* suggests that Thai youth might be more likely than American youth to develop Overcontrolled problems, and that the reverse might be true of Undercontrolled problems. On the other hand, the *pattern-specific form of the threshold model* suggests that Thai parents and other adults might be especially likely to be distressed by, and seek help for, Undercontrolled problems. This, in turn, suggests the contrary prediction that Thai youth might be more likely than Americans to be *referred* for Undercontrolled problems.

Method.   Our clinic sample included 760 youngsters, 376 from Thai mental health and child guidance clinics and 384 from U.S. mental health and child guidance clinics. Within each national group, the sample was perfectly balanced for age group (6–11 vs. 12–17 years), sex, and urban vs. rural place of residence, thus forming a 2 (culture) × 2 (sex) × 2 (urban/rural) factorial design with proportional cell N throughout. To insure that the cases would not reflect idiosyncratic characteristics of a single clinic in each culture, we drew from five U.S. clinics [in Washington, D.C., North Carolina, and Tennessee] and three Thai clinics [in Bangkok and two rural provinces]. Cases were drawn from clinic records blindly, with the constraints that all design cells within each culture contain equal numbers, and that neither the culture, sex, nor urban–rural factors be confounded with age.

Procedure.   For all youngsters, trained data recorders reviewed the full written report of the intake interview with parents (or guardians), and listed verbatim each of the child problems reported to admitting clinicians. The pairs of coders achieved good inter-judge agreement on problems recorded. (Thai $r = .96$; U.S. $r = .99$). Thai problems were then translated into English through three waves of translation and back translation.

Over- and Undercontrolled problems.   All Thai and U.S. problems were coded for whether they represented Overcontrolled, Undercontrolled, or Other problems. Each problem was first coded for its correspondence to any problem appearing on the CBCL; the two coders agreed on 96.7% of these judgments, and more than 80% of the problems listed for each culture were judged to have a CBCL equivalent. For those problems, the coders agreed 95.1% of the time as to which CBCL problem was the appropriate match. Those problems having *no* CBCL equivalent were used to develop the TYC, as discussed earlier. Next, we computed an Overcontrolled and Undercontrolled score for each youngster, by (1) calculating the number of each child's problems that fit the empirically derived Overcontrolled syndrome for that child's age × sex group, and (2) dividing this total by the number of all problems on the CBCL that load on the syndrome. The resulting score thus represented the proportion of all *possible* Overcontrolled problems that each youngster's list of referral problems included. These decimal values were multiplied by 100, to produce percentages; to correct for variations in the productivity of parents, we divided the adjusted Overcontrolled score by the total number of problems listed for the child, then multiplied by 10 (the approximate ceiling for numbers of problems listed). Parallel procedures were followed in computing an Undercontrolled score.

Results and Implications

Analyses involved $2 \times 2 \times 2 \times 2$ (culture $\times$ age $\times$ sex $\times$ urban/rural) ANOVAs focused on total problems, Overcontrolled problems and Undercontrolled problems. There were numerous significant effects. Only those most relevant to the proposed research can be described here.

Over- and Undercontrolled problems in the Thai and U.S. samples. The ANOVA on total problems revealed no overall culture effect. However, there were highly significant culture effects on both Overcontrolled problems, $F (1,744) = 57.52$, $p < 0.0001$, and Undercontrolled problems, $F (1,744) = 81.52$, $p < 0.0001$. The two effects ran in opposite directions: Overcontrolled problems were more common in the Thai than the American sample (means: 6.24 and 3.31), but Undercontrolled problems were more common in the American sample than the Thai sample (means: 12.04 and 7.70). These results, shown in Fig. 5.1, appear consistent with the suppression-facilitation model: They support the possibility that child problems involving aggression or the outward expression of distress may be more often discouraged or suppressed in the Thai than in the American cultural context, and/or that child problems involving

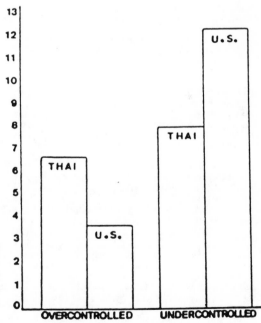

FIG. 5.1. Mean scores for Thai and U.S. youngsters on Overcontrolled and Undercontrolled problems. Reprinted by permission of the American Psychological Association.

inhibition and the internalization of distress may be facilitated more by Thai than by American cultural patterns.

This latter possibility was further suggested by a frequency analysis of individual referral problems. As an illustration, Table 5.2 lists the 12 most common referral problems in each national sample. As the table shows, the most common reason for referral in both national samples was poor school performance, an

TABLE 5.2
Twelve Most Common Referral Problems in the U.S. and Thailand

	Type	U.S %	Thai %	[Thai vs. US] X	p-Value
Most Common in U.S. Sample					
1. Poor school work	U	33.9%	35.9%	.4	n.s.
2. Disobedient at home	U	19.3%	6.1%	29.5	.001
3. Temper tantrums, hot temper	U	15.4%	11.7%	2.2	n.s.
4. Gets into fights	U	14.3%	.8%	49.3	.001
5. Disobedient at school	U	14.1%	2.9%	30.3	.001
6. Physically attacks people	U	12.5%	7.4%	5.4	.05
7. Lying or cheating	U	11.5%	3.5%	17.5	.001
8. Steals outside the home	U	10.4%	4.5%	9.5	.005
9. Can't concentrate, pay attention	U	10.2%	6.4%	3.6	.10
10. Agrues a lot	U	9.9%	3.2%	13.8	.001
11. Demands attention	U	8.9%	1.1%	24.3	.001
12. Can't sit still, hyper-active	U	8.6%	5.6%	2.6	n.s.
Most Common in Thai Sample					
1. Poor school work	U	33.9%	35.9%	.4	n.s.
2. Somatic problems (esp. headaches) with no known physical cause	O	6.3%	29.3%	69.3	.001
3. Absentminded, forgets easily	N	2.6%	17.0%	44.4	.001
4. Fearful or anxious	O	3.4%	12.8%	22.6	.001
5. Lacks motivation to study/learn	N	4.7%	12.0%	13.2	.001
6. Sleep problems	O	1.0%	11.7%	36.5	.001
7. Underactive, lacks energy	O	.5%	11.7%	41.6	.001
8. Temper trantrums, hot temper	U	15.4%	11.7%	2.2	n.s.
9. Stubborn, sullen, irritable	M	4.7%	9.8%	7.5	.01
10. Nervous movements, twitching	O	2.1%	9.0%	17.6	.001
11. Strange behavior	O	1.0%	9.0%	25.6	.001
12. Worrying	O	2.6%	7.4%	9.4	.005

Note. Columns show the percentage of youngsters in the U.S. and Thai samples, respectively, for whom each problem was reported, and results of chi square tests comparing the U.S. and Thai figures. The Type column shows the problem type, as determined by factor analyses of the CBCL: U=loads exclusively or predominantly on the Undercontrolled syndrome; O=loads exclusively or predominantly on the over-controlled syndrome; M=loads on both syndromes with about equal frequency across various age X sex groups; N=not included in factor analyses, because not listed on the CBCL.
Reprinted by permission of the American Psychological Association.

Undercontrolled problem. One other Undercontrolled problem, temper tantrums, appeared in the top twelve for both national samples. Beyond these two commonalities, though, Thai and U.S. patterns diverged markedly. All 12 most common U.S. referral problems were Undercontrolled, and 8 of these were significantly more common in the U.S. than the Thai sample (see χ^2 and p-value columns in the table). By contrast, 7 of the 12 Thai problems were Overcontrolled, and all of these were significantly more common in the Thai than the U.S. sample. In addition, the two non-CBCL Thai problems—absentmindness and low motivation for study—both seem to involve dysfunctional internal state rather than Undercontrolled behavior. Particularly striking in the Thai sample was the high frequency of somatic problems having no known physical cause; headaches, in particular, were reported for 23% of Thai youngsters. This, too, suggests the possibility of internalized distress. Alternatively (or in addition), it might suggest the possibility that Thai parents are especially sensitive to, and prone to refer their children for, problems of an apparently physical/medical nature.

CONCLUSION: SUPPORT FOR THE SUPPRESSION-FACILITATION MODEL

Overall, the findings provide some support for the suppression-facilitation model, but not for the adult distress threshold model. It is possible, though, that the threshold model was not supported here because the impact of the suppression-facilitation process was so strong. It might be, for example, that Thai youngsters show so much more, or so much more severe, Overcontrolled behavior than American youth that the relative preponderance or severity across the two cultures makes findings like ours almost unavoidable. However, given an Overcontrolled and an Undercontrolled child who have equally numerous or severe problems, it is still possible that Thai parents and other adults would give treatment priority to the Undercontrolled child (as suggested by the pattern-specific form of the threshold model). It is also possible that Thai adults might be less concerned than Americans about problems of *either* type—Over- or Undercontrolled (as suggested by the general form of the model). Both possibilities were explored in the next step of our program.

III. Attitudes of Thai and American Adults toward Child Problems [Weisz, Suwanlert, Chaiyasit, Weiss, Walter, and Anderson (1988)].

To investigate these two "threshold" possibilities, we asked Thai and American adults to make a series of judgments about two children, one with Overcontrolled problems, the other with Undercontrolled problems. In each country, we surveyed the judgments of three adult groups who serve as "gatekeepers" to child mental health care: parents, teachers, and child clinical psychologists. We asked the adults to judge how serious the problems of each child were, and to indicate which child had a greater need for "help from a specialist." The general form of the threshold hypothesis was assessed by testing main effects of culture—i.e., Thai–U.S. differences (e.g., in perceived "seriousness") that transcended differences in problem type. The pattern-specific form of the threshold hypothesis was assessed by testing differential differences—that is, Thai–U.S. differences that differed in pattern depending on whether Over- or Undercontrolled problems were involved.

Method

In the 2 (culture) $\times$ 3 (adult group) $\times$ 2 (Over- vs. Undercontrolled problem) $\times$ 2 (sex of child) $\times$ 2 (context information) $\times$ 2 (order) experimental design, problem was a within-subjects factor. Thai and American parents, teachers, and clinical psychologists, all read one vignette describing an Overcontrolled child and one vignette describing an Undercontrolled child. Half read vignettes about boys, half about girls. For half, the Overcontrolled child was placed within context A (one particular description of the child's strengths and the impact of the child's problems on school adjustment), and the Undercontrolled child in another (B); for half, this pairing was reversed. Finally, order was counterbalanced, with half receiving the Overcontrolled vignette first, and half the Undercontrolled vignette. The full sample numbered 461, with 233 Americans and 228 Thais. Each national sample included similar numbers of parents, teachers, and clinical psychologists who work with children. Analyses involved procedures (e.g., general linear models approaches) that control for nonorthogonality produced by unequal cell Ns. Parents and teachers were randomly selected (*we* randomly selected them, using school rosters) from 9 elementary schools in the U.S. (in Maryland, North Carolina, Tennessee, and Virginia), and 10 elementary schools in Thailand. Psychologists who work with children were randomly selected from the *National Registry of Health Care Providers in Psychology*, in the U.S., and from the membership roster of the Thai Psychologists Association, in Thailand. With systematic follow-up mailing and phoning, return rates ranged from 72% to 94%.

Materials. Each adult read two vignettes describing a child. In one vignette, the description included 8 problems which have been found to load on the broadband Overcontrolled syndrome for both boys and girls: dependency on adults, fear of going to school, nervousness, anxiety, refusal to talk, shyness and timidity, sadness and depression, and worrying. The other vignette included 8 problems which load on the Undercontrolled syndrome for boys and girls: arguing, cruelty to others, getting into fights, disobedience in school, lying, physically attacking people, teasing, and threatening people. The vignettes went through three waves of translation and back translation. One wave involved a professional translation agency, two involved bilingual social scientists. After each vignette, the adults answered several questions about the child involved, using 7-point Likert scales. These included:

1. How serious is this child's problem?
2. If you were this child's parent, how worried would you be about his (her) behavior?
3. If you were this child's teacher, how worried would you be about his behavior?
4. Do you think this child's behavior will improve in a year or two?, and
5. Compared to other primary school students in general, how unusual is this child?

After reading both vignettes, respondents were asked to make a treatment priority judgment: "Comparing the two children you just read about, which child has a greater need to be taken to a specialist for counseling or help?"

Results and Implications

Seriousness and other ratings: Support for the general form of the threshold model.   The $2 \times 3 \times 2 \times 2 \times 2 \times 2$ (culture $\times$ adult group $\times$ sex of child $\times$ Over- vs. Undercontrolled problems $\times$ content combination $\times$ vignette order) GLM analyses yielded some intriguing effects. On all five of the Likert ratings, there were strong main effects of culture, all F values > 25.0, all p values < 0.001. As Figure 5.2 shows, Thais, compared to Americans, rated the problems (both Over- and Undercontrolled) as less serious (means: 4.47 vs. 5.24), less worrisome to a parent (5.15 vs. 5.88) or teacher (4.85 vs. 5.76), less unusual (4.44 vs. 4.97), and *more* likely to improve in time (4.70 vs. 3.37). This last finding suggests that Thais may have rated seriousness and worrisomeness relatively low partly because they were more confident than Americans that the problems would improve over time. Moreover, the culture difference on the improvement question suggests that the other culture effects are not mere response style artifacts—i.e., that Thais simply give lower ratings on Likert scales; in the improvement question, Thais gave *higher* ratings than Americans. Overall, the findings support the general form of the threshold model, indicating that Thai adults express lower levels of concern or distress over child problems—be they Over- or Undercontrolled—than do American adults.

Treatment priority judgments: Only marginal support for the pattern-specific form of the threshold model.   Responses to the treatment priority question (see above), because they involved two-choice data, were analyzed using a log linear

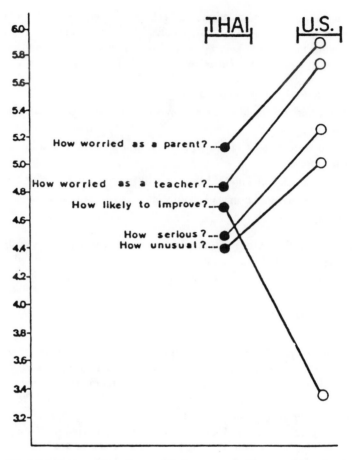

FIG. 5.2.   Thai and American adults' answers to five questions about child problems (Over- and Undercontrolled combined). Numbers reflect mean ratings on Likert scales ranging from 1 to 7. Reprinted by permission of the American Psychological Association.

approach which generates main and interaction effects analogous to ANOVA, but which uses the chi square distribution to test the effects. The $2 \times 3 \times 2 \times 2 \times 2 \times 2$ analysis revealed only a marginal culture effect, $X2\ (1) = 3.76$, $p = 0.05$. As shown in Fig. 5.3, Americans were about equally likely to rate the Overcontrolled child (49%) and the Undercontrolled child (51%) as more in need of treatment; Thais, by contrast, were somewhat more likely to rate the Undercontrolled child as more in need of treatment (60% vs. 40%). This finding, despite its marginal significance, is shown in Fig. 5.3. The figure is included to illustrate a pattern of findings that would, if significant, be consistent with the pattern-specific form of the threshold model. Having presented the figure, though, I must emphasize that our analyses yielded no significant findings in support of that form of the model.

IV. Population Prevalence of Child Problems in Thailand and the U.S. [Weisz, Suwanlert, Chaiyasit, Weiss, Achenbach, & Walter, 1987].

Our first study focused on clinic referral problems and generated support for the suppression-facilitation model. Our second study focused on adults' attitudes toward child problems and generated support for the threshold model. What these studies did not provide, however, was a crucial piece of the cross-cultural puzzle: Information on the prevalence of clinically significant problems in Thai and American youngsters who have not been referred to clinics. Such epidemiologic information is needed if we are to understand how cultural forces affect the psychological development of *most* children in the two cultures, since most will never be referred to child clinicians. In the Child Prevalence Study, we sought such epidemiologic information, in the form of CBCL (in the U.S.) and TYC (in Thailand) reports completed for randomly selected boys and girls in the two countries.

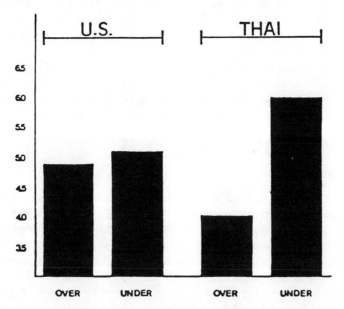

FIG. 5.3. American and Thai responses to "Which child has a greater need to be taken to a specialist for counseling or help?" Numbers reflect the percentage of adults who rated the need as greater for the Overcontrolled and the Undercontrolled child, respectively.

Method

Research Design and Sample. The research design was a 2 (culture) × 2 (sex) × 3 (age level) factorial. The Thai sample included 60 boys and 60 girls at ages 6–7, 8–9, and 10–11 (30 boys and 30 girls at each *yearly* age level); the U.S. sample [obtained by Achenbach & Edelbrock, 1981] included 100 boys and 100 girls at ages 6–7, 8–9, and 10–11 (50 boys and 50 girls at each yearly age level). The Thai sample was drawn from elementary schools, a good source for a representative sample, since a strictly enforced law requires all Thai children to complete 7 years of schooling. A sample of 38 elementary schools was selected from various regions to mirror the combination of urban, suburban, and semi-rural regions sampled in the U.S. We selected 29 public and 9 private schools, to mirror the proportions of such schools nationwide. From each school, we randomly selected grade levels, classes, and a maximum of one child from each selected class (e.g., "the 7th child on the alphabetical class list"). Some 91.5% of those Thai parents who were asked to participate did so and completed the full TYC (administered by an interviewer); the corresponding U.S. rate was 82.3%.

Procedure. Two trained interviewers administered the TYC to Thai parents (inter-interviewer reliability: $r = 0.91$). Five trained interviewers administered the CBCL to U.S. parents (inter-interviewer reliability: $r = 0.96$). Working entirely in the language of the country, each interviewer proceeded through a standardized introduction, then all items of the TYC or CBCL. They also asked whether the target child had been taken to a specialist of any kind for testing or for help with a problem; children for whom the "testing or help" involved psychological problems were dropped from the sample later (but retained for future analyses) to insure that the sample included only *non*-clinic youngsters.

Results and Implications

The primary analyses were 2 × 2 × 3 (culture × sex × age level) ANOVAs focused on the parallel portions of the TYC and CBCL (i.e., the 118 specific problems listed on both checklists, plus two open-ended items: "other physical problems" and "additional items"). The dependent variables included, (1) *total problem score* [i.e., the sum of all 1 and 2 ratings made by parents across the 118 specific problems and the two open-ended items], (2) *Overcontrolled score* [i.e., the sum of all 1 and 2 ratings on problems that load on the broad-band Over-controlled syndrome (Achenbach & Edelbrock, 1983), adjusted to correct for the number of such problems in factor analyses of boys vs. girls], (3) *Undercontrolled score* [i.e., adjusted sum of Undercontrolled syndrome problems], and (4) *each of the 118 individual problems*, considered independently. Given the number of significance tests calculated, we took two steps to minimize the risk of interpreting significant findings that might arise by chance. First, we set alpha at .01 for all tests. Second, in analyses of the 118 individual problems we calculated the percentage of variance accounted for by each effect, and we applied Cohen's (1977) criteria for judging the magnitude of ANOVA effects: Effects accounting for 1%–5.9% of the variance are considered *small*, 6.0%–13.8% are *medium*, and > 13.8% are *large*.

Total problems.   We first conducted a $3 \times 2 \times 2$ (age $\times$ sex $\times$ culture) ANOVA on the total problems that were identical for the TYC and CBCL, plus "other physical problems" and "additional problems." The analysis revealed a main effect of culture, $F (1,948) = 12.37, p < 0.001$. Thai children had higher problem scores than American children, but the difference was only 3.4 points on the 240-point scale (means: 24.2 and 20.8). The culture effect accounted for 1.28% of the variance in total problem scores, which made it "small" by Cohen's (1977) criteria. No other main or interaction effects were significant.

Over- and Undercontrolled problems.   Overcontrolled problem scores showed only one significant effect, a main effect of culture: Thais had higher Overcontrolled scores than Americans (means: 19.3 and 16.6), $F, (1,948) = 7.96, p < 0.005$. Following Cohen's (1977) criteria, the effect was small, accounting for 1.24% of the variance in Overcontrolled scores.

Undercontrolled scores, by contrast, showed no significant culture effect; but boys scored higher than girls (means: 27.1 and 22.0), $F (1,948) = 18.74, p < 0.0001$. Again the effect was small, accounting for 1.79% of the variance in Undercontrolled scores. The sex difference is consistent with a substantial body of literature on Undercontrolled behavior in boys and girls (see Rutter & Garmezy, 1983).

On Over- and Undercontrolled problems, the findings with regard to culture should be considered in the light of our Referral Problems Study, described earlier. In that study, like this one, we found evidence that Thai youngsters showed more Overcontrolled behavior problems than their American counterparts. However, in the Referral Problems Study we also found much more evidence of Undercontrolled behavior in American than in Thai youth, a finding not replicated in the present Prevalence Study. Is a Thai-U.S. difference in Undercontrolled problems pronounced among *clinic-referred* youngsters but not among normal randomly selected youth? Explaining this phenomenon in the light of cultural difference would be a challenging task. However, before pursuing such a task, we should consider an alternative possibility, related to the incompleteness of the data set thus far: The Referral Problems Study spanned the 6–17-year age range, whereas the Prevalence Study included only children younger than 12. Findings of the former study suggested that Thai adolescents (at least those who are clinic-referred) may well be more susceptible to Overcontrolled problems, and less susceptible to Undercontrolled problems, than Thai children or American children or Adolescents. This suggest the patterns identified in the present Prevalence Study may present an incomplete picture. To fill out the picture, we need to extend the Prevalence Study to include adolescents. Such an extension is planned as one part of our continuing investigations.

Individual problems.   In our ANOVAs of individual problems, we found significant ($p < 0.01$) culture effects on 54 of the 118 specific problem items. As might be expected, the individual Overcontrolled problems were more likely to show significantly higher scores among Thai than American children than the reverse. When we calculated the percentage of variance accounted for by each of the significant effects, and applied Cohen's (1977) criteria, we found that 39 of the culture differences qualified as "small," 4 as "medium," and 2 as "large." The other nine accounted for less than 1% of the variance. Table 5.3 shows the six medium and large effects, which are generally in the direction that would be suggested by the cross-cultural literature and by our earlier findings. Of particular interest is the fact that four of the six problems have somatic overtones, and all of these were more prevalent in Thailand than the U.S.—a trend reminiscent of our findings in the Referral Problems Study.

The findings presented here have implications for the theoretical models outlined at the beginning of the chapter, as they apply to Thailand and the U.S. The findings also have general implications for the cross-cultural study of developmental psychopathology. In the remainder of the chapter I address implications of both types while summarizing some of the main findings of the research.

CHILD PSYCHOPATHOLOGY IN THAILAND AND THE U.S.: HOW WELL DO THE FINDINGS FIT THE THEORETICAL MODELS?

First let us consider the findings thus far as they bear on the suppression-facilitation and threshold models.

Suppression-Facilitation Model

According to the suppression-facilitation model, cultural patterns may directly affect the prevalence of various problems in children, with some types of problem behavior suppressed or discouraged while other types are fostered by pre-

TABLE 5.3
Six Problems Showing the Most Pronounced Thai-U.S. Differences in Prevalence, and Percent of Variance Accounted for By Each Difference

Problem (and CBCL/TYC Problem Number	Direction	P	Variance
88. Sulks a lot	Thai > US	.0001	23%
51. Feels dizzy	Thai > US	.0001	15%
49. Constipated, doesn't move bowels	Thai > US	.0001	13%
71. Self-conscious or easily embarrassed	US > Thai	.0001	7%
24. Doesn't eat well	Thai > US	.0001	6%
102. Underactive, lacks energy	Thai > US	.0001	6%

vailing cultural patterns. We considered the implications of this model for two broad patterns of problem behavior. *Are Overcontrolled child problems fostered by Thai cultural patterns?* One possibility we considered was that Overcontrolled problems in children might be fostered by the Thai emphasis on deference, inhibition, and self-control. Our findings in both the Clinic Referral Study and the Child Prevalence Study support this notion. Together, the two studies suggested that Overcontrolled problems may be somewhat more prevalent among Thai than American youngsters, in both clinic-referred and random samples. Moreover, both studies suggested that among the various Overcontrolled problems, problems involving somaticizing may be the ones to which Thai youngsters are particularly susceptible.

Are Undercontrolled child problems fostered by American cultural patterns? We also considered the possibility that Undercontrolled problems might be more prevalent among American than Thai youngsters. In support of this idea, much of the literature suggests that American adults are more tolerant than Thai adults of aggression, open expression of feelings, and other Undercontrolled behavior in children. Our findings, though, offered only mixed support for this idea. The Clinic Referral Study showed much higher levels of Undercontrolled behavior reported for clinic referred American than Thai youngsters. However, the Child Prevalence Study revealed no such difference between randomly sampled Thai and American children.

Adult Distress Threshold Model

According to the adult distress threshold model, cultures may influence adults' attitudes toward child behavior, helping to determine how distressing child problems will be to the adults and how likely it is that the adults will seek help through clinical or other intervention. As already suggested, cultures may differ in their distress threshold for child problems generally or for particular problem patterns. Let us consider, here, how the findings reflect on the two forms of the threshold model.

General form of the threshold model: Do Thai and American adults differ in their level of concern over child problems generally? It was suggested earlier that Thai adults might show lower levels of distress than American adults over child problems generally. This seemed possible because the literature suggests that several aspects of Thai Buddhism might mitigate adults' distress over such concerns as children's problems. Moreover, it seemed possible that adults' concern over child problems might depend in part on the adults' exposure to the literature of child psychology, and Americans certainly have more of such exposure than do Thais. Whatever the reasons, our data certainly did point to lower levels of distress over child problems among Thai than American adults. When Thai and American adults were given identical descriptions of child problem behavior, the Thai adults rated the child problems as less serious, less unusual, and more likely to improve with time, and they rated themselves as less likely to be worried if they were the target child's parent or teacher.

Pattern-specific form of the threshold model: Do Thai and American adults differ in their relative levels of concern over Under- vs. Overcontrolled child problems?   The pattern-specific form of the threshold model holds that cultures may differ differentially in the level of concern they provoke over differing patterns of child problem behavior. The research described here focused on Over- and Undercontrolled problems. The available ethnographic literature suggested that thresholds for adult distress in Thailand, but not in the U.S., would be set at relatively low levels for Undercontrolled child behavior, and at higher levels for Overcontrolled child behavior. Our data, though, provided only one marginal finding in support for this notion. Only when we presented adults with a forced choice, asking them whether the Over- or Undercontrolled child had a greater need for help from a specialist, did we find any evidence of such a differential difference. On that forced choice question, Thai adults more often gave treatment priority to the Undercontrolled child than the Overcontrolled child, whereas American adults were equally likely to assign treatment priority to the two children. However, that culture × Over- vs. Undercontrolled interaction attained only borderline significance, and none of our other analyses offered even this level of support. As a whole, then, our data did not support the pattern-specific form of the threshold model.

Taking stock: Relations among the findings.   The findings of the research completed thus far suggest several processes by which culture may be related to patterns of child psychological dysfunction in Thailand and the U.S. One is tempted to speculate about relations among the findings. For example, perhaps the high level of somaticizing found among Thai youth (Clinic Referral Study and Child Prevalence Study) results partly from the fact that Thai adults are not very concerned about problems that seem purely psychological (Adult Attitudes Study). Such speculation should not be overdone at this point, however. The fact is that we will need to fill significant gaps in our base of information before drawing conclusions about the meaning of our findings. However, even at this early point in the process, the data suggest a number of general lessons for those of us interested in the cross-cultural study of developmental psychopathology.

SOME LESSONS FROM THE FINDINGS THUS FAR

1. *Cultures that are evidently quite different in their beliefs and practices with regard to child rearing may nonetheless be quite similar in the prevalence of various child problems in their general population.*

Substantial differences between cultures in values, beliefs, and patterns of child-rearing may not necessarily translate into major cross-cultural differences in patterns of child psychopathology. Despite marked cultural differences between Thailand and the U.S., as outlined earlier, Thai and American parent reports showed considerable similarity in the population prevalence of child problems. Thai and American means for total problems differed by only 3.4 points on a 240-point scale. Of 118 specific problems, 64 showed no significant cross-cultural difference despite the powerful statistical tests afforded by our sample of 960 children. Of the 54 problems on which Thai and American children did differ significantly, only six showed cross-cultural effects accounting for as much as 6% of the variance; thus, only six of 118 specific problems could be considered "medium" or "large" in magnitude by Cohen's (1977) standards. In summary, the findings suggest that problem prevalence is generally quite similar among Thai and American children. [Similar findings were recently reported in a comparison of Dutch and American children, by Achenbach, Verhulst, Baron, and Akkerhuis (1987).]

The overall similarities found for so many different problems certainly raise an important developmental possibility: much of what we see in the way of child problems in various parts of the world may be so strongly influenced by developmental forces that even wide variations in culture may not alter the picture dramatically. We will be able to provide further information relevant to this possibility as we collect prevalence data for adolescents in Thailand and the U.S. In any event, as such data accumulate from various cultures, we should be better and better able to suggest which patterns of child disturbance are most strongly influenced by social forces and which may be shaped by more culture-transcendent forces, such as biological and cognitive development.

2. *Despite similarities in the general population prevalence of many problems, some theoretically meaningful clusters of child problem behavior may still differ in prevalence across cultures; identifying such differences, and exploring their origins, may enhance our understanding of how social forces influence developmental psychopathology.*

As noted earlier, the numerous similarities we have identified between American and Thai patterns of child psychopathology have not meant that the differences are unimportant. Consider, for example, the fact that Overcontrolled problems were noted significantly more often for Thai than for American youngsters in our study of clinic referred youngsters and in our epidemiologic study of randomly sampled children. This difference is quite consistent with our theoretical interpretation of the literature on Thai culture and its emphasis on inhibition and self-control. The findings reported here do not provide any final explanation as to the mechanism by which such cross-national differences might have been produced. Indeed, one can imagine operant processes, modeling, and even psychodynamic processes similar to those discussed by Freud—any or all of which might play a role. However, the identification of cross-national differences is a necessary first step in the process of understanding the processes by which societies influence patterns of child dysfunction.

3. Despite similarities in the general population prevalence of many problems, cultures may still differ markedly in the problems for which children are referred to mental health specialists.

Although our epidemiologic study revealed numerous similarities between Thai and U.S. patterns, we found quite striking cross-national differences in the problems for which youngsters were actually referred for treatment. Such differences are made possible, in part, by the fact that clinic referral is so overdetermined. Referral depends on: (1) the youngster's behavior, (2) an adult's judgment that the behavior is maladaptive, (3) an adult's belief that intervention by others can produce change, and that the appropriate other might be a mental health specialist, and (4) the availability of a mental health specialist. Cross-national differences on any of these four factors might account for differences in the observed patterns of clinic referral. It is even possible, for example, that certain types of child behavior in Thailand are more likely to be referred to the Abbot of the local Buddhist temple than to a clinical psychologist. Studying such natural pathways to intervention needs to be a part of cross-cultural research on developmental psychopathology. Studying clinic referral patterns is a useful first step, but it is only one step.

4. Evidence continues to accumulate that boys show undercontrolled behavior problems more often than do girls, across cultures.

In the epidemiologic study presented here, boys showed higher Undercontrolled behavior problem scores than did girls. This sex difference was underscored in tests at the level of individual problems. Of the 118 problems, 21 showed sex effects; 14 resulted from higher scores among boys than girls, whereas 7 showed the reverse sex difference. Of the problems for which girls showed higher prevalence, none was a consistently Undercontrolled problem (see principal components analysis in Achenbach & Edelbrock, 1983); of the 14 problems for which boys showed higher prevalence, 12 were consistently Undercontrolled.

These findings should be of special interest because they arose in a culture where boys receive special training in the tenets of Therevada Buddhism, including nonaggression, politeness, and humility. Indeed, it could be argued that Thailand is one of the few places in the world where the cultural traditions might be expected to moderate the traditional sex differences in Undercontrolled behavior. Yet the sex differences emerged in Thailand, as in the U.S.; these were main effects of sex, most not qualified by sex × culture interactions. The robustness of these sex differences across such different cultures offers some support to the notion that they reflect culture-transcendent developmental forces.

5. *Cultural differences may be associated not only with different adult attitudes toward child problems, but also with different adult beliefs regarding etiology and appropriate treatment.*

To fill out our picture of cross-cultural differences in the area of developmental psychopathology, it will be important to understand differences in prevailing beliefs about etiology and treatment. In our Adult Attitudes Study, Thais were particularly likely to attribute child problems to faulty child rearing, socialization, or teaching; more than half made that attribution for both Over- and Undercontrolled problems. Americans, by contrast, were particularly fond of personality trait and psychodynamic etiological theories; they were quite unlikely to attribute responsibility directly to parents or other socializing agents.

We found equally striking cross-cultural differences in the treatments our adults proposed for disturbed children. For both Over- and Undercontrolled problems, Thai adults favored verbal interventions whereas Americans favored behavioral approaches involving reward and punishment contingencies. Viewed broadly, this collection of findings suggests that a child who shows disturbed behavior may well meet with very different adult interpretations and very different intervention preferences depending on the cultural context within which the child shows the behavior.

6. *Cross-cultural differences may be found not only across nations but across different professional groups; indeed, psychologists may form a kind of "professional culture," formed via a socialization process analogous to that occurring within a national culture.*

In our Adult Attitudes Study, Thai and American psychologists concurred in a number of judgments—agreeing in some instances where other Thai and American adults showed cross-cultural differences. For example, when adults from the two cultures rated the "seriousness" of the problem behavior children showed in the vignettes, we found cross-national differences among parents and teachers, but not among psychologists. In interpreting this finding, it is useful to note that most Thai psychologists receive instruction via western textbooks and articles, and from teachers and supervisors who attended western universities. Indeed, most child clinical training around the world has its origins in the west. Such training is, of course, a kind of professional socialization analogous in some respects to the socialization that occurs within a national culture. Psychologists in various parts of the world may thus partake of a "professional culture" which may mitigate effects of their national culture.

7. *Cross-cultural research on child psychopathology poses real methodological challenges; consider the problem of parent reports.*

Most worthwhile research ventures pose significant methodological problems. Cross-cultural research on child psychological problems is no exception. The methods we have used thus far seem appropriate to the early stages of the research. However, the methods are subject to a number of *uncontrolled* cultural influences.

Consider, for example, our use of parent reports in the Child Prevalence Study. Parent reports on the occurrence of various child problems are certainly influenced by the actual occurrence and intensity of those problems. However, the parent reports may also be influenced by cultural context—in at least three ways. First, the cultural milieu may color adults' judgments about what is *appropriate* for children at a given age; such judgments could help determine whether parents report, for example, that their child "talks too much" (item No. 93 on the TYC and CBCL). The amount of talking considered *normal* by American parents might well be considered *too much* by parents in a culture where children are expected to be quiet. Second, cultural context may color adults' judgments about what is *usual* for children at a given age; such judgments could influence the likelihood that parents would report, for example, that their child is "unusually loud" (item No. 104). Third, parent reports may be influenced by culture-bound definitions of concepts embedded in the problem items. For example, the Thai definition of "swearing" (item No. 90) includes language that would be considered merely impolite in the U.S.; swearing, in Thailand, includes calling a peer a lizard, or insulting a peer's parent. Thus, the fact that Thai parents in our study reported twice as much swearing among their children as did American parents may reflect cross-cultural differences in the breadth of a definition, as much as anything.

Concerns such as these need to be raised for two reasons. First, it is important to recognize the limitations of our methods lest we overinterpret findings. Second, raising such concerns can help point the way to more refined methods, or at least a richer methodological diversity. In the case of child psychopathology, it may be worthwhile, in the long run, to supplement parent (and other) reports with direct observations of child behavior. Before this can be done effectively, though, we will need to use systematic reports of those who know the children to identify those behavior problems that are high enough in base rate to warrant observational research. This is but one example of the methodological challenges posed by research on child psychopathology across cultures.

8. Findings from different cross-cultural studies may not necessarily fit together to form a seamless conceptual fabric.

Finally, I want to emphasize that my experience with cross-cultural research in this area has not been quite the additive process I had envisioned at the outset. Despite the best of intentions on the part of my colleagues and me, not all of our findings fit together neatly. Let me close the chapter with an example that was briefly noted earlier. Our Child Prevalence Study revealed very similar levels of Undercontrolled behavior in Thai and American children—no significant difference on a composite Undercontrolled score, and few significant differences on individual Undercontrolled behaviors, despite a very large sample which afforded high power. Our Adult Attitudes Study revealed that, when forced to make treatment priority judgments, Thai adults were at least marginally more likely than American adults to give priority to an Undercontrolled rather than an Overcontrolled child. So, Undercontrolled child problems appear to be about equally likely in Thailand and the U.S., and when they occur our evidence suggests that Thai adults may be somewhat more likely than American adults to give them priority over Overcontrolled problems for treatment referral. This would seem to suggest that when one tallies the problems for which Thai and American youngsters are referred to clinics, Undercontrolled problems should be more prevalent in the Thai referrals than in the U.S. referrals. What did we find when we carried out such tallies? Precisely the opposite pattern.

Since we put all these findings together, my colleagues and I have identified several possible reasons why the one finding that would have made everything fit together may have eluded us. But, despite our post-hoc reasoning, we continue to be perturbed by the feeling that we may not yet fully understand everything about child psychopathology in Thailand and the United States. The feeling is frustrating. But Piaget noted, some time ago, that perturbation can be good for us, warding off the illusion of understanding, and preventing premature foreclosure on issues that deserve sustained attention.

ACKNOWLEDGMENTS

The research described here was carried out with a number of colleagues. I am particularly grateful to Somsong Suwanlert and Wanchai Chaiyasit, who have coordinated the Thai components of the research, and to Bahr Weiss, Wanni Anderson, Bernadette Walter, and Thomas Achenbach, for a variety of other contributions. I also gratefully acknowledge the continuing support of the National Institute of Mental Health, through grant #5 R01 MH38240.

REFERENCES

Achenbach, T. M. (1978). The Child Behavior Profile: I. Boys aged 6–11. *Journal of Consulting and Clinical Psychology, 46* 478–488.
Achenbach, T. M., & Edelbrock, C. S. (1978). The classification of child psychopathology: A review and analysis of empirical efforts. *Psychological Bulletin, 85,* 1275–1301.
Achenbach, T. M., & Edelbrock, C. S. (1981). Behavioral problems and competencies reported by parents of normal and disturbed children aged 4–16. *Monographs of the Society for Research in Child Development, 46,* No. 188.
Achenbach, T. M., & Edelbrock, C. S. (1983). *Manual for the Child Behavior Checklist and Revised Child Behavior Profile.* Burlington, VT: University of Vermont Department of Psychiatry.
Achenbach, T. M., Verhulst, F. C., Baron, G. D., & Akkerhuis, G. W. (1970). Epidemiological comparisons of American and Dutch children: I. Behavioral/emotional problems and competencies reported by parents for ages 4 to 16. *Journal of American Academy of Child and Adolescent Psychiatry, 26,* 317–325.

Boesch, E. (1977). Authority and work attitudes of Thais. In K. Wen & K. Rosenburg (Eds.), *Thai in German eyes* (pp. 176–231). Bangkok: Kledthai.

Brislin, R. W. (1970). Back-translation for cross-cultural research. *Journal of Cross-Cultural Psychology, 1,* 185–216.

Cohen, J. (1977). *Statistical power analysis for the behavioral sciences.* (Rev. ed.). New York: Academic Press.

Collins, L. F., Maxwell, A. E., & Cameron, C. (1962). A factor analysis of some child psychiatric clinic data. *Journal of Mental Science, 108,* 274–285.

Conners, C. K. (1970). Symptom patterns in hyperkinetic, neurotic, and normal children. *Child Development, 41,* 667–682.

Daksinganadhikorn, P. (1973). *Buddhism,* 2nd edition revised. Bangkok: World Fellowship of Buddhists.

Draguns, J. G. (1982). Methodology in cross-cultural psychology. In I. Al-Issa (Ed.), *Culture and psychopathology.* Baltimore: University Park Press.

Gardiner, H. W. (1968). Expression of anger among Thais: Some preliminary findings. *Psychologia, 11,* 221–228.

Gardiner, H. W., & Suttipan, C. S. (1977). Parental tolerance of aggression: Perceptions of preadolescents in Thailand. *Psychologia, 20,* 28–32.

Hayashki, K., Toyama, B., & Quay, H. C. (1976). A cross-cultural study concerned with differential behavioral classification: I. The Behavior Checklist. *Japanese Journal of Criminal Psychology, 2,* 21–28.

Jahoda, G. (1977). In pursuit of the emic-etic distinction: Can we ever capture it? In Y. H. Poortinga (Ed.), *Basic problems in cross-cultural psychology.* Amsterdam: Swets & Zatlinger.

Jumsai, M. L. M. (1980). *Understanding Thai Buddhism.* Bangkok: Chalermnit Press.

Kennedy, S., Scheirer, J., & Rogers, A. (1984). The price of success: Our monocultural science. *American Psychologist, 39,* 996–997.

Kingshill, C. (1960). *Ku daeng—the red tomb: A village study in northern Thailand.* Chiangmai, Thailand: The Prince Royal's College.

Moore, F. J. (1974). *Thailand: Its people, its society, its culture.* New Haven, CT: Hraf Press.

National Identify Office (Kingdom of Thailand). (1984). *Thailand in the 80s.* Bangkok: Muang Boran Publishing House.

Peterson, D. R. (1965). Structural congruence and metric variability in a cross-cultural study of children's behavior problems. *Archivo di Psycologia,* Neurologia, e Psychiatrica, *2,* 174–187.

Phillips, H. P. (1965). *Thai peasant personality.* Berkeley: University of California Press.

Quay, H. C., & Parskeuopoulos, I. N. (1972, August). *Dimensions of problem behavior in elementary school children in Greece, Iran, and Finland.* Paper presented at the 20th International Congress of Psychology, Tokyo, Japan.

Quay, H. C. (1979). Classification. In H. C. Quay & J. S. Werry (Eds.) *Psychopathological disorders of childhood* (2nd ed., pp. 1–42). New York: Wiley.

Rutter, M., & Garmezy, N. (1983). *Developmental psychopathology.* In P. Mussen (Gen. Ed.) and E. M. Hetherington (Vol. Ed.), *Handbook of Child Psychology, Vol. IV* (pp. 775–911). New York: Wiley.

Sangsingkeo, P. (1969). Buddhism and some effects on the rearing of children in Thailand. In W. Caudill & T. Y. Lin (Eds.), *Mental health research in Asia and the Pacific* (pp. 286–295). Honolulu: East-West Center Press.

Suvannathat, C. (1979). The inculcation of values in Thai children. *International Social Science Journal, 31,* 477–485.

Wagatsuma, H. (1977). Problems of language in cross-cultural research. *Annals of the New York Academy of Sciences, 285,* 141–150.

Weisz, J. R., Suwanlert, S., Chaiyasit, W., & Walter, B. R. (1987). Over- and Undercontrolled referral problems among Thai and American children and adolescents: The wat and wai of cultural differences. *Journal of Consulting and Clinical Psychology, 55,* 719–726.

Weisz, J. R., Suwanlert, S., Chaiyasit, W., Weiss, B., Achenbach, T. M., & Walter, B. A. (1987). Epidemiology of behavioral and emotional problems among Thai and American children: Parent reports for ages 6–11. *Journal of the American Academy of Child and Adolescent Psychiatry, 26,* 890–898.

Weisz, J. R., Suwanlert, S., Chaiyasit, W., Weiss, B., Walter, B. A., & Anderson, W. W. (1988). Thai and American perspectives on Over- and Undercontrolled child behavior problems: Exploring the threshold model among parents, teachers, and psychologists. *Journal of Consulting and Clinical Psychology, 56,* 601–609.

6 Stress and Coping in Early Development

Megan R. Gunnar
University of Minnesota

Sarah Mangelsdorf
University of Michigan

Roberta Kestenbaum
Sarah Lang
Mary Larson
Debra Andreas
University of Minnesota

How individuals function under stress is central to our understanding of both normative and pathological development (Garmezy & Rutter, 1983). An adequate understanding of the organization of stress responses requires an analysis of both behavior and physiology (Levine, 1982). Although stress-sensitive physiological and behavioral systems often respond together, responses also diverge at times. This divergence, sometimes described as dissociation, reflects both one reason why stress is so difficult to define objectively and the specificity of the roles played by different systems in an organism's adaptation to difficult circumstances (Gunnar, 1986).

In this chapter, we explore the relations between behavioral, hormonal, and relationship systems believed to play important roles in the developing child's ability to manage stress and challenge. Several questions will be addressed. First, because competence and vulnerability can be viewed as antonyms, we consider relations between behavioral indices of competence and physiological measures of stress reactivity. Is it the case that the competent child is less stress vulnerable? Second, a secure parent-child relationship has been shown to be linked with the development of competence. Thus, we ask how the quality of the parent-infant relationship mediates the young child's physiological reactions to stressful events? And third, a child's reactions to stressful circumstances may be mediated, more generally, by their capacity and strategies for coping with stress. Therefore, we consider what we know about the development of the coping process and how coping strategies mediate the child's emotional and physiological reactions to stressful, challenging events.

In these analyses we focus on normative development; however, we hope that a better understanding of these issues with normal children will provide information useful in understanding pathological development as well. As often noted, the study of normal and pathological development goes hand-in-hand: the study of pathological development throwing into relief our understanding of normal developmental processes, and the study of normal development serving as a springboard for our understanding of pathology (e.g., Cicchetti, 1984).

COMPETENCE AND STRESS

Competence is what we strive for in ourselves and our children, and a decrease in competence is often used to index the deleterious consequences of neglect and abuse (Wald, Carlsmith, Leiderman, & Smith, 1983). Competence, however, is culturally defined; and while it would seem likely that the competent individual in any culture would be one who was not excessively vulnerable to stress, it does not necessarily follow that competence and relative stress-immunity go hand in hand. Arguments over the linkage between competence and stress are classic in research on coping and health (Carver & Scheier, 1985). Often these arguments revolve around types of coping behaviors that protect the individual from experiencing emotional trauma and physiological stress, but at the same time reduce active problem solving versus those that allow the individual to deal with the problem, but at the cost of great emotional trauma and physiological stress. Who is more competent, the person who is less stressed or the one who deals more directly with the problem? Because active, problem-focused coping is typically seen as more competent than avoidance and denial in our culture (Cohen & Lazarus, 1973), in many instances the stressed problem solver is voted more competent. However, are higher stress levels typically associated with behavioral competence, and from a developmental perspective, what is the relation between competence and stress during childhood?

Fear and wariness of the unknown are typically associated with activation of hormonal stress systems, including increased sympathetic-adrenomedullary activity as reflected in elevated heart rate and increased production of adrenaline and noradrenaline, and heightened pituitary-adrenocortical activity as reflected in increased cortisol production (Borysenko, 1984). Because of this, a number of researchers have assumed that inhibited, fearful individuals may have a lower threshold for stress reactivity than do uninhibited, bold individuals. Kagan and his colleagues (e.g., Kagan, Reznick, & Snidman, 1987) have examined this question using several cohorts of preschool children preselected to be either extremely socially inhibited or socially bold. Tested repeatedly across the preschool years, fearful, inhibited children were found to have higher and more stable heart rates during laboratory testing, and in one study they found higher home and laboratory cortisol concentrations in these children as compared to bold, uninhibited children. In a similar vein, in an unselected sample, Fox and his colleagues (1987, cited in Fox, 1988, in press)) recently examined the relations between difficult temperament, ease of entry into nursery school, and vagal tone. Vagal tone reflects the strength of the parasympathetic influence on heart rate. Kagan's inhibited children with high and unvarying heart rates had poor vagal tone or greater sympathetic than parasympathetic influence. In their study, Fox and his colleagues found that preschoolers with difficult temperaments and those who had difficulty entering preschool had poor vagal tone. Both of these studies support the idea that behavioral competence is associated with low stress reactivity.

There are a number of other studies, however, that contradict this conclusion. Several studies with adults have shown that personality measures associated with competence, specifically ego strength (Roessler, Burch, & Mefferd, 1967) and emotional stability (Lambert, Johansson, Frankenhaeuser, & Klackenberg-Larsson, 1969), correlate with higher rather than lower levels of arousal in the adrenal-medullary system. Similarly, personality measures associated with lowered competence, specifically depressive tendencies (Frankenhaeuser & Patkai, 1965), have been found to correlate with lower levels of adrenaline excretion during stress. In behavioral studies with adults, Frankenhaeuser and her colleagues (e.g., Frankenhaeuser & Andersson, 1974) have repeatedly found that individuals who show a greater adrenaline response to work demands also perform tasks faster, more accurately and with better endurance, especially under low to moderate stimulus demands. This greater competence may place individuals at risk for coronary disease (i.e., Type A behavior); however, Frankenhaeuser (1980) has noted that this is the case only if these individuals lack a sense of control over important aspects of their environment.

These data are similar to data reported by Rose and his colleagues (1982) in a study of adrenocortical activity among air traffic controllers. On the whole, these researchers found few personality correlates of basal cortisol activity. However, when they examined groups of air traffic controllers who showed large versus small elevations in cortisol to increased work demands, a number of relations emerged. Specifically, the high responders were judged by their peers to be more competent, reported themselves to be more satisfied with their work, weighed closer to their ideal weight, and reported that their supervisors gave them more freedom. In sum, using adult subjects it appears that more competent individuals tend to be higher stress responders regardless of whether adrenomedullary or adrenocortical measures of stress reactivity are used. It is worth noting that in at least one study using nonhuman primates a similar pattern emerged. Coe, Smith, and Levine (1985) found that alpha or dominant male squirrel monkeys exhibited higher basal and stress levels of cortisol than did males lower on the dominance hierarchy.

Furthermore, it appears that the positive correlation between competence and stress-reactivity is not confined to adults. Johansson, Frankenhaeuser, and Magnusson (1973) found that among school children, IQ and achievement were positively correlated with catecholamine excretion, especially in boys. These high adrenaline and noradrenaline producing children were also judged by their teachers to be livelier, happier, and better adjusted than their lower stress hormone producing peers. Mattsson, Gross, and Hall (1971) reported similar findings for cortisol. Using a group of 10 hemophiliac boys, they noted that the high cortisol excretors at home and in the hospital were the boys who were the best adapted, most competent, and most mature. The two lowest cortisol excretors were the most poorly adapted. They engaged in intense, careless motor activity, were very irritable, exhibited uncontrolled emotional outbursts, and were the least competent overall.

How can we reconcile these two very disparate types of results? Several alternatives come to mind. First, what stresses competent individuals may be somewhat different from what stresses less competent individuals. Thus, whether competence is positively or negatively associated with stress may depend on the testing situation. Second, stress appears to result from a combination of uncertainty and engagement (Rose, 1980). That is, if a situation or outcome is uncertain, if it matters to the person, and if the person remains engaged in trying to control the outcome, then resources are mobilized and stress results. On a day to day basis, competent individuals may remain more engaged and may select situations of mild to moderate uncertainty more readily. Thus, they may experience more daily, moderate stress. However, because of this pattern of greater engagement and skill development, they may protect themselves from periods of intense stress resulting from helplessness in the face of events that can not be avoided. We return to this possibility later when we consider approach and avoidance modes of coping with stressful information. Third, and finally, it is possible that the causal arrow also runs from stress to competence. That is, slightly higher basal levels of stress hormones may facilitate more competent behavior because the individual is physiologically better prepared to deal with challenge. Several studies with infants support this possibility.

Recently, Spangler and his colleagues (Spangler, Meindel, & Grossmann, 1988) examined basal cortisol concentrations in newborns. Some newborns had high daily average concentrations with a good deal of variability in concentrations across different samples. Others had low daily average concentrations with little variation from one sample to the next. When these researchers examined observations of irritability in the nursery and scores on the Brazelton Newborn Behavioral Assessment Exam they found that the high, variable group was less irritable and behaved more competently during the Brazelton. We (Gunnar, Isensee, & Fust, 1987) have also found that among extremely healthy newborns, higher cortisol values following the Brazelton exam are associated with more competent state regulation behavior during testing. Finally, among older infants, we (Gunnar, Mangelsdorf, Larson, & Hertsgaard, 1989) have found that higher home baseline cortisol concentrations are sometimes associated with less behavioral distress during maternal separation. In sum, there may be a physiological basis for competence or better behavioral organization, however, that basis may involve higher rather than lower basal concentrations of stress hormones.

PARENT-CHILD RELATIONSHIP

Recent analyses of competence trace its roots to the early parent-child relationship (Sroufe, 1983). Specifically, patterns of stable, warm, and responsive caregiving are seen as giving rise to a secure attachment relationship and internal working models of the self that support the development of competence (Main, Kaplan, & Cassidy, 1985). As just discussed, there may be linkages between competence and stress reactivity. As suggested by the attachment-competence research, these linkages may be mediated, in part, by the quality of the parent-child relationship. However, when the issue is stress and stress reactivity, it seem likely that the quality of the parent-child relationship may have direct effects as well. Surprisingly, we know very little about the effects of attachment security on the developing child's physiological stress responding.

There is, however, good evidence that the presence of the mother facilitates exploration and reduces behavioral distress in infants and toddlers exposed to novel environments (Bowlby, 1969). Furthermore, these effects are greater in secure rather than insecure relationships (e.g., Main, 1973). There is also good evidence in other mammals that the presence of the attachment figure reduces physiological stress reactions to novel situations. For example, 16-day-old rats show dramatic increases in heart rate that do not habituate even after fairly long periods in a novel environment. In contrast, in rats of the same age, heart rate quickly returns to baseline when an anesthetized, lactating female is placed in the novel cage with them (Richardson, Siegel, & Campbell, 1988).

Infant rhesus monkeys also show dramatic buffering effects of the mother's presence (Gonzalez, Gunnar, & Levine, 1981). In a study of separation cortisol responses, mothers, infants averaging 7-months-of-age, and adult, nonlactating females were first captured out of their social groups and adapted to individual-sized cages. During this time mother-infant pairs were housed together. Capturing the animals, although done as gently as possible, involved temporary disruption of the social group, distress vocalizations, and threat gesturing. Three hours after capture, all subjects were blood sampled for plasma cortisol. Adult females, both mothers and nonmothers, exhibited significant increases in cortisol that declined to baseline by 3 to 5 days after capture. In contrast, the infants failed to show any evidence of a stress response to capture (see Fig. 6.1). Levine and his colleagues (Coe & Levine, 1981) have also shown that in squirrel monkeys, contact with the mother buffers the infant from responding to brief bouts of handling.

There may be limits, however, to the buffering effect of the mother's presence on the infant's physiological responses to stressful circumstances. For example,

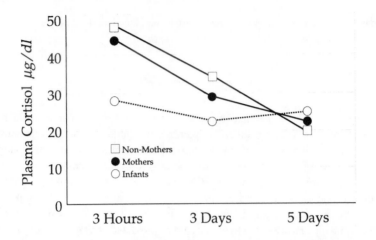

Adaptation Period: Time Post Capture

FIG. 6.1. Plasma cortisol following capture from social group and during adaptation to individual-sized cages in non-mothers housed separately and mothers and infants housed as dyads. Adapted from Gonzales et al. (1981).

although the mother's presence buffered the adrenocortical response of 7-month-old rhesus monkeys to capture and handling, at an average age of 12 months these infants were tested again in another study. The protocol for that study (Gunnar, Gonzalez, & Levine, 1980) also called for capture from the social group and housing either with mother or with a peer. Compared to baseline cortisol levels, all subjects showed a stress response to capture even when housed with their mothers. The failure to obtain the buffering effect could not have been due to the prior separation, as only half of the subjects were separated in the earlier study and all failed to show the buffering effect at 12 months. It may, however, have been due to developmental changes in the attachment rela-tionship. In rhesus there is a dramatic increase in infant independence between 7 and 12 months, and the latter part of the first year also sees an increase in maternal rejection or weaning of the infant (Hinde & Spencer-Booth, 1967). Surprisingly, the relations between developmental changes in the frequency of attachment-related behavior and the impact of the mother's presence on the infant's physiological stress reactivity have received little attention.

Thus far none of the studies described involved examination of the effects of the quality of the mother-infant relationship. Most of the work on relationship quality has been conducted using human children, and little of it has involved examination of physiological stress reactions. Sroufe and Waters (1977), how-ever, did examine heart rate responses during and following separation. They found that the return of the mother more rapidly reduced elevated heart rates in infants from secure, as compared to insecure, mother-infant relationships. Even more dramatic results have been obtained in infant rhesus. Following a 2-week separation, we (Gunnar, Gonzales, Goodlin & Levine, 1981) found that reunion with the mother actually triggered a stress response in infants from less secure relationships, whereas this was not the case for secure infants. In our study, security was measured by the extent to which the infant rather than the mother was responsible for maintaining dyadic proximity. The more the responsibility was prematurely shifted to the infant, the more stress the infant experienced during reunion. Interestingly, while infants from more imbalanced or insecure relationships were more stressed during reunion, they were slightly less stressed by separation than infants from more balanced or secure relationships (see Table 6.1). A discussion of the effects of relationship security on separation reactions follows.

Another way to analyze the influence of relationship quality on the buffering effect of maternal presence is to examine surrogate reared infants. There are now a number of studies indicating that infant primates will organize their attachment behaviors around cloth surrogate mothers and will use the surrogate to reduce behavioral distress and facilitate exploration in novel settings (Harlow, 1958). However, there is considerable debate over whether or to what extent the infant is truly attached to the surrogate. As noted by Levine (1980), physiological measures of surrogate-reared monkey's reactions to separation differ sharply from the responses of monkeys reared with real mothers. Specifically, the physiological response to separation is less intense, of shorter duration, and less specific. At best the surrogate would seem to be a marginal attachment figure. However marginal, the presence of the surrogate appears to be as effective as the presence of a real mother in reducing heart rate (e.g., Candland & Mason, 1969) and cortisol (e.g., Hill, McCormack, & Mason, 1973) to novel situations. These data raise questions about whether it is the attachment bond or merely the

TABLE 6.1
Relations Between Hinde's % Approach - % Leave Index and Adrenocortical Responses to Separation and Reunion in Rhesus Macaque Infants

% Approach - % Leave[a]	Rank Order	Delta Cortisol[b]	
		Separation	Reunion
0.46	5	+9.3	+27.1
0.31	4	+13.7	+12.7
0.29	3	+26.5	+20.5
0.19	2	+27.3	+1.0
0.00	1	+29.8	-0.7

[a]High values reflect increasing infant responsibility for mother-infant proximity.

[b]Cortisol expressed in μg/dl as a difference from the average of the three adaptation days shown in Fig. 6.1

Data adapted from Gunner et al. (1981).

opportunity to engage in species-typical coping behaviors (e.g., clinging) that buffers the infant's stress reactions in the mother's presence.

If it is the opportunity to engage in coping behaviors that is important, then rejecting surrogates should provide less buffering than nonrejecting surrogates. Unfortunately, there are no published data on physiological stress reactions in the presence versus the absence of rejecting surrogates. In addition, the data on attachment responses to rejecting surrogates are mixed. Harlow and his colleagues noted that rejecting surrogates (those that shot blasts of air at the infant intermittently) elicited as much proximity and clinging as nonrejecting surrogates. In contrast, Kaplan (1981), using more subjects and a different species, found that infants raised on airblast surrogates spent much less time in contact with the surrogate than those raised on nonrejecting surrogates.

To summarize, the mother's presence reduces behavioral distress and facilitate exploration of novel environments in human and nonhuman primates. These effects appear to be enhanced in more secure relationships. There is good evidence in other mammals that the mother's presence also buffers physiological stress reactions, however, there may be limits to this buffering effect. There is also some evidence in both human and monkey infants that reunion with the mother is more stress reducing if the preseparation relationship is secure rather than insecure. Finally, there is little data on the impact of relationship security on physiological responses to novel or stressful circumstances in the mother's presence.

Part of the problem in studying the impact of relationship quality on the stress-reducing benefits of the mother's presence is that the mother's absence is itself one of the most potent stressors of early childhood. The effects of separation on behavior has been studied extensively in human children and in nonhuman primates (e.g., Bowlby, 1973). The initial reaction of many infants by the end of the first year is to protest the separation. There have also been a number of studies on the physiological correlates of separation in infant monkeys (Kalin & Carnes, 1984). In general, separation elicits dramatic, transient increases in heart rate, body temperature, adrenaline, and cortisol. As the duration of separation increases, these physiological responses change, partly as a function of species and partly as a function of environments. For example, in rhesus infants housed singly during separation, cortisol returns to near baseline levels by 24 hours following separation (Gunnar et al., 1981.) In squirrel monkeys, this relatively rapid return to baseline is not observed (Coe & Levine, 1981), unless the squirrel monkey is left in its home group, in which case cortisol levels begin to decline within an hour of the mother's removal (Coe, Weiner, Rosenberg, & Levine, 1985).

While separation conditions and species are associated with differences in physiological and behavioral reactions to separation, within species and conditions large individual differences are also frequently noted. This is true of both human and nonhuman primate infants. To what extent are these differences linked to the quality of the infant-mother relationship? This is currently a heatedly debated issue related to how attachment quality is measured in human infants. The most frequently used technique to determine attachment security is the Strange Situation developed by Ainsworth and Wittag (1969). In this assessment, the infant experiences several brief (3 minute) separations from mother sometimes in the presence of a strange adult female and sometimes alone. Security of attachment is judged largely by the infant's reactions to the mother's return (Ainsworth, Blehar, Waters, & Wall, 1978). Two groups of insecure infants are identified. One group, the "A" or avoidant attached, display little upset during separation and ignore mother upon her return. A second group, the "C" or resistant attached, are extremely upset by separation and do not appear to gain much comfort from the mother upon her return. Finally, one group of secure infants, "B's," are identified. These babies are characterized by their positive greeting of mother upon her return. Secure infants who cry during separation seek contact and calm upon the mother's return, while secure infants who are not upset by separation greet the mother happily upon her return.

As the descriptions imply, there is a range of distress reactions noted during the Strange Situation, and it is the causes of the distress that are currently debated. According to one line of argument, the amount of distress during the testing is a function of the infant's temperament, and distressed temperament determines attachment classification. Thus, Kagan (1982) has argued that "A's" are temperamentally very low on distress. "B's" are moderate on distress, and "C's" are temperamentally very high on distress. According to this argument, quality of attachment does not mediate the infant's reaction to the stress of separation, it is confounded with it. Not surprisingly, attachment theorists do not agree. Most recently they have argued that temperament and attachment are orthogonal constructs, and their orthogonality is reflected in attachment subclassifications (Belsky & Rovine, 1987). That is, the "B" or secure classification is further broken down into 4 subclassifications, the first two (B1 and B2) describe infants who are no more distressed than "A" infants by separation, the latter two (B3 and B4) describe infants who are upset by separation, with B4 infants being as upset as "C" infants. Belsky and Rovine (1987) recently showed that prior measurements of temperament obtained early in the first year could predict the division between Low Criers (A, B1, and B2) and High Criers (B3, B4, and C), but not the division between "A" and "B" or "B" and "C" infants.

If true, then these data suggest that a secure relationship does not influence the distress caused by the mother's absence. We (Gunnar et al., 1989) recently examined this issue with infants at 9 and again at 13 months. At both of these ages we subjected the infants to maternal separations and measured the cortisol response. At 9 months, the separations were part of the Louisville Temperament Assessment exam developed by Matheny and Wilson (1981). This allowed us to also obtain an objective measure of distressed temperament. At 13 months, the separations were part of the Strange Situation, which allowed us to obtain measures of attachment classification. Our results were striking.

First, we did obtain evidence of a slight increase in cortisol in response separation, but there was considerable individual variation, and compared to nonhuman primate infants the responses was very small. Second, we found that distressed temperament at 9 months strongly predicted separation distress at 13 months in the Strange Situation. We also found that the magnitude of the cortisol increase to separation was modestly correlated with the measure of distressed temperament. Infants with more distressed or irritable temperaments showed greater increases in cortisol in response to separation. What about attachment quality? It was not related to either the 9 month temperament measure nor to the cortisol measures.

These data are remarkably similar to Sroufe and Waters (1977) earlier results showing that heart rate during separation could not be predicted by attachment classification. They are dissimilar to the data on rhesus infants that suggested a greater cortisol response to separation among more secure infants. However, species differences might well account for this difference. In humans, then, the data thus far suggest that the security of the infant's attachment relationship does not play a role in either the baby's behavioral or physiological distress reactions at least to brief separations. Variations in distress and physiological reactions to separation appear to be related to the infant's temperament and not to the security of his or her relationship with mother. What we do not know, however, is whether these conclusions can be extended to truly pathological relationships or to more traumatic or longer separations.

COPING

Everything that we have discussed thus far can be seen as part of research on coping. Indeed, the study of stress cannot be separated from the study of coping. This is because in almost any theory of stress, the stressfulness of an event is viewed as a function of the individual's ability to cope with that event. Thus, cognitive theories of stress such as Lazarus' (1977) describe stress as the outcome of the individual's appraisal of threat relative to her appraisal of coping resources. Similarly, in Levine's (1985) psychobiological model, stress is a function of uncertainty about outcomes and one's control over outcomes. Finally, we (Gunnar, Marvinney, Isensee, & Fisch, 1989) have recently argued that stress is the result of sudden changes in demands that the organism is unprepared to meet. This latter definition is similar to Murphy's (1974) and, because it is not couched in cognitive terms, would seem more appropriate to the study of stress in early development.

There are numerous theories of coping. Yet despite Murphy's early work, we have only a sketchy understanding of the development of coping strategies and processes. Several beginning attempts at developmental models are described later. However, it may be useful first to consider a nondevelopmental analysis. Roth and Cohen (1986), in a recent review, argued that while the study of coping covers a broad area, and though the coping process is complex, there is a striking coherence in much of the literature. Specifically, they noted that two basic orientations or modes of coping can be identified in nearly all coping theories. These two modes summarize cognitive and emotional activity organized around either approaching or avoiding stressful information. They note, in addition, that both approach and avoidance modes have their benefits and their costs. Avoidant strategies can be beneficial in that they reduce stress and can prevent anxiety from being crippling. Their costs include interference with appropriate actions, and in the extreme, disruptive avoidance behavior that results in failures to learn from or integrate the stressful experience. Approach strategies, on the other hand, can be beneficial because they lead to appropriate action. Their costs include increased stress and, in the extreme, maladaptive or nonproductive worry and hypervigilence. This discussion should be reminiscent of the discussion of competence and stress earlier in this chapter.

Roth and Cohen (1986) point out that while individuals may differ in the extent to which they organize their coping around avoidance and approach strategies, in many situations both modes are required to cope effectively. However, in effective coping, approach and avoidance modes may vary in their primacy across time. Avoidance strategies may be useful in the short run as they allow the individual to deal gradually with the stressor without becoming emotionally and physically overwhelmed. Approach strategies may be necessary in the long run in order to remove or manage the objective effects of the stressor. In addition, in effective coping both modes may be present at the same time. For example, an individual may engage in avoidance of certain aspects of the stressful situation in order to approach and deal more effectively with other aspects. To date, developmental analyses of coping have not been oriented towards examining the organization of approach versus avoidance strategies. In the following discussion, we consider to what extent such an orientation might provide a useful guide.

Although there are few developmental models of coping, per se, a concern with coping is not new to developmental theory. Interest in how the developing child maintains emotional and physical integrity in the face of environmental perturbations is a theme running through the clinical and personality literature from psychoanalytic theory to current self-control theories (Connell & Wellborn, in press; Freud, 1938). The roots of coping are typically traced to early social relations, particularly those with the primary caregiver or attachment figure (Bowlby, 1969; Mahler, Pine, & Bergman, 1975; Sander, 1975). In her earliest relations, the infant learns both an orientation to the world as benign or threatening and a sense of her power to control outcomes. Both orientations should influence whether coping actions become primarily directed towards approach or avoidance. As noted earlier, it is expected that a secure attachment history facilitates the development of competence (Sroufe, 1983), and competence should help direct the child towards approach-oriented coping. Also, social learning theory would suggest that in addition to learning basic coping orientations, the infant and young child might learn specific coping responses and interpretive stances from interaction with and observation of the caregiver (Bandura, 1977). Recently, in the research on social referencing, such effects have been demonstrated to occur as early as the first year (Campos & Stenberg, 1981; Feinman, 1983).

The emphasis on the early attachment relationship accords well with the research on stress in the presence and absence of the mother discussed earlier. However, this orientation provides only the basic outline for the study of coping development. Much work is needed to fill in, on a more microanalytic level, just what it is that infants and young children do to cope in different situations, how their strategies change with development, and how they differ among children. Research and theorizing of this sort is just beginning. Unfortunately, to date, none of the work has involved physiological measures, thus we do not know how different coping actions or orientations might map on to different physiological reactions to events during early childhood.

Gianino and Tronick (1988) and others (see Field, this volume) have argued that while the mother or attachment figure may serve as the infant's most potent coping resource, disruptions of the relationship may also serve as a potent source of stress. These disruptions need not involve separation. Indeed, failure of the caregiver to respond to the infant's signals may be an equally important, and perhaps for some infants a more chronic source of stress. This has been studied in both normal (Gianino & Tronick, 1988) and disturbed (Field, this volume) relationships using the "still face" paradigm. Accordingly, the mother and infant are seated enface. The mother plays with the infant as she normally would for several minutes, then for several minutes she maintains a neutral, nonresponsive or still face. In a study of 3-, 6-, and 9-month-olds, Gianino and Tronick analyzed the behaviors the infants engaged in during the still face period. They scored attempts to signal the mother, both positive and negative; attempts to disengage, including simple looking away and looking towards objects; and attempts at self-calming, including nonnutritive sucking. Signaling can be viewed as an approach behavior using the Roth and Cohen (1986) framework, while the other categories of strategies would all seem to involve various avoidance techniques. Overall, there was an increase in the frequency of signaling between 3 and 9 months. The increase was for negative signals. Furthermore, while the 3-month-olds exhibited more of what might be termed reactive distress, the negative signals of the 9-month-olds were more angry and agentic in nature. The other major developmental change they noted was in the use of object attend. Compared to 3-month-olds, 9-month-olds more often regulated their emotional reactions or coped by distracting themselves with objects. In addition, they were more capable than the younger infants of moving back and forth between signaling (approach) and object attend (avoidance). These data clearly indicate that both approach and avoidance are part of the normal infant's coping repertoire from early in development, and that normal infants show an increase in the flexible use of the coping modes with development during the first year.

In another study, Cohn and Tronick (1983) had mothers display depressed rather than neutral affect. This study was conducted only with 3.5-month-olds. Interesting, very little positive signaling or approach behavior was seen. Instead, infants cycled between avert gaze (avoidance) and distress. In infants of truly depressed mothers, Field (this volume) reports a general reduction in interactive bids, and a flattening of affect that extends to interactions with other adults. Perhaps this mode of behavior reflects a general avoidance mode of coping developing that is becoming rigid or defensive in these infants.

While Tronick and his colleagues have focused on one type of stressor arising from the parent-infant relationship, Kopp (1989) has recently attempted to outline a more general model of coping or emotion regulation during the first 3 years of life. She notes that in the first days and months, reflex actions serve as the basis for emotion regulation. As the infant develops some control over her attention, attention regulation enters the coping repertoire. Caregivers must facilitate the infant's attempts to regulate emotion, especially during the early months. As the infant learns to associate the caregiver with the reduction of distress and the enhancement of positive affect, social signaling enters the coping repertoire. During the second half of the first year, both attention regulation and social signaling become more sophisticated and elaborated. Attention regulation is increasingly more flexible, and increasingly involves the infant's use of objects as a source of distraction. Social signaling becomes more specific as the infant learns to cue specific needs and desires. Cognitive limitations serve as the major developmental constraints on coping during the early years. Thus, it is not until the infant is cognitively mature enough to engage in planful problem solving that coping actions oriented towards the approach mode begin to appear with much frequency. Finally, with the development of language a whole new level of coping opens up for the child.

Kopp's models provides a useful framework to begin more extensive analyses of the development of coping. However, as she notes, many of the pieces of the model remain to be clarified empirically. Recently my students and I have begun several empirical analyses of the coping strategies infants use in different situations. In one study (Hornik & Gunnar, 1987), we examined the strategies employed by 12- and 18-month-olds when confronted with a caged, live rabbit located across the room from where the mother was seated. All of the infants found the rabbit interesting and all appeared to want to pet it; however, with the exception of a few extremely bold infants, most were wary about approaching and touching the rabbit on their own. The coping problem for the infants was to either control their wariness in order to approach the rabbit or to somehow get the mother and rabbit closer together. In analyzing the strategies used, we were struck by the richness of the repertoires of even the youngest infants. We noted four major categories of strategies: Attachment behavior, Self-calming or Self-stimulation, Attention Regulation, and Direct Control or Problem Solving (see Table 6.2). The attention regulation category appeared the most elaborated among these toddlers, including such actions as approach to the rabbit while attending to other aspects of the room, diverting the mother's attention when she tried to focus the infant on the rabbit, and distraction through the use of other objects. Attention regulation has appeared as a major category of coping behavior in all of the models of coping development discussed thus far. It is perhaps worth noting that currently Rothbart and Posner (1985) are analyzing the development of attentional strategies as a major factor in self-regulation as it relates to temperament.

Finally, in our study, only one coping category yielded evidence of developmental change between 12 and 18 months. This was the category of direct control or problem solving. Only 18-month-olds were observed to actively attempt to alter the testing situation. They attempted this by actively trying to pull or push the mother over to the cage. When this did not work, some tried to push the cage over to mother. When this did not work, one little girl got her mother's keys out of the purse, went to the door and said "Go." The emergence of active, problem solving as an aspect of coping at about this age is predicted in Kopp's model. However, because this type of problem solving involves the child taking direct control of events, its developmental roots may lie in earlier experiences with control in stressful situations.

Of all of the factors influencing the stressfulness of different situations, the opportunity to control outcomes appears to be the most important (Weinberg & Levine, 1980). Indeed, this variable is so potent that actual control is not necessary: the perception or expectation of control is sufficient to dramatically reduce

TABLE 6.2
Coping Strategies Used by Wary 12- and 18-Month-Olds in
Exploring a Live, Caged Rabbit

Category and Behavior	% of Children
Attachment Behavior:	
Proximity to Mother	90%
Fuss to Mother	57%
Self-Calm	
Self-Stimulation	90%
Nervous Laughter	48%
Attention Regulation	
Distract Self	76%
Divert Mother	48%
Devious Approach	29%
Direct Control	
Direct Control	33%
Leave Taking	10%

behavioral and physiological responses to even very aversive events (Averill, 1973). The research on use of the attachment figure as a coping resource fits well within the control framework. In the attachment figure's presence the infant has control over engaging in numerous coping actions (approach, touch, cling), while in her absence the infant's control over coping resources is greatly reduced. In addition, through signaling specific needs to the caregiver, the infant gains what can be called mediated control over outcomes (Gunnar, 1983).

In several studies, my students and I have attempted to understand when control becomes important in determining the infant's reactions to potentially stressful events. Using a fear-eliciting toy monkey (Gunnar, 1980; Gunnar-vonGnechten, 1978), the effects of permitting infants to turn on the toy themselves versus experiencing the same pattern of toy activations uncontrollably was examined. By 12 months, infants consistently responded with less crying and more approach in the controllable versus uncontrollable condition. However, this effect was not obtained at 6 and 9 months. Recently, Mangelsdorf (1987) examined infant's reactions to adult strangers who varied in how responsive they were to the infant's signals, and thus in their controllability. Six-month-olds were found not to be affected by this aspect of the stranger's behavior. By 12 months, however, the infant's reactions to the stranger were strongly affected by her controllability.

Both these studies suggest that while infants are responsive to contingent stimulation much earlier in infancy (e.g., Watson, 1967), it is not until near the end of the first year that they use information about their control over events to appraise the threat potential of situations. It is not surprising, then, that it is not until well after 12 months that, in novel settings, infants begin to actively seek out ways of directly controlling or altering circumstances. What we do not know is how the infant's history of control within the parent-infant relationship influences either the effectiveness of direct control in reducing distress or the extent to which the infant actively attempts to directly control stressful circumstances.

INTEGRATION AND IMPLICATIONS

As in any relatively new area, there are more questions than answers. Competence, which we value in ourselves and our children, does not appear to buffer us from stress. Instead, it appears to be correlated with greater stress reactivity. This makes sense if we hypothesize that the coping behavior associated with competence are likely to involve approach more than avoidance strategies. Approach strategies are likely to bring the child into contact with stressful elements of situations, and to keep the child engaged and invested in a way that supports greater stress reactivity. In contrast, less competent individual are likely to use more avoidance strategies. These strategies are more likely to reduce stress, at least temporarily. However, as Kagan et al.'s (1987) work has shown, when inhibited children (whom we can expect to be more avoidant children) are forced to confront threatening situations, they show dramatic stress reactions. Thus, the relations between competence and stress may reverse under conditions in which avoidance strategies are not available or effective. The above hypotheses, of course, remain to be tested.

The review of the parent-infant data also revealed as many questions as answers. Although there has been a great deal of research on attachment quality or security, we do not know whether or how this dimension of the parent-infant relationship is related to physiological stress. Because a secure relationship has been linked to the development of competence, we might hypothesize that, in general, children from secure relationships will be more stress-reactive than children from insecure relations. Furthermore, we might expect this stress-reactivity to be mediated by the greater use of approach strategies among children from secure relationships. However, as in the case of the inhibited children discussed earlier, we might also expect that the relations between security and stress would reverse under conditions in which insecure children were not able to effectively use avoidance strategies. Again, these hypotheses remain to be tested.

It is also surprising how little we know about the effect of relationship quality on the stress buffering effects of the mother's presence. We might, however, predict that the presence of the mother in secure relationships has a greater buffering power than the presence of a mother in an insecure relationship. This, in fact, might serve to link attachment security more directly to approach coping strategies. Specifically, if the mother's presence is more stress buffering, then the secure infant might be able to use more approach strategies than the insecure infant, thereby developing an orientation towards approach over avoidance strategies. These predictions would be fairly straightforward to examine.

In addition to the above questions, we clearly need more information about the development of specific strategies. Again, if approach versus avoidance can serve as a useful distinction in the study of the development of coping, then what we need to identify are the strategies that fall into these categories and their ontogeny. This may be a necessary first step in addressing some of the attachment security and coping questions already outlined.

Finally, we have framed this chapter around normal development. However, especially in the area of stress and coping, a dual focus on normal and pathological development would seem most useful. It is very possible that some of the conclusions arrived at in this review would not apply to children from pathological relationships. One likely candidate suggested earlier is the absence of a link between attachment history and stress reactions to separation. Specifically, separation stress-reactions may differ among children with more and less pathological attachment histories. Another is the conclusion that the mother's presence is stress buffering. In addition, an analysis of the development of coping strategies in children from pathological relationships may also tell us something about the extremes of human adaptability, as well as make us more sensitive to the functions of what might appear maladaptive behaviors in these children.

REFERENCES

Ainsworth, M. D. S., & Wittig, B. A. (1969). Attachment and the exploratory behavior of one-year-olds in a strange situation. In B. M. Foss (Ed.), *Determinants of infant behavior Vol. 4* (pp. 113–136). London: Methuen.

Ainsworth, M. D. S., Blehar, M. C., Waters, E., & Wall, S. (1978). *Patterns of attachment: A psychological study of the strange situation.* Hillsdale, NJ: Lawrence Erlbaum Associates.

Averill, J. (1973). Personal control over aversive stimuli and its relationship to stress. *Psychological Bulletin, 80,* 286–297.

Bandura, A. (1977). *Social learning theory.* Englewood Cliffs, NJ: Prentice-Hall.

Belsky, J., & Rovine, M. (1987). Temperament and attachment security in the strange situation: An empirical rapprochement. *Child Development, 58,* 787–795.

Borysenko, J. (1984). Stress and coping, and the immune system. In J. D. Matarazzo, S. M. Weiss, J. A. Herd, N. E. Miller, & S. M. Weiss (Eds.), *Behavioral health* (pp. 248–260). New York: Wiley

Bowlby, J. (1969). *Attachment and Loss: Attachment* (Vol. 1). New York: Basic Books.

Bowlby, J. (1973). *Attachment and Loss: Separation* (Vol. 2.). New York: Basic Books.

Campos, J., & Stenberg, C. (1981). Perception, appraisal and emotion: The onset of social referencing. In M. Lamb & L. Sherrod (Eds.), *Infant social cognition: Empirical and theoretical considerations* (pp. 273–314). Hillsdale, NJ: Lawrence Erlbaum Associates.

Candland, D. K., & Mason, W. (1969). Infant monkey heart rate: Habituation and its effects of social substitutes. *Developmental Psychobiology, 1,* 254–256.

Carver, C., & Scheier, M. (1985). Self-consciousness, expectancies, and the coping process. In T. Field, P. McCabe, & N. Schneiderman (Eds.), *Stress and coping* (pp. 305–330). Hillsdale, NJ: Lawrence Erlbaum Associates.

Cicchetti, D. (1984). The emergence of developmental psychopathology. *Child Development, 55,* 1–7.

Coe, C. L., & Levine, S. (1981). Normal responses to mother-infant separation in non-human primates. In D. F. Klein & J. Raplan (Eds.), *Anxiety: New research and changing concepts* (pp. 155–157). New York: Raven Press.

Coe, C. L., Smith, E. R., & Levine, S. (1985). The endocrine system of the squirrel monkey. In L. A. Rosenblum & C. L. Coe (Eds.), *The handbook of squirrel monkey research* (pp. 191–218). New York: Plenum Press.

Coe, C. L., Wiener, S., Rosenberg, L., & Levine, S. (1985). Physiological consequences of maternal separation and loss in the squirrel monkey. In L. A. Rosenblum & C. L. Coe (Eds.), *The handbook of squirrel monkey research* (pp. 127–148). New York: Plenum Press.

Cohen, F., & Lazarus, R. S. (1973). Active coping processes, coping dispositions, and recovery from surgery. *Psychosomatic Medicine, 35,* 375–380.

Cohn, J., & Tronick, E. Z. (1983). Three-month-old infant's reactions to simulated maternal depression. *Child Development, 54,* 185–193.

Connell, J., & Wellborn, J. (in press). Self-system processes from a motivational perspective. In M. Gunnar & L. A. Srofe (Eds.), *Self Processes in Development, Minnesota Symposia on Child Psychology, Vol. 23* . Hillsdale, NJ: Lawrence Erlbaum Associates.

Feinman, S. (1983). How does the baby socially refer? Let us count the ways: A reply to Campos. *Merrill-Palmer Quarterly, 29.*

Fox, N. A. (1988, in press). Heart rate variability and self-regulation: Individual differences in autonomic patterning and their relation to infant and child temperament. In S. Reznick & J. Kagan (Eds.), *Perspectives on behavioral inhibition.* Chicago: University of Chicago Press.

Frankenhaueser, M. (1980). Psychobiological aspects of life stress. In S. Levine & H. Ursin (Eds.), *Coping and health,* 1st edition. New York: Plenum Press.

Frankenhauser, M. & Andersson, K. (1974). Note on interaction between cognitive and endocrine functions. *Perceptual & Motor Skills, 38,* 557–558.

Frankenhaeuser, M., & Patkai, P. (1965). Interindividual differences in catecholamine excretion during stress. *Scandinavian Journal of Psychology, 6,* 117–123.

Freud, S. (1938). Psychopathology of everyday life. In A. A. Biell (Ed.), *The Basic Writings of Sigmund Freud* (pp. 35–180). New York: Random House.

Garmezy, N., & Rutter, M. (1983). *Stress, coping and development in children.* New York: McGraw-Hill.

Gianino, A., & Tronick, E. (1988). The mutual regulation model: The infant's self and interactive regulation, coping and defensive capacities. In T. Field, P. McCabe, & N. Schneiderman (Eds.), *Stress and Coping Across Development.* Hillsdale, NJ: Lawrence Erlbaum Associates.

Gonzales, C., Gunnar, M., & Levine, S. (1981). Behavioral and hormonal responses to social disruption and infant stimuli in female Rhesus monkeys. *Psychoneuroendocrinology, 6*(1), 55–65.

Gunnar, M. (1980). Control, warning signals and distress in infancy. *Developmental Psychology, 16*(4), 281–289.

Gunnar, M. (1983). Discussion of Field's research. In M. Perlmutter (Ed.), *Minnesota Symposia on Child Psychology, Vol. 16* (pp. 35–40). Hillsdale, NJ: Lawrence Erlbaum Associates.

Gunnar, M. (1986). Human developmental psychoneuroendocrinology: A review of research on neuroendocrine responses to challenge and threat in infancy and childhood. In M. Lamb, A. L. Brown, & B. Rogoff (Eds.), *Advances in Developmental Psychology, Vol. 4* (pp. 51–103). Hillsdale, NJ: Lawrence Erlbaum Associates.

Gunnar, M., Gonzales, C., & Levine, S. (1980). The role of peers in modifying behavioral distress and pituitary-adrenal response to novel environments in year-old Rhesus monkeys. *Physiology and Behavior, 25,* 795–798.

Gunnar, M. R., Gonzales, C., Goodlin, B., & Levine, S. (1981). Behavioral and pituitary-adrenal responses during a prolonged separation period in infant rhesus macaques. *Psychoneuroendocrinology, 6,* 66–75.

Gunnar, M. R., Isensee, J., & Fust, S. (1987). Adrenocortical activity and the Brazelton Neonatal Assessment Scale: Moderating effects of the newborn's biomedical status. *Child Development, 58,* 937–944.

Gunnar, M. R., Mangelsdorf, S., Larson, M., & Hertsgaard, L. (1989). Attachment, temperament and adrenocortical activity in infancy: A study of psychoendocrine regulation. *Developmental Psychology, 25,* 355–363.

Gunnar, M. R., Marvinney, D., Isensee, J., & Fisch, R. O. (1989). Coping with uncertainty: New models of the regulations between hormonal, behavioral and cognitive processes. In D. Palermo (Ed.), *Coping with uncertainty.* Hillsdale, NJ: Lawrence Erlbaum Associates.

Gunnar-vonGnechten, M. (1978). Changing a frightening toy into a pleasant toy by allowing the infant to control its actions. *Developmental Psychology, 14*(2), 157–162.

Harlow, H. F. (1958). The nature of love. *American Psychologist, 13,* 673–685.

Hill, S., McCormack, S. A., & Mason, W. (1973). Effects of artificial mothers and visual experience on adrenal responsiveness of infant monkeys. *Developmental Psychobiology, 6,* 421–429.

Hinde, R. A., & Spencer-Booth, Y. (1967). The behavior of socially living rhesus monkeys in their first two and one half years. *Animal Behavior, 15,* 169–196.

Hornik, R., & Gunnar, M. (1987, April). Towards a taxonomy of infant coping strategies. *Poster presented at the Society for Research in Child Development.* Baltimore.

Johansson, G., Frankenhaueser, M., & Magnussen, D. (1973). Catecholamine output in school children as related to performance and adjustment. *Scandinavian Journal of Psychology, 14*, 20–28.

Kagan, J. (1982). *Psychological research on the human infant: An evaluative summary.* New York: The William T. Grant Foundation.

Kagan, J., Reznick, S., & Snidman, N. (1987). The physiology and psychology of behavioral inhibition. *Child Development, 58*(6), 1459–1473.

Kalin, N., & Carnes, M. (1984). Biological correlates of attachment bond description in humans and nonhuman primates. *Progress in Neuropsychopharmacology and Biological Psychiatry, Vol. 8* (pp. 459–469). London: Pergamon Press.

Kaplan, J. (1981). Effect of surrogate-administered punishment on surrogate contact in infant squirrel monkeys. *Developmental Psychobiology, 14*, 523–532.

Kopp, C. (1989). Regulation of distress and negative emotions: A developmental view. *Developmental Psychology, 25*, 343–354.

Lambert, W. W., Johansson, G., Frankenhaueser, M., & Klackenberg-Larsson, I. (1969). Catecholamine excretion in young children and their parents as related to behavior. *Scandinavian Journal of Psychology, 10*, 306–318.

Lazarus, R. S. (1977). Cognitive and coping processes in emotion. In A. Monat & R. Lazarus (Eds.), *Stress and coping.* New York: Columbia University Press.

Levine, S. (1980). A coping model of mother-infant relationships. In S. Levine & H. Ursin (Eds.), *Coping and health* (pp. 87–100). New York: Plenum.

Levine, S. (1982). Comparative and psychobiological perspectives on development. In W. A. Collins (Ed.), *The concept of development: Minnesota Symposia on Child Psychology, Vol. 15* (pp. 29–54). Hillsdale, NJ: Lawrence Erlbaum Associates.

Levine, S. (1985). A definition of stress? In G. P. Moberg (Ed.), *Animal Stress* (pp. 51–69). Bethesda, MD: American Physiological Society.

Mahler, M., Pine, F., & Bergman, A. (1975). *The psychological birth of the human infant.* New York: Basic Books.

Main, M. (1973). *Play, exploration and competence as related to child-adult attachment.* Unpublished doctoral dissertation. The Johns Hopkins University.

Main, M., Kaplan, N., & Cassidy, J. (1985). Security in infancy, childhood, and adulthood: A move to the level of representation. In I. Bretherton and E. Waters (Eds.), Growing points in attachment theory and research. *Monographs of the Society for Research in Child Development, 50*, 66–106.

Mangelsdorf, S. (1987). *The development of social appraisal processes in infancy.* Unpublished doctoral dissertation, University of Minnesota, Minneapolis.

Matheny, A. P., & Wilson, R. S. (1981). Developmental tasks and rating scales for laboratory assessment of infant temperament. *JSAS Catalog of Selected Documents in Psychology, 11*, 81–82. (Ms. No. 2367).

Mattsson, A., Gross, S., & Hall, T. (1971). Psychoendocrine study of adaptation in young hemophiliacs. *Psychosomatic Medicine, 33*, 215–255.

Murphy, L. B. (1974). Coping, vulnerability, and resilience in childhood. In D. Hamburg & Coelho (Eds.), *Coping and adaptation* (pp. 69–100). New York: Basic Books.

Richardson, R., Siegel, M. A., & Campbell, B. A. (1988). Effects of maternal presence on the fear response to an unfamiliar environment as measured by heart rate in rats as a function of age. *Developmental Psychobiology, 21*, 613–635.

Roessler, R., Burch, N. R., & Mefferd, R. (1967). Personality correlates of catecholamine excretion under stress. *Journal of Psychosomatic Research, 11*, 181–185.

Rose, R. M. (1980). Endocrine responses to stressful psychological events. Advances in psychoneuroendocrinology. *Psychiatric Clinics of North America, Vol. 3*(2), 251–276.

Rose, R. M., Jenkins, D. C., Hurst, M., et al. (1982). II. Biological, psychological and work correlates. *Psychoneuroendocrinology, 7*, 113–123.

Roth, S., & Cohen, L. J. (1986). Approach, avoidance, and coping with stress. *American Psychologist, 41*, 813–819.

Rothbart, M. K., & Posner, M. I. (1985). Temperament and the development of self-regulation. In H. Hartlage & C. G. Telzrow (Eds.), *Neuropsychology of individual differences: A developmental perspective* (pp. 93–123). New York: Plenum Press.

Sander, L. W. (1975). Infant and caretaking environment: Investigation and conceptualization of adaptive behavior in a system of increasing complexity. In E. J. Anthony (Ed.), *Explorations in Child Psychiatry*, (pp. 129–166). New York: Plenum.

Spangler, G., Meindel, E., & Grossmann, K. A. (1988, April). Behavioral organization and adrenocortical activity in newborns and infants. Poster presented at *6th Biennial International Conference on Infant Studies*, Washington, D. C.

Sroufe, L. A. (1983). Infant-caregiver attachment and patterns of adaptation in preschool: The roots of maladaptation and competence. In M. Perlmutter (Ed.), *Development and policy concerning children with special needs. Minnesota Symposia on Child Psychology, Vol. 16* (pp. 41–84). Hillsdale, NJ: Lawrence Erlbaum Associates.

Sroufe, L. A., & Waters, E. (1977). Heart rate as a convergent measure in clinical and developmental research. *Merrill-Palmer Quarterly, 23*, 3–27.

Wald, M., Carlsmith, M., Leiderman, P. H., & Smith, C. (1983). Intervention to protect abused and neglected children. In M. Perlmutter (Ed.), *Development and policy concerning children with special needs. The Minnesota Symposia on Child Psychology, Vol. 16* (pp. 207–232). Hillsdale, NJ: Lawrence Erlbaum Associates.

Watson, J. S. (1967). Memory and "contingency analysis" in infant development. *Merrill-Palmer Quarterly, 13*, 55–67.

Weinberg, J., & Levine, S. (1980). Psychobiology of coping in animals: The effects of predictability. In S. Levine & H. Ursin (Eds.), *Coping and health*, (pp. 39–60). New York: Plenum Press.

7 Maternal Depression Effects on Infant Interaction and Attachment Behavior

Tiffany Field
University of Miami Medical School

The infant's ability to form attachments develops in the context of an interactive relationship with the mother. Mothers (or caregivers) learn to read their infants' affective displays (facial expressions, vocalizations, and gaze behavior) and modulate their stimulation and arousal-modulation needs. When this occurs, the infant's affect appears to be positive, the interaction harmonious (both behaviorally and physiologically), and a normal attachment or relationship seems to develop, thereby fostering the infant's social/emotional development. If the mother (caregiver) is affectively unavailable or unresponsive, as is the depressed mother, behavioral and physiological disorganization will invariably ensue, manifested by disturbances in the infant's affective and physiological functions. These may contribute to later disturbances in attachment and ultimately to disturbed affective development.

Unfavorable affective development has been reported for children reared by depressed mothers as opposed to mothers with other diagnoses or normal mothers (Cytryn, McKnew, Bartko, Lamour, & Hamovitt, 1982; Grunebaum, Cohler, Kauffman, & Gallant, 1978; Rolf, Crowther, Teri, & Bond, 1984; Sameroff & Seifer, 1983). Because children of depressed parents are at higher risk themselves for depression, several researchers have suggested the strategy of studying infants and toddlers of parents who have experienced depression (Cantwell, 1983; Cicchetti & Aber, 1986). Although infant depression is not a recognized DSM III-R category (American Psychiatric Association, 1987), there have been times, historically, when it was considered a clinical entity (Kashari, Husain, Shokim, Hodges, Cytryn, & McKnew, 1981). We believe that the depressed mother may predispose her infant to developing "depressed" behavior during the infancy stage. Despite suggestive data on risk factors for developing depression, there are very few studies in the literature on the early interactions of depressed mothers and their infants.

This chapter reviews that limited literature as well as data from our laboratory on the early behavior of infants of depressed mothers. These data will then be critically examined in the context of the methodological limitations of the interaction and attachment paradigms for understanding the unique problems of the depressed mother and her infant and in the context of a developmental model for infant depression. It should be noted that these studies have included mothers presenting different types of depression, some of them simulated depression, some postpartum depression, and some more chronic depression; thus the mothers have experienced clinically and etiologically different forms of depression. In addition, the infants, while manifesting *depressed* affect would not necessarily be considered clinically depressed. Although early depressed affect deriving from early mother-infant interactions may be a precursor or prototype of later clinical depression in childhood or adulthood, the absence of longitudinal studies on these infants precludes any speculation about the prognostic significance of infant depressed affect.

DEPRESSED MOTHER-INFANT INTERACTIONS

Young infants of depressed mothers have typically been studied in the face-to-face interaction paradigm. In this situation, the mother is simply asked to play for a few minutes with her infant and the mother's and infant's behaviors are then coded from videotaped interactions. One of the first studies on the effects of maternal depression on infant behavior was one in which maternal depression was simulated by normal mothers (Cohn & Tronick, 1983). Mothers behaved spontaneously and then were asked to "look depressed" during interactions with their 6-month-old infants. Although it was not clear that their infants responded to their "looking depressed" in the same way that infants would respond to naturally depressed mothers, the interactions in which mothers were instructed to "look depressed" resulted in disorganized, distressed behavior on the part of the infant. During this manipulation, the infants more frequently looked wary, averted their gaze, protested, and attempted to elicit responses from the mother, much like the infant interacting with the still-face mother attempts to reinstate a normal interaction (Tronick, Als, Adamson, Wise, & Brazelton, 1977). In the study by Cohn and Tronick (Cohn & Tronick, 1983; Cohn, 1987) distressed behavior of infants continued even after the mothers resumed their normal behavior (see Fig. 7.1). While this study was only a simulation, infants of *naturally* depressed mothers became accustomed to their mother's behavior and may no longer seem to be distressed by this behavior. This appears to be the case based on more recent studies on infants of naturally depressed mothers (postpartum depression). In a study by Field (1984), infants of naturally depressed mothers

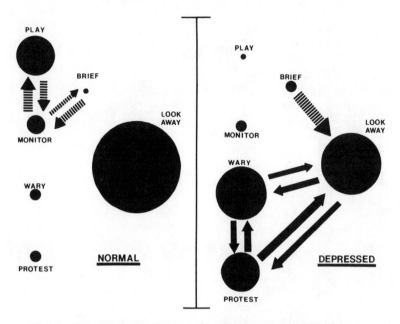

FIG. 7.1.   State transition diagrams for the depressed and normal conditions. The relative proportion of infant time spent in each state is
indicated by size of the circle representing that state. The thickness of
the arrows represents the relative size of the conditional probabilities
of event sequence transitions. Striped arrows indicate those transitions for which conditional and unconditional probabilities do not significantly differ, $p < .05$. Taken from Cohn (1987).

were compared to infants of nondepressed mothers who were invited to "look
depressed." The Beck Depression Inventory (Beck, Ward, Mendelson, Mach, &
Erbaugh, 1961) was used to identify mothers experiencing postpartum depression. Face-to-face interactions of these depressed mothers and their infants were
compared to the interactions of nondepressed mothers and their infants. In addition, baseline and interaction heart rate were recorded for both the mothers and
infants, and activity level was measured by the use of an actometer (motion
recorder) attached to the infant. The mothers and infants engaged in three face-
to-face play interactions including a spontaneous interaction, an interaction in
which the mother was asked to "look depressed" and a "reunion" interaction in
which the mother was again asked to behave naturally. These interactions were
videotaped and then coded for a number of infant behaviors including positive
facial expressions, negative facial expressions, vocalizations, looking away,
protesting, and looking wary, and for the mother, positive facial expressions,
negative facial expressions, vocalizations, looking at the infant, and tac-
tile/kinesthetic stimulation.

As can be seen in Table 7.1, during the "looking depressed" situation the

TABLE 7.1

Infant and Mother Behaviors During Spontaneous, "Depressed," and "Reunion" Interactions [Mean (M), Repeated Measures (R), and Interaction (I) Effects]*

Behaviors	Nondepressed			Depressed			Effect and p Level
	Spontaneous	Depressed	Reunion	Spontaneous	Depressed	Reunion	
Infant Behaviors							
Positive facial expressions (frequency)	8.5_a	4.0_b	4.5_b	3.0_c	2.0_c	2.0_c	M^1I^1
Negative facial expressions (frequency)	1.5_a	8.0_b	6.5_b	5.5_b	5.0_b	4.5_b	I^1
Vocalizations (frequency)	7.0_a	3.0_b	3.5_b	2.0_c	1.5_c	1.5_c	M^2I^1
Looking away (% time)	21_a	48_b	39_b	38_b	32_b	33_b	I^2
Protesting (% time)	5_a	42_b	37_b	15_c	16_c	17_c	M^2I^4
Looking wary (% time)	7_a	36_b	31_b	11_c	14_c	13_c	M^3I^4
Activity	17_a	26_b	23_b	9_c	11_c	12_c	M^2I^1
Heart rate	148_a	159_b	154_b	140_a	142_a	145_a	M^1I^1
Mother Behaviors							
Positive facial expressions (frequency)	21.5_a	2.0_b	16.5_a	5.0_b	4.0_b	3.5_b	M^3I^4
Negative facial expressions (frequency)	2.5_a	8.0_b	3.0_a	9.0_b	11.5_b	10.5_b	M^1I^1
Vocalizations (frequency)	53_a	21_b	48_a	22_b	26_b	27_b	M^2I^2
Looking at infant (% time)	93_a	89_a	95_a	58_b	65_b	62_b	M^3
Tactile/Kinesthetic stimulation (% time)	39_a	11_b	33_a	21_c	11_b	18_c	M^2R^2
Heart rate	79_a	87_b	81_a	71_c	78_c	74_c	M^1I^1

*Means bearing different subscripts (a, b, c) are different at $p<.05$ or less; SDs can be obtained from the author.
$^1p<.05$, $^2p<.01$, $^3p<.005$, $^4p<.001$. Taken from Field (1984).

infants of nondepressed mothers (versus those of depressed mothers) were more disturbed, showed more frequent negative facial expressions, protests, and looking wary behavior, and higher activity levels and heart rate. Thus, the request to "look depressed" appeared to alter significantly the behavior of nondepressed mothers and their infants, but the behavior of naturally depressed mothers and their infants was not affected by this manipulation. These data on the nondepressed mothers and their infants support those of Cohn and Tronick (1983), suggesting that these infants noticed a change in their mothers' affect and modified their own affective behavior and responsivity to the mothers "looking depressed." Much of the infants' behavior in this study (as in the Cohn and Tronick study) appeared to be an attempt to reinstate a normal interaction. Failing this, the infants' distressed behavior (looking away, looking wary, and protesting) carried over into their subsequent "reunion" interaction. This would suggest a carry over of affective behavior or the establishment of a "mood" in the infant. Elevated activity level and corresponding increases in heart rate during the "looking depressed" interaction suggest that this may have been an anxiety-provoking situation both for the nondepressed mothers and their infants.

The naturally depressed mothers, in contrast, did not appear to change their behavior across the three situations. The infants of the depressed mothers also appeared unaffected by these manipulations. The infants of naturally depressed mothers behaved less positively during the spontaneous interaction and showed little change during the "looking depressed" interaction. These infants may not have been as distressed by their mothers being invited to "look depressed" because they had become accustomed to the mothers' depressed behavior. Infants of truly depressed mothers may have developed a passive coping, depressed style of interacting. The lower heart rate may also be a manifestation of their helplessness or passive coping.

Lower heart rate has been associated with situations of helplessness or passive coping (Obrist, Lawler, Howard, Smithson, Martin, & Manning, 1974) and has been attributed to decreased sympathetic adrenergic activity or increased parasympathetic activation or vagal tone. Infant primates who do not have control in stressful situations show behaviors very similar to the behaviors of infants of depressed mothers (Reite, Short, Seiler, & Pauley, 1981). During brief periods of stress, infant monkeys typically show agitated behavior and physiological arousal whereas during more prolonged stress, their activity and physiology are depressed. The primate infant has been said to be actively coping in the former situation and passively coping in the latter. Thus, the infant monkey data appear analogous to the data of this study. The behavior of infants of depressed mothers appeared to *mirror* the behavior of their mothers. This suggests that by experiencing frequent lack of control during early interactions, these infants may have developed a passive-coping, depressed style of interaction. Their "depressed mood" persisted across interactions and may be a well established "defensive posture" that would appear in situations regardless of the stimulation provided.

This could be an early precursor of anxious/resistant attachment as described by Cicchetti and Aber (1986).

In a more recent study of naturally depressed mothers, Cohn and his colleagues (Cohn, Matias, Tronick, Connell, & Lyons-Ruth, 1986) also noted a persistent depressed mood in infants despite the variations in interaction styles of their depressed mothers. They sampled a group of 13 depressed mothers who were diagnosed by the Center for Epidemiological Studies Depression Scale (CESD) (Radloff, 1977). When the infants were 6-months-old they were filmed together with their mothers in a face-to-face interaction. During these interactions, the mothers were extremely variable in their positivity or level of engagement and intrusiveness or expression of anger. A small number of mothers showed the pattern similar to clinical descriptions of depressed mothers. These mothers were disengaged for 75% or more of the interaction time (see Fig. 7.2). They slouched back in their chairs, turned away from the infant, or spoke to the infant in an expressionless voice with little facial expression. A second group of mothers also showed low proportions of positive expression but high rates of

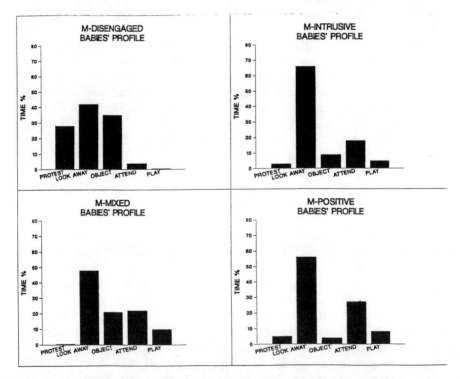

FIG. 7.2.   Individual differences among depressed mothers in the percent of time spent in behavioral states during face-to-face interactions with their infants. Taken from Cohn et al. (1986).

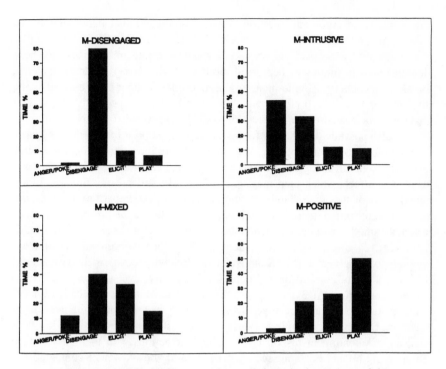

FIG. 7.3. Individual differences among infants in the percent of time spent in behavioral states during face-to-face interactions with their depressed mothers. Taken from Cohn et al. (1986).

eliciting behavior. They appeared to want to engage their infants and used many eliciting behaviors but did not seem able to expand their affective range of neutral positive affective expression and were positive in their affective expression at least 35% of the time. Despite these variations in the mothers' behavior, the infants' behavior was far less variable (see Fig. 7.3). The infants were typically highly withdrawn and seldom showed positive affective expression. According to Cohn and colleagues (1986), the most disturbing behavior for these infants was the pattern of maternal disengagement. Apparently not even high rates of poking provoked comparable upset.

The way in which depressed behavior is transmitted from mother to infant is unknown, although genetic susceptibility and/or perinatal factors cannot be ruled out as a possible origin, particularly in light of the Sameroff and Seifer (1983) data suggesting that infants of depressed mothers are at unusually high risk for developing depression. Another possibility is that depressed affect emerges in very young infants as a function of their early interactions with postpartum-depressed mothers. This depressed affect may derive from the infants mimicking their mothers' behaviors or simply from minimal maternal stimulation. Although this remains an empirical question, these data suggest that depression in the mother can be transmitted to her offspring as early as the first few months of life. To date, only "depressed" affect and elevated heart rate and cortisol have been demonstrated in infants of depressed mothers (Field, Healy, Goldstein, Perry, Bendell, Schanberg, Zimmerman, & Kuhn, 1988). Without other clinical signs, such as depressed sleep architecture, it would be highly speculative to suggest that the clinical syndrome of depression could be experienced as early as infancy.

It is also possible that these infants were depressed prior to experiencing early interactions with their mothers. That is, they may have shown depressed-like behavior from birth, suggesting a genetic or temperamental basis for the infants' depressed affect, which then may be reinforced by a depressed mother. In another study of this kind, mothers who were identified prepartum as being depressed were filmed interacting with their infants during the postpartum period, when the mothers remained depressed (Field, Sandberg, Garcia, Vega-Lahr, Goldstein, & Guy, 1985). After their delivery, the newborn infants of these mothers were given a Brazelton Neonatal Behavior Assessment (Brazelton, 1973) and were noted to have "depressed" activity level and responsivity to social stimulation. At 3 months postdelivery, the mothers who had been depressed during pregnancy received scores meeting the criterion for depression on the Beck Depression Inventory and showed flat affect and low activity levels as well as less contingent responsivity during interactions with their infants (see Table 7.2). Infants of depressed mothers in turn showed fewer contented expressions, more fussiness, and lower levels of physical activity than infants of nondepressed mothers. It is not clear from these data whether the infants' diminished activity level and responsivity during their early interactions were merely a behavioral style that persisted from birth, or one that largely developed from 3 months of exposure to the depressed behavior modeled by their mothers, from minimal maternal stimulation, and from the infants' repeated failure to reestablish normal interactions (Tronick, Ricks, & Cohn, 1982).

A more extensive longitudinal study across pregnancy and early infancy would be required to assess the origins of this depressed behavior in young infants. Nonetheless, the importance of studying the effects of maternal depression on infant affect is highlighted simply by the incidence of the problem, ranging from 10–12% for postpartum depression and 40–70% for postpartum blues, with residual effects after 1 year in approximately 4% of mothers, and a recurrence rate reported between 20 and 30% (Davidson, 1972; Grundy & Roberts, 1975).

Another question, not addressed in these studies, is whether the depressed affect of these infants is specific to interactions with their depressed mothers or whether the infants have already developed a *depressed* style of interacting that has generalized to their interactions with nondepressed adults. Thus, in a subsequent study we compared interactions of infants with their depressed mothers to their interactions with nondepressed adult strangers. Because stranger fear reput-

TABLE 7.2
Mean Rating Scale Scores and P Levels Based on Bonferroni T Tests (df = 23)

	Depressed	Control	p Level
Infant Interaction Behaviors			
State	1.5	2.6	.01
Physical activity	1.6	2.5	.01
Head orientation	2.0	2.2	n.s.
Gaze behavior	2.1	2.3	n.s.
Facial expressions	1.4	2.1	.05
Vocalizations	1.5	1.6	n.s.
Fussiness	1.3	2.2	.01
Summary rating	1.6	2.2	.05
Mother Interaction Behaviors			
State	1.6	2.4	.05
Physical activity	1.8	2.7	.01
Head orientation	2.4	2.5	n.s.
Gaze behavior	2.3	2.5	n.s.
Facial expressions	1.7	2.4	.05
Vocalizations	1.8	1.9	n.s.
Silence during infant gaze aversion	1.5	1.3	n.s.
Imitative behaviors	1.4	2.2	.05
Contingent responsivity	1.5	2.3	.05
Gameplaying	1.4	2.2	.05
Summary rating	1.7	2.3	.05
Questionnaire Ratings			
CCTI-Emotionality	20	13	.01
EASI-Emotionality	18	12	.01
Childrearing Attitudes	05	01	.05
Locus of Control	28	15	.01
State Anxiety	38	29	.05
Trait Anxiety	51	28	.01
Beck Depression	22	04	.01

edly does not emerge until later in the first year of infancy, we hoped that the unfamiliarity of the comparison adult would not confound the comparison of these interactions.

In this study (Field et al., 1988), depressed and nondepressed mothers were recruited when the infants were 3- and 6-months-of-age from a sample of Black and Hispanic mothers. The mothers were classified as depressed or nondepressed based on their responses to two inventories, the Beck Depression Inventory (BDI) and the Profile of Mood States (POMS: McNair, Lorr, & Droppleman, 1971). If the mothers received a score of less than 9 on the BDI, they were classified as nondepressed; a score greater than 12 classified them as depressed.

Mothers and infants were videotaped in a 3-minute face-to-face interaction, with mothers asked to pretend they were playing with their infant at home. Following this interaction, the infant was situated face-to-face with a non-depressed *stranger* of the same ethnicity as the mother. Because pilot data revealed no mother/stranger order effects and because we did not want to influence the mother's interaction behavior by observing the stranger-infant interaction, the order of these interaction situations was not counterbalanced. The strangers were selected based on two criteria, experience with infants, and demonstration of affectively responsive behaviors in face-to-face interactions with this age infant. Simultaneous with the videotaping of the interaction situations, the mothers' and infants' heart rates were recorded to determine whether, as in the previous study, there were differences in the physiological activity of the depressed mother-infant and nondepressed mother-infant dyads and whether there was greater synchrony in the physiological rhythms of the nondepressed mother-infant dyads. Following the interaction situations, saliva samples were taken from the mothers and infants by placing a syringe along the gum line. These samples were subsequently assayed for cortisol levels to determine the differential stressful effects of these interactions on the nondepressed and depressed mother-infant dyads.

Hypotheses could be made in both directions based on the existing literature. That is, the literature on mothers' simulated "depression" (Cohn & Tronick, 1983), still-faced behavior (Tronick et al., 1977), and imitative behavior (Field, 1977), for example, showed that infants readily change their behavior when the adult's behavior was modified, as if the infant's behavior is very much affected by the "mood state" or type of behavior displayed by the adult. In this context the infant would notice that the stranger's behavior was different and would be expected to behave differently with the adult stranger whose behavior is not "depressed" or is different from that of the mother. However, if the infant's behavior has been "depressed-like" since birth and/or the mother has reportedly been depressed since pregnancy as in the Field et al. (1985) study, then it is conceivable that the infant has developed a *depressed* style of interacting that might generalize to other adults. Still another possibility is that infants who typically experience interactions that are depressed in nature, e.g., unanimated, unstimulating interactions, may experience that interaction situation as generally stressful in which case the infants may appear generally depressed in this context, irrespective of their interaction partner.

Physiological measures (heart rate and cortisol) were used to tap the infant's physiological response to the interaction situation. Elevated heart rate has been reported during stressful interactions such as those in which the mother was asked to remain still-faced (Stoller & Field, 1982), or in which the mother is overstimulating (Field, 1981). Although cortisol levels have not been used as an index of stress in the early mother-infant interaction situation, elevated cortisol levels have been noted in infants experiencing other forms of stressful interaction, for example, following the Brazelton assessment (Gunnar, Malone, & Fish, 1984; see also, Gunnar, Mangelsdorf, Kestenbaum, Lang, & Larson, this volume). Again, based on the literature, different hypotheses could be formulated about these measures. If the infants have become accustomed to these types of interactions, they would perhaps be less stressed by them, as they appeared to be in the Field et al. (1985) study on prolonged maternal depression. In this case no elevations in heart rate or cortisol would be expected. If, however, the interaction situation is stressful, higher heart rate and cortisol levels might be expected. Unfortunately, because of the limited literature on these types of mother-infant dyads and the limited use of physiological measures in young infants in the early interaction context, no definitive hypotheses could be made.

Based on ratings of the interaction rating scale, depressed mothers and their infants showed less positive interaction behavior than the nondepressed mothers and their infants (see Table 7.3). This finding is not surprising given that at least three of the studies in the literature reported less optimal interaction behavior in *depressed* mother-infant dyads as already described (Cohn et al., 1986; Field, 1984; Field et al., 1985). In addition, the depressed mothers received lower ratings than the nondepressed strangers on most of the interaction behaviors. This finding would be expected based on comparisons between depressed and nondepressed mothers since the strangers were also not depressed. Less predictable were the findings that the infants of depressed mothers performed more poorly than the infants of nondepressed mothers when interacting with a stranger. And, they did not differ in most behaviors as a function of interacting with their mother or the stranger. These findings suggest that the infant's depressed style of interacting generalizes from interactions with their mother to those of nondepressed adults. An exception to this generalization is that the infants of depressed mothers showed more head and gaze aversion with their mothers than with the stranger. This is probably not surprising since the stranger was novel, and might, therefore, be expected to elicit more looking behavior from the infant. In addition, looking away behavior is more notably frequent during infants' interactions with their depressed mothers, suggesting that gaze aversion may be more stimulus-specific, i.e., more frequently elicited by depressed maternal behavior than are other infant behaviors (Cohn et al., 1986., Field, 1984).

Also less predictable was the apparent negative effect the infants of depressed mothers had on the nondepressed stranger's behavior. Even though the strangers were naive to the classification of the infants, the strangers performed less optimally with infants of depressed versus infants of nondepressed mothers on several behaviors including state, physical activity, vocalizations, contingent responsivity, and gameplaying. Consistent with the suggestion that infants affected the strangers' behavior were the findings that infants of depressed mothers were no different than their peers on head orientation and gaze behavior with the stranger, and the stranger, in turn, did not differ on these behaviors with the two groups of infants. Thus, as might be expected in interactions of this kind, there are strong reciprocal influences, a phenomenon which invariably confounds any attempts to determine causality or directionality. However, because there was no a priori reason to expect that a nondepressed adult would behave differently with infants of depressed than infants of nondepressed mothers, the negative influence of the former infants' behavior seems to be the most parsimonious interpretation of these data. The infants' depressed style of interacting appeared not only to

TABLE 7.3

Interaction Ratings of Infants (of Depressed and Nondepressed Mothers), Mothers (Depressed and Nondepressed) and Strangers in Mother Interaction and Stranger Interaction Situations (Interobserver Reliabilities are in Parentheses)

Mothers	Mother Situation		Stranger Situation		Effect
	Depressed	Nondepressed	Depressed	Nondepressed	
Infant Interaction Behaviors					
State (.82)	1.66a	2.66b	1.97a	2.52b	G^4
Physical activity (.81)	1.78a	2.66b	2.06a	2.61b	G^4
Head orientation (.92)	1.63a	2.28b	2.00b	2.30b	I^2
Gaze behavior (.83)	1.83a	2.55b	2.25b	2.52b	I^2
Facial expressions (.84)	1.63a	2.48b	1.81a	2.34b	G^4
Vocalizations (.87)	1.46a	2.07b	1.66a	1.83b	G^4
Fussiness (.95)	1.88a	2.59b	2.00a	2.30b	G^4
Summary rating	1.69a	2.42b	1.98a	2.36b	G^4
Mother/Stranger Interaction Behaviors					
State (.83)	1.51a	2.72b	2.59b	2.96c	$G^2 I^2$
Physical activity (.86)	1.32a	2.55b	2.13c	2.65b	$G^1 I^3$
Head orientation (.94)	2.70a	3.00b	3.00b	3.00b	N.S.
Gaze behavior (.92)	2.80a	3.00b	2.94b	3.00b	N.S.^{4}
Facial expressions (.81)	1.46a	2.55b	2.22b	2.48b	$G^3 I^4$
Vocalizations (.95)	1.32a	2.52b	1.97c	2.43b	$G^3 I^3$
Silence during infant gaze aversion (.82)	1.46a	2.20b	1.97b	2.09b	I^3
Imitative behaviors (.90)	1.05a	1.72b	1.35b	1.52b	I^3
Contingent responsivity (.83)	1.34a	2.45b	1.88c	2.39b	$G^2 I^4$
Gameplaying (.96)	1.05a	1.76b	1.19a	1.52b	$G^1 I^4$
Summary rating	1.59a	2.45b	2.13c	2.41b	$G^1 I^3$

Note. *Means bearing different subscripts (a, b, and c) are different at $p < .05$ or less revealed by post hoc comparison of adjacent groups. Higher scores are optimal for all ratings. Taken from Field et al. (1988).

G = group effect.

I = group X mother/stranger interaction effect.

$^1 p < .05$, $^2 p < .01$, $^3 p < .005$, $^4 p < .001$.

generalize to their interactions with nondepressed strangers, but also seemed to elicit depressed-like behavior in the nondepressed adult. This suggests that, as in a transactional process, the infants' depressed behaviors also elicit and reinforce the depressed mothers' behaviors.

The elevated heart rate of the infants of depressed mothers suggests that these infants were sympathetically aroused during their interactions with their mothers (Field, 1984). Similarly, their lower vagal tone suggests lower parasympathetic activity during these interactions (Porges, McCabe, & Yongue, 1982). Higher sympathetic arousal, and, conversely, lower parasympathetic activity generally occur in stressful situations (McCabe & Schneiderman, 1984), suggesting that infants of depressed mothers were stressed during interactions with their mothers. Surprisingly, however, heart rate was not elevated during their interactions with the stranger. This might have been expected since their behavior generalized to their interactions with the stranger. The greater amounts of looking at the stranger, most likely accompanied by heart rate decelerations (Graham & Clifton, 1966), could have attenuated the expected elevation in heart rate. Unfortunately, second-by-second behaviors were not coded. In a future study, time-locked behavior and heart rate could be analyzed to determine the correspondence between looking behavior and cardiac deceleration.

Elevated cortisol levels in infants of depressed mothers also suggest they were sympathetically aroused or stressed during these interaction sessions (Gunnar et al., 1984). Curiously, cortisol values of depressed mothers were no different than those of nondepressed mothers. Because cortisol levels are typically not elevated in chronically depressed individuals, this finding raises the possibility that these mothers had been depressed for longer than the postpartum period. This would not be surprising, as others have reported a very high incidence of chronic depression among low SES samples of this kind (Brown & Harris, 1975; Lyons-Ruth, Zoll, Connell, & Grunebaum, 1986). Another possibility is that the generally limited attentiveness and blunted sensitivity of the depressed mothers to their infants' behavior may have resulted in this being a nonstressful situation for them, thus attenuating any expected stress-related cortisol elevations in the depressed mothers.

For intervention purposes one would have hoped to have seen more optimal interaction behavior on the part of the infants of depressed mothers when they interacted with nondepressed adults. However, these data suggest a persistence in *depressed* interaction behavior across interaction partners for infants of depressed mothers as early as 3-months-of-age, at least in these brief interactions. It is not clear whether the infants' depressed affect persists or would change if the mothers' depression subsided, and it is also unclear how this behavior develops in the infant. We have speculated elsewhere that the infant may be depressed from birth via genetic and/or perinatal factors, as in a temperament trait. The infant may then exhibit a pattern of depressed behavior that elicits a predictable set of responses from both the mothers and strangers. Neonatal data on infants, such as those reported in Field et al. (1985) are essential to determine what role the infant might have in the developing of interaction patterns observed in depressed mothers and their infants.

Alternatively, infants' depressed behavior may derive from mothers modeling depressed behavior and the infants, in turn, mimicking the behavior, as in a social learning process (Field, 1984). It may also derive from limited stimulation and arousal modulation provided by the mother, as in stimulus deprivation related depression. The infant may develop a learned helplessness or passive coping style in the face of repeatedly unresponsive maternal behavior. Finally, a related interpretation is offered by Tronick and Gianino (1986).

> Eventually, the infants' accumulation of interactive experience with the depressed mother — and, in particular, the continued "success" his or her self-directed behaviors have in reducing the intensity and acuteness of the negative affect — have a structural effect. The infants' self-directed behaviors will then dominate his or her style of interacting with the mother. In addition, the infant will develop a representation of self as ineffective and of the mother as unreliable. Once this representation becomes established, the infant utilizes it to guide his or her interaction with others, distorting those interactions as well. (p. 9)

Whatever the developmental origins of this behavior may be, the persistence of the infants' depressed style of interacting across interaction partners highlights the need for additional developmental and process-oriented research on this problem.

DEPRESSED MOTHER-INFANT ATTACHMENTS

Although early interactions have traditionally been studied in a mother-infant face-to-face paradigm, attachments have been studied almost exclusively in the strange situation (Ainsworth, Blehar, Waters, & Wall, 1978), a series of separations from and reunions with the mother as well as encounters with a stranger. The strange situation traditionally yields an attachment classification of an insecurely attached-avoidant (A-type), securely attached (B), insecurely attached-resistant (C), or variants thereof, and more recently a "D" type or disorganized/disoriented type of infant (Main, Kaplan, & Cassidy, 1985). Just as early face-to-face interactions between depressed mothers and infants have rarely been studied, infants of depressed mothers have rarely been studied in the strange situation context. Although the data yielded by those few studies that are in the literature on depressed mother-infant attachment classifications are mixed, they are suggestive of disturbances in the mother-infant relationship.

In one of the most comprehensive studies on the attachment of depressed mothers and their infant, Lyons-Ruth and her colleagues (Lyons-Ruth et al.,

1986) assessed a sample of depressed mothers and their 1-year-old infants in the strange situation paradigm. Although the same sample of mothers has been assessed in early face-to-face interactions by Cohn et al. (1986), (data already reviewed in this paper), and although they have not yet presented data on relationships between the early interaction behavior of these depressed mothers and their infants and their later attachment classifications, it would appear that attachment disturbances in these dyads may have had early precursors in their early interactions. Maternal depression assessed at the beginning and end of this study (6- to-18-month interval) by the Center for Epidemiological Studies Depression Scale (CES-D) (Radloff, 1977) was remarkably stable in this low-income sample (R = .73). Only nine mothers changed from the depressed to the nondepressed group or vice-versa over the time period studied, and those changes were evenly balanced between increased and decreased depression. In addition to the strange situation paradigm, naturalistic mother-infant interactions were videotaped at the home when the infants were 1 year old. Although both infant and maternal behavior were coded, the authors reported only maternal behavior in this paper. Several aspects of the mothers' interactive behavior toward the 1-year-olds were significantly related to the mothers' depression scores. Increasing maternal depression was correlated with increased maternal covert hostility and increased interfering manipulation as well as decreased flatness of affect in mother-infant interaction. Thus, higher maternal depression scores were related to greater affectivity, more covert hostility, and more interference with infants' goal-directed activity.

Despite the significant linear relationships reported between maternal depression and maternal interaction behavior, no linear relations were noted between maternal depression and infant attachment behavior. The incidence of insecure infant attachment did not differ among the depressed and nondepressed mothers, nor did the mothers' depression scores correlate with infant reunion behaviors in the strange situation, such as infant avoidance or resistance at reunion. However, when the incidence of insecure attachment was plotted by severity of maternal depression scores a curvilinear relationship was noted (see Figure 7.4). Lyons-Ruth et al. (1986) suggest that their data are very consistent with those of Spieker and Booth (1985) who studied a similar low-income sample and found that mothers of avoidant infants reported the lowest mean depression score while mothers of avoidant/resistant infants (a classification they termed A/C) gave the highest mean depression scores, with mothers of secure infants scoring in the middle-range. Similarly, in the Lyons-Ruth et al. sample, infants whose mothers reported the least frequent depressed symptoms and infants whose mothers reported the most frequent symptoms were about equally likely to show insecure attachment. Mothers, on the other hand, who reported mild to moderate depressive symptoms were more likely to have securely attached infants. Infants of mothers reporting the least depressive symptoms (potentially suggestive of denial) were more often classified as avoidant, while infants of mothers with the

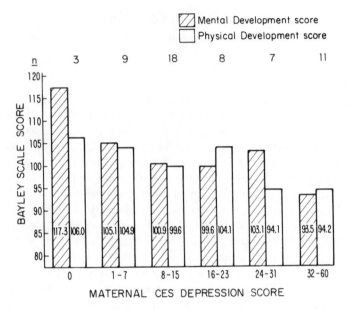

FIG. 7.4. Maternal depression and secure and insecure attachment in infants. Taken from Lyons-Ruth et al. (1986).

most severe depressive symptoms were more frequently classified as avoidant or unstable avoidant attachment. The unstable avoidant classification refers to behavior in which there is marked avoidance of the mother at the first reunion by proximity or contact seeking at the second reunion. In both the Spieker and Booth (1985) and the Lyons-Ruth et al. (1986) samples, mothers of unstable avoidant infants were more depressed than other mothers in the sample. As Cicchetti (1987) has suggested, these unstable avoidant infants may have been more appropriately assigned to the disorganized/disoriented category. As Main et al. (1985) have suggested D type infants may have experienced *depressed* mothering.

According to Lyons-Ruth et al. (1986) "It is not surprising that infant avoidance, including unstable avoidance, was found to be more frequent among infants of depressed mothers, since previous analyses had indicated that depressed mothers exhibit more covert hostility and since covert hostility was found to be related to infant avoidance, including unstable avoidance (Lyons-Ruth, Connell, Zoll, & Stahl, in press).

The increase in infant avoidance among the least depressed mothers is more puzzling but does fit with our hypothesis that mothers giving zero scores on the depression scale might fit Main's description of the rigidly controlled mothers likely to have avoidant infants. All three mothers giving zero depression scores had avoidant infants. A number of other mothers reporting low depression scores also had avoidant infants, but they did not show marked signs of the negative interactive behaviors characterizing both the zero-score mothers and the highly depressed mothers. Thus, the curvilinear relationship between insecure attachment and depression is consistent with, but not completely explained by, the maternal behaviors when the infants observed were twelve-month-old'' (pp. 75–76).

In a sample of older (2- and 3- year-old) children (N = 99), similar data were reported by Radke-Yarrow, Cummings, Kuczynski, and Chapman (1985). This sample was comprised of the offspring of bipolar depressive (manic-depressive) mothers (N = 14), mothers with major unipolar depression (N = 42), mothers with minor depression (N = 12), and mothers with no history of affective disturbances (N = 31). The mothers' diagnosis was made by a standard psychiatric interview, the Schedule for Affective Disorders and Schizophrenia (SADS) (Spitzer & Endicott, 1977). The mothers were also rated on the severity of this psychopathology on the Global Assessment scale (GAS) (Spitzer, Endicott, & Robins, 1978). In addition to the assessment of the strange situation behavior and attachment classification of the infants, the mothers' affective behavior was observed during an interaction with the child. The results suggested that insecure (A, C, and A/C patterns) attachments were more common among children and mothers with a major depression (bipolar or unipolar) than among children and mothers with minor depression or among children with normal mothers. Insecure attachments were more frequent in infants with mothers of bipolar depression than in those of mothers with unipolar depression. Histories of most severe depression in the mother were associated with A/C attachments. The mothers' emotional expressions and interaction with their children in situations other than the strange situation predicted patterns of attachment: Mothers who expressed more negative and less positive emotion tended to have insecurely attached children.

In the Rochester Longitudinal Study (Sameroff, Seifer, & Zax, 1982) similar groupings of mothers and their infants were observed in the strange situation at 1 year. Although the diagnostic group of primary interest was children of mothers who were schizophrenic (N = 29), three other comparison groups of infants were observed including those of mothers who received a diagnosis of neurotic depression (N = 58), personality disorders (N = 40), or no mental illness (N = 57). At the 1-year assessment of strange situation behavior there were no differences between the depressed and no-mental-illness groups in mother and child behavior as well as their interactions during home observations.

In a similar study using an adaptation of the strange situation, (Gaensbauer, Harmon, Cytryn, & McKnew, 1984), no differences were noted between 12-month-old infants of mothers who were manic-depressive, infants of mothers who were unipolar depressive, and infants of the control group mothers on attachment classifications. However, the infants of depressed parents compared with the control children were more fearful in freeplay and reunion, and sadder at maternal separation and reunion. Although there were no differences in the percentage of infants securely attached to affectively ill and healthy parents at 12 months (77% for each group), at 18 months there was a dramatic decrease in the percentage of securely attached infants belonging to affectively ill parents (14%) but not with the infants of healthy parents (58%).

These results are similar to short-term longitudinal findings reported by Egeland and Sroufe (1981). As part of a larger longitudinal study on children at developmental risk due to poverty, Egeland and Sroufe (1981) assessed infants' security of attachment at 12 months and again at 18 months for a subsample of infants whose maltreating mothers were "psychologically unavailable" (but not physically abusive) as compared to a group more at risk for maltreating their infants due to psychosocial disadvantages. For the subsample of infants of psychologically unavailable mothers, the number of securely attached infants fell from 57% at 12 months to 0% at 18 months. This compared to a slight rise from 67% to 71% in secure attachments among the control infants also in the same period of time from 12 to 18 months. Although the psychologically unavailable mothers were not formally diagnosed as clinically depressed, Egeland and Sroufe's (1981) descriptions of their interactions with their infants and toddlers resembled both clinical and research descriptions of depression in adult social interaction and in parental caretaking behavior.

In a review of these data Cicchetti and Aber (1986) suggest that maternal depression does not seem to affect seriously the attachment relationship over the first year as much as it does over the second year. They then speculate about why at least two of the investigations have reported secure attachments at 12 months but insecure at 18 months in infants of depressed mothers.

> Given the depressed mothers' seemingly paradoxical combination of unavailability and overprotectiveness, the new linguistic and locomotor capacities of the infant which emerged during the first half of the second year of life must be experienced by the mother as particularly difficult and challenging. As long as the newborn and young infant did not demand too much active interaction or availability, as long as the young infant did not tax the mother's capacity to support and endure her child's active exploration in the environment, the attachment relationship could develop in seemingly typical fashion. But when the older infant/young toddler begins to walk and talk, the stress on maternal caretaking capacities becomes too great and the basic nature of the attachment relationship is transformed from one of security to one of insecurity. (p. 103; see also Bermersderer & Cohler, 1983)

Cicchetti and Aber (1986) also raised the possibility that the "children of depressed parents only appear to be more affected during the second year of life rather than the first year because the researchers failed to measure the appropriate constructs during the first year or because the measures used in the first year were simply less sensitive than those used in the second year" (p. 103). It is equally possible that because the infants are walking and talking by 18 months, they may simply be showing more dramatic forms of avoidant behavior because of these newly developed skills. Nonetheless, the Lyons-Ruth et al. (1986) and the Radke-Yarrow et al. (1985) data on considerably larger samples suggest that infants of depressed mothers tend to show disturbances in attachment.

DEVELOPMENT OF DEPRESSION IN INFANTS OF DEPRESSED MOTHERS

As noted in the introduction, we believe that the depressed mother may predispose her infant to depressed affect. The question is *why* and *how* might we expect the infants of these depressed mothers to become "depressed" themselves? Although the limited literature on the early mother-infant interactions and the attachment behaviors of infants of depressed mothers suggests that these infants are showing depressed affect, depressed activity levels, limited responsivity to social stimulation, and withdrawal from attachment figures, and although these behaviors appear to generalize to other adults (Field et al., 1988), the question remains as to whether or not these behaviors chronically disturb the social-emotional development of the infant and lead to later psychopathology. Unfortunately, to date, none of the studies, with the possible exception of the Lyons-Ruth et al. (1986) study, has recorded longitudinal data that might show whether the same infants who are showing depressed behavior during early mother-interactions are also showing later attachment disturbances. However, if depression is conceptionalized, as it has been historically, as primarily a disturbance in affect regulation, and if affect regulation first develops in early infancy, and if the mother is the primary agent in facilitating the infant's development of affect regulation but is psychologically unavailable to the infant, then there is reason to believe that the early depression behavior patterns of the infant will persist in the form of chronically depressed affect.

In a model we have developed elsewhere entitled "Attachment as psychobiological attunement" (Field, 1985, 1987) we suggested that infants appear to differ in their responsivity to social stimulation from birth because of different genetic backgrounds and prenatal and perinatal experiences. Mothers learn to read their infants' signals (facial expressions, gestures, vocalizations, and gaze behavior) and modulate their stimulation to match their infant's individual stimulation/arousal modulation needs. The infant can then be affectively responsive and the interaction harmonious (both behaviorally and physiologically). Thus, normal attachment relationships could develop, thereby fostering the infant's affective development. Optimal levels of stimulation and arousal modulation are achieved then in an attachment or intimate relationship as each individual becomes attuned to the stimulation/arousal modulation needs of the other.

In mother-infant interactions the mother carefully modulates her behaviors to those of her infant to provide adequate stimulation and arousal modulation. In the optimal interaction the mother's and infant's affective behaviors and physiological rhythms become synchronized. If the mother is emotionally unavailable or affectively unresponsive, as is a depressed mother, the infant experiences acute or chronic disorganization, and the mother's and infant's behavioral and physiological rhythms become asynchronous. This is manifested in acute or chronic affective disturbance and changes in activity level, autonomic, and biochemical activity. This may occur because the infant may have been deprived either temporarily or chronically, of an important general regulator (Zeitgeber) of stimulation and behavioral and physiological rhythms (the mother), and thus fails to develop or sustain arousal modulation and organized behavioral and physiological rhythms.

A similar model, entitled "The Mutual Regulation Model," has been proposed by Tronick and Gianino (1986). According to these authors,

> the depressed mother, because of her own emotional state, fails to respond to her infant's other-directed regulatory signals and thus fails to provide the infant with appropriate regulatory help. This results in poorly coordinated actions, causing the infant to experience negative affect consistently and repeatedly. For a time, the infant may persist in attempting to repair the interactions, but, with each repetition of his or her failure, he or she more quickly turns to self-directed regulatory behaviors in order to cope with the negative affect generated by the interaction. The infant turns inward, away from social engagement, and increasingly utilizes self-directed regulatory behaviors that reduces sensitivity to inappropriate emotional feedback provided by the mother. (p. 9)

Thus, in the Field model the mother is considered a source of arousal regulation and in the Tronick and Gianino model the mother is seen as a source of affect regulation. In both models, the infant is viewed as needing help with arousal/affect regulation while the mother (depressed mother) is viewed as being unavailable to provide this help. Although it is unlikely that all infants of depressed mothers will themselves develop depression, it may be that some infants require more external regulation or do not have other sources of help to compensate for their mothers' emotional unavailability. The effects of the mother's failure to facilitate arousal/affect regulation are clearly evidenced in the disturbed interaction patterns observed in depressed mothers and their infants. Whether these early regulation disturbances predispose the infants to later disturbances in attachment or whether the attachment disturbances derive from contemporaneous maternal child care patterns, (e.g., the overprotectiveness that has been noted in depressed mothers of older infants) is unclear. Further, the attachment disturbances may relate to continuing disturbances in affect regulation. Disturbances in affect regulation have also been noted in older infants. An illustration is provided by Gaensbauer et al. (1984) who noted that infants of depressed parents tend to prolong the experience and expression of affect (i.e., they experience a slow recovery time from a disruptive emotion), as if the infants are carrying affect into subsequent experiences when its expression is most relevant to coping with prior experiences. Gaensbauer et al. report that these infants exhibit more fear in situations where one would normally experience less fear (for example, during freeplay and during reunions with the mother at 12 months) and they exhibit less fear in situations where more would be expected (for example, during maternal separations at 15 months). Although Gaensbauer et al. (1984) suggested that these data may provide evidence for a genetic component and etiology for affective disorders, they also caution that "the mechanisms whereby genetic vulnerability combines with environmental and developmental factors to produce the clinical picture are not well understood" (p. 223). Genetic vulnerability or prenatal conditions may contribute to the development, for example, of an infant temperamental trait such as emotional lability, but it would seem that the absence of external regulation from the infant's caregiver would significantly exacerbate any disturbed patterns already noted in the infant.

Some have suggested that the withdrawal behaviors noted in the infant of the depressed mother during early interactions (Tronick & Gianino, 1986) and the avoidant behavior noted in the later attachment/strange situation (Main, 1981) may be adaptive, or at the very least they may be considered coping behaviors. The withdrawal and turning away behavior of the young infant, for example, is viewed as adaptive in reducing infant sensitivity to the inappropriate emotional feedback provided by the mother (Tronick & Gianino, 1986). And, the avoidant response by the older infant is seen as a compromise allowing the child to stay close to the mother but without eliciting a rejection. As Main (1981) suggests, the avoidant response, in addition, helps the child to organize and maintain some degree of self-control over his or her potentially disorganizing angry feelings and aggressive behaviors. In this sense, the avoidant behavior can be viewed as adaptive. Although these infant behaviors may be adaptive in the context of relating to a depressed mother, by, for example, reducing the infant's sensitivity to the mother's emotional unavailability and rejecting behavior, they may not facilitate the infant's development of social-emotional competence. Cicchetti and Aber (1986) have raised that problem as a critical developmental question. "In particular, are certain developmental tasks which, if resolved in an alternative manner (i.e., one which may be adaptive although not competent according to generally accepted criteria), make the infant/child more prone to developing pathology in later life?" (p. 124). As they suggest, unfortunately there are no studies on how depressed children resolve the stage-salient developmental issues. But we would maintain, based on the data by Field et al. (1988) showing that infants of depressed mothers generalize their withdrawal and depressed-like behavior to adults who are not depressed, that the problem is one of developing a repertoire of social behaviors and affective responses that may be adaptive in the presence of a depressed mother but not so adaptive in the presence of peers and other adults. The same behavior that may be adaptive in the presence of a depressed mother may be incompetent behavior in the presence of other adults or peers.

As is often the case, the same data sets are being interpreted as having different developmental implications. Whereas we view the mother's depression as predisposing the infant to chronically depressed affect, others have a more optimistic view. For example, Tronick and Gianino (1986) suggest that a child's experience with a depressed mother does not necessary lead to psychopathology or negative developmental effects. Some effects may be positive. For example, an infant of a depressed mother may become exceedingly sensitive to the mother's emotional state in order to read her better and to regulate the interaction better. This sensitivity may be useful to the child in interactions with others. In addition, they note that many factors other than the infant's interactive experiences with the mother affect the course of the infant's development including other sources of social support. As Cicchetti and Aber (1986) have elaborated, there are vulnerability factors and protective factors that may be enduring and challengers and buffers that may be transient in development. These may provide self-righting opportunities by exposing the infant to the larger world of other adults and peers who may provide better models for social interaction behavior and affect regulation than the depressed mother. As Cicchetti and Aber (1986) have noted, "in any study of developmental psychopathology, one needs to look at the impact not only of the pathology on development, but also of development on the pathology" (p. 124). As is true of most other developmental phenomena and problems, the contribution of maternal depression to psychopathology in her offspring will only be made clear by longitudinal investigations of this problem.

ACKNOWLEDGMENTS

I would like to thank all the infants and mothers who participated in the research reviewed in this paper as well as my coauthors and research assistants. The research was supported by NIMH Research Scientist Development Award to Tiffany Field (#MH00331). Correspondence and requests for reprints should be sent to Tiffany Field, University of Miami Medical School, P.O. Box 016820, Miami, FL 33101.

REFERENCES

Ainsworth, M. D. S., Blehar, M., Waters, E., & Wall, S. (1978). *Patterns of Attachment.* Hillsdale, NJ: Lawrence Erlbaum Associates.
Beck, A. T., Ward, C. H., Mendelson, M., Mock, J. E., & Erbaugh, J. (1961). An inventory for measuring depression. *Archives of General Psychiatry, 4*, 561–571.
Bermersderer, S., & Cohler, B. J. (1983). Depressive reactions during separation period: Individuation and self among children of psychotic depressed mothers. In H. L. Morrison (Ed.), *Children of depressed parent.* New York: Grune & Stratton.

Brazelton, T. B. (1973). *Neonatal Behavioral Assessment Scale*. London: Spastic International Medical Publications.

Brown, G., & Harris, T. (1975). *Social origins of depressions: A study of psychiatric disorders of women*. New York: Free Press.

Cantwell, D. P. (1983). Family genetic factors. In D. P. Cantwell & G. A. Carlson (Eds.), *Affective disorders in childhood and adolescence*. New York: Spectrum.

Cicchetti, D. (1987). personal communication.

Cicchetti, D., & Aber, J. L. (1986). Early precursors of later depression: An organizational perspective. In L. Lipsitt & C. Rovee-Collier (Eds.), *Advances in infancy*, Vol. 4 (pp. 87–137). Norwood, NJ: Ablex.

Cohn, J. (1987). *Individual differences among depressed mothers and their infants during face-to-face interactions*. Paper presented at the Biennial Meeting of the Society for Research in Child Development, Baltimore, April.

Cohn, J. F., Matias, R., Tronick, E. Z., Connell, D., & Lyons-Ruth, K. (1986). Face-to-face interactions of depressed mothers and their infants. In E. Z. Tronick & T. Field (Eds.), *Maternal depression and infant disturbance* (pp. 31–45). San Francisco: Jossey-Bass.

Cohn, J. F., & Tronick, E. Z. (1983). Three-month-old infants' reaction to simulated maternal depression. *Child Development, 54,* 185–193.

Cytryn, L., McKnew, D. H., Bartko, J. J., Lamour, M., & Hamovitt, J. (1982). Offspring of patients with affective disorders. *Journal of American Academy of Child Psychiatry, 21,* 389–391.

Davidson, J. R. (1972). Postpartum mood changes in Jamaican women. *British Journal of Psychiatry, 121,* 659–663.

Egeland, B., & Sroufe, L. A. (1981). Developmental sequelae of maltreatment in infancy. In R. Rizley & D. Cicchetti (Eds.), *Developmental perspectives on child maltreatment*. San Francisco: Jossey-Bass.

Field, T. (1981). Infant gaze aversion and heart rate during face-to-face interactions. *Infant Behavior and Development, 4,* 307–315.

Field, T. (1984). Early interactions between infants and their postpartum depressed mothers. *Infant Behavior and Development, 7,* 527–532.

Field, T. (1985). Attachment as psychobiological attunement: Being on the same wavelength. In M. Reite & T. Field (Eds.), *Psychobiology of attachment and separation* (pp. 415–450). New York: Academic Press.

Field, T. (1987). Interaction and attachment in normal and atypical infants. *Journal of Consulting and Clinical Psychology, 55,* 1–7.

Field, T., Healy, B., Goldstein, S., Perry, S., Bendell, D., Schanberg, S., Zimmerman, A., & Kuhn, C. (1988). Infants of depressed mothers show "depressed" behavior even with non-depressed adults. *Child Development, 59,* 1569–1579.

Field, T., Sandberg, D., Garcia, R., Vega-Lahr, N., Goldstein, S., & Guy, L. (1985). Prenatal problems, postpartum depression, and early mother-infant interactions. *Developmental Psychology, 12,* 1152–1156.

Gaensbauer, T. J., Harmon, R. J., Cytryn, L., & McKnew, D. H. (1984). Social and affective development in infants with a manic-depressive parent. *American Journal of Psychiatry, 141,* 223–229.

Graham, F., & Clifton, R. (1966). Heart rate changes as a component of the orienting response. *Psychological Bulletin, 65,* 213–228.

Grundy, P. F., & Roberts, C. J. (1975). Observations on the epidemiology of postpartum mental illness. *Psychosomatic Medicine, 53,* 286–290.

Grunebaum, J., Cohler, B., Kauffman, C., & Gallant, D. (1978). Children of depressed and schizophrenic mothers. *Child Psychiatry and Human Development, 8*(4), 219–229.

Gunnar, M. R., Malone, S., & Fish, R. D. (1984). Psychobiology of stress and coping in the human neonate: Studies of adrenocorticol activity in response to stress. In T. Field, P. M. McCabe, & N. Schneiderman (Eds.), *Stress and coping* (pp. 179–196). Hillsdale, NJ: Lawrence Erlbaum Associates.

Kashani, J. H., Husain, A., Shokim, W. O., Hodges, K. K., Cytryn, L., & McKnew, D. H. (1981). Current perspectives on childhood depression: An overview. *American Journal of Psychiatry, 138,* 143–153.

Lyons-Ruth, K., Connell, D., Zoll, D., & Stahl, J. (in press). Infants at social risk: Relations among infant maltreatment, maternal behavior, and infant attachment behavior. *Developmental Psychology.*

Lyons-Ruth, K., Zoll, D., Connell, D., & Grunebaum, H. E. (1986). The depressed mother and her one-year-old infant: Environment, interaction, attachment and infant development. In E. Tronick & T. Field (Eds.), *Maternal depression and infant disturbance* (pp. 61–82). San Francisco: Jossey-Bass.

Main, M. (1981). Avoidance in the service of attachment: A working paper. In K. Immelman, G., Barlow, L., Petrinovich, & M. Main (Eds.), *Behavioral development: The Bielefeld Interdisciplinary Project.* New York: Cambridge University Press.

Main, M., Kaplan, N., & Cassidy, J. (1985). Security in infancy, childhood, and adulthood: A move to the level of representation. In I. Bretherton & E. Waters (Eds.), *Growing points in attachment theory and research.* Society for Research in Child Development Monographs. Chicago: University of Chicago Press.

McCabe, P., & Schneiderman, N. (1985). Psychophysiological reactions to stress. In N. Schneiderman & J. Tapp (Eds.), *Behavioral medicine: The biopsychosocial approach.* Hillsdale, NJ: Lawrence Erlbaum Associates.

McNair, D. M., Lorr, M., & Droppleman, L. F. (1971). *Profile of mood states.* Educational and Industrial Testing Service: San Diego.

Obrist, P. A., Lawler, J. E., Howard, U. L., Smithson, K. W., Martin, P. L., & Manning, J. (1974). Sympathetic influences on cardiac rate and contractility during acute stress in humans. *Psychophysiology, 11,* 405–427.

Porges, S. W., McCabe, P. M., & Yongue, B. G. (1982). Respiratory-heart rate interactions: Psychophysiological implications for pathophysiology and behavior. In J. T. Cacippo & R. E. Petty (Eds.), *Perspectives in cardiovascular psychophysiology* (pp. 233–260). New York: The Guilford Press.

Radke-Yarrow, M., Cummings, E. M., Kuczynski, L., & Chapman, M. (1985). Patterns of attachment in two- and three-year-olds in normal families and families with parental depression. *Child Development, 56,* 884–893.

Radloff, L. S. (1977). The CES-D Scale: A self-report depression scale for research in the general population. *Applied Psychological Measurement, 1,* 385–401.

Reite, M., Short, R., Seiler, C., & Pauley, J. D. (1981). Attachment, loss, and depression. *Journal of Child Psychology and Psychiatry, 22,* 141–169.

Rolf, J. E., Crowther, J., Teri, L., & Bond, L. (1984). Contrasting developmental risks in preschool children of psychiatrically hospitalized parents. In N. F. Watt, E. J. Anthony, L. C. Wynne, & J. E. Rolf (Eds.), *Children at risk for schizophrenia: A longitudinal perspective* (pp. 23–31). Cambridge, England: Cambridge University Press.

Sameroff, A. V., & Seifer, R. (1983). Familial risk and child competence. *Child Development, 54,* 1254–1268.

Sameroff, A. J., Seifer, R., & Zax, M. (1982). Early development of children at risk for emotional disorder. *Monographs of the Society for Research in Child Development, 47.* Chicago: University of Chicago Press.

Spieker, S. J., & Booth, C. L. (1985, April). Family risk typologies and patterns of insecure attachment. In J. D. Osofsky (Chair), *Intervention with infants at risk: Patterns of attachment.*

Symposium presented at the biennial meeting of the Society for Research in Child Development, Toronto.

Spitzer, R. L., & Endicott, J. (1977). DIAGNO II: Further developments in a computer program for psychiatric diagnosis. *American Journal of Psychiatry, 125,* (Suppl. 7), 12–21.

Spitzer, R., Endicott, J., & Robins, E. (1977). *Research Diagnostic Criteria for a Selected Group of Functional Disorders.* New York: Biometrics Research, New York State Psychiatric Institute, 3rd. ed.

Stoller, S. A., & Field, T. (1982). Alteration of mother and infant behavior and heart rate during a still-face perturbation of face-to-face intervention in T. Field & A. Fogel (Eds.), *Emotion and early interactions* (pp. 57–82). Hillsdale, NJ: Lawrence Erlbaum Associates.

Tronick, E., Als, H., Adamson, L., Wise, S., & Brazelton, T. B. (1977). The infant's response to entrapment between contradictory messages in face-to-face interaction. *Journal of Child Psychiatry, 17,* 1–13.

Tronick, E. Z., & Gianino, A. F. (1986). The transmission of maternal disturbance to the infant. In E. Z. Tronick & T. Fields (Eds.), Maternal depression and infant disturbance. *New Directions for Child Development* (no. 34). San Francisco: Jossey-Bass.

Tronick, E., Ricks, M., & Cohn, J. (1982). Maternal and infant affective exchange: Patterns of adaptation. In T. Field & A. Fogel (Eds.), *Emotion and early interactions* (pp. 83–100). Hillsdale, NJ: Lawrence Erlbaum Associates.

The Application of Developmental Knowledge to a Clinical Problem: The Study of Childhood Autism

Marian Sigman
University of California, Los Angeles

The understanding of childhood autism has benefited dramatically from the application of theories and methods developed in studying normal children. The classic studies carried out by Hermelin and O'Connor (1970) provided a model for this approach. In the 1980s there has been a flowering of empirical research carried out primarily in Great Britain and the United States on the psychological characteristics of autistic children. The investigators of this research were trained in a variety of disciplines including psychology, linguistics, and psychiatry but share knowledge and appreciation for the discipline of normal child development.

This chapter illustrates the application of normal developmental theory to the study of autism through a summary of the aims, methods, problems, and findings of a research program carried out by a group of investigators at UCLA. Corroborative and conflicting evidence from other research groups is interwoven in this review but I do not attempt an exhaustive survey of this fruitful area of inquiry. This review not only informs the reader about the syndrome of autism but discusses an approach to the study of psychopathology in children, which derives from and may also contribute to our understanding of normal development.

The developmental perspective is employed in this research program and in developmental psychopathology for two reasons. First, research of a particular disorder at a particular age period can be guided by understanding what tasks or competencies are important for the normal child to master at this age (Cicchetti, 1984; Sroufe & Rutter, 1984). The domains of functioning examined are selected on the basis of their salience for the developing person. Second, the use of a developmental perspective is critical for understanding and integrating the research results from a variety of studies. Without such a model, results tend to be scattered across domains and ages so that the stability and instability of strengths and weaknesses of the developing child cannot be conceptualized (Cicchetti & Schneider-Rosen, 1986). I return to a consideration of the developmental perspective at the end of this chapter.

INTRODUCTION OF THE CLINICAL PROBLEM

My interest in autistic children began in April, 1976 when one of the psychology interns whom I was supervising began to coordinate the inpatient assessment and intervention program with a young autistic child. This 4 1/2-year-old boy showed all the symptoms required by the then current psychiatric diagnostic system (APA, 1980) for the diagnosis of autism. His problems had been noted by his parents when he was about 20-months-of-age. His responses to adults were different from responses I had previously observed in young children in ways that I found difficult to characterize. While he was very affectionate to his mother, he also seemed unresponsive and, somehow, oblivious of her. He initiated no interactions with other children. He had no meaningful speech although he repeated statements and jingles that he had heard. He preferred to line objects in a row or to twirl the wheels on a truck and never seemed to pretend. Finally, we could not determine if he had delusions or hallucinations because of his lack of meaningful speech. His scores on a developmental examination were in the retarded range with his language score being even lower than his other scores. Developmental delay is characteristic of 70–80% of autistic individuals, but is not necessary for the diagnosis as there are autistic people whose intellectual abilities in every area but language are average or better. Furthermore, this little boy, with whom one could not converse, had an uncanny ability to read just about anything he saw including the name of the building where we met, the Neuropsychiatric Institute. This ability, graced with the latin name of hyperlexia, is held occasionally by autistic people.

The psychology intern, Dr. Stephen Greenspan, and I began to ask ourselves what type of concepts this child might understand given his lack of meaningful speech. For example, at the age of 4 years, even with his developmental delay, he would be expected to understand object permanence, the concept that objects continue to exist even when out of view. The research findings concerning object permanence in young autistic children were contradictory. Two studies showed that object permanence was achieved in older autistic children (Curcio, 1978; Serafica, 1971), one suggested that object permanence was delayed (Christ, 1977), while another (Bettleheim, 1967) concluded that this knowledge was held only with nonthreatening objects. We wondered how this child could develop language if he did not have the kind of object concepts considered to be necessary for language acquisition in normal children.

This question, prompted by a clinical case, formed the basis for the research investigation begun by Judy Ungerer and myself in 1979. The major aims of the research were: (1) to characterize the object concepts of young autistic children; (2) to determine the deficits in object concepts specific to autism; and (3) to portray the relation between object concepts and language acquisition in autistic children. This last objective was given particular importance by the findings that the autistic individual who had the best adjustments in later life were those who developed language skills before 5-years-of-age (Rutter, Greenfield, & Lockyer, 1967).

ISSUES IN DEVELOPMENTAL PSYCHOPATHOLOGY

Selection of Experimental and Control Samples

The choice of a sample became the next area of concern. Sample selection is a critical issue for studies in developmental psychopathology. The choices made concerning the sample itself, the basis for diagnosis, the nature of the control sample, and the matching variables all influence the research findings. In terms of the sample characteristics, we wished to study the youngest autistic children who could be diagnosed. The major reason for this was that the concepts to be investigated were those that normally develop in the first 2-years-of-life. A second reason was that we wished to study deficits that existed early in life. It seemed to me at the time that studies of older autistic children might uncover deficits that were not primary but occurred secondarily because of the child having been deviant through so many periods of development. This consideration still seems valid. However, certain deficits are not manifested until characteristics or abilities become common in normal children of a particular age. For example, to specify deficits in concrete operations one would need to study autistic children in the developmental age range of 5 to 7 years since this is when normal children typically achieve these abilities. Thus, studies of different age groups are needed to understand the whole range of strengths and weaknesses in autistic individuals.

One consequence of selecting a young group of autistic children is that the incidence of developmental delay is maximized since autistic children with better developmental skills are not recognized as early as children with poorer developmental skills. If one wishes to specify the deficits of autistic children of any age, the issue of developmental delay has to be addressed with the control group. If one does not do this, the characteristics identified may belong to developmental disabilities in general rather than to autism in particular.

These are several ways to address this issue. One way is to use a group of normal children matched on mental age with the autistic children. The flaw in the use of a normal sample as a control group is that the group is always much younger chronologically so that the experiences of the children are quite different. Another way to address the issue is to use a group of mentally retarded children. The advantage of a mentally retarded control group is that the experimental and control groups can be equated on both mental and chronological ages. However, mentally retarded subjects may have specific deficits as a function of retardation. An example that has recently emerged is in the ability to recognize emotion from photographs of faces. A number of studies have shown that affect recognition is impaired in mentally retarded individuals relative to their other cognitive abilities so that problems in affect recognition may not be specific to autism, as had been thought, but may be general to developmental delay (Hobson, Ouston, & Lee, 1989a, Maurer & Newbrough, 1987).

The inclusion of both mentally retarded and normal subjects matched on mental age allows this problem to be addressed. Given these considerations, we decided to use two control groups, mentally retarded children matched individually with the autistic children on mental and chronological ages and normal children matched individually on mental ages. This research strategy had an additional advantage. Autism is much more prevalent in males than females, with a ratio of 4 : 1, whereas mental retardation is equally common in both males and females. Our autistic samples have always been predominantly male but it has been impossible to find enough retarded children of the correct mental and chronological ages, who are also males, to compose a control group. For this reason, the normal group has been selected to contain the same number of males and females as the autistic group.

The characteristics of the control sample are also very important. The predominant form of organic mental retardation is Down's syndrome and this is certainly recognized earlier than any other type of retardation (Cicchetti & Beeghley, in press). Our autism samples generally consist of children in the age range of 3 to 5 years. Nonautistic developmentally disabled children in this age range also tend to have motor or sensory problems which makes it difficult for us to test them using standard assessments. Thus, it is quite difficult for us to locate enough mentally retarded children without Down's syndrome to use as a control sample. On the other hand, if the control sample is totally composed of children with Down's syndrome, the research comparisons may not reveal characteristics of autistic children so much as characteristics of Down's syndrome. To avoid this problem, half the children in our mentally retarded control group have Down's syndrome while the other half suffer from retardation of different origins.

The control group in any clinical study is supposed to be free of the disorder manifested by the experimental group. In some studies, this is easy to establish. For example, in studies of preterm infants, the maturity at birth of the full-term control group is easy to determine although matching the samples on other important variables, such as socioeconomic status (SES), is not easy. In other disorders, determining that the control group is really free of the diagnosis can be very difficult. In our studies, we have to ensure that the mentally retarded children are not autistic. The co-occurrence of autism and Down's syndrome is extremely rare and none of the 50 to 60 Down's syndrome children that we have seen has ever been described as autistic. In our previous studies, we recruited mentally retarded children without Down's syndrome from Regional Centers or the outpatient service at UCLA. Any child who was described as showing ''autistic features'' was excluded from the control group. In the current study, the same diagnostic procedures used for the autism sample are employed with the control groups.

Diagnostic Criteria

The issue of diagnosis is important for any clinical study. In developmental psychopathology, the specification of a group can be particularly difficult as diagnoses change over time. However, this difficulty also occurs in other fields. For example, the preterm infants of 32-week gestation used in our original studies at UCLA (Sigman, Kopp, Parmelee, & Jeffrey 1973) were quite young for surviving infants in 1971–1972 when the sample was collected. In 1988, preterm infants of 27-week gestation routinely survive because of improved medical care so the definition of a very young preterm infant has changed over this period.

Two diagnostic issues are particularly critical. One issue concerns the diagnostic system used for identifying autism. Several systems are available. The one being used clinically at UCLA when we began our studies was DSM-III (APA, 1980). The classification system was originally quite general, only requiring that certain problems in language, social, and behavior emerge before 30-months-of-age. On the other hand, the diagnosis of autism seemed much more reliable than other psychiatric diagnoses so the specificity seemed adequate. A revision of this diagnostic system, is now available, DSM-III-R (APA, 1987). The classification system is now broadened so that the definition of autism includes children with milder symptomatology. Children who would have been considered to have pervasive developmental disorders using DSM-III will now be diagnosed as autistic using DSM-III-R. The advantage of the new system is that the descriptors are more behavioral and, therefore, easier to determine. The disadvantage is that the disorder itself has been redefined.

A second issue with diagnosis centers on the individual who will be responsible for making the diagnosis. Clearly, this individual must be independent of the investigators. The diagnostician must be very experienced in the diagnosis of autism and, ideally, shown to be reliable in his or her diagnosis with other clinicians. This ideal cannot always be met, particularly with a rare disorder like autism where referrals are likely to come from several clinical sources. Furthermore, researchers can not always solve this problem by using their own diagnosticians, because referring clinicians may not want another clinician making independent diagnoses of their cases.

Our research group has used varying approaches to diagnosis. In the first study, the autistic sample was composed entirely of children who were currently or previously on an inpatient ward. Diagnosis was carried out by multiple clinicians involved in the case with an experienced psychiatrist and psychologist always involved. No member of the research group worked on this ward so diagnosis was always made independently. We had to count on the generosity of our colleagues for referrals, which was and continues to be remarkable. In our second study, most of the referrals came from the Clinical Research Center for Childhood Psychopathology which was in existence at UCLA at the time, the inpatient ward, or outpatient referrals. In the outpatient cases, the diagnoses were confirmed by one of the two clinicians who agreed to do this for us. The diagnoses of all the children were reconfirmed by the ratings of an advanced clinical psychology graduate student using the Childhood Autism Rating Scale (CARS) developed by Schopler, Reichler, and Renner (1986). In our current study, we are using the referring clinician's diagnosis, the CARS rating, and the Autism Behavior Checklist (Krug, Arick, & Almond, 1980). This checklist is filled out by an investigator during an interview with the parent.

Matching Variables

Almost any variable used in matching a control group to a clinical group can be defined in a variety of ways. In the field of autism, the measure and nature of intelligence have varied from one study to another. The major issue is whether to match the samples on a nonverbal performance scale, a verbal scale, or a scale that includes both verbal and nonverbal abilities. The argument for using a performance match is that the autistic children's abilities are underestimated with a verbal or general scale as the autistic children are always most deficient in language. The problem with this argument is that matching on performance ability is equating groups on the very best skills of the autistic group so the groups are almost sure to differ in other ways. The most conservative match is on language abilities. In this situation, the autistic children are likely to be somewhat better on performance tasks, particularly if these tasks include puzzles. Moreover, it is very difficult to match young autistic children with mentally retarded children on language abilities and chronological age since the mentally retarded children have to be severely retarded to have such low language skills and are, therefore, very difficult to test.

Investigators have approached this problem in a number of ways. Katherine Loveland and Susan Landry (Loveland & Landry, 1986) use children with specific language disabilities, rather than mentally retarded children, in their control samples. This can only be done with children from 4- to 8-years-of-age as specific language delays are usually diagnosed in this age period. Debra Fein and Lynn Waterhouse (Fein & Waterhouse, 1987) use normal children matched on a variety of tasks. Peter Hobson (1986) does separate analyses matching both on performance abilities, and for a smaller sample, on language abilities. We have occasionally used a similar approach, analyzing the results with a 2 factor (Language Level × Diagnostic Group) ANOVA. We use a general developmental scale for matching so the groups are equated on overall abilities.

Observer Bias

The most basic principle of research is that the observer should be unaware of the group membership of the individual subject. The more clearly reliable and valid a diagnostic category, the more difficult it is to establish observer naivite. For some disorders, like cerebral palsy, no observer could be unaware of the diagnosis as it is based on behavior. In the case of autism, the problem is slightly less severe. The mentally retarded children without Down's Syndrome are not clearly identifiable as different from the autistic children by observers who have less clinical experience with these disorders. For this reason, we have often used different tests and coders. Furthermore, we have used more molecular behavioral observations, done second by second, rather than molar rating scales. The amount of observer bias is minimized by coding discrete behavior patterns each second.

OBJECT CONCEPTS IN AUTISTIC CHILDREN

In our first series of studies, the object concepts of 16 autistic children, aged 3 to 5 years, with an average mental age around 2 years on the Cattell developmental scale, were examined. The concepts of the autistic children were contrasted with those of 16 mentally retarded children, 8 children with Down's syndrome, and 8 with other developmental disabilities, and with 16 normal children. The autistic and mentally retarded groups were closely matched on mental and chronological ages while the normal group was matched on mental age.

Object representation was measured using a variety of paradigms designed for studying object concepts in normal children. Sensorimotor intelligence was examined with the Casati-Lezine Scale, a measure that assesses object exploration, intentional use of tools, and object permanence. Because this scale does not include an assessment of imitation, the imitation scale of the Uzgiris-Hunt scale was also administered. Awareness of object categories was assessed with a sorting procedure, like the ones used with normal children by Ricciuti (1965) and Sugarman (1983). The children were given objects to sort on the basis of color, form, and function and their spatial and sequential behavior was observed. Functional categories consisted of representations of fruit, vehicles, animals, and furniture. Object category knowledge was also assessed with a visual differentiation paradigm in which the children were familiarized to a form, color, or functional set which was then contrasted with a new form, color, or functional stimulus. This procedure was used only with the autistic and normal samples.

The autistic, mentally retarded, and normal children had sensorimotor concepts appropriate for their mental ages (Sigman & Ungerer, 1981, 1984b). To return to the original clinical question, the autistic children were capable of remembering that objects continue to exist even when out of view. The autistic children could do a number of tasks including finding objects hidden successively under several screens, using strings to pull attached objects, using rakes to obtain objects out of reach, opening and closing match boxes, working a pivot, and even rotating a rake to use the opposite end to push a cookie out of a tube. The autistic children were no worse at any of these skills than the other children and all acted with intentionality and possessed some notion of the functional use of objects.

Object categorization skills were also similar for the three groups of children (Ungerer & Sigman, 1987). None of the children used the most sophisticated form of object sorting, which is to separate objects both sequentially and spatially into two groups. Most of the sorting was sequential touching of several members of one group or the other, and this was equally true for autistic, mentally retarded, and normal children. Objects were temporally handled according to function and form more than color. The visual differentiation paradigm gave similar results with the clearest differential preference being shown to the novel form stimulus. After the children had been familiarized to slides showing different pieces of furniture, both autistic and normal children looked longer at fruit or vehicles rather than novel examples of furniture (Sigman, Ungerer, Mundy, & Sherman, 1987). Thus, all the children seemed to differentiate on the basis of form, many could use color categories, and an equivalent number in each sample were aware of such functional categories as food, vehicles, furniture, and animals.

The autistic children were deficient in two regards. First, they were much less likely to imitate either a vocalization or gesture than the mentally retarded or normal children. This limitation in imitation has been reported in other samples (Dawson & Adams, 1984; DeMyer et al., 1972) and differentiates autistic children from those with other developmental delays.

The most notable characteristic of the autistic children was a real limitation in the functional or symbolic use of objects in play (Sigman & Ungerer, 1984b; Ungerer & Sigman, 1981). Play was observed in two different settings. One was an unstructured 16-minute episode with the child placed in the center of the room with a variety of toys and the mother and observer sitting in chairs at opposite corners. The adults did not initiate any behaviors with the child but did respond to the child's bids with encouragements to play. In the other observations, the experimenter sat opposite the child and encouraged play by handing objects to the child. If spontaneous use not was observed, the experimenter modeled and prompted particular play acts.

A coding system was employed, which had originally been designed to investigate developmental changes in the play behaviors of normal children in the second year of life (Ungerer, Zelazo, Kearsley, & O'Leary, 1981). These play skills emerge in the same age period in normal children as the sensorimotor and categorization skills described previously. Play is categorized in terms of the developmental hierarchy of simple manipulation, relational combining of objects, functional use of objects as they are conventionally used, and symbolic use of objects in which some element of pretend is involved. Functional play is subdivided according to where it is directed, to the object, self, adult, or doll. Sequences of play in which a behavior is repeated toward different object themes (such as feeding the doll, wiping her face, and putting her to bed) were also coded. The autistic children showed a variety of play acts, particularly in the structured situation. However, the autistic children showed less functional and symbolic play and fewer different doll-directed acts than the mentally retarded and normal children. While other studies had shown deficits in symbolic play (Riquet, Taylor, Benroya, & Klein, 1981; Tilton & Ottinger, 1964; Wing, Gould, Yeates, & Brierly, 1977), this investigation was the first one to examine the forms of play that normally develop early in infancy. The autistic children were lacking play behaviors while they were able to demonstrate other forms of representational behaviors that usually emerge in the same age period.

The deficit in primitive forms of representational play may reflect the same processes as the language disorder universally observed in autism. In fact, our studies have shown that the level of doll-directed functional play and symbolic play was associated with receptive language ability (Mundy, Sigman, Ungerer, & Sherman, 1987; Sigman & Ungerer, 1984b). This association is also true for normal children both concurrently and predictively (Ungerer & Sigman, 1984). However, the other object concepts, such as sensorimotor skills and categorization ability, bear no concurrent relation to language acquisition in the autistic children while these object concepts are associated with language skills in the mentally retarded and normal samples.

Given that language abilities and play behaviors were significantly associated in the autistic children, the deficit in presymbolic and symbolic play might be due to their poorer language abilities than either control group. In order to test this, a series of 2×2 ANOVAs (Diagnostic Group $\times$ Language Group) were run on the play scores. In all cases, there were no significant interaction effects and both factors, diagnostic group and language group, showed significant main effects. In other words, children with less language ability showed less mature play and autistic children, as a group, showed less mature play. The best illustration of the importance of play ability to the diagnosis of autism was that the seven *high*-language autistic children showed significantly fewer different functional and symbolic play acts than the four *low*-language retarded children. The diagnosis of autism does imply a deficit in symbolic skills over and above the deficit in language comprehension.

These findings raise an important question regarding why autistic children should be able to master certain complicated object concepts and unable to master others, both sets usually emerging at about the same age in normal children. Two explanations suggest themselves. First, the kind of representation used in symbolic play may be different than the kind manifested in sensorimotor skills and category knowledge (Wolf & Gardner, 1981). The ability to engage in pretend play may require that the child have some metarepresentational capacity, an ability to register that she or he is now operating in the pretend rather than the reality mode (Leslie, in press). Thus, the requirements for the development of symbolic play may either be cognitively more complex or more abstract and, therefore, may tax the abilities of the autistic child more than the requirements for using objects functionally. The second explanation is that symbolic development may depend on social exchange and social awareness (Vygotsky, 1978; Werner & Kaplan, 1963). If this is so, autistic children's limitations in social interactions may compromise their acquisition of symbolic skills. The impetus for our second series of investigations of young autistic children came partly from a desire to investigate the links between social behaviors and symbolic skills in these children.

SOCIAL INTERACTIONS AND SOCIAL AWARENESS OF AUTISTIC CHILDREN

The investigation of the social behaviors of autistic individuals has lagged behind the study of perceptual and cognitive processes. This is somewhat surprising given the profound and immediate sense one has that something is awry during a personal interaction with any autistic individual. In fact, as has been pointed out repeatedly, the original description of the syndrome was in terms of an inborn problem in "affective contact" (Kanner, 1943).

In our first series of studies, we did include one observation of the social responses of the children to their caregivers and a stranger. Following the 16-minute free play observation, a new individual replaced the experimenter. This was followed by a sequence of separation and reunion episodes, each of 2-minute durations, during which either the caregiver or stranger left or entered the room. The child was constrained from following the adults by a gate stretched across the end of the room. Otherwise, the child was free to do whatever she or he wished and the adults did not initiate interactions.

This observation was included to determine whether the autistic children differentiated between their caregiver and a stranger and reacted in any way to the comings and goings of the adults. This paradigm was used rather than the "strange situation" (Ainsworth, Blehar, Waters, & Wall, 1978) because we did not expect to be able to code the quality of the caregiver-child attachment relationship. We wished to have an observation in which caregiver-directed and stranger-directed behaviors could be directly contrasted and the behaviors of the autistic children compared to those of the control subjects.

The autistic children, as a group, showed a clear differentiation between their caregivers and strangers, directing more behavior to the former than the latter, particularly following the separation (Sigman & Ungerer, 1984a). About half the autistic children also seemed to respond negatively to the separation, either showing distress following separation or an increase in proximity seeking following reunion with the caregiver. We have replicated these findings with a new sample and find even clearer evidence that the autistic children respond differentially to separation and reunion with a caregiver and a strange adult (Sigman & Mundy, 1989). In our first study the social behaviors of the autistic children differed from the social behaviors of the mentally retarded and normal children in three regards, two of which have turned out to be important. First, they did not talk as much, which is not surprising given their lack of verbal skills. Second, they did not share toys with their mothers, either by lifting the toy for the mother to see or bringing it to her, as the normal and mentally retarded children frequently did. This observation has now been replicated in different settings with different partners and is discussed shortly. Third, following the last reunion, the stranger abruptly crossed the room, picked up the child without smiling or saying anything, released the child, and then returned to her seat. In the following 2 minutes, the normal children spent a fair amount of time standing next to their mothers and looking at the stranger; the mentally retarded children looked at their mother's faces, as if looking for guidance about this ambiguous individual. The autistic children went on with their behavior, showing no increased glances at the stranger or referential looks to their mothers. I return to a discussion of this observation in the following section.

The observation that the autistic children did not spontaneously share their experience with their mothers in the free play situation seems pivotal to our understanding of autism. In our second series of studies, we observed new samples of autistic, mentally retarded, and normal children in structured interactions with an experimenter and with their caregivers. The interaction with the experimenter was designed to measure the children's initiations and responses in three different forms of social interaction (Seibert, Hogan, & Mundy, 1982; Mundy, Seibert, & Hogan, 1984). In one form, the child and experimenter were involved in a social game such as tickling, singing a song, or playing with a ball. In the second, the experimenter directed the child's behavior with respect to an object, such as saying "Give it to me," and holding out his hand or the child was observed directing verbally or gesturally the behavior of the experimenter. For example, the child might hand a wind-up toy, which had wound-down, back to the experimenter to rewind or point to a toy out of reach for the experimenter to retrieve for the child. The third type of interaction involved joint attention between the child and adult with respect to an object. For example, the experimenter pointed at a picture hanging on the wall and the child's eyes followed the point or the child might show and give a toy to the experimenter or might alternate looking between the experimenter and a novel windup toy as the toy was flipping around on the tabletop.

The autistic children showed markedly less sharing of attention with the experimenter during the episodes included to measure joint attention than the mentally retarded and normal children (Mundy, Sigman, Ungerer, & Sherman, 1986). They did not demonstrate the frequent glances at the experimenter's face during an active novel event, nor did they show objects or point to objects that were within reach as frequently as did children in the other groups. On the other hand, they did participate in the two other types of social interaction. Thus, they seemed as ready to participate in social games and respond to gestures of request as did the mentally retarded and normal children.

The interactions between the autistic children and a parent were also deficient in shared attention (Sigman, Mundy, Sherman, & Ungerer, 1986). In this study, the parent was given a set of tasks to do with the child including play with a group of toys, doll play, puzzle play, a social game, and cleanup. The social behaviors of the autistic, mentally retarded, and normal children were fairly similar. However, as in the unstructured setting described earlier, the autistic children did not share toys either by holding them up in the air for the parent to see or bringing them to their mothers or fathers.

This failure of the young child to share his or her world with the parent seems to parallel the lack of understanding of the information available to anther person shown by older autistic children (Baron-Cohen, Leslie, & Frith, 1985). Several other researchers have also found the young autistic child to be deficient in his or her ability to share another's point of view. Loveland and Landry (1986) have identified a specific deficit in the use of joint attention in their studies of 5- to 7-year-old autistic children who were contrasted with verbal-ability-matched children with developmental language disorders. Several other samples of autistic children have been shown to point less to external events, follow points, or alternate looking between objects and people than mental-age matched normal samples (Curcio & Piserchia, 1978; Wetherby & Prutting, 1984). The pragmatic disorders often noted in the language of autistic children seems to result from their inability to modify their verbal communications to the needs of the listener (Prizant & Wetherby, 1987; Tager-Flusberg, 1981). Evidence is compelling that, at all ages and in both verbal and nonverbal communication, the autistic individual is limited in ability to see another person as an agent or contemplation (Werner & Kaplan, 1963).

To some extent, there is variability in this domain so that some autistic individuals show somewhat more awareness of the perspective of others than other autistic individuals. Those young autistic children in our study who shared attention somewhat more frequently with the experimenter were also more advanced in their language skills (Mundy, Sigman, Ungerer, & Sherman, 1987). This finding is consistent with the report by Sugarman (1984) who has suggested in a recent case study that person-object coordinated exchanges may be a prerequisite of language development in the young autistic child.

We had expected that those children able to share attention with other people would also be more advanced in object play skills we assessed. To our surprise, there were few significant associations between the nonverbal communication and play skills. The children who showed more sophisticated play were not necessarily the children with more awareness of others. Language acquisition seemed to have correlates in two somewhat independent systems in the autistic child, symbolic representation, and shared attention.

While the fact that most autistic children do not frequently share attention with others has been established, the basis for this limitation is still unclear. Baron-Cohen, Leslie, and Frith (1985) have suggested that the autistic individual does not possess a theory of mind, implying a cognitive limitation in *knowing* about the social world. However, the young autistic child may not look up at another person to share experiences because it may not occur to the child that others would want to share experiences or that this attentional/affective sharing would be satisfying in any way.

In the normal infant, joint attention evolves out of an earlier stage in which the infants and caregivers engage in face-to-face interaction. During this phase of "affective reciprocity" (Adamson & Bakeman, 1982) or "primary intersubjectivity" (Trevarthan, 1979), there is much sharing of affect and attention without the infant's awareness of the differentiation of the self and other. After 6-months-of-age, infants move from a focus on face-to-face interaction to interest in objects external to the dyad. In this phase of "secondary intersubjectivity" (Trevarthan, 1979), communication changes to a two-person interchange regarding a third event. This development reflects the infant's changing awareness that others can see and are interested in what they see (Rheingold, Hay, & West, 1976).

The limitation in the autistic child's ability to manifest secondary intersubjectivity may have two bases. First, the disorder may simply not appear until this stage so that the infant develops primary intersubjectivity but not secondary intersubjectivity. Second, the autistic child may be unable to engage in face-to-face mutual interaction or may do so with limited attention and affect. In this case, the disorder in secondary intersubjectivity may be secondary to a deficit in intersubjectivity itself, something like an inborn disorder in affective contact.

The direct evidence to decide between these alternative hypotheses is unavailable because autism cannot be diagnosed until 2- to 3-years-of age. The children whom we see at 3 to 5 years do participate in affective interchanges, but this may have been late in developing. The only kind of evidence now available would come from home movies of infants made before the children were diagnosed. Kubicek (1980) has shown that the social interchanges of a twin later diagnosed as autistic were characterized by neutral facial expression, lack of eye-contact, and rigid posturing as compared to the social interchanges of his normal twin brother. On the other hand, these characteristics may have been due to developmental delay rather than autism since this child is likely to have been mentally retarded as well as autistic. The confounding of developmental delay and autism in studies taken from home movies and videos limits the conclusions to be drawn from this source of evidence.

Although the hypothesis that the earliest deficit is in affective sharing cannot be tested directly, the way in which autistic children show affect and respond to affectively arousing situations and the emotional displays of others can be investigated. Our current line of research has drawn from the theories and methods developed recently on affective responsiveness of normal infants to study affective expression in autistic children.

AFFECTIVE RESPONSIVENESS OF AUTISTIC CHILDREN

The majority of studies on affect in autistic individuals have focused on the ability to discriminate between the affects shown by others. Peter Hobson (1983, 1984, 1986) has done a series of studies in which he has shown that autistic individuals have more difficulty than mentally retarded individuals in matching videotaped segments or pictures of gestures, vocalizations, or contexts to drawn or photographed pictures of facial expressions. However, in his most recent study (Hobson & Lee, 1988), autistic individuals matched on receptive language ability with mentally retarded individuals were as able to match photographs on affect as the control subjects if the whole face was available to them although their performance declined when the mouth and forehead were covered. Similarly, Fein and Waterhouse (1987) have found that children with pervasive developmental disabilities were slightly less able to match photographs on the basis of facial affect than a control sample equated on performance abilities. However, the PDD children performed no worse than a control group of equivalent receptive language abilities. In line with this, Szatmari (1986) has reported that a group of mildly autistic, nonretarded adults had little difficulty in comprehending emotional content in faces.

The evidence is strong that autistic people do not attend to faces or process information from faces in the same way as other people and may respond to them simply like perceptual patterns. First, autistic children show superior performance in recognizing faces shown upside down (Langdell, 1981; Hobson, & Lee, 1988). They tend to use the lower portion of the face in recognizing peers in contrast to normal children who use the upper portion (Langdell, 1978). Furthermore, when given a choice as to which matching cue to use, autistic children tend to use accessories (such as hats) rather than facial expression or the sex of the subject (Jennings, 1973; Weeks & Hobson, 1987). Finally, autistic children are less able to show an affect when asked to do so or imitate an affect shown by another person (Langdell, 1981).

The evidence seems clear that autistic people do not process affective and facial stimuli in the same way as others. However, this may be a comprehension problem as much as a deficit in affective contact. If the autistic individual does not see the other person as having feelings and thoughts, then facial expressions may not have any meaning as indicators of these feelings and thoughts, and the face may be treated like any other visual stimulus.

Another approach to studying affect is to observe the child's affective responses in a variety of situations. Langdell (1981) surveyed teachers and house-parents who reported that autistic children showed a range of emotions, including all affects except surprise. However, their affect was reported to be either flat or extreme and not contingent to the situation. Another study showed that the vocal responses of autistic children were idiosyncratic unlike those of normal infants and mentally retarded children which could be understood by people who did not know the children (Ricks & Wing, 1975).

Only a few studies have been done in which the children's spontaneous facial expressions have been observed and coded. The emotional displays of autistic children as they look in the mirror have been observed (Neuman & Hill, 1978; Spiker & Ricks, 1984). While these children show remarkably good self-recognition, giving clear identification of a change in their own image when rouge is put on their noses, they show much less positive affect and self-consciousness than control children. In one of the few studies of social interchange, autistic children between 2- to 4-years-of-age were observed to show fewer intervals of affect, positive or negative, and less positive affect overall when interacting with a familiar adult than mentally retarded controls (Snow, Hertzig, & Shapiro, 1987). They tended to show affect that was less partner-related than the MR children.

We are currently involved in microanalytic coding of the affect shown by our subjects during the interaction with the experimenter described earlier. Overall, the autistic children show similar patterns of affect in that they spend most of the interaction in positive or neutral affective states (Yirmiya, Kasari, Sigman, & Mundy, in press). There is a tendency for the autistic children to show less positive affect than the children in the other groups, but the difference is not statistically significant. The autistic children show more combinations of expressions and somewhat more negative affect although the total amount of negative affect is very low for the autistic children. The clarity of emotional signals is low for a portion of the autistic group. Several of the children showed very unusual blends of incongruent affects in different parts of the face. Even though these expressions are fleeting, any incongruent blend may provide a very startling signal to the social partner that something is amiss in the affective interchange. Overall, then, the affective displays of the autistic children were like those of the other children but more of the autistic children showed negative affect in a situation that was largely positive for the other children and some of the autistic children showed very peculiar, if fleeting, blends of facial affect.

Identification of facial expressions in one situation furnishes limited information. For this reason, our current research investigates the responses of autistic children to situations chosen to elicit particular affects of happiness, sadness, pride, and surprise in children. Empathetic responses to the experimenter and parent showing distress or discomfort are also observed. Finally, we are investigating the autistic children's tendency to use the affective signals of the experimenter and parent to guide their behavior in an ambiguous situation.

DISCUSSION

The issues raised by the assessment and intervention with one little boy have drawn us into investigations of the cognitive, social, and affective functions of autistic children. The theories and methods used to address the clinical issues have been drawn from the study of the development of normal children and the ways in which one achievement seems to depend on another for the normal child. To return to the original clinical case described at the beginning of this paper, we can now say something about this child's concepts, both social and nonsocial, as well as his social and emotional responses. First, at 4 years with a developmental age of about 2 years, he was most likely capable of object permanence and probably possessed considerable knowledge of percepts and objects. While he undoubtably differentiated his mother from other people and used her to fulfill his requests and needs, even occasionally his need for comfort, he had little understanding of his mother as a person with a viewpoint that could be shared. His affective responses to other people were usually appropriate for his developmental level except that he may have showed more negative and incongruous emotion, perhaps because other people were so confusing to him. His greatest deficit was in social concepts, possibly because social understanding is so complex and abstract, possibly because social understanding requires the ability to share one's emotional experiences with others, which this boy either was not born with or did not develop. Finally, his lack of symbolic play and shared perspective may have crippled his language acquisition as he had limited social needs to communicate and few of the symbols to do so. This suggests a direction for intervention with autistic children.

The aim of this research program has been to specify the developmental distortion in autism at the youngest age that children can be reliably diagnosed across a variety of domains. In some ways, the research findings can be described best using the model of infant development proposed by Daniel Stern in his book, *The Interpersonal World of the Infant*. Stern (1985) traces the development of the infant's sense of self through four stages.

In the earliest period, the infant has only subjective experiences of various organizations in formation. Through a variety of perceptual processes, the infant begins to distill and organize the abstract global qualities of experience. This domain of emergent organization remains active during the formative period of each of the subsequent domains of sense of self.

During the period from 2- to 7-months, the infant begins to form the sense of a core self and a core other. Four basic experiences are integrated to form a core self. These experiences consist of a some impression of coherence among the infant's own experiences and behaviors, a sense of affects as belonging to the infant, some memory of the self over a brief period of time, and a beginning view of the self as an agent of action. These experiences are available to the infant as part of the intense social interactions that characterize this period of development. A sense of the core other develops at the same time through the infant's experiences of being with another person who regulates the infant's affect, attention, somatic state, or cognitive engagement. The experience of being with a self-regulating other leads the infant to construct the sense of an evoked companion or a working model of relationships.

The sense of subjective self emerges between 7- to 9-months-of-age. As Stern (1985) describes, "the next quantum leap in the sense of self occurs when the infant discovers that he or she has a mind and that other people have minds as well . . . Infants gradually come upon the momentous realization that inner subjective experiences, the subject matter of the mind, are potentially shareable with someone else" (p. 124). The domain of intersubjective relatedness involves not only a sharing of intentions and motives but also of interpersonal activation experiences which include changes in states of arousal and affect. This sharing of interpersonal activation experiences, called affective attunement by Stern, leads the infant to sense forms of feelings where the subjective state of another is a referent. Behaviors of others can then be read as recognizable signifiers of inner state.

The sense of verbal self emerges around 15- to 18-months. The child's ability to coordinate schemas with external actions or words allows the child to make the self an object of reflection, engage in symbolic actions, and acquire language. The infant can then negotiate shared meaning with another about personal knowledge.

Earlier research on autism implied that autistic individuals have an impaired sense of verbal self since disorders of language are universal (Rutter, 1978). The contribution of the current set of studies has been to demonstrate that the young autistic child does not develop an intersubjective self. The autistic child has only a partial realization that inner subjective experiences are potentially shareable with someone else. Inner subjective experiences may not be shared with others because autistic children do not recognize that others have minds or autistic children may not recognize that others have minds because they are unable to attune affectively. Whatever the direction of effects, the autistic child shows a distorted sense of self at a level of development that should have occurred at 7–9 months.

The emergent self appears to have developed adequately in most autistic children. It is unclear whether the autistic child forms a core self and core other. Autistic individual do seem able to differentiate between themselves and others and seem to show a coherence in their sense of themselves. They are able to use themselves and others as agents of action. They demonstrate that they have memories of themselves in action. The evidence we have presented on social reciprocity and response to separation from the caregiver suggests that the autistic child may have some ability to form limited working models of internalized relationships. Thus, development of the core self and core other may proceed normally and the major developmental distortion in autism may be in the intersubjective self.

The failure of autistic children to form an intersubjective self may be based on cognitive or affective deficits. Stern stresses the importance of amodal information processing for self-development. Perhaps, the autistic individual is limited in the capacity for amodal information processing. Altneratively, the lack of affective attunement may be central and this may be due to some inherent affective unresponsiveness. Whatever the cause, the central task of development for the normal 7- to 9-month-old is not mastered competently by the autistic child.

The developmental perspective used in this research program has been described as the organizational approach (Cicchetti & Schneider-Rosen, 1986; Sroufe, 1979). Normal development is conceived of as a series of interlocking social, emotional, and cognitive competencies which are integrated into current modes of functioning. Pathological development is conceived of as a lack of integration of social, emotional, and cognitive competencies that are important to achieving adaptation at a particular developmental level. Because early structures often are incorporated into later structures, an early deviation or disturbance in functioning may ultimately cause much larger disturbances to emerge. On the other hand, an isomorphism in functioning across ages is not necessary. A variety of inherent characteristics of the child and qualities of the caregiving environment may alter the developmental trajectory. Furthermore, the requirements for adaptation change at different levels of development so that the child who appeared quite disordered at one age may adapt successfully at another.

The task, then, for the developmental psychopathologist, is to investigate the nature of the child's adjustment in the social, emotional, and cognitive domains at one age period and determine the relations between this level of adjustment and subsequent adaptation taking into account the mediating factors mentioned earlier. Sroufe and Rutter (1984) have pointed out that in the case of pathological conditions characterized by a distortion of the developmental process (such as autism) the developmental psychopathologist would be concerned both to investigate the nature of these developmental distortions and to do so in a way that would shed light on the developmental interrelationships between different aspects of functioning.

In autism, separate social, emotional, and cognitive competencies appear to develop rather normally but the integration of these social, emotional, and cognitive competencies is distorted. The failure to develop a sense of intersubjectivity shifts the developmental trajectory so that social-cognitive and symbolic

qualit,
that have sig, clinical implic.

systems are compromised. The incoherence in the development of autistic children is in sharp contrast to that of children with Down's syndrome who largely show coherence in development (Beeghly & Cicchetti, 1987) except for their requesting behaviors and expressive language (Mundy, Sigman, Kasari, & Yirmiya, 1988).

The organizational approach suggests that an early distortion in development may cause much larger disturbances to occur. The failure of the autistic child to develop intersubjectivity seems to mark the rest of the individual's life. Even at older ages, autistic children do not show affective or referential gestures. Furthermore, the pragmatic disorders of language that mark the syndrome are evidence of the individual's inability to shift perspective. The organizational approach stresses that distortions may not be isomorphic over time. However, for the autistic individual, disorders at 3-years-of-age often closely resemble disorders at 13 years. This is not to say that there are never changes in the forms of the behavior. The social aloofness of the 3-year-old may turn into the social intrusiveness of the 13-year-old. The lack of understanding of how to approach another person may result in different social behaviors. However, the development of autistic individuals shows tragic continuities.

The transactional model is often invoked to explain the transformation in adjustment patterns of individuals over time (Sameroff & Chandler, 1975). Although there is controversy in the field about the amount of improvement that can occur with environmental interventions, generally, autistic individuals do not seem very changeable (Howlin & Rutter, 1988). Even with good caregiving (Kasari, Sigman, Mundy, & Yirmiya, 1988), the autistic child has a devastating disorder. Thus, the transactional model may have less utility for this form of psychopathology than it generally does in developmental psychology and psychopathology.

The final question to be addressed is what the study of autistic children has taught us about normal development. In some ways, autism can be considered the only real psychopathology of infancy. Given that the autistic child develops some core self and attachment to others but still is so limited in social understanding, the autistic child may show that healthy working models of relationships require not only secure attachments but a capacity for intersubjectivity. In other words, the positive working model of the securely attached normal child may depend not only on the child having experienced contingent and sensitive responsiveness from the caregiver but also having developed the ability to understand the viewpoint of others. The failure of the autistic child to develop an intersubjective self and a symbol system and the massive effects these failures have on later development point to the critical nature of these developments in infancy. This work questions the notion that all that happens in the infancy period is sensorimotor development and that individual differences emerge later in childhood. The autistic child shows us quite clearly that certain cognitive and social skills have to be achieved in infancy if the child is not to be severely and tragically handicapped.

ACKNOWLEDGMENTS

The research reported in this paper was supported by grants NS25243 and HD17662 from the National Institutes of Health and MH33815 from the National Institute of Mental Health. The research was conducted collaboratively with Connie Kasari, Peter Mundy, Tracy Sherman, Judy Ungerer, and Nurit Yirmiya.

REFERENCES

Adamson, L., & Bakeman, R. (1982). Affectivity and reference: Concepts, methods, and techniques in the study of communication development of 6-to-18-month-old infants. In T. Field & A. Fogel (Eds.), *Emotion and early interaction*. Hillsdale, NJ: Lawrence Erlbaum Associates.

Ainsworth, M. D. S., Blehar, M. C., Waters, E., & Wall, S. (1978). *Patterns of attachment*: A psychological study of the strange situation. Hillsdale, NJ: Lawrence Erlbaum Associates.

American Psychiatric Association. (1980). *Diagnostic and statistical manual of mental disorders* (3rd Edition), DSM-III. Washington, D.C.: American Psychiatric Association.

American Psychiatric Association. (1987). *Diagnostic and statistical manual of mental disorders* (3rd Edition, Revised) (DSM-III-R). Washington, D.C.: American Psychiatric Association.

Baron-Cohen, S., Leslie, A. M., & Frith, U. (1985). Does the autistic child have a "theory of mind"? *Cognition, 21*, 37–46.

Beeghly, M., & Cicchetti, D. (1987). An organizational approach to symbolic development in children with Down syndrome. In D. Cicchetti & M. Beeghly (Eds.), *Symbolic development in atypical children*. New Directions for Child Development, no. 36. Summer. San Francisco: Jossey-Bass.

Bettleheim, B. (1967). *The empty fortress; infantile autism and the birth of the self*. New York: The Free Press.

Christ, A. E., (1977, October). *Factors affecting the cognitive assessment of psychotic children arrested at the sensorimotor stage of development*. Paper presented at the American Academy of Child Psychiatry, Toronto, Canada.

Cicchetti, D. (1984). The emergence of developmental psychopathology. *Child Development, 55*, 1–7.

Cicchetti, D., & Beeghley, M. (Eds.) (in press). *Down's syndrome in developmental perspective*. New York: Cambridge University Press.

Cicchetti, D., & Schneider-Rosen, K. (1986). An organizational approach to childhood depression. In M. Rutter, C. E. Izard, & P. R. Read (Eds.), *Depression in young people*. New York: The Guilford Press.

Curcio, F. (1978). Sensorimotor functioning and communication in autistic children. *Journal of Autism and Childhood Schizophrenia, 8*, 282–292.

Curcio, F., & Piserchia, E. A. (1978). Pantomimic representation in psychotic children. *Journal of Autism and Childhood Schizophrenia, 8*, 181–189.

Dawson, G., & Adams, A. (1984). Imitation and social responsiveness in autistic children. *Journal of Abnormal Child Psychology, 12*, 209–225.

DeMyer, M. K., Alpern, G. D., Barton, S., DeMyer, W. E., Churchill, D. W., Hingtgen, J. N., Bryson, C. Q., Pointius, W., & Kimberlin, C. (1972). Imitation in autistic, early schizophrenia, and non-psychotic subnormal children. *Journal of Autism and Childhood Schizophrenia, 2*, 264–287.

Fein, D., & Waterhouse, L. (1987, April). *Social and nonsocial tasks in PDD and young normal children*. Paper presented at the symposium on the Development of Social Cognition in Autistic

Spectrum Disorders, Biennial meeting of the Society for Research in Child Development, Baltimore, Maryland.

Hermelin, B., & O'Connor, N. (1970). *Psychological experiments with autistic children.* New York: Pergamon Press.

Hobson, R. P. (1983). The autistic child's recognition of age-related features of people, animals, and things. *British Journal of Developmental Psychology, 1,* 343–352.

Hobson, R. P. (1984). Early childhood autism and the question of egocentrism. *Journal of Autism and Developmental Disorders, 14,* 85–104.

Hobson, R. P. (1986). The autistic child's appraisal of expressions of emotion. *Journal of Child Psychology and Psychiatry, 27,* 321–342.

Hobson, R. P., Ouston, J., & Lee, A. (1989). Recognition of emotion by mentally retarded adolescents and young adults. *American Journal of Mental Retardation, 93,* 434–443.

Hobson, R. P., & Lee, A. (1988). What's in a face: The case of autism. *British Journal of Psychology, 79,* 441–453.

Howlin, P., & Rutter, M. (1987). *Treatment of autistic children.* New York: Wiley.

Jennings, W. B. (1973). *A study of the preference for affective cues in autistic children.* Unpublished doctoral dissertation, Memphis State University.

Kanner, L. (1943). Autistic disturbances of affective contact. *Nervous Child, 2,* 217–250.

Kasari, C., Sigman, Mundy, P., & Yirmiya, N. (1988). Caregiver interaction with autistic children. *Journal of Abnormal Child Psychology, 16,* 45–56.

Krug, D. A., Arick, J. R., & Almond, P. J. (1980). Autism screening instrument for education planning. Portland, Oregon: AISEP Educational Company.

Kubicek, L. F. (1980). Organization in two mother-infant interactions involving a normal infant and his fraternal twin brother who was later diagnosed as autistic. In T. M. Field, S. Goldberg, D. Stern, & A. M. Sostek (Eds.), *High-risk infants and children: Adult and peer interactions,* (pp. 99–110). New York: Academic Press.

Langdell, T. (1978). Recognition of faces: An approach to the study of autism. *Journal of Child Psychology and Psychiatry, 19,* 255–268.

Langdell, T. (1981). *Face perception: An approach to the study of autism.* Doctoral thesis, London: London University College.

Leslie, A. M. (1987). Pretense and representation: the origins of "theory of mind". *Psychological Review, 94,* 412–426.

Loveland, K., & Landry, S. (1986). Joint attention and language in autism and developmental language delay. *Journal of Autism and Developmental Disorders, 16,* 335–349.

Maurer, H., & Newbrough, J. R. (1987). Facial expressions of mentally retarded and nonretarded children: I. Recognition by mentally retarded and non retarded adults. *American Journal of Mental Deficiency, 91,* 505–510.

Mundy, P., Seibert, J. M., & Hogan, A. E. (1984). Relationship between sensorimotor and early communication abilities in developmentally delayed children. *Merrill-Palmer Quarterly, 30,* 33–48.

Mundy, P., Sigman, M., Kasari, C., & Yirmiya, N. (1988). Nonverbal communication skills in Down syndrome children. *Child Development, 55,* 235–249.

Mundy, P., Sigman, M., Ungerer, J., & Sherman, T. (1986). Defining the social deficits of autism: The contribution of nonverbal communication measures. *Journal of Child Psychology and Psychiatry, 27,* 657–669.

Mundy, P., Sigman, M., Ungerer, J. A., & Sherman, T. (1987). Nonverbal communication and play correlates of language development in autistic children. *Journal of Autism and Developmental Disorders, 17,* 349–364.

Neuman, C. J., & Hill, S. D. (1978). Self-recognition and stimulus preference in autistic children. *Developmental Psychology, 11,* 571–578.

Prizant, B. M., & Wetherby, A. M. (1987). Communicative intent: A framework for understanding social-communicative behavior in autism. *Journal of the American Academy and Adolescent Psychiatry, 26,* 472–480.

Rheingold, H. L., Hay, D. F., & West, M. J. (1976). Sharing in the second year of life. *Child Development, 47,* 1148–1158.

Ricciuti, H. N. (1965). Object grouping and selective ordering behavior in infants 12- to 24 months old. *Merrill-Palmer Quarterly, 11,* 129–148.

Ricks, D. M., & Wing, L. (1975). Language, communication, and the use of symbols in normal and autistic children. *Journal of Autism & Childhood Schizophrenia, 5,* 191–221.

Riquet, C. B., Taylor, N. D., Benroya, S., & Klein, L. S. (1981). Symbolic play in autistic, Down's, and normal children of equivalent mental age. *Journal of Autism and Developmental Disorders, 11,* 439–448.

Rutter, M. (1978). Language Disorder and infantile autism. In M. Rutter & E. Schopler (Eds.), *Autism; a reappraisal of concepts and treatment.* New York: Plenum Press.

Rutter, M., Greenfield, D., & Lockyer, L. (1967). A five-to-fifteen year follow-up study of infantile psychosis. II. Social and behavioral outcome. *British Journal of Psychiatry, 113,* 1183–119.

Sameroff, A., & Chandler, M. (1975). Reproductive risk and the continuum of caretaking casualty. In F. Horowitz (Ed.), *Review of child development research (Vol. 4).* Chicago: University of Chicago Press.

Schopler, E., Reichler, R. J., & Renner, B. R. (1986). *The childhood autism rating scale.* New York: Irvington Publishers.

Seibert, J. M., Hogan, A. E., & Mundy, P. (1982). Assessing interactional competencies: The Early Social-Communication Scales. *Infant Mental Health Journal, 3,* 244–259.

Serafica, F. C. (1971). Object concepts in deviant children. *American Journal of Orthopsychiatry, 41,* 473–482.

Sigman, M., Kopp, C. B., Parmelee, A. H., & Jeffrey, W. E. (1973). Visual attention and neurological organization in neonates. *Child Development, 44,* 461–466.

Sigman, M., & Mundy, P. (1989). Social attachments in autistic children. *Journal of the American Academy of Child and Adolescent Psychiatry, 28,* 74–81.

Sigman, M., Mundy, P., Sherman, T., & Ungerer, J. A. (1986). Social interactions of autistic, mentally retarded, and normal children with their caregivers. *Journal of Child Psychology & Psychiatry, 27,* 647–655.

Sigman, M., & Ungerer, J. (1981). Sensorimotor skills and language comprehension in autistic children. *Journal of Abnormal Child Psychology, 9,* 149–165.

Sigman, M., & Ungerer, J. A. (1984a) Attachment behaviors in autistic children. *Journal of Autism and Developmental Disorders, 14,* 231–244.

Sigman, M., & Ungerer, J. A. (1984b). Cognitive and language skills in autistic, mentally retarded, and normal children. *Developmental Psychology, 20,* 293–302.

Sigman, M., Ungerer, J., Mundy, P., & Sherman, T. (1987). Cognition in autistic children. In D. Cohen & A. Donnellan (Eds.), *Handbook of autism and pervasive developmental disorders.* New York: Wiley.

Snow, M. E., Hertzig, M. E., & Shapiro, T. (1987). Expressions of emotion in young autistic children. *Journal of the American Academy of Child and Adolescent Psychiatry, 26,* 836–838.

Spiker, D., & Ricks, M. (1984). Visual self-recognition in autistic children: Developmental relationships. *Child Development, 55,* 214–225.

Sroufe, L. A. (1979). The coherence of individual development. *American Psychologist, 34,* 834–841.

Sroufe, L. A., & Rutter, M. (1984). The domains of developmental psychopathology. *Child Development, 55,* 17–29.

Stern, D. (1985). *The interpersonal world of the infant.* New York: Basic Books.

Sugarman, S. (1983). *Children's early thought.* Cambridge, England: Cambridge University Press.

Sugarman, S. (1984). The development of preverbal communication. In R. L. Schiefelbusch & J. Pickar (Eds.) *The acquisition of communicative competence.* Baltimore: University Park Press.

Szatzmari, P. (1986, October). *Social comprehension in Asperger's Syndrome.* Paper presented at the American Academy of Child and Adolescent Psychiatry. Los Angeles.

Tager-Flusberg, H. (1981). On the nature of linguistic functioning in early infantile autism. *Journal of Autism and Developmental Disorders, 11,* 45–46.

Tilton, J., & Ottinger, D. (1964). Comparison of the play behavior of autistic, retarded, & normal children. *Psychological Reports, 15,* 967–975.

Trevarthen, C. (1979). Communication and cooperation in early infancy: A description of primary subjectivity. In M. Bullova (Ed.), *Before speech: The beginning of interpersonal communication* (pp. 321–347). New York: Cambridge University Press.

Ungerer, J. A., & Sigman, M. (1981). Symbolic play and language comprehension in autistic children. *Journal of the American Academy of Child Psychiatry, 20,* 318–337.

Ungerer, J. A., & Sigman, M. (1984). The relation of play and sensorimotor behavior to language in the second year. *Child Development, 55,* 1448–1455.

Ungerer, J. A., & Sigman, M. (1987). Categorization skills and language development in autistic children. *Journal of Autism and Developmental Disorders, 17,* 3–16.

Ungerer, J. A., Zelazo, P. R., Kearsley, R. B., & O'Leary, K. (1981). Developmental changes in the representation of objects in symbolic play from 18 to 34 months of age. *Child Development, 52,* 186–195.

Vygotsky, L. S. (1978). *Mind in society: The development of higher psychological processes.* Cambridge, MA: Harvard University Press.

Weeks, S. J., & Hobson, R. P. (1987). The salience of facial expression for autistic children. *Journal of Child Psychology and Psychiatry, 28,* 137–151.

Werner, H., & Kaplan, S. (1963). *Symbol formation.* New York: Wiley.

Wetherby, A. M., & Prutting, C. A. (1984). Profiles of communicative and cognitive-social abilities in autistic children. *Journal of Speech and Hearing Research, 27,* 367–377.

Wing, L., Gould, J., Yeates, S. R., & Brierly, L. M. (1977). Symbolic play in severely mentally retarded and autistic children. *Journal of Child Psychology and Psychiatry, 18,* 167–178.

Wolf, D., & Gardner, H. (1981). On the structure of early symbolism. In R. L. Schiefelbusch & D. O. Bricker (Eds.), *Early language: Acquisition and intervention.* Baltimore, MD: University Park Press.

Yirmiya, N., Kasari, C., Sigman, M., & Mundy, P. (in press). Facial expression of affect in autistic, mentally retarded, and normal children. *The Journal of Child Psychology and Psychiatry.*

9 Schizophrenia: A Developmental Perspective

Robert F. Asarnow
Joan Rosenbaum Asarnow
Robert Strandburg
University of California, Los Angeles

This chapter examines schizophrenia from a developmental perspective. We describe two different, though complimentary, approaches to understanding the development of the schizophrenic disorders. These approaches feature the examination of: (1) "core" impairments at different stages of the schizophrenic disorder and, (2) a description of the "natural history" (i.e., chronology of symptom development, premorbid functioning and course) of childhood onset schizophrenia. We will summarize findings from these two approaches, which may help explicate how schizophrenic disorders develop.

The newly emerging field of developmental psychopathology emphasizes the importance of examining a variety of factors—genetic, constitutional, psychological, environmental, and sociological in determining the etiology of mental disorders (Cicchetti, 1984). In addition, the developmental psychopathology perspective by highlighting the issue of continuities and discontinuities in development, underscores the importance of carefully detailing the antecedents and course of childhood behavior disorders. Our studies of the schizophrenic disorders which are reviewed here have been framed within the perspective of developmental psychopathology. These studies attempt to provide a developmental analysis of the schizophrenic disorders.

Why a developmental analysis of schizophrenia? Our research programs were stimulated by the belief that there might not be a simple cause of the schizophrenic disorders. Rather, understanding schizophrenia may require elucidating how a genetically transmitted predisposition is expressed at different stages of development and interacts with the care-giving environment to determine both whether an individual develops a schizophrenic disorder and the quality and level of psychosocial development. A developmental perspective can provide both research strategies for identifying a psychobiological predisposition to develop a schizophrenic disorder and a conceptual framework for linking those psychobiological dysfunctions to key schizophrenic symptoms and associated impairments.

We first present a vulnerability/stress model for the development of schizophrenia which provides the broad context for our work. We then describe a research strategy we have employed to identify psychobiological vulnerability factors to illustrate how a developmental perspective can elucidate a critical issue in the study of the schizophrenic disorders. Following that, we summarize a series of studies directed toward detailing the nature of psychobiological vulnerability factors and psychosocial stressors, and elucidating the links between psychobiological dysfunctions and the phenomenology of the schizophrenic disorders in children who develop a schizophrenic disorder prior to 12-years-of-age. Finally, we discuss how psychobiological vulnerability factors and psychosocial stressors may interact to determine the onset and course of schizophrenic disorders.

VULNERABILITY/STRESS MODELS OF SCHIZOPHRENIC DISORDER

Our attempts to understand the development and course of schizophrenia have been guided by a vulnerability/stress model. There is currently a wide spread consensus summarized, for example, in a recent report by the Institute of Medicine/National Academy of Sciences (Elliott & Eisdorfer, 1982) that many forms of illness result from interactions of predisposing vulnerabilities of individuals and stressors. Vulnerability/stress models belong to the general class of diathesis/stress models of schizophrenia developed in the 1960s by Falconer (1965), Meehl (1962), and Rosenthal (1970). The threshold model of Gottesman and Shields (1982) is a variant of this general class of model. The increasing acceptance of vulnerability/stress models of schizophrenia results from the failure of simpler genetic models to account for the transmission of schizophrenic symptoms and from a growing recognition of the broad range of factors which appear to determine the likelihood of developing a schizophrenic disorder and which influence the course of the disorder once it develops (Zubin, Magaziner, & Steinhauer, 1983; Gottesman & Shields 1982). Vulnerability/stress models postulate that a genetic liability to schizophrenia interacts with aspects of the environment to yield a schizophrenic outcome. These models regard schizophrenia as a set of disorders in which the genetic liability is persistent (though the effective genotype is evolving), while the manifest phenomenology is episodic.

The specific nature of the genetic predisposition to schizophrenia may be quite complex. It is quite possible that the schizophrenic disorders are etiologically heterogeneous (Cloninger, 1987). Different genes (or sets of genes) may contribute to the liability to different forms of schizophrenia. In addition, there may be forms of schizophrenia (perhaps associated with early central nervous system insults) where genetic predisposition plays less of a role.

Figure 9.1, depicts a multifactorial vulnerability/stress model of schizophrenic disorder. Variations in psychosocial adaptation and symptomatic behavior are postulated to result from the interaction between: (1) enduring psychobiological vulnerabilities, (2) socio/environmental and biological stressors, and (3) the moderating effects of individual competencies and individual and family coping responses. This model posits that a predisposition to schizophrenia is genetically transmitted, but that only those vulnerable individuals exposed to certain types or levels of stressors will develop a frank schizophrenic disorder. Those individuals with the greatest loading of vulnerability factors, the least adequate coping responses and competencies, and the greatest exposure to stress are most likely to develop a schizophrenic disorder and are likely to have an unfavorable outcome should they have a psychotic episode. Conversely, those individuals with the least loading of vulnerability factors, the most adequate coping responses, and competencies with the least exposure to stress are least likely to develop a schizophrenic disorder and will have the best outcome should they have a psychotic episode.

This framework emphasizes the study of enduring psychobiological vulnerabilities as they interact with socio-environmental stressors. The putative psychobiological vulnerability factors we have focused on are impairments in certain aspects of attention/information processing (AIP). These AIP impairments may tap the "central integrative dysfunction" (Meehl, 1962) hypothesized to be the "endophenotype" for schizophrenia. In the next section we summarize a series of studies designed to test the hypothesis that AIP impairments may index psychobiological vulnerability for some forms of schizophrenia.

Stressors are defined as transient events that demand adaptive changes from the individual and that challenge the individual's current coping and competence. We have focused on the study of acute stressors, such as intercurrent life events, and more chronic stresses, such as particular patterns of family interaction.

Protective variables are environmental and personal factors that reduce the likelihood that a given level of vulnerability to schizophrenic disorder leads to manifest schizophrenic symptomatology under a given level of stress. We have studied two classes of potential protective factors. The first are individual competencies such as general intellectual abilities and social skills that can offset the deleterious effects of vulnerability factors on psychosocial adaptation. The second class of protective factors are the repertoire of coping responses the individual has available to attenuate the effects of stressors when they occur and to compensate for the effects of his or her vulnerability (i.e., impaired AIP) by, for

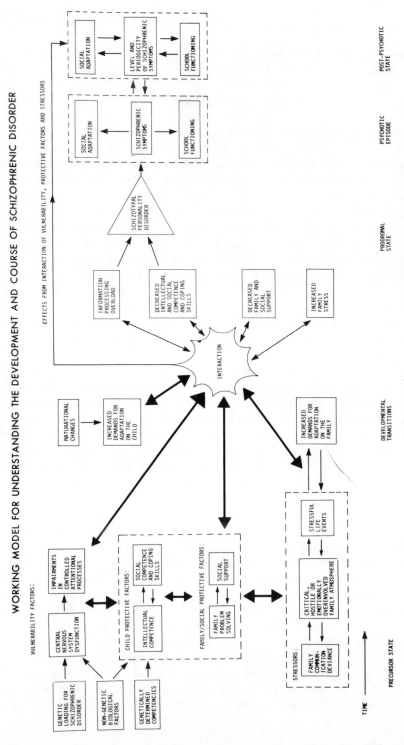

WORKING MODEL FOR UNDERSTANDING THE DEVELOPMENT AND COURSE OF SCHIZOPHRENIC DISORDER

FIG. 9.1. A heuristic vulnerability/stress model of the schizophrenic disorders.

192

example, learning to limit their exposure to social stimuli which may overload their reduced AIP capacity. Social support systems and family coping responses have analogous effects at the social systems level.

This model highlights the complex developmental pathways that need to be understood if we are to have a full understanding of the schizophrenic disorders. A key step in putting together the pieces of the "epigenetic" puzzle is identifying what the psychobiological vulnerability to schizophrenic disorder is. Identifying the psychobiological vulnerability to schizophrenic factors would provide a basis for determining which *individuals* are predisposed to develop a schizophrenic disorder as opposed to groups being statistically at risk. In turn, this would set the stage for determining how vulnerability may eventuate in psychotic symptoms. The next section reviews a series of studies that illustrate a research strategy for identifying measures that tap the psychobiological vulnerability to schizophrenic disorder.

THE CONVERGENCE STRATEGY—AN APPROACH FOR IDENTIFYING VULNERABILITY FACTORS

Schizophrenic disorders typically have their onset during the early adult years, between 18- and 35-years-of-age. The vulnerability/stress model described earlier predicts that prior to the onset of schizophrenia, during the prodromal stage of the disorder, there should be signs of vulnerability to the disorder. Similarly, subsequent to a full blown psychotic episode, during the postpsychotic stage of the disorder, there should be persistent signs of vulnerability in schizophrenic individuals. This view of schizophrenia has led to the development of an approach, the "convergence strategy" (Asarnow & MacCrimmon, 1978), to identifying tasks which index vulnerability to schizophrenic disorders. The convergence strategy is based on the assumption (see Asarnow & MacCrimmon, 1978; Cromwell & Spaulding, 1978; Zubin & Spring, 1977) that measures that detect impairments in individuals who share the trait of vulnerability to schizophrenic disorder, but who are in a different clinical state at the time of testing, are not merely reflecting clinical state but may be tapping the trait of vulnerability to schizophrenic disorder. Thus, we (Asarnow & MacCrimmon, 1978) have studied individuals during the three developmental stages of schizophrenic disorder—the premorbid, the acute, and the postpsychotic stages. Our goal was to determine if tasks could be identified that detect persistent dysfunctions in individuals vulnerable to schizophrenic disorder across variations in clinical state, and thus might index vulnerability to schizophrenic disorder.

We focused on attentional tasks as potential measures of vulnerability to schizophrenic disorder because of the prominence of attentional problems in the phenomenology of schizophrenia (cf. Kraepelin, 1919; McGhie & Chapman, 1961) and the demonstrated sensitivity of psychological laboratory measures of attention to schizophrenic impairment (see Lang & Buss, 1965; Neale & Cromwell, 1970; Neuchterlein & Dawson, 1984; Venables, 1964 for reviews). In addition, impairments in attention may lie at the interface between the biological vulnerability to schizophrenic disorder and the social dysfunction, which is an important clinical feature of these disorders.

A number of attention demanding tasks, particularly those which make extensive demands on AIP capacity (e.g., continuous performance tests, a digit span distractibility task, dichotic listening tasks and both simple and cross modal reaction time tasks), have been shown to detect dysfunction in schizophrenic patients and in nonpsychotic individuals who are statistically at risk for developing a schizophrenic disorder, such as the children of schizophrenic parents (see J. Asarnow, 1988; J. Asarnow & Goldstein, 1986; R. Asarnow 1983; Neale & Oltmans, 1980; Neuchterlein & Dawson, 1983, for reviews). We illustrate this line of research by reviewing studies conducted to determine if a partial report span of apprehension task taps a psychobiological vulnerability to schizophrenic disorder. (See Asarnow, Granholm, & Sherman, in press for review of studies of span of apprehension in schizophrenia.)

The forced choice, partial report span of apprehension task used in the studies below was originally developed (Estes & Taylor, 1964) to measure the amount of information people can extract from briefly presented (e.g., 50 msec) visual displays. This task provides an index of the efficiency of visual attentional processes by requiring subjects to indicate which of two predesignated target letters are present in arrays where the number of nontarget stimuli are varied. In a seminal series of studies Neale and his colleagues showed that hospitalized schizophrenic patients had a smaller span of apprehension than normal controls (Neale, McIntyre, Fox, & Cromwell, 1969) and nonpsychotic psychiatric patients (Neale, 1971).

To determine whether the partial report span of apprehension task taps vulnerability to schizophrenic disorder we first turned to the study of children at risk for schizophrenia. Our high-risk group were foster children whose biological mother was schizophrenic, but whose foster parents had no history of severe psychiatric disorder. These children had never been psychotic and were therefore, free of the effects of "stigmatization," medication, and institutionalization found in hospitalized schizophrenic patients. The high-risk group (see Asarnow et al., 1977, 1978, Steffy, Asarnow, Asarnow, MacCrimmon, & Cleghorn, 1984) obtained significantly lower scores than foster children without a family history of schizophrenic disorder and a community control group on a partial report span of apprehension task as well as the Spokes test from the Halstead-Reitan battery and a concept formation task. A cluster analysis of scores on the battery of attention tasks indicated that only a subset (cluster IV) of the high-risk children had impaired attentional performance. The high-risk children with impaired performance on the above tasks showed certain behavioral characteristics including social isolation, difficulties in fulfilling the student role, and difficulty in modulating aggression that had been found in retrospective studies to represent the premorbid state of schizophrenia (MacCrimmon, Cleghorn, Asarnow, & Steffy, 1980). They also obtained elevated scores on the schizophrenia scale of the MMPI.

As discussed earlier, if the partial report span of apprehension task is tapping vulnerability to schizophrenic disorder, it should detect dysfunction, not only in acutely disturbed schizophrenic patients and children at risk for schizophrenia, but also in schizophrenic patients during the post-psychotic stages of the disorder when there has been substantial abatement of acute psychotic schizophrenic symptoms. We therefore conducted a series of studies of adult schizophrenic patients during the acute and postpsychotic stages, as another test of whether the forced choice, partial report span-of-apprehension that discriminated between our high-risk and control groups was tapping a vulnerability to schizophrenic disorder.

In an initial study (Asarnow & MacCrimmon, 1978), both acutely disturbed and partially recovered schizophrenics detected significantly fewer target stimuli on ten letter arrays than did normal controls. The acute and partially recovered schizophrenics did not differ from each other. In addition, as can be seen in Fig. 9.2A, the acute and remitted schizophrenics showed the same level and pattern of performance as the subset of children in cluster IV of our high-risk study.

A subsequent study replicated and extended these findings (see Fig. 9.2B) by showing that another group of schizophrenic outpatients detected significantly fewer target stimuli than manic-depressive outpatients and normal controls on the five and ten letter arrays (Asarnow & MacCrimmon, 1981). The fact that schizophrenic patients, at least during the postpsychotic state of the disorder, could be differentiated from similarly stabilized manic depressive patients suggests that there is some degree of diagnostic specificity for span performance. Examination of the frequency distributions of the scores revealed that only a subgroup of schizophrenics were impaired on this task.

The preceding study was cross-sectional. It is possible that the cohort of partially recovered outpatient schizophrenics available for testing could have represented a subset of patients who had made the least adequate posthospitalization adjustment and were thus available for retesting. To determine whether the residual impairment found in this group might be a reflection of their minimal clinical recovery, we conducted a longitudinal study of schizophrenic patients (Asarnow & MacCrimmon, 1982). Patients were tested on the span task during inpatient hospitalization, when they were acutely disturbed, and 12 weeks later as outpatients. Schizophrenic patients continued to show impaired performance relative to normal controls (see Fig. 9.2C), tested at comparable intervals, even though there was significant improvement in both overall clinical condition and specific aspects of thought disorder over the 12 weeks. These findings corrobo-

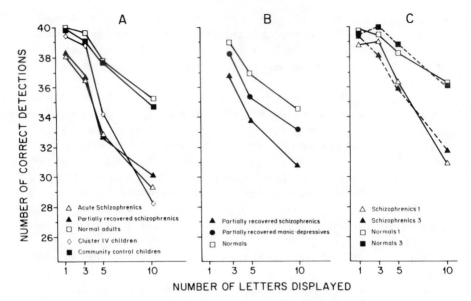

FIG. 9.2.   Mean number of correct detections of the target stimuli as a function of the number of letters displayed in span of apprehension task for: (A) Partially recovered schizophrenic and normal subjects from Asarnow and MacCrimmon (1978) and cluster IV and community control children from Asarnow et al. (1977), (B) partially recovered schizophrenic and manic-depressive patients and normal subjects from Asarnow and MacCrimmon (1981), and (C) schizophrenic and normal subjects retested over a 12-week interval from Asarnow and MacCrimmon (1982).

rated the results of the previous cross-sectional studies, indicating that the span-of-apprehension task is sensitive to schizophrenic dysfunction across wide variations in clinical state and thus may be a marker of vulnerability to schizophrenia.

Another test of whether the span-of-apprehension task is tapping a trait associated with vulnerability to schizophrenic disorder is whether it shows the temporal stability required of such a measure. We observed a highly significant correlation ($r = .72$) in the span performance of schizophrenic patients over a 12-week period (Asarnow & MacCrimmon, 1982). These findings were recently corroborated in a longitudinal study of 36 chronic schizophrenic patients (Asarnow, Marder, Mintz, Van Putten, & Zimmerman, 1988). The correlations on the ten-letter array ($r = .79$ over a 12-week interval and $r = .68$ over a 6-month interval) indicate that the span performance of schizophrenic patients is quite stable.

If the span task taps vulnerability to schizophrenia, individuals with no personal history of psychiatric disorder who show impairments on this task might be expected to manifest some of the clinical and personality traits characteristic of the schizotypic or psychosis prone individual. This hypothesis was tested by selecting subjects from temporary employment agencies who reported no history of psychiatric disorder and dividing them into groups with good and poor performance on the span of apprehension task (Asarnow, Nuechterlein, & Marder, 1983). Subjects who performed poorly on the span scored significantly higher on the schizophrenia scale of the MMPI, two indices of schizotypy (the schizoidia and schizophrenism scales), and an index of subclinical schizophrenic thinking (the magic ideation scale: Eckblad & Chapman, 1985) than the balance of the subjects. The poor-span group did not show generalized elevation on the MMPI, suggesting that there is some degree of specificity for the relationship between span-of-apprehension performance and scores on indices of schizotypy and psychotic-like experiences.

Some evidence that impaired AIP may be transmitted across generations within families is provided by a recent study (Wagener et al., 1986). This study found that the span performance of young-adult schizophrenics was significantly correlated ($r = .55$) with that of their mothers, none of whom had a history of schizophrenic disorder. Although these data do not tell us whether these correlations have a genetic basis, they do suggest that there may be familial transmission of impaired AIP (at least between male schizophrenic patients and their mothers).

In summary, the research briefly reviewed earlier indicates that the span task detects dysfunction in individuals vulnerable to schizophrenia and in schizophrenic individuals across wide variations in clinical state. This suggests that this task may tap the persistent (though subtle) "central integrative dysfunction" hypothesized to represent a vulnerability to some forms of schizophrenic disorder.

STUDIES OF SCHIZOPHRENIC CHILDREN

As already noted, the first onset of schizophrenic symptoms typically occurs during early adulthood. There is however, ample evidence that prior to adolescence some children present symptoms which meet DSM-111 criteria for schizophrenic disorder (Green et al., 1984; Russell et al., 1986; Asarnow & Ben-Meir, in press). Moreover, schizophrenia can be reliably diagnosed in children (Russell et al., 1986). Although childhood onset schizophrenia is rare, it may provide an opportunity to address one of the most vexing problems in schizophrenia research—the problem of heterogeneity. It is now widely accepted (cf. Cloninger, 1987) that the schizophrenic disorders are probably etiologically heterogeneous. Identifying more homogeneous subgroups, particularly ones with an increased genetic liability, would clearly facilitate attempts to clarify the nature of vulnerability to schizophrenic disorder. Similar to findings for a number of genetically transmitted diseases indicating that early onset of disorder is associated with a heavy genetic loading for the disease, a two-fold increase in the aggregation of schizophrenic disorders has been found among the first degree relative of prepubertal onset cases of schizophrenia as compared to adult onset cases of schizophrenia (Kallman & Roth, 1956; Kolvin, 1971). These data suggest that childhood onset schizophrenia may be a more severe, possibly more homogeneous, form of schizophrenia with an increased genetic predisposition to schizophrenic disorder.

In addition, studying childhood onset schizophrenia provides a unique opportunity to determine the *functional* significance of the psychobiological impairments which are associated with vulnerability to this disorder, by examining how these impairments effect the development of important cognitive and social abilities. Finally, by comparing adult and child onset schizophrenic individuals, we can address a key question in the field of developmental psychopathology; the similarities and possible continuities between child and adult onset forms of a disorder.

PSYCHOBIOLOGICAL STUDIES OF SCHIZOPHRENIC CHILDREN

The next set of studies attempted to detail the nature of the psychobiological vulnerability to schizophrenic disorder by determining which of the multiple cognitive processes tapped by the Estes and Taylor span task is impaired in schizophrenic children. In the first of a series of three studies, schizophrenic, mental age matched normal children, and a group of younger normal children were administered the same span task used in the studies described earlier. (See Asarnow and Sherman, 1984 for a more detailed description.) Inspection of Fig. 9.3, which presents span-of-apprehension data for the three groups, indicates that for all groups there is a decrement in performance as the number of letters in the array is increased. At all array sizes, except the one letter array, the schizophrenic children detected significantly fewer target stimuli than the mental age matched normals. The schizophrenic and younger normal groups did not differ from each other on any of the arrays.

That schizophrenic children show the same kind of impairment on the span as other groups of individuals vulnerable to adult onset schizophrenia suggests that childhood onset schizophrenia falls on the continuum of the "schizophrenia spectrum." In general, impaired information processing tends to be a characteristic of those adult schizophrenics with a poor premorbid history (Cromwell, 1975; Nuechterlein, 1977). That schizophrenic children are also impaired suggests that attentional impairments are characteristic of the more severe forms of schizophrenia, i.e., those with the earliest onset and with the poorest prognosis.

A second study tried to identify the cognitive processes underlying the impaired performance of schizophrenic children on the Estes and Taylor span task. This study attempted to determine whether schizophrenic and younger normal

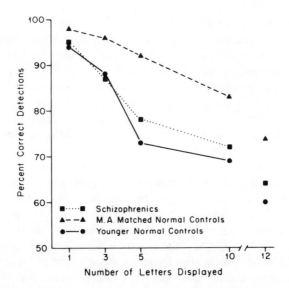

FIG. 9.3. Partial report span task: Mean number of correct detections of the target stimulus as a function of the number of letters displayed for schizophrenic and mental age matched and younger normal children. From *Child Development* (1984), *55,* 249–261. Reprinted with permission. Copyright 1984, the Society for Research in Child Development, Inc.

children, who obtained similar scores on the span task, are also similar in the processes which underlie their performance. These issues were addressed by constructing a 12 letter array version of the span task in which task parameters were manipulated to isolate the contribution of a number of cognitive processes tapped by the Estes and Taylor span task. Four cognitive processes were examined: (1) information acquisition strategies, (2) stimulus discrimination skills, (3) general response biases, and (4) fatigue/learning effects.

We were particularly interested in examining information acquisition strategies. There are major developmental changes in children between the ages of 4 and 9 in their information acquisition strategies. One of the hallmarks of these changes is the transition from stimulus features controlling the child's attention deployment to the child's acquiring information from stimuli in the service of testing hypotheses (Hagen, Jongeward, & Kail, 1976; Pick & Frankel, 1974). Do schizophrenic children have impaired span performance because they have less efficient strategies for acquiring information? While the tachistoscopic presentations used in the span preclude multiple eye movements, normal subjects selectively focus attention to a part of the visual field even under very brief stimulus presentation times (Posner, 1978). The role of information acquisition strategies was examined by determining the effect of the location of the target stimulus within the array on the accuracy of detection.

Figure 9.3 reveals that on the 12-letter arrays, as on the 10-letter arrays in Experiment I, the schizophrenic and young normal children detected significantly fewer target stimuli than MA matched normal subjects, but did not differ significantly from one another. As on the 10-letter arrays, all groups of children performed better than chance.

The results of this study suggested that the impaired performance of the schizophrenic children on the Estes and Taylor span-of-apprehension task is *not* due to: (1) a general fatigue habituation effect—they show the same increase in accuracy level over four trial blocks as do the other two groups of subjects, or (2) the differential effects of some response bias—schizophrenic children showed the same response bias as shown in the other two groups of children, a tendency to report Ts slightly more often than Fs. The impaired span-of-apprehension performance of the schizophrenic children is not due to poor stimulus discrimination skills since they responded in the same fashion as the two groups of normal children to the number of letters adjacent to the target stimulus. All three groups detected fewer target stimuli when the target was adjacent to 5 letters than when it was not immediately adjacent to any other letters or was adjacent to 8 letters.

Of great interest, the schizophrenic children showed the same pattern of information acquisition seen in the MA matched control group. As shown in Fig. 9.4 both the MA matched controls and the schizophrenic children were more

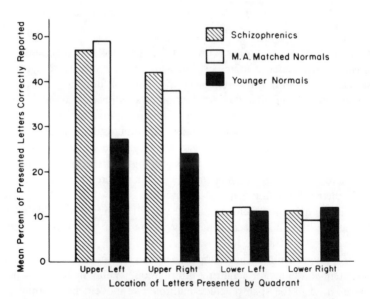

FIG. 9.4. Partial report span task: Mean percentage of trials when the target stimulus is correctly detected as a function of target letter location for schizophrenic and mental age matched and younger normal children. From *Child Development* (1984), *55,* 249–261. Reprinted with permission. Copyright 1984, the Society for Research in Child Development, Inc.

likely to detect the target stimuli when they were presented in the upper half of the screen than when they were presented in the lower half of the screen. In contrast, the younger normal children showed an equal probability of detecting the target stimuli across stimulus locations. Thus, in one important way the schizophrenic children differed from the younger children. These results suggest that the schizophrenic children were using the same information acquisition strategy as that employed by the older MA matched normal control group, but less efficiently since their overall performance levels were lower than those of the MA matched control children.

The schizophrenic children in Experiments I and II showed impaired performance on two versions of a partial report span task relative to a group of children matched to them on general intellectual abilities. This indicates that the information processing impairment found in the schizophrenic children is not simply reflecting a global impairment of intellectual abilities.

Adequate iconic and immediate memory are necessary for successful performance on the partial report span tasks employed in the previous two studies. Could the impaired performance of schizophrenic children be due to deficient iconic and/or immediate memory? We tested this hypothesis in a third study by presenting the children with another version of the span task (a full report task), which makes greater demands on iconic and immediate memory and less demands on early attentive processing than partial report span tasks. The full report span task assesses immediate an iconic memory by requiring subjects to report all of the tachistoscopically presented letters they can remember seeing. While the partial report span task also involves short term memory, the full report task places a greater demand on short term memory since stimuli have to be held in memory while the verbal response is being executed.

The schizophrenic children did not differ from the mental age matched controls in the number of letters reported in the full report span task. This suggests that the impaired performance of schizophrenic children on partial report span tasks is not due to deficient iconic and/or immediate memory. More importantly, the results of the third study indicate that subjects did not perform on the partial report span by simply naming all the letters they could retrieve from iconic and/or immediate memory. The mean number of letters reported (2 to 4) on the full report span task is far less then the number of letters which had to be processed (6 to 9) on the 12 letter partial report span task to yield the detection rates obtained in experiment II.

What strategy do children use to perform on partial report span tasks? The data from Experiment I suggest that all groups of subjects were engaged in a serial search task when performing this partial report span task. Serial processing demands focal attention. It is characterized by the direction of attention "serially to different locations, to integrate the features within the same spatio-temporal 'spotlight' into a unitary percept" (Treisman & Gelade, 1980). One of the defining characteristic of a serial mode of processing is that there is an incremental cost (increased reaction time or errors) when subjects are required to detect targets in displays with increasing numbers of distractors. This is exactly what happens on the Estes and Taylor span task in experiment one. As the number of distractors increased from 0 to 2 to 4 to 9, The target detection rates for all groups decreased. Moreover, the fact that the schizophrenic children and the younger normals showed a greater "cost" with increased number of distractors than MA matched normals suggests that their serial search is either initiated more slowly or employed less efficiently than that of the older control group.

A convergent result emerges from Experiment II. When the target is in the upper quadrants, as opposed to the lower quadrants, both the schizophrenics and the MA matched normals showed a significantly greater probability of correctly detecting the target. This suggests both the schizophrenics and older normals consistently began their serial search in the upper quadrants, and that their iconic image of the stimulus display faded before they could adequately process the lower quadrants.

From these data, we cannot determine whether the advantage of the older normals is due to their having found a better set of features to search for, or whether all groups searched for the same set of critical features, but that the older normals were more efficient either in the initiation or application of their search. Cash, Neale, & Cromwell (1972) suggested that schizophrenic adults may have special difficulty in ignoring irrelevant features and therefore may have problems with tasks involving speeded search. On the other hand, there is evidence (e.g., Russell, Consedine, & Knight, 1980) which suggests that schizophrenics may be delayed in the initiation of visual search.

There is a general consensus (Hagen et al., 1976; Pick & Frankel, 1974) that much of perceptual and attentional development in children consists of a transition towards more active control of information acquisition. This is achieved, in part, through more efficient deployment of attentional capacity. It is interesting to note that it is in precisely these later developing systems that schizophrenic children showed their characteristic impairments.

The results of these studies suggest that schizophrenic children, like other schizophrenic individuals (Callaway & Nagudi, 1982; Neale & Oltmans, 1980) show information processing impairments under conditions which entail controlled processing. Controlled processes (which are distinguished from automatic processes) are momentary sequences of mental operations that are under the subject's control and which make demand on a central, limited pool of information processing capacity.

THE DIAGNOSTIC SPECIFICITY OF AIP IMPAIRMENTS

The following studies address a key issue in developmental psychopathology—the diagnostic specificity of impairments. Are impairments in controlled attentional processes a relatively specific characteristic of children with a schizophrenic disorder, or are they a more general characteristic of children with a severe, early onset psychiatric disorder? Children with an autistic disorder are a useful comparison group because autism, like schizophrenia, is a severe, early onset disorder in which the number of male cases exceeds the number of female cases. In addition, comparing autistic and schizophrenic children addresses the long simmering debate over the relation between childhood onset schizophrenia and autism. DSM-111 used operationialized criteria to differentiate between schizophrenia and early infantile autism. These two disorders had been lumped together in DSM-11 under the rubric of "childhood schizophrenia." Even though cognitive impairments are considered to be key features of both disorders, the studies below were two of the first to directly compare the cognitive functioning of children with autistic and schizophrenic disorders.

An initial study (Asarnow, Tanguay, Bott, & Freeman, 1987) compared the performance of nonretarded autistic and schizophrenic children on three factors that have been consistently found to account for the variance on the WISC-R, a standardized measure of intellectual functioning (Wechsler, 1974). These factors (Kauffman, 1979; Sattler, 1974) are called verbal comprehension, perceptual organization, and factor three. Since there are age-related changes in the factor structure of intellectual tests, the two groups were matched in age at time of testing as well as full-scale IQ.

The autistic and schizophrenic children did not significantly differ on the verbal factor but the schizophrenic children had significantly lower scores on both the perceptual organization and factor 3 than autistic children. Of particular importance, the scores of the schizophrenic children on factor 3 were significantly lower than those of the autistic children, below the range of normal children, and significantly lower than the scores they obtained on the verbal comprehension and perceptual organization factors. Although there is dispute over the general meaning of factor 3, the subtests included in this factor (arithmetic, coding and digit span) make extensive demands on controlled attentional processes because of their requirements for working memory, attention and speed of responding (Sattler, 1974). These results are thus consistent with the hypothesis that schizophrenic children have impairments in controlled attentional processes. This impairment appears to be somewhat specific since the autistic and schizophrenic children were matched in full-scale IQ and the schizophrenic children performed within the normal range on tasks tapping overlearned abilities (such as those tapped by the verbal factor), which make less demands on controlled attentional processes.

The autistic children did not show a global deficit in language functioning, as measured by verbal IQ. The comprehension subtest was the only subtest that the autistic children scored significantly lower on than the schizophrenic children. The sensitivity of the comprehension subtest to the relatively subtle impairments found in nonretarded autistic children may result from the demands this task makes for the integration of two abilities, verbal abstraction (Rutter, 1983) and social cognition (Sigman, Ungerer, Mundy, & Sherman 1986), hypothesized to be core cognitive impairments in autism.

Further evidence that there is some diagnostic specificity for the impairments in controlled attentional processes shown by schizophrenia children is provided by a study (J. Asarnow, Goldstein, & Ben Meir, 1988), which found that schizophrenic children and children meeting DSM-III criteria for schizotypal personality disorder had significantly lower scores on factor 3 than children with major depressive and dysthymic disorders. Interestingly, schizophrenic and schizotypal children have similar levels of performance on factor 3 suggesting that AIP deficits are present in schizotypal children (as they are in other groups at risk for schizophrenia).

To further circumscribe the cognitive impairment found in schizophrenic children, we (see Schneider & Asarnow, 1987) tested subjects on two neuropsychological tasks which make extensive demands on controlled attentional processes, the Wisconsin Card Sorting Test (WCST, Grant & Berg, 1981) and Rey's Tangled Line Test (RTLT, Rey, 1964). The WCST requires subjects to sort cards containing figures that differ in number, form, and color into categories according to a single sorting principle that must be discovered by the subject. This task makes extensive demands both on verbal mediation and the subject's ability to engage in temporally extended problem solving. Thus, the WCST taps the hypothesized core deficits in both autism and schizophrenia. Autistic, (Hoffman & Prior, 1982; Kumagai, 1984) and schizophrenic (Fey, 1951; Stuss et al., 1983) individuals show deficits on this task. To tease apart the core cognitive impairments underlying the performance of the autistic and schizophrenic children on the WCST, both groups were explicitly taught the appropriate sorting principles half way through this task. If autistic children are unable to use language to mediate and regulate their behavior, teaching them a verbal strategy should have little effect on their sorting performance. In contrast, previous studies (e.g., Koh, 1978) have indicated that when schizophrenic individuals are taught the appropriate strategy their performance can be normalized on certain memory tasks. Consequently, it was predicted that teaching schizophrenic children the correct sorting principle would improve their WCST performance while autistic children would not improve.

The RTLT is a guided visual search task which requires subjects to visually track a series of tangled lines. As this task requires controlled attentional processes for an extended period of time, it was predicted that schizophrenic children would show impaired performance on this task.

The foregoing tests were administered to groups of schizophrenic, autistic, and normal control children matched in mental and chronological age. As predicted, the schizophrenic children performed significantly worse on the RTLT than the normal children. Schizophrenic children made significantly more perseverative responses than normal children on the WCST.

The major difference between the schizophrenic and autistic children was that the schizophrenic children increased the number of nonperseverative errors (random responding) from the first to the second half of the WCST while autistic and normal children showed no change. Providing a sorting strategy, contrary to our predictions, did not facilitate the performance of the schizophrenic children on the WCST. Rather, their performance significantly deteriorated after they were taught the relevant sorting principles. Stuss et al. (1983) also found that a similar manipulation had a deleterious effect on the WCST performance of chronic schizophrenics with prefrontal leukotomies. In addition, Pueschel (1980) found that providing schizophrenic individuals verbal directions impaired their performance on a hypothesis testing task. These findings are reminiscent of the results of Rodnick and Shakow (1940) and Steffy (1978) who found, in their reaction time studies, that relevant information sometimes impaired performance. The relevant information provided in our study requires the momentary integration of information from a variety of sources to direct an ongoing activity. Providing task relevant information to the schizophrenic child, whose momentary processing capacity may be already overburdened, may further encumber processing capacity, resulting in the seemingly paradoxical effect of further impairment in performance.

Event Related Potential Concomitants

Psychophysiological studies may provide a means of more directly examining the recruitment and allocation of processing capacity. Different components of scalp recorded event-related potentials (ERPs) index a number of discrete cognitive processes, all of which may be involved in performance on span tasks. For example, the mobilization of general attentional resources in response to a warning signal (i.e., preparedness) results in a broad negative scalp field, the contingent negative variation or CNV, which resolves following presentation of the target stimulus. Similarly, CNS activity associated with selective attention (the "Nd" or "PN" component), pattern discrimination (NA), stimulus categorization (N2), and response set or context updating (P3) produce scalp fields that can be identified in the averaged EEG record (see Donchin, Ritter, & McCallum, 1978; Ritter et al., 1984). The amplitude of these components can be viewed as an estimate of the resources allocated to each of these processes.

Although there are few ERP studies of childhood onset schizophrenia, diminished CNV, Nd, and P3 amplitudes have been well documented in schizophrenic adults (for a recent review see Pritchard, 1986). These findings suggest that adult schizophrenics may be deficient in their processing capacity and/or their allocation strategy.

We recorded EEG activity from normal and schizophrenic children during performance of the partial report version of the span task to begin to evaluate recruitment and allocation of processing capacity in these younger subjects. In our initial study of 10 schizophrenic and 13 mental age matched normals

(Strandburg et al., 1984), the results were similar to those previously observed in adults. In the schizophrenic children, CNV activity was smaller and slower to develop and resolve than in normals. N1 and P3 amplitudes were similarly reduced in this group. We interpreted this as evidence that the schizophrenics were impaired in their ability to regulate processes involved in the mobilization and allocation of attention as well as discrimination of target stimuli.

The span stimuli in this study could be grouped into four levels of difficulty., Only normal children showed an increase in N1 amplitude with each increment in task difficulty. While the N1 component is largely dependent on exogeneous factors (physical properties of the eliciting stimuli), the net ERP in this time region can also include endogenous activity associated with task specific processing which temporally overlaps (and continues beyond) the N1. For example, the Nd or PN components reflect additional CNS activity involved in selective attention (Hansen & Hillyard, 1980; Naatanen & Michie, 1979) and NA reflects activity associated with pattern discrimination (Ritter et al., 1982, 1983). These endogenous components are sensitive to task demand, thus, the variation in N1 amplitude with task difficulty in the normals in our study may reflect changes in such endogenous processing.

Evidence from both ERP and magnetoencephalography studies (magnetoencephalography measures evoked CNS magnetic activity which provides more precise information about the spatial location of neural generators) suggests that Nd (or PN) activity elicited in auditory selective attention tasks is generated in sensory cortex (see Naatanen & Picton, 1987). In addition, Knight et al. (1981) have demonstrated that the development of Nd is dependent on regulatory inputs from frontal cortex. While Nd is maximum at the vertex, the N1 effects in the visual span task were most prominent at posterior leads. Thus they more closely resemble the NA component observed by Ritter et al. (1982, 1983) in visual discrimination tasks. Ritter et al. (1983) argue that while Nd, NA and other endogenous negativities seen in this temporal region are elicited by different paradigms "they all appear to be associated with stimulus identification processes" (p. 177). It is conceivable that, as with Nd, frontal regulatory mechanisms play a role in the development of each of these endogenous, attention related components. In fact, abnormal, asymmetric frontal activity (which spanned the entire recorded epoch; see Fig. 9.5) was observed in the schizophrenic children in our study, which might explain the absence of endogenous effects in the N1 region among these children.

To determine whether these N1 differences in schizophrenic children were indeed the result of differences in endogenous processing, we recently recorded ERPs from 13 schizophrenic and 17 normal children using identical span stimuli in two conditions which differ only in task instructions (Strandburg et al., submitted). The first was a reaction time condition in which the children were required to press a button as quickly as possible to the onset of each visual span array. Following this, instructions for the partial report span task were given and

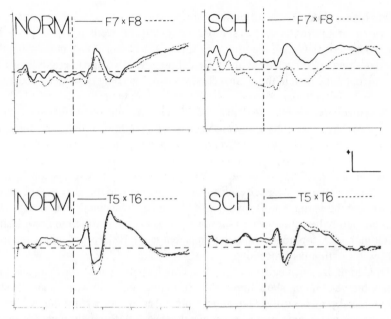

FIG. 9.5. Hemispheric differences within groups for event related potentials. Event related potentials (averaged over difficulty levels) over left (solid lines) and right hemispheres) can be compared at frontal (top) and posterior (bottom) sites in normal (left) and schizophrenic (right) children. Traces begin with the onset of an auditory warning stimulus. The vertical line which intersects the trace 500 msec later marks the onset of the visual span stimuli. The dashed horizontal line represents the zero voltage baseline with respect to a linked earlobe reference. Large calibration marks represent 250 msec intervals on the horizontal axis and 14 uV on the vertical axis. Positive up. From *Electroencephalagraphy and clinical Neurophysiology* (1984), *57*, 236–253. Reprinted with permission. Copyright 1984, Elsevier Scientific Publishers.

the stimuli from the first condition were repeated. By subtracting primarily exogenous, low task demand ERP activity recorded during the RT task from the ERPs obtained during the partial report span task, a difference potential is obtained which reflects that portion of CNS activity associated with the additional, endogenous processing required to make the span discrimination. Schizophrenic children produced significantly less endogenous activity in response to the span processing demands than normal children at all posterior leads.

It is important to emphasize that these difference potentials measure *relative* activity levels between two conditions which differ in processing demand (RT and span). While ERP amplitude measures were more negative in the N1,P2 region during span processing than during the RT condition in both normal and schizophrenic children, the difference between conditions was significant only in the normal group. In the span condition, the ERP traces were quite similar in the two groups in the N1,P2 region. They differ in net processing negativity (the difference potential) because in the RT condition the N1 is considerably larger in the schizophrenic than in the normal children. Normals may be able to handle the demands for attentional control in the RT task in an entirely automatic fashion while schizophrenics may find that the RT task requires effortful processing. Thus, they have less capacity available when the additional demands for span processing must be met. Alternatively, schizophrenic children may not differ in their processing capacity from the normal children, but rather, have an inefficient allocation strategy. They may allocate excessive capacity to the simpler RT task and fail to increase this capacity adequately in response to the greater processing demands of the partial report span task. It should also be noted, that as expected from the purely behavioral studies discussed earlier, this information processing deficit in the schizophrenic children is apparent in the ERP record within the first 200 msec of stimulus processing.

To summarize, our behavioral and electrophysiological studies suggest that schizophrenic children show impaired performance on tasks which make extensive demands on controlled attentional processes while performing relatively normally on task which make less demands. These AIP impairments appear to have some degree of diagnostic specificity. The impairments in controlled attentional processes observed in schizophrenic children may reflect abnormalities in the allocation and/or recruitment of processing capacity.

PREMORBID CHARACTERISTICS AND COURSE IN SCHIZOPHRENIC CHILDREN

The second set of developmental analyses we have employed are follow-back and follow-up studies to describe the natural history of childhood onset schizophrenia. These analyses provide a basis for checking the validity of our working hypothesis that childhood onset schizophrenia is a more severe form of schizophrenia. Our current data suggests that childhood onset schizophrenia is a particularly severe and disabling disorder that profoundly influences the child's development. Support for this conclusion derives from three major sets of findings. First, we conducted follow-back studies of schizophrenic children by examining school and medical record data generated prior to the onset of the full-blown schizophrenic disorder in order to describe the schizophrenic child's early development. We (J. Asarnow & Ben-Meir, 1988) found that schizophrenic and schizotypal children typically showed chronic or insidious patterns of dysfunction beginning in early childhood and sometimes dating from infancy. When compared to children with severe depressive disorders (major depressive and/or dysthymic disorders), schizophrenic and schizotypal children achieved significantly lower levels of premorbid social adjustment. Schizophrenic and schizotypal children showed early tendencies towards social withdrawal, poor peer relationships, low levels of scholastic achievement, poor school adaptation, and few interests.

A second study (Watkins, R. Asarnow, & Tanguay, 1988) examined the history of symptom development in schizophrenic children. Language abnormalities and delays, motor delays and hypotonia, bizarre responses to the environment, and lack of social responsiveness appeared during infancy. The scope and severity of these early symptoms was unexpected. Particularly surprising was the finding that 13 of the 18 children had marked language abnormalities and delays prior to the onset of schizophrenia. Early language abnormalities and delays are some of the most sensitive indices of central nervous system dysfunction appearing early in development.

During early childhood, additional symptoms appeared including extreme mood lability, inappropriate clinging, unexplained rage reactions, and hyperactivity. Still later, but in no case before 6 years, symptoms of formal thought disorder and flat or inappropriate affect first emerged. This was followed, usually after 9 years, by the appearance of diagnostically significant delusions and hallucinations. This temporal ordering of the emergence of severe symptoms may indicate that the children's level of cognitive development mediates the expression of schizophrenic symptoms.

Finally, early data from a follow-up study (J. Asarnow et al., 1988) of the course of childhood-onset schizophrenia spectrum and depressive disorders indicate that schizophrenic and schizotypal children frequently show persistent difficulties as they progress through adolescence. This study is still in progress and extensive data on symptomatology, social adjustment, and family adjustment patterns are forthcoming. However, data are currently available on rates of rehospitalization and out of home placement for a group of 18 schizophrenic and schizotypal children for the first 1 to 5 years following their psychiatric hospitalizations. Because the outcomes were similar for schizophrenic and schizotypal children, we combined the data of children with schizophrenia spectrum disorders (schizophrenic and schizotypal). As shown in Fig. 9.6, which presents the cumulative probability of out of home placement for children with schizophrenia spectrum and depressive disorders, out of home placement was very common for schizophrenic and schizotypal children. Although all but two children were sent home at discharge, within 13 months of hospital discharge, 57% of the schizophrenic and schizotypal children were placed out of their homes. Placement was usually in residential treatment centers for an extended period of time (the range was 60 to 730 days with some children still in placement) and was usually precipitated by out of control behavior. Rates of out of home placements were significantly higher for children with schizophrenia spectrum disorders than for

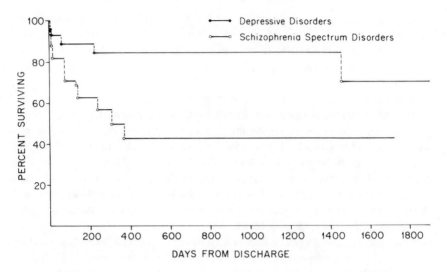

FIG. 9.6. Results of a survival analysis of probability of out-of-home placement for children with depressive and schizophrenia spectrum disorders.

children with depressive disorders. Moreover, when depressed children were placed, they tended to be placed in nontherapeutic settings such as boarding schools or foster homes. Rehospitalizations were more common among the depressed children than the schizophrenic children. Two schizophrenic children, however, were rehospitalized at discharge because even after long hospitalization they were judged to be too disturbed to be safe at home, and 5 schizotypal children (3 of whom also met criteria for depressive disorders) were rehospitalized within 2½ years of discharge. Reasons for rehospitalization included out of control behavior (5 cases), suicide attempts (1 case), and concerns about depression and out of control behavior (1 case).

These data are consistent with our working hypothesis that childhood onset schizophrenia may be a particularly severe form of schizophrenia.

FAMILIES OF SCHIZOPHRENIC CHILDREN

As noted previously we have been interested in examining the role of psychosocial stressors in determining the onset and course of disorder in schizophrenic children. To address this issue, a series of studies have focused on attributes of the family environment which may potentiate, or protect against dysfunction in children with schizophrenic and schizotypal disorders. In terms of the model described previously, some family (or environmental) attributes may be conceptualized as possible psychosocial stressors, while others may be conceptualized as possible protective factors.

One of the more robust findings in studies of families of adult schizophrenics is that interpersonal communications in these families tend to be unclear and often confusing. Much of this research has employed the construct of communication deviance. As defined by Singer and Wynne (1965), communication deviance refers to a confusing unclear communication style that leads to a disruption in the focus of attention. Results from a study by J. Asarnow, Goldstein, and Ben-Meir (1988) reveal that, similar to findings with adult schizophrenics, rates of communication deviance were significantly higher in the parents of children with schizophrenic and schizotypal disorders than in the parents of children with major depressive and dysthymic disorders. Additionally, schizophrenic and schizotypal children whose parents showed communication deviance had the most severe impairments in their psychosocial functioning (as indexed by Global Adjustment Scale scores) and the greatest AIP deficits (as indexed by factor 3 of the WISC-R).

These results are similar to those of a study of adult onset schizophrenics (Wagener et al., 1986), which found higher rates of communication deviance in mothers of schizophrenic patients with AIP impairments (as measured by a partial report span task) than in patients without an AIP impairment. Interestingly, Wagener and her colleagues found that the mothers with elevated communication deviance scores tended themselves to have AIP problems (measured by a partial report span task).

Another focus of J. Asarnow's research program has been on examining the family environments of schizophrenic children in an effort to describe the experiences of these families and to identify natural coping processes that may facilitate adaptation. A recent study with hospitalized schizophrenic and schizotypal children (Asarnow & Horton, in preparation) highlights the profound impact these disturbed children have on family life. Analysis of the parents descriptions of their family lives revealed that 67% of the parents of schizophrenic and schizotypal reported severe or extreme disruption in their homes associated with their child's difficulties. Those families experiencing the greatest disruption were families whose children had shown more chronic (vs. acute) disturbance, were exposed to high levels of other environmental stressors, and families where the mother reported a low level of support from her husband and/or significant others in her environment. When asked about how they had coped with their child's problems, most mothers and fathers described active cognitive coping strategies such as trying to take things one day at a time or think about the difficulty from another perspective. In contrast, when asked what advice they would offer to other parents in a similar situation, parents suggested a more behavioral approach involving problem-solving behaviors and seeking help from professionals.

MECHANISMS OF INTERACTION BETWEEN PSYCHOBIOLOGICAL VULNERABILITY AND PSYCHOSOCIAL STRESSORS

The vulnerability/stress model of schizophrenic disorder implies that psychobiological vulnerability and psychosocial stressors are *independent* factors which either have additive or interactive effects in determining the onset and/or course of schizophrenic disorder. These factors are depicted as independent for reasons of both parsimony in model testing and the current "dualistic" conception of the relation between internal, biological and external environmental factors. The results of our studies to date are largely consistent with predictions derived from a vulnerability/stress model. Relative to both normal controls and psychiatric contrast groups, schizophrenic children have both greater rates of psychobiological vulnerabilities (as measured by a variety of AIP tasks) and a greater risk of exposure to putative psychosocial stressors such as communication deviance.

Our data, however, are *not* consistent with the assumption that psychobiological vulnerability factors and psychosocial stressors are independent factors. Rather, our studies of both childhood (J. Asarnow et al., 1988) and adult (Wagener et al., 1986) onset schizophrenics suggest that schizophrenic individuals with the greatest psychobiological vulnerability are the most likely to be exposed to parental communication patterns which may tax the childs fragile attentional processes. If persistent, these parental communication patterns may act as psychosocial stressors.

The highly significant correlations we have observed between the scores of young adult schizophrenics and their mothers on a partial report span task raise the possibility that, consistent with our working model, AIP impairments in some schizophrenic individuals may be genetically transmitted. Of course, between generation correlations does not prove genetic transmission. Moreover, these findings need to be replicated. Some additional evidence that the AIP impairments tapped by the partial report span task may be under some degree of genetic control comes from a recent Swedish study (Bartfai, personal communication) of normal female monozygotic twins who were either reared apart or together. Both groups of monozygotic twins showed significant correlations in their span performance. In addition, the monozygotic twins who were reared apart and together did not differ in the magnitude of their correlations. This twin data suggest that individual variations in span performance are under some degree of genetic control.

Taken together, our studies of child and adult onset schizophrenic patients and their parents and normal monozygotic twins suggest that there may be two, nonmutually exclusive mechanisms by which individual vulnerability measures and aspects of the family environment may interact to codetermine whether an individual develops schizophrenic disorder and the course of the disorder once it emerges. The first mechanism is that there are different risks of exposure to stressful family transactions for schizophrenic patients with and without impairments in controlled attentional processes. In Wagener's study almost all of the schizophrenic patients with poor performance on the span of apprehension task had parents with elevated communication deviance scores. Conversely, relatively few of the schizophrenic patients with good performance on the span of apprehension task had elevated communication deviance scores. The stressful effect on schizophrenic patients of exposure to family transactions with high loadings of CD has been emphasized in a number of previous studies (see Goldstein, 1987 for a review). It appears that patients with poor span of apprehension performance have a much greater risk of being exposed to stressful communication patterns than patients who do not have poor span performance. One link between the schizophrenic patient's attentional impairment and his parents elevated communication deviance scores may be that some of the behaviors assessed by the CD measure may reflect the parents own attentional impairments. Alternatively, the CD measure may index additional parental characteristics.

A second way individual differences in the efficiency of controlled attentional processes might predispose schizophrenic individuals to respond differentially to certain family transaction patterns is that the effects of the same family transaction pattern are experienced differently by patients depending upon the integrity of their AIP processes. There is some evidence that certain skills which are important for the development and maintenance of social relationships make extensive demands on an individual's ability to monitor and switch between multiple sources of information. For example, studies of children's friendship formation indicate the importance of empathy, the reading of internal cues, and sensitivity to the affective reactions of others for developing successful friendships (Asarnow & Callan, 1985; Dodge, Pettit, McClaskey, & Brown, 1986; Rubin & Krasnor, 1986; Zahn-Waxler, Ianotti, & Chapman, 1982). Those schizophrenic patients with impaired attentional processes may be particularly unable to respond to this variety of cues presented in real time (Asarnow & Goldstein, 1986; Sherman & Asarnow, 1984).

It may be precisely those schizophrenic patients who, because of their own AIP impairments, are the most vulnerable to the effects of confusing, ambiguous, and affectively laden family transactions who are the individuals most likely to be exposed to such transactions. Exposure to these transactional stresses may further impair the patients attentional functioning, reducing the patient's ability to cope with these stressful transactions. This process, in at least those forms of schizophrenia characterized by the presence of attentional impairments in schizophrenic patients and their mothers, is consistent with epigenetic or transactional models of schizophrenia. Our results underscore the importance of conducting process oriented studies to rigorously elucidate the ways in which the psychobiological vulnerabilities tapped by certain AIP tasks interact with specific patterns of family transactions in real time to influence the development and course of schizophrenic disorders.

CONCLUSION

That both children at risk for schizophrenia and schizophrenic children can be differentiated from normal controls and psychiatric contrast groups using measures found in previous research to characterize adult onset schizophrenics indicates that there is some homotypic similarity between childhood and adult variants of schizophrenia. Furthermore, it supports the efficacy of the strategy of applying measures developed in work with adult forms of a behavior disorder to determine the similarity of adult disorders with putative childhood variants. The demonstration of some degree of homotypic continuity between childhood and adult onset schizophrenia is not the end of the story however. Rather, it sets the stage for the most important questions for a developmental psychopathologist interested in understanding the schizophrenic disorders. How does the age of onset of psychosis affect subsequent cognitive and affective development? Are the factors that contribute to the development of hallucinations different from the factors that contribute to the development of thought disorder, flattened affect, and impaired reality testing? How are the CNS impairments (which may be genetically transmitted) that predispose some individuals to develop certain schizophrenic symptoms altered by the environment? What types of environmental stressors are required to elicit a schizophrenic psychosis in vulnerable individuals? What are the individual competencies and environmental protective factors that can buffer the effects of stressors on vulnerable individuals? Answers to these questions will flesh out the epigenetic puzzle of schizophrenia as well as contribute to our understanding of the interplay between cognition and affect in normal development.

ACKNOWLEDGMENTS

The research described in this chapter was supported by grants from the John D. and Catherine T. MacArthur Foundation to Robert Asarnow, Joan Asarnow, and Michael J. Goldstein, and the University of California, Los Angeles node of the Network on Risk and Protective factors in Major Mental disorders and by NIMH grant MH30897 to the UCLA Child Psychiatry Clinical Research Center.

REFERENCES

Asarnow, J. R., & Goldstein, M. J. (1986). Schizophrenia during adolescence and early adulthood: A developmental perspective *Clinical Psychology Review, 6,* 211–235.
Asarnow, J. R. (1988). Children at risk for schizophrenia: Converging lines of evidence. *Schizophrenia Bulletin, 14,* 613–631.

Asarnow, J. R., & Ben-Meir, S. (1988). Children with schizophrenia spectrum and depressive disorders: A comparative study of onset patterns, premorbid adjustment, and severity of dysfunction. *Journal of Child Psychology and Psychiatry, 29,* 477–488.

Asarnow, J. R., & Callan, J. W. (1985). Boys with peer adjustment problems: Social cognitive processes. *Journal of Consulting and Clinical Psychology, 53,* 709–717.

Asarnow, J. R., Goldstein, M. J., & Ben-Meir, S. (1988). Parental communication deviance in childhood onset schizophrenia specturm and depressive disorders. *Journal of Child Psychology and Psychiatry, 29,* 825–838.

Asarnow, J. R., Goldstein, M. J., Carlson, G. A., Perdue, S., Bates, S., & Keller, J. (1988). Childhood-onset depressive disorders: A follow-up study of rates of rehospitalization and out-of-home placement among child psychiatric inpatients. *Journal of Affective Disorders, 15,* 245–253.

Asarnow, J. R., & Horton, A. (1989). *Coping and stress in families of child psychiatric inpatients: Parents of children with depressive and schizophrenia spectrum disorders.* Manuscript in preparation.

Asarnow, R. F. (1983). The Search for the Psychobiological Substrate of Schizophrenia: A perspective from studies of children at risk for schizophrenia. In R. Tarter (Ed.), *The child at psychiatric risk.* New York: Oxford University Press.

Asarnow, R. F., Granholm, E., & Sherman, T. (in press). Span of apprehension in schizophrenia. In S. Steinhauer, J. Gruzelier, & J. Zubin (Eds.), *Handbook of schizophrenia: Neuropsychology, psychophysiology and information processing.* Amsterdam: Elsevier Science Publishers.

Asarnow, R. F., & MacCrimmon, D. J. (1978). Residual performance deficit in clinically remitted schizophrenics: A marker of schizophrenia? *Journal of Abnormal Psychology, 87,* 597–608.

Asarnow, R. F., & MacCrimmon, D. (1981). Span of apprehension deficits during the post-psychotic stages of schizophenia: A replication and extension. *Archives of General Psychiatry, 38,* 1006–1011.

Asarnow, R. F., & MacCrimmon, D. J. (1982). Attention/information processing, neuropsychological functioning and thought disorder during the acute and partial recovery phases of schizophrenia: A longitudinal study. *Psychiatry Research, 7,* 309–319.

Asarnow, R. F., Marder, S. R., Mintz, J., Van Putten T., & Zimmerman, K. (1988). The differential effect of low and conventional doses of neuroleptic on schizophrenic patients with good and poor information processing abilities. *Archives of General Psychiatry, 45,* 822–826.

Asarnow, R. F., Neuchterlein, K. H., & Marder, S. R. (1983). Span of apprehension performance, neuropsychological functioning and indices of psychosis-proneness. *Journal of Nervous and Mental Disease, 171,* 662–669.

Asarnow, R. F., & Sherman, T. (1984). Studies of visual information processing in schizophrenic children. *Child Development, 55,* 249–261.

Asarnow, R. F., Steffy, R. A., MacCrimmon, D. J., Cleghorn, & J. M. (1977). An attentional assessment of foster children at risk for schizophrenia. *Journal of Abnormal Psychology. 86,* 267–275.

Asarnow, R. F., Steffy, R. A., MacCrimmon, D. J., & Cleghorn, J. M. (1978). The McMaster Waterloo project: An attentional and clinical assessment of foster children at risk for schizophrenia. In L. C. Wynne, R. L. Cromwell, & S. Matthysse, (Eds.), *The nature of schizophrenia: New approaches to research and treatment.* New York: Wiley.

Asarnow, R. F., Tanguay, P. E., Bott, L., & Freeman, B. J. (1987). Patterns of intellectual functioning in non-retarded autistic and schizophrenic children. *Journal of Child Psychology and Psychiatry, 28,* 273–280.

Callaway, E., & Nagudi, S. (1982). An information processing model for schizophrenia. *Archives of General Psychiatry, 3,* 339–347.

Cash, T. F., Neale, J. M., Cromwell, R. L. (1972). Span of apprehension in acute schizophrenics: Full-report procedure. *Journal of Abnormal Psychology 3,* 322–326.

Cicchetti, D. (1984). The emergence of Developmental Psychopathology. *Child Development*, *55*, 1–7.

Cloninger, C. R. (1987). Genetic principles and methods in high-risk studies of Schizophrenia. *Schizophrenia Bulletin*. 13, 515–524.

Cromwell, R. L. (1975). Assessment of schizophrenia. In M. Rosenzweig, & L. Porter, (Eds.), *Annual Review of Psychology*. Palo Alto, CA: Annual Reviews.

Cromwell, R., & Spaulding, W. (1978). How schizophrenics handle information. In W. E. Fann (Ed.), *The phenomenology and treatment of schizophenia*. New York: Spectrum.

Dodge, K. A., Pettit, G. B., McClaskey, C. L., & Brown, M. M. (1986). Social competence in children. *Monographs of the Society for Research in Child Development*, *51*(2), Serial No. 213.

Donchin, E., Ritter, W., & McCallum, W. (1978). Cognitive psychophysiology: The endogenous components of the ERP. In E. Callaway, P. Tueting, & S. Koslow (Eds.), *Event-related brain potentials in man* (pp. 349–442). New York: Academic Press.

Eckblad, M., & Chapman, L. J. (1985). Magical ideation as an indication of schizotypy. *Journal of Consulting and Clinical Psychology*, *51*, 215–225.

Elliott, G. R., & Eisdorfer, C. (1982). *Stress and human health: Analysis and implications of research*. New York: Springer.

Estes, W. K., & Taylor, H. A. (1964). A detection method and probabilisitc models for assessing information processing from brief visual displays. *Proceedings of the National Academy of Science*, *52*, 446–454.

Falconer, D. S. (1965). The inheritance of liability to disease to certain diseases estimated from the incidence among relatives. *Annals of Human Genetics*, *31a*, 51–76.

Fey, E. T. (1951). The performance of young schizophrenics and young normals on the Wisconsin Card Scoring Test. *Journal of Consulting Psychology*, *15*, 311–319.

Goldstein, M. J. (1987). Family interaction patterns that antedate the onset of Schizophrenia and related disorders: A further analysis of data from a longitudinal prospective study. In K. Hahlweg & M. J. Goldstein (Eds.), *Understanding major mental disorders: The contribution of family interaction research*. New York: Family Process Press.

Gottesman, I. E., & Shields, J. (1982). Schizophrenia: The epigenetic puzzle. Cambridge, England: Cambridge University Press.

Grant, D. A., & Berg, E. A. (1981). *Wisconsin Card Sorting Test*. Odessa, FL: Psychological Assessment Resources.

Green, W., Campbell, M., Hardesty, A., Grega, D., Padron-Gayol, M., Shell, J., & Erlenmeyer-Kimling, L. (1984). A comparison of schizophrenic and autistic children. *Journal of the American Academy of Child Psychiatry*, *23*, 399–409.

Hagen, J., Jongeward, R., & Kail, R. (1976). Cognitive perspectives on the development of memory. In H. Reese (Ed.), *Advances in child development and behavior* (Vol. 10). New York: Academic Press.

Hansen, H. C., & Hillyard, S. A. (1980). Endogenous brain potentials associated with selective auditory attention. *Electroencephalography and Clinical Neurophysiology*, *49*, 277–290.

Hoffman, W. L., & Prior, M. R. (1982). Neuropsychological dimensions of autism in childrn: A test of the hemispheric dysfunction hypothesis. *Journal of Clinical Neuropsychology*. *4*, 27–41.

Kallman, F. J., & Roth, B. (1956). Genetic aspects of preadolescent schizophrenia. *American Journal of Psychiatry*, *112*, 599–606.

Kauffman, A. S. (1979). *Intelligent testing with the WISC-R*. New York: Wiley.

Knight, R. T., Hillyard, S. A., Woods, D., & Neville, H. J. (1981). The effects of frontal cortex lesions on event-related potentials during auditory selective attention. *Electroencephalogy Clinical Neurophysiology*, *52*, 571–582.

Koh, S. D. (1978). Remembering of verbal materials by schizophrenic young adults. In S. Schwartz (Ed.), *Language and cognition in schizophrenia* (pp. 55–99). Hillsdale, NJ: Lawrence Erlbaum Associates.

Kolvin, I. (1971). Psychoses in childhood—A comparative study. In M. Rutter (Ed.), *Infantile autism: Concepts, characteristics and treatment.* Edinburgh: Churchill Livingstone.

Kraepelin, E. (1919/1913). *Dementia praecox and paraphrenia* (Translated by R. M. Barclay). Edinburgh: E & S Livingstone.

Kumagai, T. (1984). Card sorting responses in autistic children: The frontal dysfunction hypothesis. *Japanese Journal of Special Education, 21,* 17–23. (From *Psychological Abstracts,* 1984, 71, Abstract No. 28849).

Lang, P. H., & Buss, A. H. (1965). Psychological deficit in schizophrenia: Interference and activation. *Journal of Abnormal Psychology, 70,* 77–106.

MacCrimmon, D. J., Cleghorn, J. M., Asarnow, R. F., & Steffy, R. A. (1980). Children at Risk for Schizophrenia: Clinical and attentional characteristics. *Archives of General Psychiatry, 37,* 6771–674.

McGhie, A., & Chapman, J. (1961). Disorders of attention and perception in early schizophrenia. *British Journal of Medical Psychology, 34,* 103–119.

Meehl, P. E. (1962). Schizotaxia, schizotypy, schizophrenia. *American Psychologist, 17,* 827–838.

Naatanen, R., & Michie, P. T. (1979). Early selective attention effects on the evoked potential. A critical review and reinterpretation. *Biological Psychology, 8,* 81–136.

Naatanen, R., & Picton, T. (1987). The N1 wave of the human electric and magnetic response to sound: A review and an analysis of the component structure. *Psychophysiology, 24,* 375–425.

Neale, J. M. (1971). Perceptual span in schizophrenics. *Journal of Abnormal Psychology, 77,* 196–204.

Neale, J. M., & Cromwell, R. L. (1970). Attention and schizophrenia. In B. A. Maher (Ed.), *Progress in experimental personality research* (Vol. 5). New York: Academic Press.

Neale, J. M., McIntyre, C. W., Fox, R., & Cromwell, R. L. (1969). Span of apprehension in acute schizophrenics. *Journal of Abnormal Psychology, 74,* 593–596.

Neale, J. M., & Oltmans, T. F. (1980). *Schizophrenia.* New York: Wiley.

Nuechterlein, K. H. (1977). Reaction time and attention in schizophrenia: A critical evaluation of the data and theories. *Schizophrenia Bulletin, 13,* 373–428.

Nuechterlein, K. H., & Dawson, M. E. (1984). Information processing and attentional functioning in the developmental course of schizophrenic disorders. *Schizophrenia Bulletin, 10,* 160–203.

Pick, A. D., & Frankel, G. W. (1974). A developmental study of strategies of visual selectivity. *Child Development, 45,* 1162–1165.

Posner, M. I. (1978). *Chronometric explorations of mind.* Hillsdale, NJ: Lawrence Erlbaum Associates.

Pritchard, W. S. (1986). Cognitive event-related potential correlates of schizophrenia. *Psychological Bulletin, 100,* 43–46.

Pueschel, K. M. (1980). *Neuropsychological assessment and "hypothesis testing" in schizophrenic and brain damaged patients.* Unpublished manuscript.

Rey, A. (1964). *L'Examen clinique en psycologie* (The clinical exam in psychology). Paris: Presses Universitaires de France.

Ritter, W., Ford, J. M., Gaillard, A. W. K., Harter, M. R., Kutas, M., Naatanen, R., Polich, J., Renault, B., & Rohrbaugh, J. (1984). Cognition and event-related potentials: I. The relation of negative potentials and cognitive processes. In R. Karrer, J. Cohen, & P. Tueting, (Eds.), *Brain and information: Event-related potentials. Annals of the New York Academy of Sciences, 25,* 24–38.

Ritter, W., Simson, R., & Vaughan, H. G. Jr. (1983). Event-related potential correlates of two stages of information processing in physical and semantic discrimination tasks. *Psychophysiology, 20,* 168–179.

Ritter, W., Simson, R., Vaughan, H. H. Jr., & Macht, M. (1982). Manipulation of event-related potential manifestations on information processing stages. *Science, 218,* 909–911.

Rodnick, E. H., & Shakow, D. (1940). Set in the schizophrenic as measured by a composite reaction time index. *American Journal of Psychiatry. 97*, 214–220.

Rosenthal, D. (1970). *Genetic theory and abnormal behavior.* New York: McGraw Hill.

Rubin, K. H., & Krasnor, L. R. (1986). Social cognitive and social behavioral perspectives on problem-solving. In M. Perlmutter (Ed.), *Minnesota symposium on child psychology (Vol. 18, pp. 1–68).* Hillsdale, NJ: Lawrence Erlbaum Associates.

Russell, A., Bott, L., & Sammons, C. (1986, October). *The phenomenology of prepubertal onset schizophrenia.* Paper presented at the meeting of the American Academy of Child Psychiatry, Los Angeles.

Russell, P. N., Consedine, C. E., & Knight, R. G. (1980). Visual and memory search by process schizophrenics. *Journal of Abnormal Psychology, 2,* 109–114.

Rutter, M. (1983). Cognitive deficits in the pathogenesis of autism. *Journal of Child Psychology and Psychiatry, 24,* 27–41.

Sattler, J. M. (1974). *Assessment of children's intelligence.* Philadelphia: W. B. Saunders.

Schneider, S. G., & Asarnow, R. F. (1987). A comparison between the cognitive/neuropsychological impairments of non-retarded autistic and schizophrenic children. *Journal of Abnormal Child Psychology, 15,* 29–46.

Sherman, T., & Asarnow, R. F. (1985). The cognitive disabilities of the schizophrenic child. In M. Sigman (Ed.), *Children with dual disabilities: Mental retardation and mental illness.* Orlando, FL: Grune & Stratton.

Sigman, M., Ungerer, J., Mundy, P., & Sherman, T. (1986). Cognition. In D. J. Cohen & A. Donnellan (Eds.), *Handbook of autism and pervasive developmental disorders.* New York: Wiley.

Singer, M. T., & Wynne, L. C. (1965). Thought disorder and family relations of schizophrenics: IV. Results and implications. *Archives of General Psychiatry, 12,* 201–209.

Steffy, R. A. (1978). An early cue sometimes impairs process schizophrenic performance. In L. Wynne, R. Cromwell, & S. Matthysse (Eds.), *The nature of schizophrenia: New approaches to research and treatment.* New York: Wiley.

Steffy, R. A., Asarnow, R. F., Asarnow, J. R., MacCrimmon, D. J., & Cleghorn, J. M. (1984). The McMaster-Waterloo Project: Multifaceted strategy for high-risk research. In N. Watt, E. J. Anthony, L. C. Wynne, & J. E. Rolf (Eds.), *Children at risk for schizophrenia: A longitudinal perspective.* New York: Wiley.

Strandburg, R. J., Marsh, J. T., Brown, W. S., Asarnow, R. F., & Guthrie, D. (1984). Event-related potential concomitants of information processing dysfunction in schizophrenic children. *Electroencephalography and Clinical Neurophysiology, 57,* 236–253.

Strandburg, R. J., Marsh, J. T., Brown, W. S., Asarnow, R. F., Guthrie, D., & Higa, J. (submitted). *Processing negativities in a complex discrimination task: II. Abnormalities in Schizophrenic children.*

Stuss, D. T., Benson, D. F., Kaplan, E. F., Weir, W. S., Naesser, M. A., Lieverman, I., & Ferrill, D. (1983). The involvement of orbitofrontal cerebrum in cognitive tasks. *Neuropsychologia, 21,* 235–248.

Treisman A. M., & Gelade G. (1980). A feature integration theory of attention. *Cognitive Psychology, 97,* 136–145.

Venables, P. H. (1964). Input dysfunction and shizophenia. In B. A. Maher (Ed.), *Progress in experimental personality research* (Vol. 1). New York: Academic Press.

Wagener, D. K., Hogarty, G. E., Goldstein, M. J., Asarnow, R. F., & Browne, A. (1986). Information processing and communication deviance in schizophenic patients and their mothers. *Psychiatry Research, 18,* 365–377.

Watkins, J. M., Asarnow, R., & Tanguay, P. E. (1988). Symptom development in childhood onset schizophrenia. *Journal of Child Psychiatry. 29,* 865–878.

Wechsler, D. (1974). *Wechsler Intelligence Scale for Children-Revised.* New York: Psychological Corporation.

Zahn-Waxler, C., Iannotti, R., & Chapman, M. (1982). Peers and prosocial development. *Peer relationships and social skills in childhood* (pp. 133–162). In K. Rubin & H. Ross (Ed.), New York: Springer-Verlag.

Zubin, J., Magaziner, J., & Steinhauer, S. R. (1983). The metamorphosis of schizophrenia: From chronicity to vulnerability. *Psychological Medicine, 13,* 551–571.

Zubin, J., & Spring, B. (1977). Vulnerability: A new view of schizophrenia. *Journal of Abnormal Psychology, 86,* 103.

10 Age of Onset, Temporal Stability, and Eighteen-Month Course of First-Episode Psychosis

William G. Iacono
University of Minnesota

Morton Beiser
University of British Columbia

In 1981, together with colleagues Tsung-Yi Lin and Jonathan Fleming, we launched a long-term prospective study of schizophrenia by recruiting a large sample of individuals experiencing their first episode of psychosis. This study, which operated under the acronym MAP (for Markers and Predictors of schizophrenia), was concerned with how a number of different factors contribute to variability in the onset, presentation, and course of disorder in a cohort of 175 psychotic patients. Potential predictors selected for this study included specific clinical features and definitions of psychosis (Beiser, Fleming, Iacono, & Lin, 1988), psychophysiological markers (Iacono, 1985), anomalies in brain morphology, (Iacono, Smith, Moreau, Beiser, Fleming, Lin, & Flak, 1988), labeling by the self and significant others (Beiser, Waxler-Morrison, Iacono, Lin, Fleming, & Husted, 1987), life stress, role demands, coping abilities, and social support.

Our goal was to identify and recruit all individuals in our catchment area who made their first-lifetime contact with a helping agency or professional because of psychotic symptoms. Although difficult and expensive, studying first-episode cases has many advantages compared with inquiries that include or focus on chronic disorder. Chronicity limits diagnostic and prognostic variability, obscures the effects of psychosocial factors, and produces subjects whose biological abnormalities may be secondary to the long-term effects of illness, treatments, and institutionalization. To avoid the possible bias associated with recruiting only institutionalized patients from a single facility (Cohen & Cohen, 1984), we cast a broad net in an effort to come as close as possible to obtaining a total sample—all residents of a Canadian coastal city experiencing an episode of psychosis for the first time in their lives. Subjects were recruited from multiple sources both within and outside the traditional mental health care system. Because there is no consensus on how best to classify psychotic disorders, we used several diagnostic systems that provide a range of operational definitions for schizophrenia and affective psychosis.

As these introductory remarks indicate, the MAP project has many facets and objectives, not all of which can be addressed in this chapter. We are taking this opportunity to address three issues from a developmental perspective. One involves individual differences in the age of onset of psychosis, both within and among different categories of psychosis and between the sexes. Another concerns the developmental course of disorder as manifested in the temporal stability of diagnostic assignment during the year and a half that follows the first psychotic episode. The last relates to the prediction of the short-term outcome of psychosis.

OVERVIEW OF THE MAP PROJECT

Although schizophrenia was the focus of the MAP investigation, this project is unique among studies of first-episode schizophrenia with regard to the comprehensiveness of the sample and the inclusion of all cases of nonorganic psychosis regardless of diagnosis. The decision to study psychosis generally rather than only schizophrenic and related psychoses such as schizophreniform and schizoaffective disorder accomplished three important objectives. First, it provided comparison groups of patients who, like the schizophrenic subjects, were also experiencing their first bout of psychotic symptoms. Second, it provided an opportunity to use and evaluate different operational definitions of schizophrenia and other psychotic disorders without relying on a sample that was preselected for having a particular type of disorder or that was derived from a single source. Many reports that have contrasted diagnostic approaches have selected their study samples by choosing patients who have an initial diagnosis of schizophrenia (e.g., Bland & Orn, 1978; Klein, 1982; Stephens, Astrup, Carpenter, Shaffer, & Goldberg, 1982) or schizophrenia-related disorder (Sartorius et al., 1986). While such studies can provide valuable information regarding how different operational definitions of schizophrenia work if the initial inclusion criteria are sufficiently broad, they provide little insight into the consequences of using different operational definitions of affective psychosis. Other studies have selected patients from a single source (e.g., Endicott, Nee, Fleiss, Cohen, Williams, & Simon, 1982; Helzer, Brockington, & Kendell, 1981; Klein, 1982; McGlashen, 1984; Stephens et al., 1982), thus leaving the generalizability of their results undetermined. Third, the inclusion of all instances of nonorganic psychosis resulted in a unique sample of patients with psychotic mood disorders who were experiencing their first episode. To our knowledge, such a sample has not been studied before. Compared to those individuals with major affective disorder without psychotic features, little is known about psychotic patients with mood disorders.

To recruit study participants, a referral network was established to identify all persons in Vancouver, British Columbia (a metropolitan area of 1.25 million), who experienced their first episode of psychosis from February, 1982 through September, 1984. Although differing in important ways, the subject recruitment strategy and the basic design of the study were similar to that of the World Health Organization (WHO) Collaborative Study on Determinants of Outcome of Severe Mental Disorders (Sartorius et al., 1986). To minimize selection bias, we established a referral network that was comprised of agencies at which individuals experiencing a first episode of psychosis might appear. These included psychiatric hospitals, psychiatric services of general hospitals, university and college counseling services, community mental health centers, private counseling services, employment and immigration counseling agencies, psychiatrists in private practice, and a one-in-six probability sample of general practice physicians. Approximately 13% of the study participants were referred from sources other than inpatient hospital services.

Research assistants maintained regular contact with the referral sources which were supplied with a definition of psychotic behavior purposely broad and inclusive enough to ensure identifying all potential participants. Upon receiving a referral, project staff screened all relevant material to determine if the patient satisfied the following inclusion criteria:

1. Currently psychotic, i.e., experiencing hallucinations or delusions, displaying grossly disorganized behavior, showing marked loss of drive, social withdrawal, severe excitement, overwhelming anxiety or fear, and gross self-neglect.

2. Experiencing a first episode of disorder, i.e., not treated prior to the present episode with antipsychotic, antimanic, or antidepressant drugs.

3. Age between 15 and 54 years.

4. Absence of organic cerebral illness, chemical dependence, severe mental retardation, or a chronic physical disorder.

5. Lived in the Vancouver metropolitan area for at least 6 months.

Potential subjects, including doubtful and borderline cases, were initially retained for the project with their final disposition decided by the results of a thorough clinical investigation that included administration of a semistructured interview (the Present State Examination or PSE, 9th edition; Wing, Cooper, & Sartorius, 1974) within 3 months from the beginning of treatment by a clinical psychologist or psychiatrist, review of clinical charts, and interviews with family members and friends.

Following the completion of all data gathering on each subject, the research staff met to pool information gained from the PSE and ancillary sources. At least two experienced diagnosticians, including one Ph.D. level clinical psychologist and one psychiatrist, attended each of the clinical case conferences. The function of the case conferences was to establish the presence of symptoms and signs relevant to diagnosis. The method resembled a "best estimate" approach to diagnosis (Leckman, Sholomskas, Thompson, Belanger, & Weissman, 1982) in that it is assumed that the optimal diagnostic assignment is the one made on the basis of the most complete information.

Five different diagnostic systems were used to classify participants. These were the Diagnostic and Statistical Manual-Third Edition (DSM-III; American Psychiatric Association, 1980), the Research Diagnostic Criteria (RDC; Spitzer, Endicott, & Robins, 1977, 1978), the criteria of Feighner et al. (1972), the International Classification of Diseases-Ninth Edition (ICD-9; World Health Organization, 1978), and the 12-point flexible system of Carpenter, Strauss, and Bartko (1973). With the exception of ICD-9, each of these systems has an explicit set of criteria for making diagnoses. ICD-9, which is quite similar to DSM-II (American Psychiatric Association, 1968), offers more clinical latitude and less operational specificity than the other systems. In order to adapt the fairly loose ICD-9 psychotic disorder categories for research purposes, the project clinicians prepared a checklist of symptoms and diagnostic criteria derived from the clinical constructs described in the ICD-9 manual. The checklist consisted of a listing in outline form of the symptoms and criteria contained in the descriptive paragraphs in the manual. The use of this checklist insured that we attended to all of the ICD-9 descriptive criteria in a comprehensive fashion. ICD-9 is the official classification system in Canada; our use of ICD-9 approximates the way it was used in this country at the time the MAP project was initiated.

To optimize diagnostic reliability, all of the symptoms and diagnostic criteria associated with the psychotic disorders described in each diagnostic system were reviewed for each patient to determine whether each symptom was present or absent. Then the diagnostic algorithms specified for each system were strictly followed to arrive at a diagnosis. Only subjects who satisfied the criteria for an active psychotic disorder in at least one diagnostic system were retained for study.

Of 318 potential subjects identified during the intake period, we successfully recruited 193. However, 18 of these individuals failed to satisfy the project inclusion criteria following our clinical review. Hence, 175 patients participated in the study. The remaining 125 individuals either refused to give informed consent (n = 94) or disappeared or moved away before we could approach them (n = 31).

The very similar age and sex characteristics of the participants and nonparticipants are summarized in Table 10.1. There were no significant differences in the mean age or distribution of ages of the participants vs. the nonparticipants. There were also no significant differences in the sex distribution between the two

TABLE 10.1

A Comparison of the Age and Sex of MAP Participants and Nonparticipants

Age at First Treatment Contact for Psychotic Symptoms (in Years)

| | Percent of Patients by 5-Year Interval | | | | | | Age | | |
Group	16-20	21-25	26-30	31-35	36-40	41+	M	SD	Range
All Participants	33	33	15	7	5	7	25.2	8.1	16-50
Males (n=119)	32	35	15	6	5	7	25.0	7.8	16-50
Females (n=56)	34	27	16	11	4	9	25.7	8.9	16-50
All Nonparticipants[a]	34	22	18	14	6	7	25.8	8.3	16-49
Males (n=70)	37	23	19	11	6	7	25.1	7.8	16-49
Females (n=50)	30	20	16	18	6	6	27.1	9.0	16-49

[a]Five nonparticipants (2 males, 3 females) were not included in this table because information about their ages was not made available.

groups. However, there were more male than female cases of psychosis for the 175 participants, 68% of whom were male, (Yates corrected chi-square $= 21.97$, df $= 1$, $p < .001$) as well as for the combined group of 300 patients, 64% of whom were male (Yates corrected chi-square $= 21.87$, df $= 1$, $p < .001$).

To establish short-term outcome, we conducted follow-up assessments 9 and 18 months following intake. Nine months after they entered the study, subjects were interviewed by trained master's level research assistants with another structured interview, the Diagnostic Interview Schedule or DIS (Robins, Helzer, Cro᠁ghan, & Ratcliff, 1981), which was abbreviated to focus on assessment of the ⸓unctional psychoses. The 18-month follow-up included a re-administration of the PSE by a project clinician and an interview with a significant other to collect corroborative data about the patient. Both the DIS and the PSE covered psychiatric status during the month preceding the interview. On both follow-up occasions, information was collected pertaining to occupational and school activity, treatment, medication, psychoactive substance use, living situation, and social activity. In addition, medical records from area clinics and hospitals were reviewed for each subject. Clinical case conferences were again held to establish patient diagnosis at the time of the 9- and 18-month assessments and to assign Global Assessment Scale (GAS) ratings (Endicott, Spitzer, Fleiss, & Cohen, 1976).

Attrition is a concern in all longitudinal studies. At the time of the 9-month assessment, we re-interviewed 120 of our 175 psychotic subjects. At 18 months our participation rate actually improved, with 129 re-interviews. Four of our subjects died over this period. Since death is an analyzable outcome, our true attrition rate over 18 months was 42 subjects or 24%. The "true" drop-outs either could not be located, had moved such a distance that following them was impractical, or refused to participate. Comparing those present at 18 months with the dropouts, we found that remainers were on average slightly younger and came from slightly higher socioeconomic backgrounds. There were no significant differences in education or gender proportions. The distribution of patients across DSM-III psychiatric diagnoses also did not differ between the retained and lost-to-follow-up samples. In light of these data, it is unlikely that differential drop-out had much effect on our results. There may be some bias towards better prognosis in our retained sample because parental social class does predict adjustment (Turner, 1968). However, younger psychotic patients tend to have poorer outcome, a factor that could offset any advantage associated with social class.

The diagnoses of the 175 MAP project participants are presented in Table 10.2. For the purposes of this presentation, RDC and Feighner "probable" diagnoses were combined with "definite" to define cases of disorder. For the 12-point flexible system, the presence of 6 or more symptoms was used to define schizophrenia. The proportion of subjects diagnosed as having schizophrenia varies considerably across diagnostic systems. ICD-9, which has the broadest

TABLE 10.2
Number of Psychotic Patients by Diagnostic Category
for Each Diagnostic System (Total n = 175)

Diagnosis	ICD-9[a]	12-Point	RDC	DSM-III	Feighner
Schizophrenia	114	70	64	54	41
Schizophreniform	--	--	--	31	--
Schizoaffective	--	--	54	6	--
Mania	28	--	25	38	16
Depression	23	--	20	35	21
Paranoia[b]	7	--	--	7	--
Other	3	105	12	4	97

Note. Dashed lines indicate that the diagnostic category does not exist for the indicated diagnostic system.

[a]Manic depressive psychosis was broken down into subtypes depending on whether the patient's first eposide was manic or depressed. Mixed cases were classified manic.

[b]Includes all psychosies in ICD-9 and DSM-III that are referred to as "paranoid."

definition of schizophrenia, generated 2.78 times as many patients with this diagnosis as the Feighner system, which has the narrowest characterization of schizophrenia. DSM-III, on the other hand, provides the broadest notion of mania (bipolar disorder) and major depression, with the Feighner system again being the most conservative. Both the 12-point and Feighner approaches categorize the majority of patients as having an undiagnosed psychosis. For the 12-point system, this occurs because schizophrenia is the only disorder that can be diagnosed. The large number of Feighner system unspecified psychoses stems from the rather rigidly narrow and exclusive criteria used to diagnose schizophrenia and affective psychosis; most psychotic patients simply cannot be assigned a specific diagnosis using this conservative approach. Both DSM-III and RDC have schizophrenia-related diagnostic categories (schizophreniform and schizoaffective disorder, respectively) that do not appear in other systems.

AGE OF ONSET AND SEX DISTRIBUTION

Because the MAP project was designed to recruit every case of first episode psychosis, it provides a valuable opportunity to examine schizophrenia from an epidemiological perspective. However, since recruitment was not population based but derived instead from a specific set of referral sources, the MAP project cannot be considered a study of incidence. In addition, we were restricted by the rules of informed consent, so no data other than age, sex, and chart diagnosis were available on the potential participants who were not successfully recruited into the study. Nevertheless, the data present an opportunity for heuristic investigations of age and sex trends. As Rutter and Sroufe have noted (Rutter, 1988; Sroufe & Rutter, 1984), the developmental perspective considers age and sex as key variables. They reflect, either alone or in combination, different levels and processes of biological maturation, variations in social status and educational attainment, and differences in the duration and kinds of experiences encountered. Information about age and sex differences associated with schizophrenia may ultimately provide insights to the underlying biological and psychosocial factors that contribute to the development of this disorder.

Such data also have important implications for the diagnosis and genetics of schizophrenia. If it is the case, as the Feighner and DSM-III systems specify, that those with an age of onset over 40 and 45, respectively, are not schizophrenic, then such individuals should not be so classified and specific research programs on the etiology and treatment of late-onset schizophrenic-like psychoses should be launched. Likewise, in family studies, relatives of those with schizophrenia can be considered as having passed through the age of risk by age 40–45 and the age correction of family data should be adjusted to reflect this knowledge. In addition, analysis of the differences in age of onset and sex distribution between this study and others provides an opportunity to analyze research in this field and formulate questions that can be addressed in future investigations.

Schizophrenia is characterized as equally prevalent in males and females (American Psychiatric Association, 1980, 1987) with females having an age of onset that is about 5 years later (Lewine, 1981; Loranger, 1984). Much of the data concerning the age of onset of schizophrenia are derived from incidence studies which define onset as the age at first psychiatric hospital admission. These investigations, which use unspecified criteria of unknown reliability to diagnose schizophrenia, report the average age of onset of schizophrenia to be as high as 32–36 years in males and 36–43 years in females (Larson & Nyman, 1970; McCabe, 1975; Slater & Cowie, 1971), with the age of risk extending beyond 60 (Bland, 1977; Häfner, 1987; McCabe, 1975; Munk-Jørgensen, 1985, 1986; Ni Nullain, O'Hare, & Walsh, 1987; Slater & Cowie, 1971; Strömgren, 1987; Wing, 1986). More recent studies using diagnostic criteria and data gathering instruments of proven reliability, have generated statistics suggesting that the average age of onset is under age 28 for women and under age 23 for men (e.g., Baron, Gruen, Asnis, & Kane, 1983; Bellodi, Morabito, Macciardi, Gasperini, Benvenuto, Grossi, Marzorati-Spairani, & Smeraldi, 1982; Levanthal, Schuck, & Rothstein, 1984; Loranger, 1984).

Findings from the MAP Study

Table 10.3 gives the proportion of males and females by diagnostic category and presents means and standard deviations for age at entry to our study. For the purposes of this presentation, age of onset is considered as the age at first contact with a helping agency or professional for the treatment of psychotic symptoms. Because for the vast majority of our subjects this time was associated with hospitalization, our operational definition of onset is similar to that used in registry-based epidemiological studies, all of which use hospital first admissions to identify cases, and to that employed in the WHO study reported by Sartorius et al. (1986), which used a community-based referral method similar to ours to recruit cases. However, since people do not necessarily seek help at the first signs of psychosis and because psychotic symptoms are not necessarily the first indication of the onset of a psychotic disorder, it should be noted that our definition of onset does not date the age at which signs of illness first appeared. Many of our subjects, and especially those diagnosed schizophrenic, experienced prodromal symptoms for some time before florid psychotic symptoms emerged. For these individuals, the actual age of disorder onset could predate the appearance of psychotic symptoms and entry into the mental health treatment system by many months.

The most striking feature of Table 10.3 is that regardless of diagnostic definition, there are three times as many schizophrenic men as women. Although not quite as pronounced, the same unbalanced sex distribution characterizes DSM-III schizophreniform and RDC schizoaffective disorder. Across diagnostic systems, the sex ratio for mania and depressive psychosis is about 1.0. While this finding may appear unusual given that major depression is diagnosed in twice as many women as men, it should be noted that all MAP subjects with this diagnosis were psychotic and suffering their first episode. Little is known about the pattern of gender distribution to be expected in such a sample which probably makes up less than a third of those institutionalized with a diagnosis of major depression (Eagles, 1983). Moreover, an unspecified proportion of these patients will ultimately be shown to have bipolar disorder, which is not clearly more common in females (e.g., Robins et al., 1984). Paranoid and other psychoses are also dominated by males although for some diagnostic systems, sample sizes are too small to reach any firm conclusions.

A second finding evident in Table 10.3 is that, regardless of the diagnostic system employed, there is no sex difference in the age of onset for schizophrenia. The same holds true for DSM-III schizophreniform disorder and RDC schizoaffective disorder. By contrast, women with depressive psychosis are older than men with the same diagnosis. For both sexes, people with diagnoses of paranoid and other psychoses who enter the treatment system are older than those with affective and schizophrenic disorders. These findings are more striking in Table 10.4, which indicates the peak 5-year period or quinquennium for the development of DSM-III defined psychoses. Most people who enter the treatment system with a diagnosis of schizophreniform disorder were young: almost half were under 21 and almost three quarters were under 26. Major depression and bipolar disorder peak in the 21–25 year period, while first treatment contact for the majority of other psychoses (which for the purposes of Table 10.4 include schizoaffective, paranoid, brief reactive, and atypical psychoses) occurs much later in life. These age variations across categories are statistically significant

TABLE 10.3

Sex Distribution and Age of Onset by Diagnostic Category Within Each Diagnostic System

Diagnosis	Sex	ICD-9 %	ICD-9 Age M	ICD-9 Age SD	12-Point %	12-Point Age M	12-Point Age SD	RDC %	RDC Age M	RDC Age SD	DSM-III %	DSM-III Age M	DSM-III Age SD	Feighner %	Feighner Age M	Feighner Age SD
Schizophrenia	M	75	24	6.3	76	23	5.7	75	22	4.9	76	23	5.5	73	23	5.1
	F	25	23	7.5	24	23	7.1	25	20	4.2	24	21	4.7	27	20	4.5
Schizophreniform	M	--	--	--	--	--	--	--	--	--	71	22	4.4	--	--	--
	F	--	--	--	--	--	--	--	--	--	29	22	5.5	--	--	--
Schizoaffective	M	--	--	--	--	--	--	70	25	6.7	83	25	9.4	--	--	--
	F	--	--	--	--	--	--	30	25	8.7	17	44	--	--	--	--
Mania	M	54	28	8.5	--	--	--	56	28	8.8	53	27	8.0	50	31[a]	10.2
	F	46	24	6.7	--	--	--	44	25	6.9	47	26	7.9	50	22[a]	4.2
Depression	M	52	22	3.7	--	--	--	55	22[a]	3.7	66	24	6.2	52	22	3.7
	F	48	31[a]	10.2	--	--	--	45	31[a]	11.3	34	30[a]	10.1	48	31[a]	10.9
Paranoia	M	57	41	12.2	--	--	--	--	--	--	57	41	12.2	--	--	--
	F	43	38	7.9	--	--	--	--	--	--	43	38	7.9	--	--	--
Other	M	100	38	12.5	63	27	8.8	67	40	10.7	100	31	12.1	72	26	8.4
	F	0	--	--	37	27	9.4	33	37	6.7	--	--	--	28	27	9.3

[a]Age of males and females significantly different at the .05 level (two-tailed test).

TABLE 10.4
Age of Onset and SDM-III Diagnosis

DSM-III Diagnosis	Age of Onset (1% of Patients)					Age Range
	16-20	21-25	26-30	31-35	36+	
Schizophrenia n=54	<u>43</u>	30	20	4	4	16-37
Schizophreniform n=31	<u>45</u>	36	13	7	0	16-33
Bipolar n=38	26	<u>32</u>	16	11	16	17-45
Major Depression n=35	23	<u>43</u>	14	9	11	17-42
Other n=17	12	18	6	12	<u>53</u>	17-50
All Patients n=175	<u>33</u>	<u>33</u>	15	7	12	16-50

Note. Underlined entries indicate most common 5-year period for age of onset.

(chi-square = 44.51, df = 16, $p < .001$). To conserve space, the psychiatric classification by age of onset distribution is presented only for DSM-III diagnoses. However, the other diagnostic systems yield a very similar picture.

Table 10.5 illustrates that despite the broad range of approaches used to diagnose this disorder, the finding regarding age of onset is constant. Does this finding imply that for all diagnostic systems it is equally unlikely that an older individual will be diagnosed schizophrenic? The answer to this question, as Table 10.6 illustrates, is no. Table 10.6 was prepared by determining the propor-

TABLE 10.5
Age of Onset for Schizophrenia by Diagnostic System

Diagnostic System	Age of Onset (% of Patients)					Age Range
	16-20	21-25	26-30	31-35	36+	
ICD-9 n=114	<u>39</u>	32	17	5	7	16-45
12-point n=70	<u>41</u>	34	14	4	6	16-44
RDC n=64	<u>44</u>	33	19	5	0	16-35
DSM-III n=54	<u>43</u>	30	20	4	4	16-37
Feighner n=41	<u>44</u>	32	20	5	0	16-35

Note. Underlined entries indicate most common 5-year period for age of onset.

TABLE 10.6
Of All the Patients Who Decompensate During an Age
Period, the Percentage of the Total Who Are
Schizophrenic as a Function of Diagnostic System

Diagnostic System	Age of Onset in Years				
	16-20 n=57	21-25 n=57	26-30 n=27	31-35 n=13	36+ n=21
ICD-9	77	65	70	46	38
12-point	51	42	37	23	19
RDC	49	37	44	23	0
DSM-III	40	28	41	15	10
Feighner	32	23	30	16	0

tion of individuals who presented within the social and health care systems with a diagnosis of schizophrenia during a specified quinquennium. For example, in the 16–20 age range, of the 57 subjects presenting for help, 23 or 40% were labeled schizophrenic by DSM-III, 28 or 49% were similarly diagnosed by RDC, etc. Table 10.6 indicates that, in general, the less restrictive the diagnostic conceptualization of schizophrenia (as defined by the number of cases so identified), the greater the proportion of patients in any 5-year age bracket that will receive a diagnosis of schizophrenia. Although in general, older subjects were less likely to be diagnosed schizophrenic than younger subjects, older participants were more likely to be assigned this label under a classification scheme with a broad definition of schizophrenia.

To summarize, the following conclusions are supported by these data:

1. Among psychotic subjects making a first helping contact for the treatment of their psychotic symptoms, the ratio of males to females with schizophrenia was about 3 to 1.

2. There were no sex differences in the age of onset for schizophrenia.

3. In this sample, schizophrenia was a disorder of adolescence and young adulthood; fewer than 13% of the cases had an onset after age 31.

4. The above three findings are independent of the breadth of the criteria used to define schizophrenia.

5. There is a correlation between the narrowness of the definition of schizophrenia and the likelihood of a late-onset patient being diagnosed schizophrenic. The narrower the operational definition, the less likely it is that a late onset case will be diagnosed schizophrenic.

6. Nonschizophrenic psychoses show a later age of onset than do schizophrenia and the schizophrenia-related psychoses.

7. Age of onset of the functional psychoses is highly variable, ranging from the earliest age at which we examined subjects, 16, to age 50.

Comparison of MAP Findings with Those of Other Investigators

The very high proportion of males in the MAP sample and the fact that first-episode male and female schizophrenics are equal in age contradicts some of the literature on schizophrenia. How can these discrepancies between our data and other published reports be reconciled?

The effect of nonparticipants. One possibility is that the MAP nonpartici-pants were largely older and female, thus biasing the sample towards youth and male sex. Table 10.1 illustrates, however, that there was no difference in the age distribution between participants and nonparticipants and that nonparticipants were, like participants, more apt to be male. It could be that the nonparticipant group contained a disproportionate number of schizophrenic patients and that the schizophrenics in this group were more likely to be female and older. None of these notions is well supported by the data. Relying on the diagnoses assigned the nonparticipants by their primary care therapists, 59% fell into the schizo-phrenia spectrum (schizophrenic, schizophreniform, or schizoaffective disor-der). This rate is similar to the 52% of participants who received these DSM-III diagnoses. Of the nonparticipants who were given one of these labels, only 41% were female. Although this is a somewhat larger percentage than is evident in the similarly diagnosed MAP participants (25%), the difference in the proportion of females in the two samples is not statistically significant. Combining the partici-pants and nonparticipant schizophrenia spectrum patients still generates a sample that is 68% male. Finally, of the nonparticipants with a spectrum psychosis, 85% were under 31. The corresponding number for those who participated was 91%. Hence, it does not appear that nonparticipating patients with schizophrenia-related diagnoses were substantially older than participants.

The "baby-boom" hypothesis. Another way to evaluate our findings is to consider trends in the birth rate in the several decades preceding the MAP study. If 15–25 years prior to the initiation of the MAP project there was a great increase in the birth rate, then the population could have a disproportionately large sample of individuals entering the period of greatest risk for the develop-ment of schizophrenia (ages between 16 and 25 years, see Table 10.5). Because we sampled from this group over a 2-year period, it could be that we were able to identify many of the males, who are at greater risk during this period, but that we missed females who would have entered their greatest period of risk after our recruitment of patients had terminated. That is, had we recruited patients over a more extended period of time, our early recruitment of a disproportionate number of young males with schizophrenia would have been offset by later recruitment of a disproportionate number of females. However, as can be seen from Table 10.7, which presents census data collected by Statistics Canada for

TABLE 10.7
Number of Males and Females Living in the Greater Vancouver
Metropolitan Area in 1981

Age Range	Males	Females	Totals
15-24	111,510	111,830	223,340
25-34	115,180	117,330	232,510
35-44	83,650	81,460	165,110
45-54	69,885	66,665	136,550

1981, the year the MAP study began, there were fewer individuals aged 15–24 than there were individuals aged 25–34 living in the Vancouver metropolitan area. Hence, there was no shortage of older females. Despite this fact, few females in the 25–34 year age range appear to have experienced a first episode of schizophrenia.

The contribution of substance abuse.   Illicit drug use is more prevalent in the 1980s than it was when the data for most epidemiological studies of schizophrenia were collected. The wide-spread use of street drugs and excessive alcohol consumption by adolescents and young adults could contribute to a lowering of the age of onset of schizophrenia by producing drug psychoses that resemble schizophrenia, by triggering the expression of the underlying diathesis at an earlier age than in the past, or by causing a combination of aberrant behaviors that leads to earlier entry into the treatment system than would otherwise have occurred.

Individuals who satisfied DSM-III criteria for substance dependence were excluded from the MAP project, but those who met the criteria for substance abuse were recruited. Because it was difficult to determine if impaired social and occupational functioning, one of the criteria for DSM-III substance abuse, was attributable to the substance use or other Axis I psychopathology, we diagnosed substance abuse as either definite or probable based on our degree of confidence that we could make this differentiation. All patients who received the designation of definite or probable substance abuse showed a pattern of pathological use for at least 1 month.

Whether or not drugs and alcohol play a role in the genesis of schizophrenia is unknown, but the drug-use behavior of first-episode patients may provide some insights. One way to approach this issue is to compare DSM-III schizophrenia with schizophreniform disorder. The latter is a diagnostic classification that differs from schizophrenia only in that the 6-month criterion for symptom duration is not met. Since the MAP project is a study of first-episode disorders, the chief way in which schizophrenic and schizophreniform psychoses differ is in the prodromal clinical state, with schizophrenia more likely to show an insidious onset that is associated with a lower level of premorbid competence. This was the case in our patients as evidenced by a comparison of the level of adaptive functioning for these two groups, using DSM-III Axis V, which showed that the schizophrenics were clearly functioning at a lower level than patients with schizophreniform disorder (t (83) = 3.46, $p < .001$).

If drug use is associated with the precipitation of psychosis, it might be expected that drug involvement will be more important in patients who are better compensated and less likely to be victims of an insidious process. In this fashion, drug/alcohol abuse was more clearly associated with schizophreniform than schizophrenic disorder. Twelve percent (6/52) of those diagnosed schizophrenic met criteria for probable or definite chemical abuse compared to 39% (12/31) of schizophreniform patients (Yates corrected chi-square = 6.93, df = 1, $p < .01$). Interestingly, although the sample is small, of those schizophreniform patients who were abusing drugs at intake, all but two subjects (20%) were ultimately classified as having schizophrenia once all the clinical material collected over the 18-month follow-up period was reviewed. By contrast, of those not abusing chemicals at this time, only 44% went on to receive a diagnosis of schizophrenia. Although no unequivocal conclusions can be drawn from these data, the pattern of results is consistent with the hypothesis that drug/alcohol use may contribute to the development of schizophrenia. These results also suggest that caution should be exercised comparing incidence data across periods of time associated with marked change in the availability and use of psychoactive substances.

If males are more likely than females to abuse chemicals, drug use could differentially affect the distribution of schizophrenia across the sexes. However, male and female MAP participants appear not to be differentiable according to their pattern of drug use at intake into the project. Sixty-three percent of men and 67% of women either did not use drugs or alcohol or ingested these substances only occasionally. Moreover, there was no difference in the proportion of men and women who abused chemicals: 19% of men and 17% of women were classified as definitely or probably abusing drugs and/or alcohol.

The operational definition of schizophrenia. Compared to earlier studies, the MAP project has identified an excess of males with schizophrenia. Could this be a function in the change in diagnostic practices over the last several decades? Most of the research reporting approximately equal proportions of men and women with schizophrenia is derived from studies using hospital diagnoses based on loose criteria such as those found in ICD-8 and DSM-II, two systems that consider schizoaffective disorder to be a subtype of schizophrenia. More recent and narrow diagnostic systems such as RDC and DSM-III greatly reduce the likelihood that psychotic patients with affective syndromes will receive a schizophrenic diagnosis. Because women are considerably more likely to have major affective disorder than men (e.g., Slater & Cowie, 1971) and schizophrenic women are more apt to display affective features than men (e.g., Goldstein & Link, 1988; Tsuang, Dempsey, & Rauscher, 1976), one consequence of this shift in approach might be to exclude disproportionately more women than men from the schizophrenic category.

This hypothesis has been evaluated in two studies by Lewine and associates (Lewine, Burbach, & Meltzer, 1984; Lewine, Strauss, & Gift, 1981). In the first of these investigations, Lewine et al. (1981) concluded that the broadest and narrowest sets of diagnostic criteria yielded a sex ratio of about 1.0, but intermediate approaches yielded an excess of males. This study has been criticized by Loranger (1984) who noted that the patient sample was too small to be conclusive, especially with regard to the effect of applying restrictive criteria for the definition of schizophrenia. For example, only two patients satisfied RDC criteria and only nine qualified for a Feighner diagnosis of schizophrenia.

In the more recent of these reports, Lewine et al. (1984) compared the male to female sex ratio when six different sets of operational criteria were used to diagnose schizophrenia. The broadest criteria were provided by the New Haven Schizophrenia Index (Astrachan et al., 1972) which classified 231 patients as schizophrenic, 53% of whom were male. ICD-9 and DSM-III were not used, but the 12-point, RDC, and Feighner systems were. The Feighner system offered both the narrowest definition of this disorder and the greatest excess of males: The yield was only seven patients, all male. The male : female sex ratio among RDC diagnosed schizophrenics was 2.8, which is very similar to that observed for RDC schizophrenia in the MAP project (3.0). The application of the 12-point flexible system by Lewine et al. relied on a "criterion score of 5." It is not clear whether this means that a score over 5 defines schizophrenia, as it did in the MAP project, or whether the presence of this disorder is defined by scores of 5 and above. In any event, the 12-point system as applied by Lewine et al. (1984) yielded a schizophrenic sample that was 58% male. This frequency of men differs significantly from that identified in the MAP project using the 12-point system, whether a cut-off of 6 (which yielded 76% men, Yates corrected chi-square = 5.64, df = 1, $p < .05$) or 5 (which yielded 73% men, Yates corrected chi-square = 5.36, df = 1, $p < .05$) is used.

Clearly, the conclusion of Lewine et al. (1984) is not supported by data from the MAP study. As Table 10.3 indicates, the breadth of the diagnostic criteria used to classify schizophrenia has no bearing on the sex ratio. Moreover, the sex ratios reported by Lewine et al. (1984) for the 12-point-flexible and Feighner systems do not match those calculated from MAP data for these two diagnostic approaches. However, for the Feigner system, the sample size of Lewine et al. is too small to reach firm conclusions.

A number of factors could have contributed to the discrepancy between our findings and those of Lewine et al. (1984). All of the patients evaluated by Lewine et al. came from a single hospital with 74% coming from a unit described as exclusively for patients referred to the hospital for special evaluation and research. The use of such a patient base may have generated a less representative sample than was obtained by the MAP project which drew inpatients and outpatients from a wide array of sources.

Another difference between the studies was that the MAP project included only patients experiencing their first episode. The Lewine et al. sample was not so restricted. The correlation between male excess and narrowness of diagnostic criteria could stem from the possibility that their male patients were more likely to be chronic than their females. Because more conservative diagnostic systems are more likely to diagnose chronic patients as schizophrenic, the findings reported by Lewine et al. could be a product of the known sex differences in the chronicity of schizophrenia (e.g., Lewine, 1981; Watt, Katz, & Shepherd, 1983). A final factor that differentiates these studies concerns the requirement that all MAP participants have psychotic symptoms. The absence of such a requirement in the Lewine et al. study may have led to the inclusion of many nonpsychotic cases. For example, it is possible to be diagnosed schizophrenic with the New Haven and 12-point flexible systems without having hallucinations, delusions, or thought form disorder. The possibility that the Lewine et al. study included many less severe, nonpsychotic cases is supported by the fact that the most conservative system, that of Feighner, diagnosed only 7 (2%) of Lewine et al.'s initial sample of 310 patients as schizophrenic compared to 41 (23%) of 175 MAP subjects. If such nonpsychotic cases were composed mainly of women, the narrower diagnostic systems, which emphasize specific psychotic symptoms and tend to relegate people with affective symptoms to other diagnostic categories (Goldstein, 1988; Westermeyer & Harrow, 1984), would be less likely to diagnose them as schizophrenic. In Denmark, where the diagnosis of schizophrenia is an extremely narrow one, Munk-Jørgensen (1986) found that the incidence of schizophrenia, based on first-hospital admissions, was more than two times higher in males than females.

It should be apparent, however, that the Lewine et al. data are not entirely inconsistent with the MAP findings because the RDC sex ratios obtained in the two studies are the same and Lewine et al.'s Feighner data are also consistent, though inconclusive. If it is assumed that the Lewine et al. study included many nonpsychotic individuals and that the RDC, which gives great emphasis to specific psychotic symptoms, eliminated such cases, then the two studies are in agreement in showing that when symptomatically mild or less definite cases of schizophrenia are eliminated, the sex ratio greatly favors males.

Sex ratio as a function of age of onset.   Flor-Henry (1985) has noted that the male-to-female sex ratio varies with the age of onset of schizophrenia. For example, in one study of first hospital admissions (McCabe, 1975), the sex ratio was 4.0 for patients with an age of onset under 20. Males continued to outnumber females until age 40. After that age, women outnumbered men. As can be seen from Table 10.8, other studies have also demonstrated that males are disproportionately represented among those with an early age of onset (see also Babigian, 1975; Bland, 1977; Hafner, 1987; Lewine, 1980; Lewine et al., 1981; Strömgren, 1987; Wing, 1986). The study of Baron et al. (1983) does not show this pattern, but this study retrospectively assigned the age of onset to a sample of

TABLE 10.8
Mean Age at Onset and Percentage of Individuals
Developing Schizophrenia by Age 25

Study	Country	Mean Age		Percent	
		M	F	M	F
Slater & Cowie (1971)[a]	UK	32	36	33	25
McCabe (1975)[a]	Denmark	32	43	40	20
Baron et al. (1983)[b]	USA	20	21	87	86
Loranger (1984)	USA				
First Treated		20	25	82	58
First Hospitalized		22	27	74	46
MAP DSM-III	Canada	23	21	75	77

[a]Based on when patients were first hospitalized.
[b]Determined by when patients first satisfied research diagnostic criteria for schizophrenia.

consecutive admissions that met RDC criteria for chronic schizophrenia. Because it is likely that chronic patients, whether male or female, will have had an early age of onset, Baron et al.'s not finding delayed onset in women may be specific to their use of such a sample. Nevertheless, it is of interest that the results of Baron et al. parallel those of the MAP project.

Of the investigations listed in Table 10.8, that of Loranger (1984) is most comparable to the MAP project. Unlike the other reports, Loranger's study, like the MAP investigation, took place in North America, used DSM-III to diagnose schizophrenia, and calculated age of onset when patients were first treated rather than when they were first hospitalized. The studies also differ in important ways. Loranger's study was based on a chart review with diagnoses of schizophrenia made in retrospect. Of the 884 cases with a DSM-II chart diagnosis of schizophrenia (latent and schizoaffective cases were excluded) that served as Loranger's initial sample, all doubtful cases were eliminated, leaving only 200 deemed to satisfy the more restrictive DSM-III criteria. Less than a third of these cases were first admissions. The patient source was a private university affiliated hospital that served a wealthy suburban New York community. Among Loranger's investigation, 10% of the men and 49% of the women had married. The corresponding figures from the MAP project were about the same for men (12%), but quite different for women (17%). The operational definition of first treatment was not specified by Loranger. In the MAP project, it is defined as the age at which someone appeared in the health care or social service system and was noted, for the first time, to have psychotic symptoms. Because some patients may have been in treatment before they developed psychotic symptoms, it is possible that the two studies are using different methods for defining the time of first treatment. Most of the MAP patients were hospitalized at or shortly after the time of their first helping contact, so the MAP definition of age of onset probably falls between Loranger's dating of age at first treatment and age at first hospitalization (which is also presented in the Table).

Comparing Loranger's data to that of the MAP project, it is apparent that the age of onset for the males diagnosed schizophrenic is very similar. The corresponding female data sets do not match; the MAP women show a younger age of onset with a considerably larger fraction developing schizophrenia prior to age 25. This disparity and the unequal balance between males and females in the MAP study can be explained if for some reason the MAP project systematically eliminated many schizophrenic women with an age of onset over 25 who would have been considered first episode cases in other studies. This could have happened if women with a relatively late age of onset for psychotic symptoms had been treated earlier in their lives with neuroleptic or antidepressant drugs. Such individuals would not have satisfied our criteria for a first episode and would have been excluded from study. Because they have better premorbid competence and more affective and briefer symptoms (e.g., Klorman, Strauss, & Kokes, 1977; Tsuang, Dempsey, & Rauscher, 1976), women with psychiatric disorders are more likely to be treated by general practitioners than are men who are more apt to be referred to psychiatric specialists. It is important to note that in British Columbia patients must be first assessed by a general practitioner before being referred to any specialist. Differences between the sexes in the presentation of psychopathology coupled with this gating mechanism may have resulted in women being more likely than men to be cared for by general practice physicians. Even if women were eventually referred for psychiatric care, if they had previously been treated by a general practitioner with neuroleptic or antidepressant drugs, they would have been disqualified from our study.

The quality of epidemiological data on schizophrenia.   Another approach to evaluate why the sex and age of onset findings from the MAP project are dissimilar to those presented in other reports is to examine the quality of the data in earlier reports. In general, these data suffer from various limitations, most of which are frequently ignored.

Many of the studies examining age of onset and the distribution of schizophrenia across the sexes are based on statistics collected in Northern European countries. National differences in the diagnosis of functional psychosis have been common and continue to the present day. In a brief review of the proportion of first admissions to psychiatric hospitals with various ICD-8 diagnoses, Saugstad (1985) points out that great differences exist in the diagnosis of schizophrenic, affective and reactive psychoses in England and Wales, Denmark, and Norway, all countries that have provided much of the epidemiological data on schizophrenia. England and Wales use a broad concept of affective disorder with 43% of first admissions so diagnosed. In contrast, only 6% of first admissions in Norway are classified as affective. Reactive psychosis, historically an uncommonly used category in the U.S., is the most common diagnosis in Denmark. This label was applied to 37% of cases, a rate that makes reactive psychosis five times more common than schizophrenia in Denmark, where an extremely narrow concept of schizophrenia is used (Munk-Jørgensen, 1986; WHO, 1973, 1979). For these reasons, it is difficult to compare incidence figures even from European sources. For example, using a very narrow definition of schizophrenia, Munk-Jørgensen, (1986) calculated a first hospitalization incidence rate of 5.7 per 100,000 population in Denmark, while Wing and Fryers (1976), using a different definition of the disorder, established a rate twice as high in England. A report like that of McCabe (1975), which reviews the demographic characteristics of first-admission psychoses in Denmark over a 1-year period, is similarly difficult to interpret. The reactive psychoses in the McCabe study composed 49% (743 of 1525 cases) of the admissions for functional psychosis.

Many other features of previous epidemiological investigations make comparison between them and the MAP project difficult. In addition to questions about what constitutes schizophrenia in a given country, in some studies the schizophrenia category has been intentionally broadened to include nonschizophrenic cases. Slater and Cowie's (1971, p. 73) data on age at first hospitalization, which has been reproduced by Gottesman and Shields (1982) to illustrate the age of onset distribution for schizophrenia, combines schizophrenia with paranoia. In a preliminary report of the WHO study of first-contact incidence of schizophrenia, Sartorius et al. (1986) noted that certain reactive psychoses and paranoid psychosis were included in their broad definition of schizophrenia and Ni Nullain et al. (1987) included paranoid states in their least restrictive categorization of schizophrenia. All of these studies (Ni Nullain et al., 1987; Sartorius et al., 1986; Slater & Cowie, 1971) identified a substantial number of individuals with schizophrenia with an age of onset over 40. Because paranoid psychoses show a peak age of onset after 40 and are more common in women (Kendler, 1982), the inclusion of such delusional patients will boost the number of older persons, especially women, who are counted as schizophrenic. Such practices will not only attenuate the magnitude of the male : female ratio, they will also greatly inflate estimates of the average age of onset of schizophrenia. Note also that schizophrenia in older women is unlike that in men or younger women in that older females express more paranoid symptoms (Forrest & Hay, 1971), a finding that is consistent with the possibility that many cases of diagnosed schizophrenia in older women may better be considered cases of paranoid psychosis.

Other issues center on when incidence data were collected and how a first episode is defined. Most studies rely on admission figures that predate 1970 (e.g., Helgason, 1964; Larson & Nyman, 1970; McCabe, 1975; Slater & Cowie, 1971; Strömgren, 1987). Clinical, diagnostic, and research practices have obviously changed over the last several decades (cf. Eagles & Whalley, 1985; Ni Nullain et al., 1987); it is not clear how patients diagnosed 20 or more years ago would be classified today. Nor is it evident that patients who were hospitalized in the 1950s and 1960s would necessarily be hospitalized in the 70s and 80s when community care and day hospital treatment have received much greater emphasis (e.g., Weeke, Munk-Jørgensen, Strömgren, & Dupont, 1986).

Another indication of why it is hazardous to compare incidence data collected at different points in time arises from a study by Eagles and Whalley (1985). These investigators found a 40% decline in the diagnosis of schizophrenia among first admissions to Scottish hospitals over a 10-year period beginning in 1969. Munk-Jørgensen (1985) notes that annual reports from the National Danish Psychiatric Register show a 35% decline in the number of first admission schizophrenics from 1970–1982. The reasons for these declines are uncertain, but may include a genuine drop in the incidence of schizophrenia, changing diagnostic and data collection procedures, and increased utilization of community care resources.

The definition of onset used in these European studies is age at first hospitalization. Age of onset figures are thus affected by hospital policy and factors such as distance to hospital and the availability of beds. Such an approach necessarily eliminates those whose psychosis is not severe enough to warrant hospitalization and assigns a late age of onset to someone who may have undergone lengthy outpatient treatment prior to entering hospital. It also undoubtedly leads to an unknown number of cases being counted twice and others, even if hospitalized, not being counted at all. Some hospitals record as a "first admission" the first inpatient stay at that particular hospital. This practice has been a concern historically and continues today (e.g., Brown, Parkes, & Wing, 1961; Eagles & Whalley, 1985; Ni Nullain et al., 1987). Hence, individuals who seek treatment at different hospitals or who are itinerant may be counted as first admissions on more than one occasion. In addition, many of those who are not diagnosed schizophrenic at first admission may eventually receive this diagnosis. Working from the Danish National Psychiatric Register, Munk-Jørgensen (1985) examined a cohort of patients who were first admitted in 1972 and who were diagnosed schizophrenic either in that year or sometime prior to October, 1983. Only about half the males and 39% of the females originally received the diagnosis of schizophrenia. The remainder were not classified as schizophrenic until a subsequent hospitalization.

Concluding remarks. While epidemiological investigations are a logical place to look for clues and hypotheses regarding the development of schizophrenia, few conclusions can be drawn from the existing literature. Issues such as sex differences and age of onset, which are tied together, remain unclear. Epidemiological studies are complicated by an unevenness in the quality of research practices used to collect data and by a lack of consensus as to what constitutes schizophrenia. In some countries, first-episode schizophrenia is diagnosed in those over age 65. This practice has continued in Europe through the present decade (e.g., Munk-Jørgensen, 1985; Ni Nullain et al., 1987), while in the United States the official diagnostic system from 1980–87, DSM-III, arbitrarily imposed an age cutoff of 45 (this requirement has been dropped in DSM-III-R). Obviously, until some resolution of national differences in diagnostic approach is reached, it will be difficult to integrate epidemiological data from different countries.

Both the study of Lewine et al. (1984) and the MAP project can be viewed as consistent in showing that, if one conceptualizes schizophrenia as a disorder that is defined primarily by the presence of manifest psychotic symptoms, males are more likely to be afflicted with the disorder than females. Moreover, if one assumes that schizophrenia with an age of onset over 40 is indeed rare, then many of the studies that report age of onset figures that are substantially higher than those found in the MAP project achieve this result by including many older patients, especially women, for whom the diagnosis of schizophrenia may be inappropriate. Eliminating these cases would leave a data set that much more closely resembles that of the MAP project. This would be true not only for the average age of onset of schizophrenia, but for the sex distribution as well, since under the age of 40, males do appear to outnumber females in most studies.

It is noteworthy that this association between schizophrenia and the male sex is supported by recent findings from other sources as well. In a study of the entire population of a relatively isolated Danish island from 1935–1983, Strömgren (1987) found a decrease in the prevalence of schizophrenia, but only for females. Ni Nullain et al. (1987) reported that in Ireland, the first admission rate in 1983 for male schizophrenics was 42.4 per 100,000 population compared to 28.3 for females. In their study of first admissions in three Irish countries, these investigators identified 94 cases, 65% of which were men. Munk-Jørgensen (1985, 1986) identified 587 cases from the Danish national registry from 1972–1983; 63% were male. Using data collected by Statistics Canada, Bland (1984) calculated the rate of first admission schizophrenia to be 31 per 100,000 for males, and 22 per 100,000 for females. He also determined that in the year 1978, approximately 121,000 men and 80,000 women had or had had schizophrenia.

NINE AND EIGHTEEN MONTH OUTCOME OF FIRST EPISODE PSYCHOSIS

As Masten (1988) has noted, developmental psychopathologists are interested not only in developmental patterns regarding the onset and prevalence of disorders, but also in changes in individuals already manifesting disorder. In this section, we consider the developmental course of those afflicted with psychosis from two rather different perspectives. In the first, we examine the continuity of psychopathology over time by determining the extent to which membership in a diagnostic category is stable. In the second, we examine the relationship of diagnosis, age of onset, and sex to global adjustment during the 18 months following the onset of psychotic symptoms.

Diagnostic Stability

Knowledge about the temporal stability of disorder has obvious and important prognostic implications. Disorders that are continuously present may be viewed as more severe and debilitating than those that are more episodic. The validity of a nosological system can be evaluated in part by the constancy of membership in its categories. Over time, few individuals in a particular category should be reclassified as having other disorders and few originally diagnosed with other syndromes should subsequently find themselves in the category. The assumption is that the more stable the membership in a diagnostic category, the more likely it is that the members of that category share a common psychopathological process (Beiser, Iacono, & Erickson, 1989).

Developmental considerations enter into both the definition of disorder and assessments of the validity of a diagnostic construct. The definition of bipolar and unipolar depression, for example, require tracking the episodic course of these disorders to document the presence or absence of interspersed manic episodes. Several of the ICD-9 subtypes of schizophrenia (acute, schizoaffective, and residual) are defined from a developmental vantage point. As will be seen in a subsequent section, DSM-III also takes the developmental course of disorder into account to differentiate schizophrenia from schizophreniform disorder and affective psychosis. An important question is whether a classification approach that takes course into account generates more valid diagnostic categories than one that is entirely symptom based.

When investigating diagnostic stability, it is important to evaluate all the major disorders within a diagnostic system because the breadth of a diagnostic category will partially determine the constancy of membership within that category. For example, if there is a great latitude in the range of symptoms that define a category, then membership within the group will remain relatively constant because even a remarkable change in the constellation of symptoms in a given individual may still satisfy the inclusion criteria. However, a broad definition of one disorder is likely to be associated with narrowness in another (e.g., ICD-9 employs a broad definition of schizophrenia but a restrictive concept of affective disorder, see Table 10.1). The exclusiveness of a narrowly defined category diminishes the likelihood of diagnostic constancy because slight alteration of an individual's clinical picture might lead to that person's elimination from the category. The exception to this latter generalization concerns disorders that although narrowly defined, have diagnostic criteria that are both highly sensitive and specific, probably because they identify homogeneous groups of individuals suffering from a disorder with a specific etiology. Many physical disorders are of this type. Because narrowness in one category is often associated with breadth in another, it is necessary to examine the membership of both over time to assess the validity of either. Learning that those initially labeled schizophrenic continue with this diagnosis presents only half the picture. It is also imperative to determine that those diagnosed with affective psychosis do not subsequently appear as schizophrenic.

While previous studies have demonstrated that the major functional psychoses show impressive diagnostic stability (see Beiser et al., 1989, for a review), these studies suffer from several limitations, including:

1. retrospective reliance on hospital chart data which are compromised by the lack of standardized information gathering and inconsistent application of diagnostic criteria,

2. reliance on chronic case samples which can be expected to have a more stable clinical picture than a sample derived from first-episode cases, and

3. assessments at only two points in time that are quite remote from each other, thus leaving unclear diagnostic status during the long intervals between assessments.

We examined diagnostic stability in the MAP project by comparing diagnostic outcomes across four of the five systems we used to diagnose schizophrenia. The 12-point flexible system was dropped from this analysis because data pertinent to this system's diagnostic criteria were not collected at 9 months. Figure 10.1 illustrates how the remaining four systems compare for the diagnosis of schizophrenia. All subjects represented in the figure had an intake diagnosis of schizophrenia in the indicated system. However, subjects who were not available for the 18-month assessment were deleted from this analysis. Hence, as the figure caption indicates, the number of subjects represented in each system diagnosis is less than the number who participated in the intake phase of the study.

The figure indicates that for ICD-9, RDC, and DSM-III, over half the patients diagnosed schizophrenic at intake still satisfied the criteria at 9 and 18 months. These three systems differ, however, in that those with DSM-III schizophrenia are less likely to be recovered (i.e., fall into the ''not symptomatic'' category; for this analysis, cases diagnosed as schizophrenia in remission were categorized as not symptomatic) at 9 and 18 months. It is also evident that for each of these systems, there is relatively little likelihood that a person originally diagnosed schizophrenic will subsequently receive an alternate diagnosis.

The consequences of a Feighner diagnosis of schizophrenia are quite different. This system is the least stable of the four, not only because it diagnoses the smallest fraction of patients as schizophrenic at the two follow-up points, but also because a large portion of patients are reclassified as having another or ''undiagnosed'' psychosis. Taken together, these data suggest the Feighner crite-

NINE MONTHS

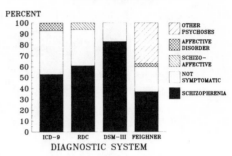

FIG. 10.1. Nine- and 18-month diagnoses of subjects with a diagnosis of schizophrenia at intake. The designation "not symptomatic" indicates that patients did not satisfy the criteria for any of the psychotic disorders in the respective diagnostic system. The number of subjects originally diagnosed schizophrenic who were available for follow up at 18 months was as follows for each diagnostic system: ICD-9, n = 83; RDC, n = 46; DSM-III, n = 40; Feighner, n = 27.

EIGHTEEN MONTHS

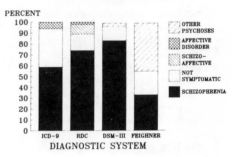

ria are overly narrow and less valid than the definitions provided in the other systems.

Figure 10.2 displays the comparable data for the major affective disorders which parallel those for schizophrenia. The major difference in diagnostic constancy between schizophrenia and affective psychosis is the much larger proportion of affective patients who recover after the initial episode. Schizophrenia is clearly a more chronic disorder than affective psychosis regardless of the diagnostic approach.

DSM-III Major depression and bipolar disorder were combined into a single category for Fig. 10.2. However, with one exception, there was no difference in the picture of diagnostic stability across these two DSM-III affective disorder subtypes. The rather interesting exception involved 20% of those originally diagnosed as having DSM-III major depression developing a manic episode over the 18-month course of the study and being reclassified as bipolar.

The affective disorder group can also be subdivided into patients who at intake experienced mood congruent versus incongruent psychotic symptoms. Mood congruent features are those which are thematically related to depressed or manic mood (e.g., delusions of guilt or grandeur); all other psychotic symptoms are incongruent (e.g., delusions of thought control or persecution). Although

NINE MONTHS

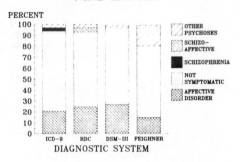

DIAGNOSTIC SYSTEM

EIGHTEEN MONTHS

FIG. 10.2. Nine- and 18-month diagnoses of patients with an intake diagnosis of affective psychosis. The number of subjects who originally received an affective disorder diagnosis and who participated in the follow-up assessments at 18 months was as follows: ICD-9, n = 39; RDC, n = 32; DSM-III, n = 52; Feighner, n = 27.

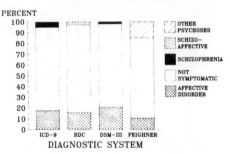

DIAGNOSTIC SYSTEM

Pope and Lipinski (1978) have persuasively argued that the presence of mood incongruent symptoms in an individual with affective features is not sufficient to call for the diagnosis of schizophrenia, these symptoms nonetheless are often referred to as "schizophrenic" (even when they appear in patients with mood disorders), and there is some data suggesting that affective patients with mood incongruent features have more in common with schizophrenia than do their mood congruent counterparts (e.g., Farmer, McGuffin, & Gottesman, 1987). Given this background, the diagnostic stability of mood congruent versus incongruent affective psychosis is of some interest. The affective disorder sample was evenly split along this dimension; there was no difference in diagnostic stability over 9 and 18 months between these two affective subtypes. It is noteworthy in particular that mood incongruent patients did not show an increased tendency to appear as schizophrenic over the course of the study. Indeed, none of the over 50 patients with affective disorder had schizophrenia at nine months, and only one, a subject originally diagnosed mood congruent, had schizophrenia at 18 months.

Another conclusion that can be drawn from these figures is that the DSM-III method of differentiating affective from schizophrenic psychosis works well. The differentiation of these two types of disorder has always been difficult, especially when an affective syndrome appears concurrently with mood in-congruent psychotic features. The other diagnostic systems effectively avoid this problem by assigning such patients to special classes: schizophrenia-schizoaffec-tive subtype (ICD-9), schizoaffective disorder (RDC), and undiagnosed psycho-sis (Feighner). Although DSM-III also has a schizoaffective disorder category, it is the only disorder in the manual that has no defining criteria, a factor that has greatly diminished its use and utility. With first-episode patients, DSM-III deals with this classification dilemma by taking a developmental approach. The pri-mary factor that determines the diagnosis is when the affective syndrome ap-peared relative to the psychotic symptoms. Schizophrenia takes precedence if the psychotic symptoms came first; affective disorder is diagnosed if psychotic symptoms appear after the mood disturbance. That this approach is reasonable is evidenced by the fact that very few patients originally diagnosed with one of these disorders switch to the other at 9 or 18 months. Unfortunately, this useful strategy for differentiating these two psychoses has been dropped in DSM-III-R (American Psychiatric Association, 1987).

Figure 10.3 displays the diagnostic constancy for RDC schizoaffective disor-der. For this figure, patients were divided according to schizoaffective subtype. Those who are "mainly schizophrenic" are primarily characterized as having

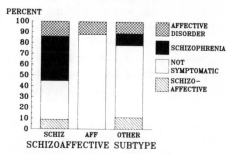

FIG. 10.3. Nine- and 18-month follow-up diagnoses of 43 sub-jects with an intake diagnosis of RDC schizoaffective disorder. Subjects were subdivided into the three RDC schizoaffective subtypes mainly schizophrenic (SCHIZ, n = 25), mainly affec-tive (AFF, n = 10), and other (n = 8).

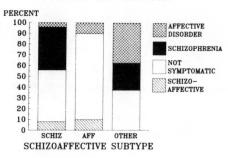

prodromal features often associated with schizophrenia (e.g., social withdrawal) or a period in which psychotic symptoms were present in the absence of depression or mania. Patients whose psychosis was never present in the absence of mood disturbance and who displayed good premorbid adjustment are referred to as "mainly affective." "Other" describes individuals who fit neither of these subtype definitions. The figure illustrates that substantial fractions of subjects initially categorized as schizoaffective were reclassified schizophrenic or affective over time. Indeed, over all subtypes combined, the continued diagnosis of schizoaffective disorder was less likely than either of these two reclassification diagnoses. Note that mainly schizophrenic patients were especially likely to be rediagnosed schizophrenic and that none of the mainly affective subjects ultimately became schizophrenic. These findings call into question the validity of RDC schizoaffective disorder and suggest that many of these patients actually have a schizophrenic or affective psychosis.

Figure 10.4 reveals a similar picture for the Feighner undiagnosed psychosis category. The data are not quite as clear as for the RDC schizoaffective diagnosis, but it must be remembered that this category has the largest membership of any in the Feighner system and includes many types of cases other than those with a schizoaffective picture.

A final category of special interest is represented in Figure 10.5. Schizophreniform disorder was introduced into the DSM in 1980 and little is known about the consequences of using this diagnosis. In this case, diagnostic consistency between the intake diagnosis and that at the follow-up times is represented by the "not symptomtic" category on the chart. This situation arises because if the symptom picture for a schizophreniform case persists beyond 6 months, the diagnosis becomes schizophrenia. The figure confirms the provisional nature of this diagnosis because at 18 months more cases were diagnosed

FEIGHNER OTHER PSYCHOSES

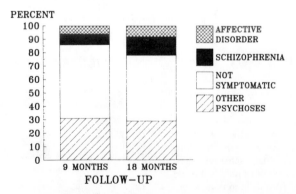

FIG. 10.4. Nine- and 18-month follow-up diagnoses of 75 patients with a Feighner intake diagnosis of undiagnosed (other) psychosis.

DSM–III SCHIZOPHRENIFORM

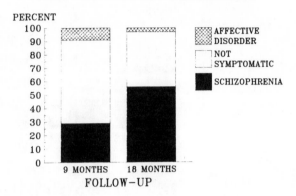

FIG. 10.5. Nine- and 18-month follow-up diagnoses of 27 patients with an intake diagnosis of DSM-III schizophreniform disorder.

schizophrenic than were viewed as not symptomatic. However, an interesting difference exists between the proportion of schizophrenic cases apparent at nine and 18 months. The fact that this proportion grows over this interval is due to many of those who were not symptomatic at 9 months relapsing and satisfying the criteria for schizophrenia by the time of the final assessment.

These diagnostic stability data suggest that schizophrenia is the most chronic of these disorders and that there is little change in the symptom picture between 9 and 18 months. In all systems, affective disorders appear to have a better prognosis. An outcome similar to that of the affective disorders is evident for each system's specialty diagnoses: RDC schizoaffective disorder, DSM-III schizophreniform disorder, and Feighner undiagnosed psychosis.

Global Adjustment Following Psychosis

Figure 10.6 confirms that this prognostic summary holds when the GAS (a modified version of which is currently Axis V in DSM-III-R) is used to evaluate outcome as well. Scores on this scale, which range from 1 to 100, reflect social and occupational adjustment as well as level of symptomatology. High scores are indicative of good adjustment. A rating of 61 or more on the GAS was used to define "good outcome." Scores in the 61–70 range define a level of adjustment that is associated with some mild symptoms or difficulty in several areas of functioning. The individual is characterized as one whom most untrained people would not consider to be "sick." Figure 10.6 indicates that the broader the definition of schizophrenia, the better the outcome on the GAS. This conclusion is supported by the observation that almost twice as many ICD-9 subjects diagnosed schizophrenic have a good outcome as do Feighner patients with this diagnosis. The same relationship between the breadth of the diagnostic construct

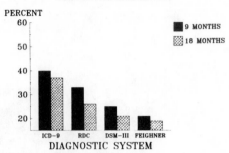

SCHIZOPHRENIA

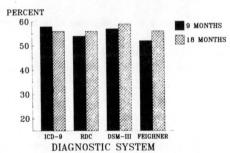

AFFECTIVE PSYCHOSIS

FIG. 10.6. Percentage of subjects in each diagnostic system who obtained Global Assessment Scale scores over 60 at 9 and 18 months.

and outcome does not appear to hold for affective psychosis: The proportion of affective patients with a good outcome is independent of the diagnostic approach. Chi square tests were used to compare the proportions of good outcome cases associated with schizophrenic and affective diagnoses for each diagnostic system. These analyses confirmed the observation from Fig. 10.6 that affective psychosis has better 9- and 18-month outcomes than schizophrenia for all four diagnostic approaches. These findings are consistent with those of Möller and associates (Möller, Schmid-Bode, Cording-Tommel, Wittchen, Zaudig, & von Zerssen, 1988) who also used the GAS to quantify outcome in patients with these disorders.

The corresponding 9- and 18-month percentages of individuals with a GAS score over 60 for the specialty diagnoses were: RDC schizoaffective disorder, 50% and 51%; DSM-III schizophreniform disorder, 58% and 48%; Feighner undiagnosed psychosis, 50% and 48%. These proportions indicate that the outcome of these disorders is more similar to that of affective psychosis than it is to schizophrenia. Finally, it should be noted that regardless of patient diagnosis, there is little change in outcome from 9 to 18 months.

We have shown that schizophrenia and affective psychosis differ in age of onset, sex distribution, and outcome in our sample. Interesting developmental issues concern the extent to which course of disorder varies as a function of age of onset and sex. Because young adults tend to be more competent and have more social resources than adolescents, they can be expected to cope more successfully with their psychosis and therefore should be better able to recover. Sex may also be an important predictor of outcome; psychotic women (at least those with schizophrenia) tend to have a milder course of disorder than do men (e.g., Angermeyer, Goldstein, & Kuehn, 1988; Munk-Jørgensen, 1986; Goldstein, 1988; Salokangas, 1983; Watt, Katz, & Shepherd, 1983). The relationship between these variables is represented in Fig. 10.7, which illustrates that trends in the data support both of these contentions (only 18-month outcome data are presented since the 9-month outcomes were virtually identical). However, the results of a two-factor (sex × age of onset) analysis of variance (ANOVA) confirmed that women have a better outcome than men, $F(1,123) = 5.45$, $p < .05$, but not that older age is associated with better 18-month adjustment, $F(2,123) = 1.35$. The sex by age interaction effect also failed to attain significance, $F(2,123) = .48$. Additional ANOVAs were carried out to determine if age of onset predicted 18-month GAS outcome for schizophrenia and affective psychosis as defined by each diagnostic system. All main effects for age of onset and diagnosis by age of onset interactions were nonsignificant, indicating that no matter how these disorders were defined, age of onset was not related to the outcome of either type of psychosis.

The relative contribution of diagnostic class ‟membership and sex to GAS outcome is highlighted in Fig. 10.8 for each classification system. With one exception, four separate two factor (diagnosis × sex) ANOVAs calculated on these data generated the expected significant ($p < .05$) main effects for diagnosis, and sex, but no significant interactions. The only exception to this pattern of results was associated with ICD-9 which failed to yield a significant diagnosis

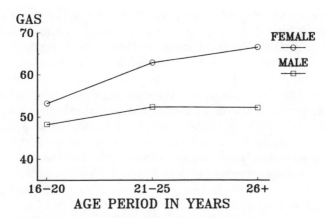

FIG. 10.7. Eighteen-month Global Assessment Scale (GAS) scores as a function of age of onset (in years) and sex.

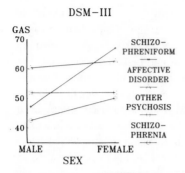

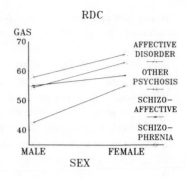

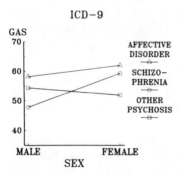

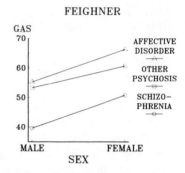

FIG. 10.8. Sex differences in 18-month Global Assessment Scale (GAS) ratings as a function of diagnostic class membership within each of four classification systems.

main effect ($p < .20$). Follow-up contrasts of the GAS ratings of males and females were carried out for each category of disorder within each diagnostic system to determine whether women showed better adjustment than men. These analyses confirmed that (1) DSM-III schizophrenic and schizophreniform women had a better outcome than men with these diagnoses, (2) schizophrenic women had better 18-month adjustment scores than men using RDC and ICD-9 but not the Feighner system (which identified a small sample of only 8 women with schizophrenia), and (3) no significant difference between the sexes was evident for any other diagnostic category in any classification system. Because the number of individuals with "other psychoses" was small, no firm conclusions can be reached regarding the effect of sex on the outcome of these disorders. These results, coupled with those from Fig. 10.6 and 10.7, indicate that although women and individuals with affective disorder tend to have good 18-month global adjustment, sex is a much stronger predictor of outcome for schizophrenia (and DSM-III schizophreniform disorder) than it is for affective psychosis.

What the Diagnostic Approach Tells Us about Prognosis

Taking a developmental approach to psychiatric diagnosis sheds light not only on the prognosis of psychotic disorders, but also on the relative validity of different diagnostic systems. All four systems generated relatively similar data for affective psychosis. These psychoses were associated with a better outcome than schizophrenia; at 9 and 18 months, affective psychotics showed higher levels of functioning on the GAS and were more likely to be in remission. In addition, individuals with these diagnoses tended to retain them if they were symptomatic at either of the two follow-up times. However, consistent with past research (e.g., Stephens, 1978), all four diagnostic approaches identify a small subgroup of schizophrenic patients with a relatively good outcome (see Figs. 10.1 and 10.6).

With regard to the diagnosis of schizophrenia, all the diagnostic systems except that of Feighner et al. (1972) indicated that individuals initially categorized schizophrenic were unlikely at a future time to be reclassified as having a different psychosis. ICD-9, RDC, and DSM-III diagnoses of schizophrenia did differ, however, with respect to their prognostic implications. DSM-III identified subjects who were least likely to remit and who had a poor GAS outcome. In general, the diagnostic outcomes for affective psychoses and schizophrenia indicate than when patients are symptomatic following their first psychotic episode, their clinical pictures remain consistent with their intake diagnosis.

Although the Feighner diagnosis of schizophrenia was associated with the lowest GAS score at 18 months, this value differed little from that associated with DSM-III schizophrenia. Compared to DSM-III, the Feighner system definition of schizophrenia shows temporal instability. Given this limitation of the Feighner approach plus the fact that it does not identify a group of patients with a distinctly poorer outcome than DSM-III, DSM-III appears to be the best system for identifying schizophrenics with a poor prognosis.

The finding that membership in a diagnostic group remains constant over time renders less likely one possible explanation of why there were not more women with a diagnosis of schizophrenia in the MAP project. The absence of additional and older women could have been due to their initially being misdiagnosed as having depressive psychosis. Note, for example, that women with a diagnosis of depression (Table 10.3) were significantly older than men with this disorder. If it were the case that older females were erroneously categorized as depressed, many women with affective psychoses could be expected to be reclassified as schizophrenic at follow-up. In fact, however, such reclassifications were too rare to make any difference.

The course of psychosis shows little change between 9 and 18 months. As Fig. 10.6 illustrates, this finding appears to be independent of diagnosis and diagnostic system. As such, it indicates that following a first episode of psychosis, most of the postpsychotic adjustment takes place before 9 months has elapsed. These findings suggest that short-term prognostic formulations regarding the 18-month outcome of these disorders can be made from information available shortly after the time of the first psychotic break. Other factors, besides diagnosis and sex, may be useful for this purpose. The MAP project intake assessment included a host of psychophysiological vulnerability variables (described in Iacono, 1985) as well as measures of premorbid competence, coping abilities, social support, stressful life experiences, role stress, and psychopathological symptoms, many of which will undoubtedly prove useful prognosticators of disorder course. In addition, the MAP subjects have now completed a 5-year follow-up assessment, thus making it possible to examine post first-episode adjustment over a longer time span.

FINAL REMARKS

Developmental psychopathology is a relatively new and emerging field, rooted in the study of children with behavior disorders and in the longitudinal investigation of children at risk for schizophrenia (Cicchetti, 1984, 1989). Although Zigler and Glick (1986) have introduced a timely volume that illustrates how adult disorders can be understood within a framework of general developmental principles, the vast majority of investigators of adult psychopathology have largely ignored the developmental perspective, even when their data lend themselves to interpretation from this vantage point. Indeed, partly due to this lack of precedence and our unfamiliarity with developmental psychology, it has been difficult for us to reconceptualize our approach to the MAP project using this perspective. We feel we have just begun this process with this chapter in which, following the lead of Rutter (1988), we have considered developmentally relevant variables such as age of onset, sex, and course of disorder. To reduce the dependency of our findings on specific conceptual definitions of schizophrenic and affective psychosis, we have examined these variables using various operational criteria. This approach has enabled us to uncover results that are independent of the system used to diagnose disorder. Hence, we have shown that regardless of the diagnostic system, male subjects suffering their first episode of schizophrenia outnumbered females three to one, the period of highest risk for schizophrenia was late adolescence/early adulthood, few individuals over the age of 35 received this diagnosis, there were no sex differences in the age of onset of schizophrenia, nonschizophrenic psychoses show a later age of onset than schizophrenia, affective psychosis had a better outcome than schizophrenia, 9 and 18-month outcomes were very similar, age of onset of disorder did not predict outcome, and women with schizophrenia showed a better 18-month adjustment than men.

These findings raise a number of issues for future research. We have challenged the notion that schizophrenia is equally prevalent in men and women and shown that our data, coupled with some recent investigations of the incidence of schizophrenia, suggest that men with this disorder outnumber women. We have also found, consistent with past research, that the course of schizophrenia is milder for women than men. These findings suggest that men may be more biologically vulnerable and less able to adapt than women with this psychosis. Different vulnerabilities and psychosocial circumstances are undoubtedly also associated with variability in age of onset and outcome, both within and among disorders. Insight into the causes of these individual and disorder differences could be gained from future studies (and additional analyses of MAP data) that investigate possible biological and psychosocial factors associated with psychopathology from an interactive, developmental vantage point.

Our data suggest that all four of the diagnostic systems we used generate somewhat similar findings if the focus is on either schizophrenia or affective psychosis. However, if comprehensive classification of all subjects rather than selection of a group with a specific diagnosis is the goal, there are obvious consequences associated with the choice of one system over another. Both the RDC and Feighner systems leave large numbers of subjects in diagnostic categories (RDC: schizoaffective disorder, 31% of the total; Feighner: undiagnosed psychosis, 55% of the total) that, because they have temporally unstable membership, are of uncertain validity.

DSM-III also has an unstable diagnostic designation, schizophreniform disorder (18% of the total), which by definition is a provisional diagnosis. Unlike the other systems, DSM-III relies on the pattern of development of psychosis for differential diagnosis. The sequencing and duration of symptoms is used to separate schizophrenia, affective psychosis, and schizophreniform disorder. Our data indicate that this approach works relatively well in that schizophrenic and affective diagnoses were more stable using this sytem than any of the others and that these two types of psychosis demonstrated markedly divergent outcomes.

Our data are consistent with other reports indicating that even when using the relatively narrow definition of schizophrenia provided by DSM-III, many patients have a relatively good outcome (Helzer, Kendell, & Brockington, 1983; Möller et al., 1988; Watt et al., 1983). About 20% of the patients initially diagnosed schizophrenic were not symptomatic 18 months following their first psychotic episode, and about a quarter of schizophrenic patients demonstrated a good outcome on the GAS. On the other hand, DSM-III schizophrenia, compared to the ICD-9 and RDC conceptualizations of this disorder, appears to be a more homogeneous, chronic psychosis. DSM-III achieves such homogeneity by requiring that 6 months of disturbed behavior be present before the diagnosis is made, in effect assigning the diagnosis after 6 months of poor outcome has been established. It is thus perhaps not surprising that generally poor outcome is evident as well at 9 and 18 months. Zigler and Glick (1986) note that although homogeneity within diagnostic classes is often viewed as desirable, disorders may in fact be heterogeneous with respect to some of their attributes. It remains to be seen whether DSM-III (and DSM-III-R) is simply homogenizing schizophrenia by greatly reducing the proportion of good outcome cases (and reclassifying them as having another form of psychosis) or purifying what has long been a fuzzy category. In future papers, we will be using data from the MAP project to help resolve this issue. We hope to accomplish this in part by determining the extent to which patients with DSM-III psychoses are more like other members of their diagnostic class than they are similar to members of other diagnostic categories on a variety of biological and psychosocial measures.

ACKNOWLEDGMENTS

The research described in this chapter was supported by grants from the Medical Research Council of Canada and Health and Welfare Canada. Data analysis was supported by a grant from the Gradute School of the University of Minnesota. The authors would like to thank John Allen and Irving Gottesman for comments on an early draft of this paper.

REFERENCES

American Psychiatric Association (1968). *Diagnostic and statistical manual of mental disorders, second edition.* Washington, D.C.: American Psychiatric Association.

American Psychiatric Association (1980). *Diagnostic and statistical manual of mental disorders, third edition.* Washington, D.C.: American Psychiatric Association.

American Psychiatric Association (1987). *Diagnostic and statistical manual of mental disorders, third edition, revised.* Washington, D.C.: American Psychiatric Association.

Angermeyer, M. C., Goldstein, J. M., & Kuehn, L. (1989). Gender differences in schizophrenia: Rehospitalization and community survival. *Psychological Medicine,*

Astrachan, B., Harrow, M., Adler, D., Brauer, L., Schwartz, A., Schwartz, C., & Tucker, G. (1972). A checklist for the diagnosis of schizophrenia. *British Journal of Psychiatry, 121,* 529–539.

Babigian, H. M. (1975). Schizophrenia: Epidemiology. In A. M. Freedman, H. I, Kaplan, & B. J. Sadock (Eds.), *Comprehensive textbook of psychiatry.* Baltimore: Williams & Wilkins.

Baron, M., Gruen, R., Asnis, L., & Kane, J. (1983). Age-of-onset in schizophrenia and schizotypal disorders. *Neuropsychobiology, 10,* 199–204.

Beiser, M., Iacono, W. G., & Erickson, D. (1989). Temporal stability in the major mental disorders. In L. N. Robins, & J. E. Barrett (Eds.), *The validity of psychiatric diagnosis.* (pp. 77–98) New York: Raven Press.

Beiser, M., Fleming, J. A. E., Iacono, W. G., & Lin, T-Y. (1988). Refining the diagnosis of schizophreniform psychosis. *American Journal of Psychiatry, 145,* 695–700.

Beiser, M., Waxler-Morrison, N., Iacono, W. G., Lin, T-Y., Fleming, J. A. E., & Husted, J. (1987). A measure of the "sick" label in psychiatric disorder and physical illness. *Social Science and Medicine, 25,* 251–261.

Bellodi, L., Morabito, A., & Macciardi, F., Gasperini, M., Benvenuto, M. G., Grassi, G., Marzorati-Spairini, C., & Smeraldi, E. (1982). Analytic considerations about observed distribution of age of onset in schizophrenia. *Neuropsychobiology, 8,* 93–101.

Bland, R. C. (1977). Demographic aspects of functional psychoses in Canada. *Acta Psychiatrica Scandinavica, 55*, 369–380.

Bland, R. C. (1984). Long term mental illness in Canada: An epidemiological perspective on schizophrenia and affective disorders. *Canadian Journal of Psychiatry, 29*, 242–246.

Bland, R. D., & Orn, H. (1978). 14-year outcome in early schizophrenia. *Acta Psychiatrica Scandinavica, 58*, 327–338.

Brown, G. W., Parkes, C. M., & Wing, J. K. (1961). Admissions and readmissions to three London mental hospitals. *Journal of Mental Science, 107*, 1070–1079.

Carpenter, W. T., Strauss, J. S., & Bartko, J. J. (1973). Flexible system for the diagnosis of schizophrenia: Report from the WHO international pilot study of schizophrenia. *Science, 182*, 1275–1278.

Cicchetti, D. (1984). The emergence of developmental psychopathology. *Child Development, 55*, 1–7.

Cicchetti, D. (1989). An historical perspective on the discipline of developmental psychopathology. In J. Rolf, A. Masten, D. Cicchetti, K. Nuechterlein, & S. Weintraub (Eds.), *Risk and protective factors in the development of psychopathology.* New York: Cambridge University Press.

Cohen, P., & Cohen, J. (1984). The clinician's illusion. *Archives of General Psychiatry, 41*, 1178–1182.

Eagles, J. M. (1983). Delusional depressive inpatients 1892–1982. *British Journal of Psychiatry, 143*, 558–563.

Eagles, J. M., & Whalley, L. J. (1985). Decline in the diagnosis of schizophrenia among first admissions to Scottish mental hospitals from 1969–78. *British Journal of Psychiatry, 146*, 151–154.

Endicott, J., Nee, J. Fleiss, J., Cohen, J., Williams, J. B. W., & Simon, R. (1982). Diagnostic criteria for schizophrenia: Reliabilities and agreement between systems. *Archives of General Psychiatry, 39*, 884–889.

Endicott, J., Spitzer, R. L., Fleiss, J. L., & Cohen, J. (1976). The Global Assessment Scale: A procedure for measuring overall severity of psychiatric disturbance. *Archives of General Psychiatry, 33*, 766–771.

Farmer, A. E., McGuffin, P., & Gottesman, I. I. (1987). Twin concordance for DSM-III schizophrenia: Scrutinizing the validity of the definition. *Archives of General Psychiatry, 44*, 634–641.

Feighner, J. P., Robins, E., Guze, S. B., Woodruff, R. A., Winokur, G., & Munoz, R. (1972). Diagnostic criteria for use in psychiatric research. *Archives of General Psychiatry, 26*, 57–63.

Flor-Henry, P. (1985). Schizophrenia: Sex differences. *Canadian Journal of Psychiatry, 30*, 319–322.

Forrest, A. D., & Hay, A. J. (1971). Sex differences and the schizophrenic experience. *Acta Psychiatrica Scandinavica, 47*, 137–149.

Goldstein, J. M. (1988). Gender differences in the course of schizophrenia. *American Journal of Psychiatry, 145*, 684–689.

Goldstein, J. M., & Link, B. G. (1988). Gender and the expression of schizophrenia. *Journal of Psychiatric Research, 22*, 141–155.

Gottesman, I. I., & Shields, J. (1982). *Schizophrenia: The epigenetic puzzle.* Cambridge, England: Cambridge University Press.

Häfner, H. (1987). Epidemiology of schizophrenia. In H. Häfner, W. F. Gattaz, & W. Janzarik (Eds.), *Search for the causes of schizophrenia* (pp. 47–74). Berlin: Springer Verlag.

Helgason, T. (1964). Epidemiology of mental disorders in Iceland. *Acta Psychiatrica Scandinavica, 40*, 11–173. (Supplement 173).

Helzer, J. E., Brockington, I. F., & Kendell, R. E. (1981). Predictive validity of DSM-III and Feighner definitions of schizophrenia: A comparison with research diagnostic criteria and CATEGO. *Archives of General Psychiatry, 38*, 791–797.

Helzer, J. E., Kendell, R. E., & Brockington, I. F. (1983). Contributions of the six-month criterion to the predictive validity of the DSM-III definition of schizophrenia. *Archives of General Psychiatry, 40,* 1277–1280.

Iacono, W. G. (1985). Psychophysiologic markers of psychopathology: A review. *Canadian Psychology, 26,* 96–112.

Iacono, W. G., Smith, G. N., Moreau, M., Beiser, M., Fleming, J. A. E., Lin, T-Y., & Flak, B. (1988). Ventricular and sulcal size at the onset of psychosis. *American Journal of Psychiatry, 145,* 695–700.

Kendler, K. S. (1982). Demography of paranoid psychosis (delusional disorder): A review and comparison with schizophrenia and affective illness. *Archives of General Psychiatry, 39,* 890–902.

Klein, D. N. (1982). Activity-withdrawal in the differential diagnosis of schizophrenia and mania. *Journal of Abnormal Psychology, 91,* 319–325.

Klorman, R., Strauss, J., & Kokes, R. (1977). The relationship of demographic and diagnostic factors to measures of premorbid adjustment in schizophrenia. *Schizophrenia Bulletin, 3,* 214–225.

Larson, C. A., & Nyman, G. E. (1970). Age of onset in schizophrenia. *Human Heredity, 20,* 241–247.

Leckman, J. F., Scholomskas, D., Thompson, W. D., Belanger, A., & Weissman, M. M. (1982). Best estimates of lifetime psychiatric diagnosis: A methodologic study. *Archives of General Psychiatry, 39,* 879–883.

Leventhal, D. B., Schuck, J. R., & Rothstein, H. (1984). Gender differences in schizophrenia. *Journal of Nervous & Mental Disease, 172,* 464–467.

Lewine, R. R. J. (1980). Sex differences in age of symptom onset and first hospitalization in schizophrenia. *American Journal of Orthopsychiatry, 50,* 316–322.

Lewine, R. R. J. (1981). Sex differences in schizophrenia: Timing or subtypes? *Psychological Bulletin, 90,* 432–444.

Lewine, R., Burbach, D., & Meltzer, H. Y. (1984). Effect of diagnostic criteria on the ratio of male to female schizophrenic patients. *American Journal of Psychiatry, 141,* 84–87.

Lewine, R. J., Strauss, J. S., & Gift, T. E. (1981). Sex differences in age at first hospital admission for schizophrenia: Fact or artifact? *American Journal of Psychiatry, 138,* 440–444.

Loranger, A. W. (1984). Sex differences in age at onset in schizophrenia. *Archives of General Psychiatry, 41,* 157–161.

Masten, A. (1988). Toward a developmental psychopathology of early adolescence. In M. D. Levine & E. R. McAnarney (Eds.), *Early adolescent transitions* (pp. 261–278). Lexington, MA: D. C. Heath.

McCabe, M. S. (1975). Demographic differences in functional psychoses. *British Journal of Psychiatry, 127,* 320–323.

McGlashen, T. H. (1984). Testing four diagnostic systems for schizophrenia. *Archives of General Psychiatry, 41,* 141–144.

Möller, H. J., Schmid-Bode, W., Cording-Tommel, C., Wittchen, H.-U., Zaudig, M., & von Zerssen, D. (1988). Psychopathological and social outcome in schizophrenia versus affective/schizoaffective psychoses and prediction of poor outcome in schizophrenia: Results from a 5–8 year follow-up. *Acta Psychiatrica Scandinavica, 77,* 379–389.

Munk-Jørgensen, P. (1985). The schizophrenia diagnosis in Denmark: A register-based investigation. *Acta Psychiatrica Scandinavica, 72,* 266–273.

Munk-Jørgensen, P. (1986). Schizophrenia in Denmark: Incidence and utilization of institutions. *Acta Psychiatrica Scandinavica, 73,* 172–180.

Ni Nullain, M., O'Hare, A., & Walsh, D. (1987). Incidence of schizophrenia in Ireland. *Psychological Medicine, 17,* 943–948.

Pope, H. G., & Lipinski, J. F. (1978). Diagnosis in schizophrenia and manic-depressive illness: A reassessment of the specificity of "schizophrenic" symptoms in light of current research. *Archives of General Psychiatry, 35,* 811–828.

Robins, L. N., Helzer, J. E., Croughan, J., & Ratcliff, K. S. (1981). National Institute of Mental ealth Diagnostic Interview Schedule: Its history, characteristics, and validity. *Archives of General Psychiatry, 38,* 381–389.

Robins, L. N., Helzer, J. E., Weissman, M. M., Orvaschel, H., Gruenberg, E., Burke, J. D., & Regier, D. A. (1984). Lifetime prevalence of specific psychiatric disorders in three sites. *Archives of General Psychiatry, 41,* 949–958.

Rutter, M. (1988). Epidemiological approaches to developmental psychopathology. *Archives of General Psychiatry, 45,* 486–495.

Salokangas, R. K. R. (1983). Prognostic implications of the sex of schizophrenic patients. *British Journal of Psychiatry, 142,* 145–151.

Sartorius, N., Jablensky, A., Korten, A., Ernberg, G., Anker, M., Cooper, J. E., & Day, R. (1986). Early manifestations and first-contact incidence of schizophrenia in different cultures. *Psychological Medicine, 16,* 909–928.

Saugstad, L. (1985). In defense of international classification. *Psychological Medicine, 15,* 1–2.

Slater, E., & Cowie, V. (1971). *The genetics of mental disorders.* London: Oxford University Press.

Spitzer, R., Endicott, J., & Robins, E. (1977). *Research diagnostic criteria, third edition.* New York: New York State Psychiatric Institute.

Spitzer, R. L., Endicott, J., & Robins, E. (1978). Research diagnostic criteria: Rationale and reliability. *Archives of General Psychiatry, 35,* 773–782.

Sroufe, L. A., & Rutter, M. (1984). The domain of developmental psychopathology. *Child Development, 55,* 17–29.

Stephens, J. H. (1978). Long-term prognosis and follow-up in schizophrenia. *Schizophrenia Bulletin, 4,* 25–47.

Stephens, J. H., Astrup, C., Carpenter, W. T., Jr., Shaffer, J. W., & Goldberg, J. (1982). A comparison of nine systems to diagnose schizophrenia. *Psychiatry Research, 6,* 127–143.

Strömgren, E. (1987). Changes in the incidence of schizophrenia? *British Journal of Psychiatry, 150,* 1–7.

Tsuang, M., Dempsey, T., Rauscher, F. (1976). A study of "atypical schizophrenia": Comparison with schizophrenia and affective disorder by sex, age of admission, precipitant, outcome, and family history. *Archives of General Psychiatry, 33,* 1157–1160.

Turner, R. J. (1968). Social mobility and schizophrenia. *Journal of Health and Social Behavior, 9,* 194–203.

Watt, D. C., Katz, K., & Shepherd, M. (1983). The natural history of schizophrenia: A 5-year prospective follow-up of a representative sample of schizophrenics by means of a standardized clinical and social assessment. *Psychological Medicine, 13,* 663–670.

Weeke, A., Munk-Jørgensen, P., Strömgren, E., & Dupont, A. (1986). Changes in utilization of Danish psychiatric institutions. I. An outline of the period 1957–1982. *Comprehensive Psychiatry, 27,* 407–415.

Westermeyer, J. F., & Harrow, M. (1984). Prognosis and outcome using broad (DSM-II) and narrow (DSM-III) concepts of schizophrenia. *Schizophrenia Bulletin, 10,* 624–637.

Wing, J. K. (1986). Epidemiological research using psychiatric case registers. In G. H. M. M. ten Horn, R. Giel, W. H. Gulbinat, & J. H. Henderson (Eds.), *Psychiatric case registers in public health* (pp. 14–25). Amsterdam: Elsevier Science.

Wing, J. K., & Fryers, T. (1976). *Statistics from the Camberwell and Salford psychiatric registers 1964–1974.* London: Institute of Psychiatry, University of Manchester.

Wing, J. K., Cooper, J. E., & Sartorius, N. (1974). *The measurement and classification of psychiatric symptoms.* New York: Cambridge University Press.

World Health Organization (1973). *Report of the international pilot study of schizophrenia.* Geneva: World Health Organization.

World Health Organization (1978). *Mental disorders: Glossary and guide to their classification in accordance with the ninth revision of the International Classification of Diseases.* Geneva: World Health Organization.

World Health Organization (1979). *Schizophrenia: An international follow-up study.* New York: Wiley.

Zigler, E., & Glick, M. (1986). *A developmental approach to adult psychopathology.* New York: Wiley.

11

Resilience in Development: Implications of the Study of Successful Adaptation for Developmental Psychopathology

Ann S. Masten
University of Minnesota

While it has long been recognized that certain experiential hazards place a child at risk for developmental problems or psychopathology, pervasive individual differences in observed adaptational outcomes of children at risk have raised a critical question: How is it that some children experience adversity and successfully negotiate the risks to their development while others fail to do so? This question has led a variety of investigators to focus more attention on the study of *resilience,* the positive side of adaptation under extenuating circumstances.

Until recently, successful adaptation had been ignored by most scientists, particularly by students of psychopathology, who, dominated by a disease model, concerned themselves primarily with symptoms, classification, prognosis, treatments, and risk factors (Rutter, 1985; Masten & Garmezy, 1985). However, a transformation is now taking place in the theoretical conceptualizations and approaches to understanding the development of psychopathology. The current interest in resilience is a marker of this transformation.

This chapter briefly examines the roots, the methods, the fruits, the failures, and the future of the study of resilience as it bears on developmental psychopathology as an emerging integrative framework for understanding and investigating adaptation and its vicissitudes. The experiences and results of one research program in particular, the "Project Competence" studies of stress resistance in children at Minnesota, is used to illustrate the origins and directions of this field of endeavor.

THE ROOTS OF RESILIENCE AS A FOCUS OF RESEARCH

Three major roots of the recent interest in resilience are risk research, stress research, and studies of adaptation emphasizing competence. Although chronologically not the first root, the study of children at risk for psychopathology and other developmental deviations is probably the most influential root for developmental psychopathology as well as the entry point for a number of key investigators who began to link the research areas of psychopathology, development, stress, and competence.

The study of children at risk for schizophrenia, for example, was pioneered on a clinical case level by Bender (1937) and Fish (1957) and on a larger scale by Mednick and Schulsinger (1968) beginning in the 1960s. The high-risk strategy of research grew out of the search for causes of this disorder and early genetic studies indicating that offspring of a schizophrenic parent had about a ten-fold increased risk for this disorder compared to a random sample of the population (Gottesman & Shields, 1982). The history and results of the consortium of these high-risk investigators have been described in detail elsewhere (Garmezy, 1974; Garmezy & Streitman, 1974; Goldstein & Tuma, 1987; Watt, Anthony, Wynne, & Rolf, 1984). Of concern here is the impact of these studies on approaches to understanding psychopathology.

These risk studies required a longitudinal perspective, which immediately confronted the investigators with the issues of assessment, continuity, and development. To monitor development, many of these investigators turned to broad-based multiple measures of adaptation at different age levels and known risk factors for development, such as maternal status, birth complications, intellectual functioning, and family interaction (Garmezy & Phipps-Yonas, 1984). With no known marker of genetic vulnerability, some investigators looked to characteristics associated with the disorder in adults, attempting to extend the same variables downward to identify likely precursors of these characteristics, raising a host of issues about the equivalence of the same measure at different ages or the same contruct with different age-appropriate measures.

Another methodological problem faced by these high-risk investigators that contributed to the growth of developmental psychopathology was the question of control groups: What was the most informative context for comparison? Matched normal controls were commonly chosen to identify features of high-risk children that distinguished them from children with similarly disadvantaged backgrounds since target status often was confounded with multiple socioeconomic risk factors. Randomly selected normal controls, on the other hand, provided a developmental context for identifying how well the target children were functioning compared to the population. Finally, psychiatric controls provided information on the specificity of problems uniquely manifested by the offspring of a parent with schizophrenia in comparison to children whose parents were impaired by other mental illnesses.

The results of these studies are not all in by any means, but after 2 decades of research (see Goldstein & Tuma, 1987; Watt et al., 1984), the yield from these studies holds some surprises. One of these is how little, with a few notable exceptions, has been learned thus far about the specific risk for schizophrenia, while how much has been learned about general risks for good and poor adaptation. For example, the severity of a parent's mental dysfunction appeared to have more relation to problems in their children than did the specific nature of their disturbance (Watt et al., 1984). Similarly, the chronic stress and disadvantage that accompany low-socioeconomic status and poverty clearly jeopardized the development of many children, whether or not they theoretically were at risk for schizophrenia (Sameroff, Barocas, & Seifer, 1984). Moreover, the quality of the caregiving environment, as reflected in family discord, stability, and socioeconomic status, was implicated in study after study as markedly related to psychosocial development (Goldstein & Tuma, 1987).

An impressive degree of normative development has been observed in studies of high-risk children. Perhaps this should not be surprising; only a small fraction of children at risk by virtue of a biological mother with schizophrenia are expected to manifest this disorder at some time in their lives. Nonetheless, there was a quality of surprise in the growing recognition that high-risk children often develop normally, particularly if the caregiving environment is reasonably good, and also manifest adaptive strengths. This conclusion led to an awakening of interest in the positive adaptation of high-risk children. This awakening has been chronicled by Norman Garmezy (1981, 1987), one of the first of the consortium investigators to highlight competence and resilience in his high-risk studies. Garmezy had long been interested in the relation of premorbid competence and schizophrenia (Garmezy & Rodnick, 1959), so his focus on competence was a natural outgrowth of his earlier work with adults.

The high-risk studies of schizophrenia have been handicapped by the difficulties of assessing risk itself. Changes in diagnostic criteria for schizophrenia presented one problem; another was the lack of reliable markers of genetic vulnerability (see Goldstein & Tuma, 1987; Watt et al., 1984). Without clear designation of who is at risk and for what, it is virtually impossible to identify the processes that increase or ameliorate the risk for schizophrenia (Garver, 1987). For example, what appears to be a protective factor may actually be a marker of lower risk (Rutter, in press). The full potential of the high-risk studies will not be realized until better designation of risk is achieved. An exciting prospect for the future is the possibility of identifying vulnerability markers and then reanalyzing the extraordinary data collected by these investigators, with a precise measure of risk.

Another important result of the search for the causes of schizophrenia was the diathesis-stressor model (Gottesman & Shields, 1972, 1982). It describes a process whereby genetic vulnerabilities, including those specific to schizophrenia as well as general vulnerabilities to stress, and genetic assets, combine with environmental factors in the development of the organism to produce different courses of disorder even in individuals with the same genetic makeup or multiple pathways to the same disorder in people with different genetic liabilities. Inherent in this model is the possibility that favorable characteristics or favorable environments, in terms of such qualities as temperament, intelligence, or parenting may ameliorate the expression of genetically based vulnerabilities, while comparable individual differences in constitution or environment may exacerbate them. Based on a polygenetic model of schizophrenia, this perspective also emphasized the complex multifactorial nature of gene-environment interaction.

The complexity of interactions between a vulnerable individual and his or her environment was also the focus of the *transactional* model articulated by Sameroff and Chandler (1975) in their influential review of perinatal risk research. This formulation illustrates once again how prospective studies of high-risk children contributed to a developmental model of adaptation.

Historically, studies of infants at risk due to prenatal or perinatal factors such as prematurity, low birth weight, brain damage, or maternal malnutrition, for example, predate the investigations of children at risk for schizophrenia (Kopp & Krakow, 1983; Masten & Garmezy, 1985). Initially, these studies were almost always retrospective in design and focused on negative sequelae. The developmental vulnerabilities of infants with pregnancy or birth complications were well documented by investigators such as Pasamanick and Knobloch (1960, 1961), who noted a dramatic link between such complications and socioeconomic disadvantage. Subsequently, however, as prospective longitudinal data became available, the diversity of outcomes became more impressive, leading Sameroff and Chandler (1975) to conclude that in many cases, infants at risk developed normally, except in cases of manifest brain injury or when there was socioeconomic risk. Indeed, they concluded, environmental socioeconomic factors were often more powerful indicators of risk than the constitutional risk factors.

The role of socioeconomic status as a modifier of prenatal risk was clearly implicated in a landmark study of infants at risk on the Hawaiian island of Kauai (Werner, Bierman, & French, 1971; Werner & Smith, 1977, 1982). The study began in 1954 with a cohort of all known pregnancies on the island and continues to follow the development of this cohort. The Kauai data showed that significantly greater deficits resulted from a combination of perinatal risk and disadvantaged home environment. On the other hand, children from advantaged homes suffered few or no long-term consequences of perinatal risk, unless there was evidence of severe neurological impairment. The protective/vulnerability influence of poverty status appeared to be a function of the quality of the caregiving environment, particularly the stability and supportiveness versus instability and disorganization of the family.

Eventually, the combination of observed diversity in outcomes and a growing Zeitgeist led these investigators to identify a resilient group of high-risk children in this sample and compare them with matched controls (Werner & Smith, 1982). Resilient children differed in personal and family attributes. For example, they had been healthier and more socially responsive infants and they grew up in families with fewer children, more spacing between them, and extended kinship and community social support networks. Thus, there appeared to be a number of compensatory factors or protective factors that either lowered the effective risk from the outset or ameliorated it in development.

While risk research proceeded with offspring of schizophrenia and other risk groups, the study of stress in children was beginning to emerge, addressing the "stressor" side of the equation. Here again, a shift in perspective occurred, led for the most part by several bridging figures in psychiatry and psychology, who were concerned with the role of adversity in the development of psychopathology.

While the concept of life stress influencing mental and physical health dates back at least to the last century (Garmezy & Rutter, 1985; Mason, 1975), the empirical study of environmental stress developed rapidly following the work of Hans Selye and Holmes and Rahe. Selye's (1936, 1956) work in delineating a general physiological response of the body to unusual demands led to hundreds of studies relating environmental challenges to disease. Another surge of studies followed the publication by Holmes and Rahe (1967) of a method to assess life change by counting and summing weighted life events. Shortly thereafter, Coddington (1972a, 1972b) created a set of life-event scales for children, with different scales for different age groups.

Life stress as indexed by such scales has been linked to a wide variety of outcomes in children as well as adults, ranging from cancer to behavior problems (Johnson, 1986). Most of these studies focused on negative outcomes, yet during the decade of the 1970s when stress research with children expanded, several prominent voices were pointing to the phenomenon of resilience, including E. James Anthony (1974), Norman Garmezy (1971; Garmezy & Nuechterlein, 1972), and Michael Rutter (1979b). It is interesting to note that this viewpoint was heralded by investigators of psychopathology and high-risk children.

It soon became evident in the life-event literature that individual differences might play a considerable role in the psychological functioning of children following cumulation of negative life events (Compas, 1987; Garmezy & Rutter, 1985; Johnson, 1986). Simple correlations of life stress and outcome measures tended to be small although persistent, whereas attributes such as sex, age, and socioeconomic status were linked with outcome.

Another major approach to the study of stress in children that blossomed in the 70s and 80s was the focus on a single type of major life event or stressor, such as divorce, in an attempt to increase the homogeneity of the stressor. It soon became evident, however, that this method did not avoid the complications of multiple stressors, as researchers examined the context of the stressor and began prospective studies. Life events rarely occur in isolation or at one point in time. Divorce, for example, is a complex series of interrelated events and stressors embedded in the ongoing lives of individuals and families. Both the multiplicity of events and context proved to be important correlates of outcome. In the case of divorce, such factors as sex, age at separation, history of marital discord, custody arrangements, and time since divorce, seemed to play a role in the subsequent adaptation of children (Emery, 1982, Hetherington, 1979).

A thorny issue for the stress researchers has been the question of prestressor adaptation. Most studies begin after a stressor has occurred, so that it is unclear whether observed behaviors stem directly from the stressor. The importance of this issue is illustrated by studies of divorce. It was widely acknowledged from a decade of research that children, particularly boys, often respond to this experience with increased disruptive-aggressive behavior (Emery, 1982; Hetherington, 1979). Data drawn from the Blocks' longitudinal study (Block, Block, & Gjerde, 1986) suggested, however, that boys from families who will subsequently divorce were already exhibiting a variety of externalizing behavioral problems (e.g., aggression, disobedience, impulsivity) years *before* the divorce occurred. These findings do not mean that the events surrounding the divorce itself are not stressful, but rather that they must be examined in the context of prior functioning.

Investigators of high-risk and high-stress children were influenced by a third tradition in psychology, the study of positive adaptation, which developed in personality theory and research from early psychoanalytic concepts of ego, defense, and adaptation (Loevinger, 1976) and evolved in the concepts of competence, coping, mastery, and ego-resiliency (Block & Block, 1980; Murphy & Moriarty, 1976; and White, 1959). This root of resilience is represented by the theoretical work of Robert White and the longitudinal studies of Lois Murphy and her colleagues in Topeka as well as Jeanne and Jack Block in Berkeley.

Lois Murphy's interest in vulnerability and coping began in the 1930s (Murphy & Moriarty, 1976), and led to a longitudinal study of coping initiated in 1953 with colleagues in Topeka, Kansas. Their purpose, as stated in their initial grant application was as follows: "To initiate the study of children's efforts to cope with their own problems and to explore the relation of these efforts to aspects of temperament and resources for growth" (Murphy & Moriarty, 1976, p. xi). To achieve this goal, they observed 32 children in great detail from infancy to adolecence. While formal assessments were obtained at different ages, the heart of the study lay in the detailed observations of the children's responses to naturally occurring stressors, such as injuries, deaths in the family, and events common to the cohort, including a tornado and Kennedy's assassination. In method, the intensive study of such a small sample is probably best described as an aggregate of case histories, with rich clinical observations and interesting patterns of correlations. Despite the small sample and the concomitant limitations of statistical rigor and empirical controls, this study continues to influence investigators of vulnerability, stress, and resilience (Masten & Garmezy, 1985).

Murphy's group viewed adaptation as a complex interplay of a child's vulnerabilities, genetic and acquired, and the challenges and opportunities that unfold in their lives. They noted normative developmental changes in adaptational style in conjunction with newly emerging resources, such as the increasing abilities to control the environment evident in the first year of life, maturational changes (for example, in appearances or energy) that accompany puberty, and changing demands from the environment. They observed long-lasting developmental problems only in the most vulnerable infants who also encountered severe trauma. Most children in this generally advantaged sample, despite some vulnerabilities and some stressful experiences, developed well, and the diversity of their coping strategies is striking. These investigators observed that the impact of stressors depended both on the current vulnerability and resources of the child and the intensity and duration of the stress. Incapacity in a previously capable mother due to mental or physical difficulties was observed to produce "drastic changes" in the quality of their children's adaptation. They suggested that the timing of such changes was critical: Heightened effects resulted when environmental stress occurred during a period of developmental challenge or sensitivity, especially if the stressors taxed the area of functioning undergoing change.

Resilience was viewed as an inherent human capacity to recover from adversity, to restore equilibrium of functioning. They also observed that successful mastery of earlier manageable stressors seemed to promote a positive self-image and better subsequent coping with stress. Robert White's theory of competence held a similar view of human nature.

In a seminal paper published in 1959, White integrated trends in animal research on exploratory behavior, ego theory in psychoanalysis, and cognitive development in infants to present a theory of competence asserting that effective transactions with the environment are intrinsically motivated, implying that humans as well as other species are active seekers of experiences that lead to competence. Satisfying this motive, presumably evolved due to its adaptive value, yields feelings of efficacy.

The Berkeley longitudinal study initiated by Jeanne and Jack Block in 1968 focused on two constructs influenced also by psychoanalytic theory: ego-control and ego-resiliency. Ego-resiliency, related to Robert White's concept of competence and Murphy's concept of coping, referred to the flexibility and resourcefulness of functioning, the ability to "modify one's behavior in accordance with contextual demands." Ego control referred to the degree of impulse control and modulation. In their study, the Blocks have investigated the development of these two constructs by assessments of over 100 children followed from ages 3 to 18. Each assessment consisted of extensive testing, observations, and ratings, wide-ranging in content, that changed with developmental level. Prototype definitions of the two constructs of interest were obtained for each age level by consensual descriptions of clinicians using the 100-item personality ascriptors in the California Q-sort. A child's actual Q-sort was then correlated with each prototype at each age. Considerable stability has been shown in these two constructs of ego resiliency and control (Block & Block, 1980; Block & Gjerde, 1986).

The combination of these two dimensions suggested two positive styles of adaptation: the resilient undercontroller, described as energetic, curious, resilient to stress, interesting, and so forth, and the resilient overcontroller, described as compliant, calm, relaxed, and empathic (Block & Block, 1980). Not surprisingly, social competence at different ages is associated with ego-resiliency.

Thus it happened that a concern with resilience emerged from research on vulnerability and risk, bolstered by work on adaptation and competence. Whenever vulnerability or risk was studied prospectively or conceptualized in the context of normal development, ideas about resilience followed in the wake of observed differences in the quality of adaptation. Lois Murphy's early study was relatively unique in observing vulnerability and coping longitudinally in a normative sample. Rutter's (1972, 1979a) systematic reviews of the maternal deprivation literature highlighted diversity in outcome as did Sameroff and Chandler's (1975) influential review of perinatal risk factors, each noting the evidence of positive adaptation despite risk. Garmezy, by example and writing, turned the attention of numerous risk researchers to the question of successful adaptation despite adversity. Each of these investigators were able to draw on the theoretical work of Jack and Jeanne Block, Robert White, and others. There was also, of course, a significant degree of cross-fertilization of ideas among such investigators. When the ideas of risk, stress, competence, and resilience came together, a broader view of adaptation emerged that was fundamental for developmental psychopathology.

The second part of this chapter focuses on one example of research concerned with resilience of children under adversity that evolved from a high-risk research program.

PROJECT COMPETENCE: STUDIES OF COMPETENCE UNDER ADVERSITY

About 10 years ago, several studies were initiated by a team of researchers at the University of Minnesota with the goal of understanding more about competence in children under conditions that challenged development, including a sample of children with congenital heart defects and consequent surgeries (O'Dougherty, 1981; O'Dougherty, Wright, Garmezy, Loewenson, & Torres, 1983), a sample of physically handicapped children (Raison, 1982; Silverstein, 1982) who were mainstreamed into regular classrooms, and a normative community sample of children with exposure to heterogeneous life stressors. This discussion focuses on this last group, the largest cohort in the Project Competence studies.

The evolution of "Project Competence" reflects the recent historical shift from a negative focus on vulnerability and risk to a broader perspective on adaptation focused on competence, protective factors, and resilience, as well as risk. The founder of this research program, Norman Garmezy (1987), has described the path that led him from studies of adult schizophrenia and premorbid competence to children of mentally ill parents at risk for psychopathology, to adaptation in disadvantaged children or children who had recently experienced stressful life events.

One way to conceptualize the approach of this project to understanding resilience is in terms of resources and challenges to adaptation. A simple model of a person's adaptation to challenge would include the nature of the challenge, the resources available to meet the challenge, and factors that moderate either the nature of the challenge or the availability of resources. We refer to vulnerability and resilience when characteristics of person or environment yield a process of exacerbation or amelioration, respectively, of threats to development.

This model, of course, is a grand oversimplification of the complex processes that occur as individuals adapt over time. When our knowledge is limited, however, simplification may be necessary to give us a handle on the phenomenon. Figure 11.1 presents a general model of the ingredients in the process of negotiating challenges to development. At Time 1, there is an individual whose current quality of adaptation can be assessed. Current behavior presumably reflects a long process of person-environment transactions at many levels. Much effort is being focused in this literature on measuring the quality of current adaptation. One of the implications of the risk literature vis-à-vis resilience was the attention it brought to bear on the assessment of competence, adding positive measures of adaptation to the long tradition of measuring behavioral problems. Predictors of current adaptation also have been studied extensively. Again, it became clear that in addition to risk factors, assets or resources must be included.

This model also assumes that an individual walks around with a set of potential strengths and weaknesses described here as vulnerabilities, resources, and protective factors. Some of these attributes are personal, what we describe by measures of personality, intelligence, appearance, or health, for example. Others belong to a person by virtue of their connections to various systems of social or economic interactions, including for example, parents, money, or status.

Three overlapping categories are suggested in the depicted model. *Resources* refer to attributes that contribute to adaptation directly: either as assets or, if lacking, as liabilities. *Vulnerabilities* refer to attributes that may jeopardize adaptation because they increase the effect of challenges, stressors, or risk factors. Some vulnerabilities may be specific, linked to a particular problem, such as a genetic susceptibility to schizophrenia. Others may be general, such as a stress-

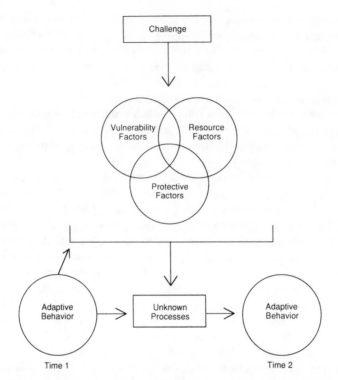

FIG.11.1.   A general model of adaptation to challenge. From Masten
et al. (1988). Reprinted with permission from the *Journal of Child Psychology and Psychiatry,* Vol. *29,* Copyright 1988, Pergamon Press.

reactive temperament. Theoretically, the effect of vulnerabilities are indirect, yet
it is conceivable that vulnerability may be so great that even normative developmental challenges exceed the capacity of the person for adaptation. Gottesman
and Shields (1982) have illustrated this process in terms of a very high genetic
diathesis for schizophrenia, yielding an insidious course over development.
Other vulnerabilities may come into play only under unusual circumstances and
hence will be observed only indirectly in combination with other factors. Some
may be constitutional while other vulnerabilities are acquired in the course of
development.

Protective attributes, those that yield resilience, also affect adaptation indirectly by reducing the effect of vulnerabilities, challenges, or risk to development. Some of these attributes may also have directly beneficial effects, hence
the overlap with resources. Other attributes, analogous to antibodies, have a
beneficial effect *only* in the presence of a specific challenge; they are activitated,
as it were, by the threat to adaptation. As with vulnerabilities, protective factors
can be innate or acquired, internal or transactional, specific or general. As

shown, some attributes may promote positive adaptation in one context and have negative effects in another, hence the overlap of vulnerabilities with both resources and protective factors.

When a stressor occurs, unknown processes ensue and changes may be observed in adaptive behavior. The time frame plays an important role here, as these processes unfold in time. An acute destabilizing event may result in rapid accommodation and recovery in less time than the interval between measurements of behavior, such that behavioral changes might not be observed.

To complicate matters further, vulnerability, resources, and protective factors may change with development or experiences. Moreover, some attributes of the person may be relatively stable, such as temperament, while others are more variable, such as social relationships.

Qualities of the challenge also play a role. Some challenges are themselves processes, such as the normative changes of puberty, or the unrelenting pressure of poverty or racial prejudice. Some stressors are acute events with no lasting effect on a person's resources. Others are catastrophic, with permanent losses of resources, such as the death of one's whole family. Clearly, even a simplistic model like this holds the threat of overwhelming complexity. Yet we must begin somewhere.

In order to evaluate the role of potential resources and protective factors in our data analyses, several models were developed to describe the relation of stress exposure to competence, taking into account a potential resource or protective/vulnerability factor (see Masten, Garmezy, Tellegen, Pellegrini, Larkin, & Larsen, 1988). Two of these models are particularly relevant to this discussion.

The compensatory model, illustrated in Fig. 11.2, describes a balance of positive and negative effects on functioning. Competence declines as a function of adversity or stress, due to the drain on resources, however, the person with more assets always functions better than the less advantaged person. From a

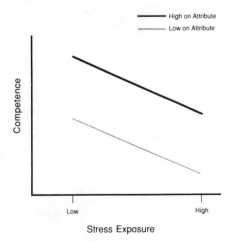

FIG. 11.2. Compensatory model, showing attribute that is related to competence. From Masten et al. (1988). Reprinted from the *Journal of Child Psychology and Psychiatry*, Vol. *29,* Copyright 1988, Pergamon Press.

statistical perspective, these effects are additive and can be described by a regression equation of this form, predicting competence (C) from attributes (A) and stressors (S): $C = B_1 A + B_2 S + D$, where B_1 and B_2 are regression weights and D is a constant (Garmezy, Masten, & Tellegen, 1984). Implicit in this model, interestingly, is one of the most basic and appealing notions about "resilience," namely, the capacity to return to better functioning when adversity abates.

The protective model, shown in Fig. 11.3, contrasts one group's decline in competence with that of a group who hold their own, as it were, under adverse conditions. We assume that a protective process underlies that maintenance of competence in the high attribute group, preventing a decline in functioning or promoting rapid recovery. This process might involve active help from a parent or the capacity to draw on ready reserves of resources represented, for example, by better problem-solving skills. Some people may simply have more reserves available, perhaps by virtue of socioeconomic differences in financial resources or by social support in the form of family and friendship. The attribute may stand in the model as a marker of accessible and relevant reserves of economic or social resources.

It should be noted that this model could also depict a vulnerability effect whereby the people disadvantaged on the attribute are affected more by the stressor, assuming this group is differentially sensitive. The key difference in interpretation, not knowing the underlying processes, rests with one's assumptions about what is normative or expected in response to the stressor or risk factor depicted on the abscissa. When outcome is worse than expected, vulnerability is inferred; when it is better than expected, resilience is inferred. The protective or vulnerability effect of a moderator also can be described in a regression equation: $C = B_1 A + B_2 S$ to $B_3 SA + D$, which adds an interaction (Attribute × Stressor) term to the prediction of competence.

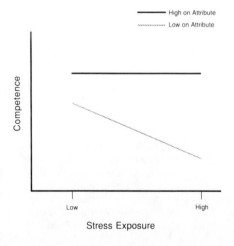

FIG. 11.3. Protective or vulnerability model, showing an attribute that modifies the relation of stress exposure or risk to competence. From Masten et al. (1988). Reprinted with permission from the *Journal of Child Psychology and Psychiatry*, Vol. 29, Copyright 1988, Pergamon Press.

When it began, this research program was unusual in its concentration on competence, which was defined in terms of effective functioning in environmental contexts important to the developmental phase of children in each cohort. Although our view of competence was inspired in part by Robert White (1959), our operational definition of competence was behavioral rather than motivational, as evidenced, for example, in behavior at home and at school, peer acceptance, and academic achievements.

Because there had not been a strong research tradition investigating competence in school-age children, particularly in relation to risk, stress, and protective factors, it was necessary to spend a good bit of time developing methods of assessing competence and potential protective factors (see Garmezy, & Tellegen, 1984; Masten et al., 1988). We needed to know more about competence and its correlates. We were interested in individual attributes, as well as contextual variables such as family characteristics, traditional "risk" factors, and threatening life events, both recent and historical. There was good reason to expect that attributes such as IQ, good quality parenting, and higher socioeconomic status would be associated with better functioning in the broadest sense and also in more specific cases; for example, IQ was expected to be a salient predictor of academic achievement. All of these qualities were traditionally associated with better outcomes or adjustment (Kohlberg, LaCrosse, & Ricks, 1972). We also sought to learn more about resilience and protective-versus-vulnerability factors that modify the relation of competence to stress exposure. We were particularly interested in identifying buffering characteristics of the individual or environment, which may ameliorate risk, because these attributes or processes may hold the key to better interventions. It may be more effective or efficient to influence the moderators of risk than it is to reduce or avoid the risk directly. Moreover, identifying protective processes might provide clues for better targeting and timing of interventions.

Potential moderating factors were identified on the basis of the literature, although at that time pertinent data were sketchy and scattered. Sex, intellectual functioning, socioeconomic status, and parenting quality were four of the most important potential moderating variables implicated in the literature both as correlates of adjustment, and moderators of risk (Garmezy, 1985; Rutter, 1979b). Other potential moderators examined as the focus of individual doctoral dissertations included humor abilities (Masten, 1982, 1986), social cognition (Pellegrini, 1980, 1985), and reflective thinking (Ferrarese, 1981; Garmezy & Tellegen, 1984).

The community sample.   The community cohort was recruited in two waves a year apart from two adjacent schools in Minneapolis (see Garmezy & Tellegen, 1984; Masten et al., 1988). Recruitment began with a mail survey of stressful life events sent to all parents of 3rd to 6th graders. Questionnaires were returned from 59% of the 612 families of children. The sample of responders to this questionnaire did not differ from nonresponders in subsequent school-wide assessments of competence based on teacher and peer ratings. From this group of 361 children, 207 (57%) were successfully recruited for an intensive series of assessments of child and parent qualities. After the first wave of recruitment, data analysis revealed that at this stage of recruitment, where families agreed to become much more involved, the resulting sample was significantly more competent and less stressed than the nonparticipants, thereby somewhat restricting the range on key attributes. To compensate as best as possible for this sampling bias, extra effort was made to recruit high-risk families in the second wave. Recruiters visited most homes families reporting high stress levels who did not spontaneously join the study and convinced 71% of these families to join, resulting in an extended range of sampling in the second wave, with no attrition bias.

The final sample were diverse in ethnic, socioeconomic, and marital background. Of the 207, 28% were minorities, 45% resided with two parents, 38% with single parents, and 17% in reconstituted households. Although an urban sample, there was a range of socioeconomic status. On the Duncan (Hauser & Featherman, 1977) index of occupational status, scores for households varied from 7 to 92.3 on a 100-point scale. The average score represented occupational levels such as skilled labor and clerical workers.

Measures in middle childhood.   Assessments, which required almost 2 years of time to complete in each sampling wave, were guided by the goals of the study and the problems inherent in a new area of investigation. Given the lack of information about the most pertinent attributes and methods to address our questions, we took a multivariate approach, attempting to measure competence, for example, in the most appropriate ways for a given age cohort, using different sources and methods for obtaining information, including "L", "O", "S", and "T" methods, to use Block's LOST acronym (Block & Block, 1980) for classifying kinds of psychological data. L-data (for "life") included demographic data, life history information, and social class. O-data (for "observational") included behavior checklists and ratings by parents, teachers, and peers. S-data (for "subjective") included questionnaires and interviews, and T-data (for "test"), included assessments of achievement and abilities.

Measures and guiding constructs of the elementary school-age assessments are listed in Tables 11.1 and 11.2. Competence was assessed by multiple measures from the perspective of different people, including a teacher rating scale, peer assessment, parent interview questions about the child, questionnaires filled out by parents, a child interview, interviewer ratings, individually administered achievement tests, and school record data on grades and standardized tests.

Stress exposure was assessed by a life event inventory modeled on Coddington's (1972a, 1972b) method and also by interview methods. The Life Event Questionnaire provided a relatively objective count of recent life events. A negative life event score was compiled by a simple tally of 30 of the 50 events on

TABLE 11.1
Project Competence Community Cohort: Outline of Measures and
Procedures in Elementary School

Year 1

Life event survey by mail: Life Events Questionnaire
Child competence assessment at school
    Teacher ratings: Devereux Elementary School Behavior
        Rating Scale (Spivack & Swift, 1967)
    Peer ratings: Revised Class Play (Masten, Morison,
        & Pellegrini, 1985)
    Achievement: School record data
Parent interviews initiated: 3 two-hour sessions (Linder, 1985)
    1. Family structure, history, activities, relationships
    2. Child's behavior, activities, relationships
    3. Contextual life events
    Developmental Questionnaire
    Home Rating Scales by interviewer
    Family Rating Scales by interviewer

Year 2

Stressful life events reassessed
Child competence at school reassessed
    (Teachers, peers, school records)
    Peabody Individual Achievement Test (Dunn & Markwart, 1970)
Child attributes assessed
    Vocabulary and Block Design from the WISC-R (Wechsler, 1974)
    Interpersonal Understanding (Selman, 1980)
    Means-Ends Problem Solving Test (Shure & Spivack, 1972)
    Matching Familiar Figures Test (Kagan et al., 1964)
    Porteus Maze Test (Porteus, 1933)
    Humor appreciation, comprehension, and production (Masten, 1986)
    Wallach-Kogan (1965) Creativity Test
Child interviews: 2 one-hour sessions (Finkelman, 1983)
    Topics: School, activities, friends, family aspirations, plans,
        self-concept, life events
    Child Interview Ratings (Finkelman, 1983; Morison, 1987)

the scale. These events were both negative and unlikely to be contaminated by the child's own behavior or competence. Interviews provided greater detail about these events and allowed for more subjective global ratings of the level of stress present in the family. The interview also provided extensive data in the history of the family, which were empirically compiled. One important composite score from these data measured the degree of family stability-instability as evidenced by events such as divorce, remarriage, moving, and changing jobs.

Potential moderators of the relations between stress exposure and competence included individual and family attributes. One focus of these measures was the family environment and resources, with variables such as socioeconomic status, social support, and quality of parenting. Another focus was cognitive abilities in the child, including assessments as divergent as IQ and humor.

Followup study. Although a followup study was not part of our initial plan, as we began to analyze the data from elementary school, we realized the potential in obtaining outcome data for this sample in late adolescence, in order to examine patterns of competence over time in relation to earlier development, interven-

TABLE 11.2
Project Competence Community Cohort: Constructs
Assessed in Elementary School

Competence
  Academic
  Social

Stress Exposure
  Negative life events
  Family stress
  Family instability

*Risk Factors or Resources
  Cognitive abilities
    Intellectual functioning (IQ)
    social cognition
    Reflexivity-impulsivity
    Humor
    Divergent thinking

  Developmental history (retrospective)
    Perinatal risk
    Health
    Early major stressors

  Family characteristics
    Demographic features
    Socioeconomic status
    Income
    Parent-child relationship
    Parenting quality
    Social network

[a]Potential vulnerability/resilience factors

ing challenges, and enduring risk and protective factors. Thus, a followup study was initiated approximately 7 years after the initial study when the cohort ranged in age from 14 to 19. Located for the followup were 189 (91%) subjects. Questionnaire data have been obtained for all but 6 of those located, 183 young people, 88% of the original participants.

The first wave of follow-up assessments were conducted by mail and thus were limited to questionnaire-type data. Even so, we obtained two perspectives by having mothers and teenage participants fill out comparable questionnaires about the teenagers. With additional funding, a second, more intensive wave of followup was initiated in 1987, including laboratory assessments, interviews of participants, interviews of the mothers, as well as additional questionnaires and self-report inventories.

An outline of the followup study procedures is presented in Table 11.3. The questionnaires of the first phase of assessment were designed to index adaptation as broadly as possible within the contraints inherent in the mail-in questionnaire method and the cooperation of subjects. Thus the questionnaires had to be reasonably brief, easy for teenagers to understand and complete, and face valid, while assessing the major aspects of competence and psychopathology germaine to this period of development. We were interested in assessing academic and/or work competence, social competence, in terms of peer friendships and love relationships, and the quality of family relationships, psychological well-being in terms of self-worth and perceived competence, and psychopathology with respect to emotional or behavior problems, symptoms, trouble with the law, and alcohol or drug problems.

Second phase assessments were designed to assess personal attributes, competence, and life stressors in more detail by interview methods and individual assessments. The young participants, now ranging in age from 16 to 21 are invited to a laboratory session at the University. This assessment includes measures of mood, humor, social cognition, and intellectual functioning, emotional and cognitive attributes linked to competence and resilience in our earlier work as well as the literature. Participants return again for a 2-hour interview primarily focused on current adaptation in multiple domains of competence. On their own, they also complete self-report measures of personality, life events, symptoms, and perceived competence. Mothers will be interviewed at home to gather additional information on their child's adaptation and the family history of life events, as well as the mother's intellectual functioning.

What have we learned thus far about competence? Although it is not yet complete, this study addresses four questions about competence:

- What is the nature of competence in middle childhood?
- What are competent children like? What are their individual and environmental resources in contrast to risk factors for reduced competence?
- Are there protective factors that appear to ameliorate the effect of stressful or high risk environments on competence?
- Is competence stable from middle childhood to late adolescence? How are patterns of adaptation linked to risk factors, stressors, and protective factors?

TABLE 11.3
Project Competence Community Cohort: Follow-Up Procedures

First Phase

    Status questionnaires (from subjects and mothers)
    Behavior checklists (from subjects and mothers)
    Competence ratings (from subjects and mothers)
    Life event questionnaires (from subjects and mothers)
    School record data (grades, achievement, attendance)

Second Phase

    Status questionnaires (subjects and mothers)
    Personality questionnaire
    Mood questionnaire
    Symptom checklist
    Competence questionnaires (from subjects, peers, mothers)
    Humor assessment
    Social cognition assessment
    IQ assessments (subjects and mothers)
    Interviews (subjects and mothers)

The first question concerns the construct validity of competence. We have attempted to measure the quality of functioning in the environment by multiple measures with multiple informants. With what result? First, we expected and found a moderately high degree of congruence in the perspectives of parents, peers, teachers, and the children themselves about the nature and quality of their behavior. Total agreement was not expected primarily because these sources see and elicit different aspects of a child's behavior and also because the measures were not directly comparable.

Table 11.4 shows the correlations among a set of competence variables derived from teacher ratings, peer assessments, school records, individual testing, parent interview, and child interview. Two conclusions might be drawn from these interrelations: First, there seems to be considerable agreement about the quality of functioning in children, even from different perspectives. The congruence of opinion is particularly notable for both disruptive-externalizing behavior and academic achievement.

Second, competence appears to be multidimensional. When the structure of competence is explored by techniques such as factor analysis, two global dimensions emerge. On one dimension, aggressive, disruptive, "externalizing" behavior problems appear at one pole and good behavior or compliance at the other. On the other dimension, sociability, leadership, active involvement, and achievement appear at one pole, while the other pole is characterized by withdrawal, social isolation, and lower achievement. In our analyses, we have chosen to keep achievement data separate because it is a well-defined area of competence that usually has been studied separately. Thus, we often focus on three aspects of competence: achievement, engaged-versus-disengaged, and disruptive-versus-well-behaved. These two global dimensions plus achievement appear to describe school functioning (Garmezy, Masten, & Tellegen, 1984) and similar dimensions emerge from child interview data (Finkelman, 1983). These two global dimensions are quite similar to the dimensions of social-emotional functioning identified by Kohn (1977) and associates in a large study in New York City of younger children. Teacher ratings of social competence and symptoms in both preschool and elementary school yielded two factors, labeled Interest-Participation versus Apathy-Withdrawal and Cooperation-Compliance versus Anger-Defiance.

The second question concerns the correlates of competence, present and past, including individual differences, family differences, and life history differences. Our extensive network of correlates, describing context of competence in childhood, may provide clues about the "etiology" of competence as well as maladaptive behavior. We expected to confirm the association with competence of traditional risk factors or resources such as socioeconomic status, IQ, and the stability or quality of parenting. High or positive scores on these characteristics were expected to be resources predictive of competence. We also expected high-risk backgrounds characterized by chronic stress to predict lower competence.

TABLE 11.4

Intercorrelations of Competence Measures in Middle Childhood

	1	2	3	4	5	6	7	8	9	10	11	12	13	14	15
Achievement															
1. PIAT total score	.73***														
2. Grade Point Average															
Teacher Ratings															
3. Cooperative/Initiating	.26***	.34***													
4. Poor comprehension/disattention	-.48***	-.60***	-.33**												
5. Disruptive/Oppositional	-.21***	-.32***	.02	.54***											
Peer Assessment															
6. Sociability/Leadership	.29***	.38***	.24***	-.48***	-.32***										
7. Sensitive/Isolated	-.23***	-.28***	.14***	.39***	.08	-.40***									
8. Disruptive/Aggressive	-.16*	-.20***	-.17**	.13*	.54***	-.16*	.08								
Parent Interview															
9. Academic Performance	.71***	.70***	.18**	-.48***	-.23***	.26***	-.26***	.16							
10. Well-behaved at school	.16*	.23***	.05	-.35***	-.51***	.25***	-.06	-.44***	.22***						
11. Attitude toward school	.29***	.36***	.03	-.48***	-.38***	.35***	-.25***	-.21**	.46***	.44***					
12. Internalizing problems	.03	-.02	.09	.08	.21**	-.19**	.06	.22**	-.05	-.16*	-.18**				
13. Externalizing problems	-.24**	-.27***	-.01	.26**	.36***	-.32***	.19**	.32***	-.34***	-.54***	-.49***	.44***			
Child Interview Ratings															
14. Engaged-Disengaged	.50***	.51***	.38***	-.35***	-.21***	.31***	-.20**	-.15*	.37***	.17**	.19**	.01	-.24***		
15. Aggressive-Disruptive	-.23***	-.32***	-.07	.24***	.45***	-.23***	.10	.33***	-.22***	-.51***	-.40***	.24***	.51***	-.48***	
16. Motivated for achievement	.41***	.43***	.25***	-.31***	-.07	.31***	-.29***	.00	.32***	.04	.17***	.03	-.18**	.62***	-.23***

*p < .05.
**p < .01.
***p < .001.

TABLE 11.5
Correlation of School Competence with Family Attributes

Family Attributes	School Competence		
	GPA	Engaged	Disruptive
SES	.29***	.20**	-.17**
Parenting quality	.38***	.36***	-.25***
Stability/Organization	.22***	.16**	-.32***
Recent life events	-.09	-.15*	.22***

*$p < .05$.
**$p < .01$.
***$p < .001$.

Similarly, we expected high levels of recent aversive life events to correspond to less effective functioning. Moreover, given the expected covariance of risk and stress, we expected these effects to be additive or cumulative.

Individual testing of attributes revealed to no one's surprise that competent children, speaking broadly of those who are more engaged, less disruptive, and higher achieving, possessed a number of assets. They obtained higher IQ scores, were more reflective problem solvers, more divergent thinkers, had better social comprehension, appreciated humor, and were able to produce funny cartoon captions (Masten, 1986; Pellegrini, 1985; Pellegrini, Masten, Garmezy, & Ferrarese, 1987). In short, competent children had an array of cognitive abilities related to effective problem-solving and social know-how.

Family assessments indicated that child competence was also associated with parental competence and socioeconomic status (SES). Table 11.5 shows correlations of several family variables with the same set of school competence composites in elementary school.

A salient dimension of family variation in this study was "Stability/Organization," a second order factor of family attributes combining family history indicators of stability and home ratings scales reflecting organized, neat, well-maintained home environments. Children with more disrupted lives, by virtue of divorce, moving, parental job changes, or disorganized homes appeared to be more at risk for disruptive behaviors. This composite index of family stability versus instability had a consistently stronger relationship with competence than the index of recent life events.

The life event score was derived from a life events questionnaire that included 50 items. To obtain a score, only 30 items were counted (1 point for each yes), excluding life events that would be confounded with competence, such as "failed a grade" or "outstanding personal achievement." Generally, this score had low but significant correlations with measures of competence, including behavior problems.

Another important aspect to the question of the context for competence concerns the distribution of resources and risk, a question not addressed by simply relating individual attributes to competence. There is considerable collinearity among all the variables discussed previously as correlates of competence, raising several issues.

One issue is the role of general cognitive ability as a mediator of many relationships, both as the common denominator of the child's individual attributes related to competence and as a possible genetic underpinning of covariance in family qualities and child competence. Our data suggest that intellectual functioning as measured by an IQ test is a pervasive marker of competence, and not just of academic achievement, although this link is the strongest. However, broader assessments of social-cognitive abilities suggest that IQ does not tell the whole story. For example, a composite measure of general social comprehension, based on a set of social problem solving and humor assessments, was related quite strongly to IQ score ($r = 77$) yet contributed significantly to the prediction of engaged versus disengaged behavior at school even when IQ variance was controlled (Pellegrini et al., 1987). Similarly, the global index of parenting quality, relates quite strongly to child IQ scores ($r = 43$) yet has been found to contribute significantly to the prediction of diverse outcomes beyond the shared variance with the child's IQ score, as will be illustrated.

Another issue concerns the covariance of environmental risk indicators. To illustrate, Table 11.6 shows intercorrelations of environmental factors that individually are significantly correlated with child competence. On the one hand, these characteristics may partly be overlapping measures of parental competence, or even more specifically, parental cognitive ability, as for example parenting quality and socioeconomic status (SES). In most analyses the effects of SES are negligible once parenting quality is taken into account. Similarly, family stability might be mediated by parental competence, although the variable appears to have unique predictive power beyond shared variance with parenting quality, particularly in predicting disruptive behavior.

Another interesting question is whether there are environments that are more hazardous, independent of how the family arrived in the environment. In our data and other studies (Johnson, 1986), there seems to be a persistent link between low income or status and more frequent life events, even events that are not under the control of the family. Thus, children of immigrants, children of incompetent parents, children of divorce, or children born to limited opportunities,

TABLE 11.6
Intercorrelations of Environmental Risk Variables

	SES	Parenting Quality	Stability
Parenting Quality	.51***		
Stability/Organization	.25***	.41***	
Recent life events	-.21**	-.27***	-.42***

*$p < .05$.
**$p < .01$.
***$p < .001$.

may share the burden of more hazardous environments. Tragically, these hazards must often be negotiated with fewer resources, whether financial, intellectual, or social.

A third issue is the effect of combined risk, whatever the source. Rutter (1979b), Sameroff (Sameroff, Seifer, Zax, & Barocas, 1987) and others in this field have analyzed the effects of combined risk, even suggesting that it is not the nature of the risk factors per se, but rather the multiplicity of risk factors that matters in predicting adaptation. The cumulative risk concept also underlies the counting up of diverse stressors in life event schedules. Almost always, combining risk factors results in better prediction, up to a point when further additions make no difference. One question in this regard is whether the cumulative effect of risk or diversity is linear or exponential. Rutter (1979b, 1983) has argued, for example, that risk factors combine interactively, supporting his view with data from the Isle of Wight studies.

Our data support the hypothesis that environmental risk, defined several ways, has cumulative effects, particularly with regard to disruptive-aggressive behavior. Simple correlations of two cumulative risk scores support this view: the life event score and the stability composite each have significant correlations with various aspects of competence. For the most part, these relations are linear rather than exponential. One exception is the relation of recent life events to disruptiveness for girls, where a significant quadratic function suggests that a curve is a better description of the relation. Girls appear to maintain lower levels of disruptiveness than do boys up to a point. At very high levels of recent life events, there appears to be a jump in the level of disruptiveness evident in girls.

Another approach to evaluating cumulative risk is to combine a set of factors each related to competence, such as socioeconomic status, IQ, sex, or parenting qualities. The result of such multiple correlations usually are better predictions of competence. In the case of our data such combinations show additive effects, despite the substantial collinearity of variance (Masten, et al., in press). One interpretation of such results is the cumulative effect of risk from disadvantage on these major individual differences. Of course, the same data support the cumulative positive effect of the resources represented by these variables.

A third basic question for this study concerns the moderators of risk and stress exposure. This question goes to the heart of the search for protective factors, a first step in the understanding the protective processes of adaptation. Protective processes may promote better outcome in a variety of ways, for example, by (a) reducing the likelihood of a risk factor occurring at all, (b) increasing the availability of compensatory resources, or (c) reducing the impact of the challenge. The correlates of adversity provide some clues about the first possibility, suggesting, for example, that parental competence or higher socioeconomic status or income reduces the likelihood of exposure to environmental hazards.

However, the search for protective factors is generally very complex and methodologically difficult because these processes are by definition interactional, implying conditional relationships and multifactorial analyses. The analysis of multivariate data, particularly with an eye to interaction effects is fraught with difficulty, ranging from the need for larger sample sizes to complexity of interpreting significant interactions of correlated variables.

Context also is very important. For example, the method of identifying the high-risk group and then comparing high versus low competence groups can be very misleading. Differences in the two groups may have more to do with general resources or the correlates of competence at all levels of risk rather than protective factors per se. Competence under adversity must be understood in the context of competence under varying conditions, particularly normally expected environments and the development of competence.

For these reasons, we approach our data and interpret results with caution. We focus on theoretically motivated questions and select only a few variables, preferably more reliable composite variables, for analysis. We recognize, moreover, that results must be evaluated in the context of other literature and interpreted as hypotheses for confirmation in other studies.

Thus far, our analyses concerned with protective factors have focused on relating school competence to stressful life events of the previous year, evaluating four major sources of individual differences strongly implicated by the literature as moderators: sex, IQ, parenting quality, and socioeconomic status (Masten et al., 1988). When all of the competence data are integrated, similar analyses will be carried out to examine the protective role of these attributes in broader contexts and across time.

To illustrate our results, this discussion focuses on disruptive-aggressive behavior. As indicated, peers and teachers agree moderately well on the presence of unruly behavior and thus the competence criterion "Classroom Disruptiveness" is a composite of peer reputation as disruptive-aggressive and teacher ratings of disruptive-oppositional behavior.

Disruptive behavior is of particular interest as it has been consistently linked to adversity, in the form of acute stress, chronic stress, and socioeconomic disadvantage. Following divorce as well as major disasters, increased disruptive behavior is often reported, particularly in boys (Emery, 1982; Garmezy & Rutter, 1985). Aggressive and antisocial behavior has also been associated with male sex, lower achievement, psychosocial disadvantage, poor supervision, and parenting skills, marital discord, and later psychopathology or antisocial behavior (Kohlberg et al., 1972; Loeber & Dishion, 1983; Loeber & Stouthamer-Loeber, in press; Robins, 1978). Thus, sex, IQ, parenting quality, and SES were viewed as potential moderators of the relation of negative life events to disruptiveness.

We viewed "Classroom Disruptiveness" as one aspect of maladaptation both because of the literature cited above, and because in our data it was negatively related to achievement and positive school involvement. Low scores generally reflect better competence; such children are viewed as well-behaved and compliant by adults and more acceptable by peers.

Our results with this variable show interesting patterns that suggest possible protective effects. First, our data suggest that general intellectual functioning may play a role in how stress exposure influences behavior. IQ has a direct relation with disruptiveness, particularly for boys. More intelligent children appear less disruptive and aggressive to their teachers, peers, parents, and to themselves. Under high-stress conditions, following a year of adverse life events, children with higher intellectual functioning are less likely to exhibit this kind of behavior (Masten et al., 1988). This interaction effect, very similar for boys and girls, is illustrated in Fig. 11.4.

Why might this be? These children have many resources, even beyond their own problem-solving skills. Other assets covary with IQ scores, and thus might be available as back-up under challenging circumstances. They may have a stronger sense of self-efficacy from past successes in contrast to children with a history of frustration and failure. This self-view may influence their interpretation of events, their frustration tolerance, and so forth. Higher IQ children also tend to be more reflective in cognitive style and their parents tend to be better educated and more resourceful. Thus, generally they are likely to have different models of stress response and different socialization histories that emphasize restraint. Finally, such children could be more discriminating in their responses to stress, more mindful of behavioral codes with teachers and peers. Socioeconomic status shows a similar interaction effect, and similar speculations might be offered in explanation. These suggestions, not exhaustive, reveal how little we actually know about the psychological mechanisms underlying an interaction effect.

The evaluation of parenting as a moderator illustrates complications intro-

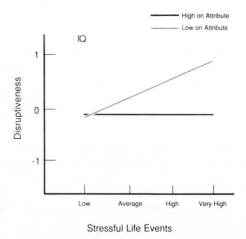

FIG. 11.4. The interaction of IQ and recent negative life events in the prediction of Clasroom Disruptiveness. Individual differences due to sex, socioeconomic status, and parenting quality are controlled. From Masten et al. (1988). Reprinted with permission from the *Journal of Child Psychology and Psychiatry,* Vol. *29,* Copyright 1988, Pergamon Press.

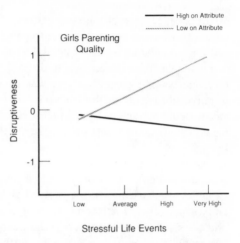

FIG. 11.5. The interaction, for girls, of parenting quality and recent negative life events in predicting Classroom Disruptiveness. Individual differences due to IQ and socioeconomic status are controlled. From Masten et al. (1988). Reprinted with permission from the *Journal of Child Psychology and Psychiatry*, Vol. *29*, Copyright 1988, Pergamon Press.

duced by sex differences. Our data, consistent with many studies, show boys to be generally more disruptive or aggressive than girls. The relation of global parenting quality to this aspect of competence and life events differs for boys and girls. There is a significant three-way interaction (sex × parenting quality × stressful life events) indicating a sex difference. Thus, parenting quality moderator effects were analyzed separately for boys and girls. For boys, no moderating effect is evident and the main effect of IQ appears to play a more significant role for boys than parenting quality.

Results for girls are illustrated in Fig. 11.5. Under high-stress conditions, girls with good parenting are not likely to be exhibiting disruptive or aggressive behavior. Their style appears to lean toward quieter behaviors or perhaps increased compliance.

Why might this be? Girls appear to be protected in some way in this context. Parents, primarily mothers, have been rated as competent, understanding, perceptive, and supportive in regard to their children. Why would this influence girls more than boys with similar parenting? Perhaps mothers are likely to interact differently with boys under stress. This has been observed in studies of postdivorce parenting (Hetherington, 1979). Girls may receive more direct support from mothers, or parents may actively try to buffer girls more than boys. Girls may also be more likely to model themselves after competent mothers. Cultural values may contribute: for example, disruptiveness may be more acceptable for boys whereas crying or withdrawal is proscribed for girls. Girls may have internalized different values and learned different ways of responding to their own distress from the processes of socialization, including modeling and other learning linked to parenting. Under stress, girls may seek and receive more support from mothers. Parenting appears to be the moderator but it may actually be a marker for any or all of these processes.

It is also possible that two distinct processes underly this finding: one primarily a sex difference, the other a parenting difference. Boys generally may respond with more aggression or disorganized activity to stress than do girls. In addition, middle-class parenting styles may promote internalizing rather than externalizing styles of response to distress. Consistent with the latter interpretation, the parenting quality index was also found to moderate the relation of negative life events to the Engaged-Disengaged dimension of school competence. Both boys and girls with higher parenting scores showed some disengagement at high stress levels in comparison to their low-stress peers with similar parenting.

Our findings thus far in regard to protective factors are both encouraging and frustrating. We find it encouraging to identify patterns in the complex network of variables we have measured, particularly patterns linked to theory and other empirical work. Unsatisfying, however, is our level of understanding of the processes underlying the patterns. Our interpretations of interactional patterns, at best, yield a series of hypotheses for further study.

One key problem is methodological. Capturing process in observations and other assessments requires a much closer level of scrutiny than is possible in the initial studies of complex behaviors. Patterns such as we have found need to be replicated in other studies, then subjected to intense study where multiple observations occur over time to monitor transactions between parent and child, and link these to, for example, school life.

While studies of process require time-intensive studies, the fourth question we are addressing in this project requires longer intervals of time to examine the prognostic significance of competence, risk, or protective factors in one part of life for later competence. The followup assessments, still in progress, provide evidence of the importance for the future of the effectiveness of functioning in middle childhood.

Results from a global assessment of outcome after approximately 7 years illustrate the directions of our findings thus far. Adolescent participants and their mothers independently completed a Status Questionnaire by mail, which included a wide array of questions. Covered by these questions were school achievement, work status, impressions of friendships, relationships with parents, activities, trouble with the law and drugs, mental and physical health, and so forth. In order to condense these data, two judges independently rated all the information provided on a set of 11 scales. Separate ratings were completed for data obtained from mothers and teenagers. Not only was interjudge agreement high, but the correlation of judgments based on mother versus teenager data was also very good. Therefore, global ratings were obtained for the 11 scales by averaging across judges and sources of information. Four of the broadest ratings of adaptation are examined here:

- Global Adaptation: Global assessment of the child's overall level of adaptation (7-point scale, 1 = very poorly adjusted, 7 = very well-adjusted);

- Psychopathology: Amount of overall psychopathology evidenced (3-point scale, 1 = none, 2 = some, 3 = definite, considerable);
- Trouble with the Law: Seriousness of this child's trouble with the law and other authorities (5-point scale; 1 = none, 5 = very serious),
- Academic Performance: How well is this child doing in school (5-point scale, 1 = well below average, 5 = well above average.)

In this order, the interrater reliabilities based on parent reports were .88, .80, .91, and .97, respectively. The correlations of judgments based on mothers' reports and judgments based on adolescents' reports were .74, .69, .70, and .70, respectively.

Competence in middle childhood was expected to show stability and predictive power, for a number of reasons. First, the literature suggests that academic achievement and antisocial behaviors particularly, have stability across the span from middle childhood to adolescence (Bracht & Hopkins, 1977; Loeber, 1982). Second, competence in middle childhood was correlated with assets and risks that were expected to show considerable stability, including IQ and the quality of parenting. Third, we assumed that children who are competent in middle childhood have weathered the normative challenges of earlier development and thus they were presumed to have adaptive qualities that would see them through the adolescent transition. Among these children, moreover, were some truly resilient children who had negotiated greater threats to development than the norm and were expected to continue on such adaptive paths.

Undoubtedly there were some children who were competent earlier yet vulnerable to unique challenges of adolescence or intervening environmental hazards. Some may have carried a genetic liability programmed to unfold only during adolescence. However, we suspected that, for the most part, the best marker of vulnerability for development in adolescence would be poor adaptation in middle childhood. Thus we predicted that the quality of adaptation in middle childhood would predict reasonably well (given the constraints of measurement error) the quality of adaptation in late adolescence.

Results supported this hypothesis, as shown in Table 11.7. Particularly salient in the pattern of correlations was the general significance of both achievement and disruptive-aggressive behavior in middle childhood for adaptation in late adolescence, broadly defined. Also as expected, major attributes of competence, particularly IQ and global parenting quality, were significantly correlated with most aspects of later adaptation (Masten, 1987).

Generally, the results we have examined thus far suggest that competence *and* the internal and external resources that usually accompany competence, are reasonably stable and predictive of later adjustment. Consistent with a diverse literature, academic achievement and externalizing behavior problems are particularly stable and broadly predictive of adaptation in late adolescence. Concomi-

TABLE 11.7

Correlations of Adaptation in Middle Childhood and Adolescence

Competence in Middle Childhood	Global Adaptation	Clinical Ratings in Late Adolescence		
		Psychopathology	Trouble With the Law	Academic Performance
Achievement				
PIAT total score	.47***	-.11	-.19**	.45***
Grade Point Average	.42***	-.09	-.16*	.43***
Teacher Ratings				
Cooperative/Initiating	.12	.01	.02	.03
Poor Comprehension/Disattention	-.34***	.05	.14*	-.32***
Disruptive/Oppositional	-.34***	.26***	.39***	-.35***
Peer Assessment				
Sociability/Leadership	.31***	-.11	-.19**	.25***
Sensitive Isolated	-.08	-.04	-.03	-.01
Disruptive/Aggressive	-.28***	.31***	.30***	-.24***
Parent Interview				
Academic performance	.38***	-.13*	-.12	.40***
Well-behaved at school	.30***	-.28***	-.40***	.33***
Attitude toward school	.42***	-.29***	-.36***	.38***
Internalizing problems	-.12	.14*	.06	-.12
Externalizing problems	-.44***	.33***	.44***	-.37***
Child Interview Ratings				
Engaged-Disengaged	.43***	-.16*	-.22***	.25***
Aggressive/Disruptive	-.43***	.38***	.42***	-.30***
Motivation/Aspiration	.44***	-.16*	-.18**	.24***

*p < .05.
**p < .01.
***p < .001.

tantly, IQ and parenting quality appear to function as broad markers of adaptive abilities and environments.

However, global stability in the group data are only part of the story. While multiple correlations are high (see Masten, 1987), a set of predictors will still only account for about half the variance in outcome. If a high- and low-risk group were identified, outcomes would show a considerable and coëxtensive range despite large mean differences in the groups. Therefore, it will be important to examine individual trajectories, particularly in relation to environmental changes, for clues to the processes of continuity and discontinuity.

Both the findings and the shortcomings of the Project Competence studies illustrate trends in this field of research endeavor. Data consistently implicate individual and family differences that seem to influence the exposure and response to environmental hazards. For example, our results add to a growing body of data that cognitive functioning and the competence of parenting moderate the relations between adversity and competence (Garmezy, 1985). Furthermore, sex appears to moderate the influence of the vulnerability or protective effect of parenting. Yet the processes by which these effects may occur are not evident, primarily because the methodology does not allow for adequate analysis of the "how" question.

In order to study process, we must get closer to the behavioral sequence, in two ways. First, we must learn when and where to look for the phenomena of interest, then observe changes over time at increasingly shorter time intervals, continually fine-tuning the reliability and specificity of our assessments. At the same time links can be made to studies of the processes that shape more specific aspects of behavior that appear to underly competence or resilience, in order to map the one approach with its microanalytic detail, only possible with highly specialized research questions, onto the other approach, which sacrifices detail for a more comprehensive picture of development. For example, studies by Patterson and his colleagues of coercive sequences of behavior between a parent and child, illustrate at a microanalytic level how parenting behavior with boys might increase or maintain the kinds of disruptive, aggressive behavior often observed in children exposed to stressful experiences, whether related to divorce, marital discord, or a major disaster.

This process of research is of course itself developmental. The first wave of resilience studies, including Project Competence, took initial steps in operationally defining and differentiating the study of successful adaptation under varying adverse conditions. The result of these efforts is better methodology, better questions, and a healthy respect for the complexity of the task before us.

CONCLUSION

Developmental psychopathology *is* the study of adaptation, its variations and vicissitudes. The awakening, historically, of investigators to the phenomenon of successful adaptation despite risk, was part of a general recognition of diversity in developmental outcomes and the complexity of developmental pathways. Resiliency, in particular, pointed to weaknesses in theory and predictions deriving from a narrow focus on psychopathology, vulnerability, and maladaptation, ignoring competence, protective factors, and resilience.

A central task now for developmental psychopathology is to understand the nature of risk, vulnerability, and protective factors as they unfold and intertwine in development to produce individual differences in the quality of adaptation. Studies of behavior under adversity may provide unique opportunities to understand the processes of adaptation. Acute environmental stressors, for example, may open an observational window into processes normally so gradual or subtle that they are impossible or impractical to observe. Similarly, studies of "transitional" periods of development when changes are rapid or challenges concentrated in time, as for example, in early adolescence (Masten, 1988), may reveal how risk, vulnerability, and protective processes work for different children. Studies of successful adaptation in very high-risk or vulnerable children may also provide clues for improving interventions with their less successful peers or reducing risk for maladaptation in other children. To understand and prevent maladaptation, we will do well to understand resilience in development; they are different parts of the same story of adaptation.

ACKNOWLEDGEMENT

The author wishes to express her deep appreciation to Norman Garmezy, Auke Tellegen, Patricia Morison, Kevin Larkin, and colleagues of Project Competence, and to the W. T. Grant Foundation and National Institute of Mental Health (MH33222) for supporting this research.

REFERENCES

Anthony, E. J. (1974). The syndrome of the psychologically invulnerable child. In E. J. Anthony & C. Koupernik (Eds.), *The child in his family: Children at psychiatric risk* (pp. 529–544). New York: Wiley.

Bender, L. (1937). Behavior problems in the children of psychotic and criminal parents. *Genetic Psychology Monographs, 19,* 229–339.

Block, J., & Block, J. H. (1980). The role of ego-control and ego-resiliency in the organization of behavior. In W. A. Collins (Ed.), *Minnesota symposia on child psychology* (Vol. 13, pp. 39–101). Hillsdale, NJ: Lawrence Erlbaum Associates.

Block, J. H., Block, J., & Gjerde, P. F. (1986). The personality of children prior to divorce: A prospective study. *Child Development, 57,* 827–840.

Block, J., & Gjerde, P. F. (1986, August). Early antecedents of ego resiliency in late adolescence. In N. Garmezy (Chair) *Roots and Correlates of Resilience Under Adversity.* Symposium of the annual meeting of the American Psychological Association, Washington, D.C.

Bracht, G. H., & Hopkins, K. D. (1977). Stability of educational achievement. In G. H. Bracht, K. D. Hopkins, & J. C. Stanley (Eds.), *Perspectives in educational and psychological measurement.* Englewood Cliffs, NJ: Prentice-Hall.

Coddington, R. D., (1972a). The significance of life events as etiologic factors in the diseases of children. I: A survey of professional workers. *Journal of Psychosomatic Research, 16,* 7–18.

Coddington, R. D., (1972b). The significance of life events as etiologic factors in the diseases of children. II: A study of a normal population. *Journal of Psychosomatic Research, 16,* 205–213.

Compas, B. E. (1987). Stress and life events during childhood and adolescence. *Clinical Psychology Review, 7,* 275–302.

Dunn, L. M., & Markwardt, F. C. (1970). *Peabody Individual Achievement Test.* Circle Pines, MN: American Guidance Service.

Emery, R. E. (1982). Interparental conflict and the children of discord and divorce. *Psychological Bulletin, 92,* 310–330.

Ferrarese, M. J. (1981). Reflectiveness-impulsivity and competence in children under stress. Doctoral dissertation, University of Minnesota. *Dissertation Abstracts International, 42,* 4928B.

Finkelman, D. G. (1983). The relationships of children's attributes to levels of competence and familial stress. Doctoral dissertation, University of Minnesota. *Dissertation Abstracts International, 44,* 2891B.

Fish, B. (1957). The detection of schizophrenia in infancy. *Journal of Nervous and Mental disease, 125,* 1–24.

Garmezy, N. (1971). Vulnerability research and the issue of primary prevention. *American Journal of Orthopsychiatry, 41,* 101–116.

Garmezy, N. (1974). Children at risk: The search for the antecedents to schizophrenia: Part II. Ongoing research programs, issues and intervention. *Schizophrenia Bulletin, 9,* 55–125.

Garmezy, N. (1981). Children under stress: Perspectives on antecedents and correlates of vulnerability and resistance to psychopathology. In A. I. Rabin, J. Aronoff, A. M. Barclay, & R. A. Zucker (Eds.), *Further explorations in personality* (pp. 196–269). New York: Wiley.

Garmezy, N. (1985). Stress-resistant children: The search for protective factors. In J. E. Stevenson (Ed.), Recent research in developmental psychopathology. *Journal of Child Psychology and Psychiatry Book Supplement,* No. 4, (pp. 213–233). Oxford: Pergamon Press.

Garmezy, N. (1987). Stress, competence, and development: Continuities in the study of schizophrenic adults, children vulnerable to psychopathology, and the search for stress-resistant children. *American Journal of Orthopsychiatry, 57*(2), 159–174.

Garmezy, N., Masten, A. S., & Tellegen, A. (1984). The study of stress and competence in children: A building block for developmental psychopathology. *Child Development, 55,* 97–111.

Garmezy, N., & Nuechterlein, K. (1972). Invulnerable children: The fact and fiction of competence and disadvantage. *American Journal of Orthopsychiatry, 42,* (Abstract) 328–329.

Garmezy, N., & Phipps-Yonas, S. (1984). An early crossroad in research on risk for schizophrenia: The Dorado Beach Conference. In N. F. Watt, E. J. Anthony, L. C. Wynne, & J. E. Rolf (Eds.), *Children at risk for schizophrenia: A longitudinal perspective* (pp. 6–18). New York: Cambridge University Press.

Garmezy, N., & Rodnick, E. H. (1959). Premorbid adjustment and performance in schizophrenia: Implications of interpreting heterogeneity in schizophrenia. *Journal of Nervous and Mental Disease, 129,* 450–466.

Garmezy, N., & Rutter, M. (1985). Acute reactions to stress. In M. Rutter, & L. Hersov (Eds.), *Child psychiatry: Modern approaches* (2nd ed., pp. 152–176). Oxford: Blackwell Scientific.

Garmezy, N., & Streitman, S. (1974). Children at risk: The search for the antecedents to schizophrenia: Part I. Conceptual models and research methods. *Schizophrenia Bulletin, 8,* 14–90.

Garmezy, N., & Tellegen, A. (1984). Studies of stress-resistant children: Methods, variables, and preliminary findings. In F. Morrison, C. Lord, & D. Keating (Eds.),*Advances in applied developmental psychology* (Vol. 1, pp. 231–287). New York: Academic Press.

Garver, D. L. (1987). Methodological issues facing the interpretation of high-risk studies: Biological heterogeneity. *Schizophrenia Bulletin, 13,* 525–529.

Goldstein, M. J., & Tuma, A. H. (Eds.). (1987). Special section on high-risk research. *Schizophrenia Bulletin, 13*(3).

Gottesman, I. I., & Shields, J. (1972). *Schizophrenia and genetics: A twin study vantage point.* New York: Academic Press.

Gottesman, I. I., & Shields, J. (1982). *Schizophrenia: The epigenetic puzzle.* Cambridge, England: Cambridge University Press.

Hauser, R. M., & Featherman, D. L. (1977). *The process of stratification: Trends and analysis.* New York: Academic Press.

Hetherington, E. M. (1979). Divorce: A child's perspective. *American Psychologist, 34,* 851–858.

Holmes, T. H., & Rahe, R. H. (1967). The social readjustment rating scale. *Journal of Psychosomatic Research, 11,* 213–218.

Johnson, J. H. (1982). Life events as stressors in childhood and adolescence. In B. B. Lahey & A. E. Kazdin (Eds.), *Advances in clinical child psychology* (Vol. 5, pp. 219–253). New York: Plenum Press.

Johnson, J. H. (1986). *Life events as stressors in childhood and adolescence.* Beverly Hills, CA: Sage Publications.

Kagan, J., Rosman, B. L., Day, D., Albert J., & Phelps, W. (1964). Information processing in the child: Significance of analytic and reflective attitudes. *Psychological Monographs, 78,* (1, Whole No. 578).

Kohlberg, L., LaCrosse, J., & Ricks, D. (1972). The predictability of adult mental health from childhood behavior. In B. B. Wolman, (Ed.), *Manual of child psychopathology.* New York: McGraw-Hill.

Kohn, M. (1977). *Social competence, symptoms and underachievement in childhood: A longitudinal perspective.* Washington, DC: V. H. Winston.

Kopp, C. B., & Krakow, J. B. (1983). The developmentalist and the study of biological risk: A view of the past with an eye toward the future. *Child Development, 54,* 1086–1108.

Linder, H. D. (1985). *A contextual life events interview as a measure of stress. A comparison of questionnaire-based versus interview-based stress indices.* Unpublished doctoral dissertation, University of Minnesota.

Loeber, R. (1982). The stability of antisocial and delinquent child behavior: A review. *Child Development, 53,* 1431–1446.

Loeber, R., & Dishion, T. J. (1983). Early predictors of male delinquency: A review. *Psychological Bulletin, 94,* 68–99.

Loeber, R., & Strouthamer-Loeber, M. (1987). The prediction of delinquency. In H. C. Quay (Ed.), *Handbook of juvenile delinquency.* New York: Wiley.

Loevinger, J. (1976). *Ego development.* San Francisco: Jossey-Bass.

Mason, J. W. (1975). A historical view of the stress field, Parts I & II. *Journal of Human Stress, 1,* 6–12, 22–36.

Masten, A. S. (1982). Humor and creative thinking in stress-resistant children. Doctoral dissertation, University of Minnesota. *Dissertation Abstracts International, 43,* 3737B.

Masten, A. S. (1986). Humor and competence in school-aged children. *Child Development, 57,* 461–473.

Masten, A. S. (1987, August). Competence and risk factors in middle childhood as predictors of adaptation in late adolescence. In A. Masten (Chair), *Competence in children at risk: Significance for developmental psychopathology.* Symposium conducted at the biennial meeting of the Society of Research in Child Development, Baltimore.

Masten, A. S. (1988). Toward a developmental psychopathology of early adolescence. In M. D. Levine & E. R. McAnarney (Eds.), *Early adolescent transitions.* Lexington, MA: Heath.

Masten, A. S., & Garmezy, N. (1985). Risk, vulnerability, and protective factors in developmental psychopathology. In B. B. Lahey & A. E. Kazdin (Eds.), *Advances in clinical child psychology* (Vol. 8, pp. 1–52). New York: Plenum Press.

Masten, A. S., Garmezy, N., Tellegen, A., Pellegrini, D. S., Larkin, K., & Larsen, A. (1988). Competence and stress in school children: The moderating effects of individual and family qualities. *Journal of Child Psychology and Psychiatry, 29,* 745–764.

Masten, A. S., Morison, P., & Pellegrini, D. S. (1985). A revised class play method of peer assessment. *Developmental Psychology, 21*, 523–533.

Masten, A. S., Morison, P., Pellegrini, D. S., & Tellegen, A. (in press). Competence under stress: Risk and protective factors. In J. Rolf, A. S. Masten, D. Cicchetti, K. Nuechterlein, & S. Weintraub (Eds.), *Risk and protective factors in the development of psychopathology.* Cambridge University Press.

Mednick, S. A., & Schulsinger, F. (1968). Some premorbid characteristics related to breakdown in children with schizophrenic mothers. In D. Rosenthal & S. S. Kety (Eds.), *The transmission of schizophrenia* (pp. 267–291). Oxford: Pergamon Press.

Morison, P. (1987). *Interview-derived attributes of children as related to competence and familial stress.* Unpublished doctoral dissertation, Minneapolis: University of Minnesota.

Murphy, L. B., & Moriarty, A. E. (1976). *Vulnerability, coping, and growth: From infancy to adolescence.* New Haven, CT: Yale University Press.

O'Dougherty, M. (1981). The relationship between early risk status and later competence and adaptation in children who survive severe heart defects. Doctoral dissertation, University of Minnesota. *Dissertation Abstracts International, 42*, 782B.

O'Dougherty, M., Wright, F. S., Garmezy, N., Loewenson, R. B., & Torres, F. (1983). Later competence and adaptation in infants who survive severe heart defects. *Child Development, 54*, 1129–1142.

Pasamanick, B., & Knobloch, H. (1960). Brain damage and reproductive casualty. *American Journal of Orthopsychiatry, 30*, 298–305.

Pasamanick, B., & Knobloch, H. (1961). Epidemiological studies on the complications of pregnancy and the birth process. In G. Caplan (Ed.), *Prevention of mental disorders in children: Initial explorations* (pp. 74–94). New York: Basic Books.

Pellegrini, D. S. (1980). *The social-cognitive qualities of stress-resistant children.* Doctoral dissertation, University of Minnesota, *Dissertation Abstracts International, 41*, 1925–1926B.

Pellegrini, D. S. (1985). Social cognition and competence in middle childhood. *Child Development, 56*, 253–264.

Pellegrini, D. S., Masten, A. S., Garmezy, N., & Ferrarese, M. J. (1987). Correlates of social and academic competence in middle childhood. *Journal of Child Psychology and Psychiatry, 28*(5), 699–714.

Porteus, S. D. (1933). *The maze test and mental differences.* Vineland, NJ: Smith.

Raison, S. B. (1982). *Coping behavior of mainstreamed physically handicapped students.* Doctoral dissertation, University of Minnesota. *Dissertation Abstracts International, 43*, 2635A.

Robins, L. N. (1978). Sturdy childhood predictors of adult antisocial behaviour: Replications from longitudinal studies. *Psychological Medicine, 8*, 611–622.

Rutter, M. (1972). *Maternal deprivation reassessed.* Harmondsworth, Middlesex: Penguin.

Rutter, M. (1979a). Maternal deprivation, 1972–1978: New findings, new concepts, new approaches. *Child Development, 50*, 283–305.

Rutter, M. (1979b). Protective factors in children's responses to stress and disadvantage. In M. W. Kent & J. E. Rolf, *Primary prevention of psychopathology, Vol. 3: Social competence in children* (p. 49–74). Hanover, NH: University Press of New England.

Rutter, M. (1983). Stress, coping, and development: Some issues and some questions. In N. Garmezy, & M. Rutter (Eds.), *Stress, coping, and development in children* (pp. 1–41). New York: McGraw-Hill.

Rutter, M. (1985). Resilience in the face of adversity: Protective factors and resistance to psychiatric disorder. *British Journal of Psychiatry, 147*, 598–611.

Rutter, M. (In press). Psychosocial resilience and protective mechanisms. In J. Rolf, A. S. Masten, D. Cicchetti, K. Nuechterlein, & S. Weintraub (Eds.), *Risk and protective factors in the development of psychopathology.* New York: Cambridge University Press.

Sameroff, A. J., Barocas, R., & Seifer, R., (1984). The early development of children born to mentally ill women. In N. F. Watt, E. J. Anthony, L. C. Wynne, & J. E. Rolf (Eds.), *Children at risk for schizophrenia: A longitudinal perspective* (pp. 482–514). New York: Cambridge University Press.

Sameroff, A. J., & Chandler, M. J. (1975). Reproductive risk and the continuum of caretaking casualty. In F. D. Horowitz, M. Hetherington, S. Scarr-Salapatek, & G. Siegel (Eds.), *Review of child development research,* (Vol. 4, pp. 187–243). Chicago: University of Chicago Press.

Sameroff, A., Seifer, R., Zax, M., & Barocas, R. (1987). Early indicators of developmental risk: Rochester Longitudinal Study. *Schizophrenia Bulletin, 13,* 383–394.

Selman, R. L. (1980). *The growth of interpersonal understanding: Developmental and clinical analyses.* New York: Academic Press.

Selye, H. A. (1936). A syndrome produced by diverse nocuous agents. *Nature, 138,* 32.

Selye, H. (1956). *The stress of life.* New York: McGraw-Hill.

Shure, M. B., & Spivack, G. (1972). Means-ends thinking, adjustment and social class among elementary school-aged children. *Journal of Consulting and Clinical Psychology, 38,* 348–353.

Silverstein, P. R. (1982). *Coping and adaptation in families of physically handicapped school children.* Doctoral dissertation, University of Minnesota. *Dissertation Abstracts International, 43,* 2635A.

Spivack, G., & Swift, M. (1967). *Devereux Elementary School Behavior Rating Scale Manual.* Devon: The Devereux Foundation.

Wallach, M. A., & Kogan, N. (1965). *Modes of thinking in young children.* New York: Holt, Rinehart, & Winston.

Watt, N. F., Anthony, E. J., Wynne, L. C., & Rolf, J. E. (Eds.). (1984). *Children at risk for schizophrenia: A longitudinal perspective.* New York: Cambridge University Press.

Wechsler, D. (1974). *Manual for the Wechsler Intelligence Scale for Children-Revised.* New York: Psychological Corporation.

Werner, E. E., Bierman, J. M., & French, F. E. (1971). *The children of Kauai: A longitudinal study from the prenatal period to age ten.* Honolulu: University of Hawaii Press.

Werner, E. E., & Smith, R. S. (1977). *Kauai's children come of age.* Honolulu: University Press of Hawaii.

Werner, E. E., & Smith, R. S. (1982). *Vulnerable but invincible: A longitudinal study of resilient children and youth.* New York: McGraw-Hill.

White, R. W. (1959). Motivation reconsidered: The concept of competence. *Psychological Review, 66*(5), 297–333.

Author Index

Subject Index